INFORMATION SYSTEMS

Policies and Procedures Manual

PRENTICE HALL
Paramus, New Jersey 07652

GEORGE JENKINS

Library of Congress Cataloging-in-Publication Data

Jenkins, George Henry.
    Information systems policies & procedures manual / George H. Jenkins. —2nd ed.
       p. cm.
    Includes index.
    ISBN 0-13-255845-9
    1. Management information systems.   2. Information resources management.
  I. Title.
    T58.6.J465   1997   96-29527
    004 '.068 ' 4—dc20   CIP

Printed in the United States of America

10 9 8 7 6 5

ISBN 0-13-255845-9

ATTENTION: CORPORATIONS AND SCHOOLS

Prentice Hall books are available at quantity discounts with bulk purchase for educational, business, or sales promotional use. For information, please write to: Prentice Hall Career & Personal Development Special Sales, 240 Frisch Court, Paramus, NJ 07652. Please supply: title of book, ISBN, quantity, how the book will be used, date needed.

PRENTICE HALL
Paramus, NJ 07652

On the World Wide Web at http://www.phdirect.com

INTRODUCTION

The *Information Systems Policies & Procedures Manual, Second Edition,* is a comprehensive, generic, and ready-to-use guidebook that provides everything needed for a thorough information systems standardization program. By using this manual as a guide, model, and frequent decision-making reference, an information systems policy and procedure program uniquely tailored to the needs of any organization can be devised. No two information systems operations could pass for twins, but they have elements in common: hardware, software and personnel. This manual defines these common threads that link all information systems operations, providing for a variety of situations; it is not a "one size fits all."

"Simplicity is the ultimate design." Often policies and procedures manuals include an overabundance of forms, but this guidebook attempts to provide a minimum. Frequently, a well-written memo or e-mail message can take the place of a form and reduce the complexity of an IS operation. The more complex, the more fence-mending is required to keep a system working. IS operations that have a formal systems and procedures manual in place are noticeably much better run.

The role of IS management is changing even more quickly than information systems technology itself. Today the IS operation is no longer found in some obscure corner of the corporate organization, but plays an interactive role in global systems.

This manual will help with the formalization of policies and procedures that are needed for a program of documentation of the IS operation. This can be done with the savings of both time and effort by using this manual which identifies standard operations documentation needed but still allows for any special needs.

End-user computing systems will grow with or without the guidance of corporate IS, but the two working together in concert will provide a synergistic dividend. This manual provides the policies and procedures which can expedite this objective.

The research conducted for this book revealed many well-run information systems operations and some real disasters. The better ones had noticeably good management and practical documentation. Expensive consultants, fad innovations, and cutting-edge technology did not always produce the desired results.

The *Information Systems Policies & Procedures Manual, Second Edition* is not a product of the academic, theoretical dream-world: it is a compilation of proven information systems policies and procedures. It is an applications manual that any seasoned information systems manager—working in either a large or small IS operation—will find useful.

ABOUT THE AUTHOR

George H. Jenkins, Ph.D. has spent 23 years as a professional IS practitioner. He began his career as an engineering programmer with General Electric, where he wrote an engineering end-user's policy and procedure manual, and later was a systems analyst with Xerox where he wrote, in only three months, an internal manual, *The Principles of Stock Keeping*. He has also worked as a DP operations manager with Columbia Record Club of CBS. He was the Administrative Coordinator for Capital Record Club and Capital Record Club of Canada where he wrote a manual on how to write policies and procedures. He was also Director for Systems and DP operations for Nicolson File Company and an administrator for Wayne County General Hospital (University of Michigan teaching hospital).

Among his other accomplishments are: writing one of the first artificial intelligence programs (which designed electric motors for General Electric); designing, programming, and successfully installing the first exponential smoothing inventory control system; installing the second on-line real-time data collection system for production control, and converting the second-largest business unit record operation to computers.

Dr. Jenkins has had articles published in the *Journal of Systems Management* and the *Data Management* magazine, and is the author of Data Processing Policies and Procedure Manual. He has also earned his CDP, CDE and CSP.

He is currently a full professor of systems analysis with the University of Findlay, where he developed a four-year degree program for systems analysts. He is a member of IIE, The Academy of Management, and The Toledo PC Users Group. Dr. Jenkins is associated with Q-Consulting of Columbus, Ohio. He is involved with reengineering and systems analysis projects there, and can be reached at *http://www.qconsulting.com*.

ACKNOWLEDGMENTS

Writing this book has been a challenge because of the technology explosion of IT. The book is dedicated to my wife Patricia Pietras-Jenkins who was willing to put up with a lot during the months of research and writing, and still encouraged me to complete the task. I would also like to especially thank my editor Jane Loeb for all of her help and dedication, which not only improved the final product but also made me a better writer.

I would like to also mention Mrs. Crisswell, of Purdue University at Fort Wayne, who helped me discover the writer in me.

CONTENTS

Chapter 3 Systems Analysis and Design—3-1

Chapter 4 Programming Procedures—4-1

Chapter 5 IS Computer Operations—5-1

Chapter 6 IS Support Operations—6-1

Chapter 10 IS Management and Audit—10-1

Chapter 11 Systems and Operations Audit—11-1

Chapter 12 IS Human Resource Management—12-1

Chapter 13 IT Training—13-1

Chapter 14 Project Management—14-1

Chapter 16 Forms Management—16-1

Chapter 18 End-User IS Operations—18-1

Chapter 1
ORGANIZATION RESPONSIBILITY

1. POLICY

1.1 ORGANIZATION RESPONSIBILITY POLICY

The purpose of the *Information Systems Policies & Procedures Manual, Second Edition*, is to provide a conformity instrument for the analysis, development, design, documentation, control of and software provision for information systems.

1.1.1 Scope

This manual provides the guidelines for policies, systems and procedures related to information systems functions at the company, the work group and the stand-alone levels. It is not intended to replace instructions by various vendors in the operations of their software or hardware.

1.1.2 Policy Objectives

The policy objectives are to:
A. Differentiate between the company, the work group and the stand-alone microcomputer operations.
B. Provide structure to the interface of various work group information systems, and to the relationship of work groups and stand-alone microcomputer systems with the company's operating system.
C. Assign the responsibility and define the authority for controlling all computer and network standards, operational standards, and training.

2. MANUAL ORGANIZATION

1.2 Manual Organization Procedures

1.2.1 Format

The manual is divided into chapters. The chapters are subdivided into sections. The sections are subdivided into subsections. The manual contains a table of contents displaying the chapters, sections, and subsections.

1.2.2 Indices Coding

A. Indices system

The reference index is in the form of:

N. Chapter number.

.N Section number.

.N.N Sub-section number. Within a sub-section, the first level of subdivision will be indented and will be identified by a capitalized alphabetic character (starting with A) followed by a period. The second subdivision level will be indented again and will be identified by a numeric character (starting with 1) followed by a period. The third subdivision level will again be indented and will be identified with a lower case alphabetic character (starting with a) followed by a period. The fourth subdivision level will also be indented and will be identified by a numeric character in parentheses (starting with 1) followed by a period. The fifth subdivision level will be indented and will be identified by a lower case alphabetic character in parentheses (starting with a) followed by a period.

B. Section and subsection titles will be upper case.

The subsequent text's first character will be upper case.

C. Numbering of pages

Pages will be numbered within each section as page "*x-x.*" For example, if the last page of a section is four, it would be numbered "4-4." The placement of page numbers will be consistent from section to section.

3. STANDARDS RESPONSIBILITIES

1.3 STANDARDS RESPONSIBILITIES PROCEDURES

1.3.1 Source of Authority

A. Information systems policies will emanate from the highest level of authority of the organization which the computer procedures will affect.

B. Forms of authority

1. The corporate computer systems manager is the authority for all company computer systems. He/she will receive policy mandates from the firm's delegated operations policymakers. These policies will be defined in writing and dated, signed, and forwarded to the corporate computer systems manager who will incorporate these policies, along with his/her own, into the company computer policies. Any financial involvement of any part of the firm's computer systems will require the co-approval of the firm's auditors, both in-house and outside, if applicable. The responsibilities of the corporate computer systems manager are defined in the corporate policies and procedures manual.

2. The manager of work group and/or stand-alone microcomputer systems, within a corporate information system operation, is the authority for these microcomputers. If the company has a corporate system with a microcomputer policies and procedures manual in place, its maintenance will be the responsibility of the corporate information systems management. The enforcement of the manual will come under the authority of the manager of the work group and/or stand-alone microcomputer systems whose responsibilities are defined in the corporate information systems policies and procedures manual.

If the manager of work group and/or stand-alone microcomputer systems receives only policy guidance from the head of the corporate information system, he/she will incorporate these policies into the microcomputer policies and procedures manual. The development, maintenance and enforcement authority will be that of the manager whose responsibilities are defined in the *Information Systems Policies & Procedures Manual, Second Edition*.

3. Managers of work group microcomputer systems, which are part of the company system, are the authority for those in that work group. The company must create a combined policies and procedures manual formulated to carry out the firm's policies for the company microcomputer system, work groups, and stand-alone microcomputer systems. The manager of work group microcomputer systems will be responsible for the procedure development, maintenance, and enforcement within his/her area of authority. The respective responsibilities for the microcomputer policy and procedure manuals will be covered in the *Information Systems Policies & Procedures Manual, Second Edition.* Any financial transactions or data access of the company's computer data base systems by work group or stand-alone systems will require the co-approval of the firm's auditors, both in-house and outside, if applicable.

4. Managers of work groups and/or stand-alone microcomputer systems in a firm that has no company information system will be the sole authority of the microcomputers. This person will be responsible for developing, maintaining and enforcing the microcomputer *Information Systems Policies & Procedures Manual, Second Edition.* The person approving will be so noted at the top right hand side of each section's first page in the manual. This will be the same person that provides the policies, or a representative.

1.3.2 Policies and Procedures Responsibility

A. All computer operations, software, supplies and supporting hardware for the firm will be the responsibility of the head of the firm's corporate computer and/or microcomputer operations. The authority to enforce the *Information Systems Policies & Procedures Manual, Second Edition,* is defined in the manual. This person has the responsibility to approve and sign all issued and all temporary policies and procedures and his/her name will be noted at the top right hand side of each section's first page in the manual. The person writing the policies and procedures will be designated by the head of the company's information system (who may elect to write it him/herself) and will be identified at the top right hand side of each section's first page after the word "By:" and under the name of the person noted as approving.

B. Firms without a corporate computer and/or microcomputer operations head will require a designated person for the microcomputer policies and procedures responsibility. This person's authority can be defined from information provided in Section 1.3.1.B.

1.3.3 Implementation

A. All corporate and work group computer systems utilizing the information systems department's management personnel are responsible for ensuring that the provisions set forth in the *Information Systems Policies & Procedures Manual* are complied with. These management persons are responsible for:

1. Insuring that all application standards are followed in their respective areas.

2. Informing the person in charge of approving the procedures if there are any problems with a procedure or if inputs from other sources do not comply with the defined procedures. This should be done in the form of a memo.

3. Providing new employees with instruction and/or documented procedures that relate to their job descriptions.

B. All stand-alone microcomputer operations will be covered by an operator's procedure manual provided by the supervisor. This manual will contain all procedure information needed for the authorized microcomputer operator to be in compliance. Also, the help desk contact will be identified for any needed assistance.

1.3.4 Manual Maintenance

Manual revisions that are permanent will be sequentially identified, after the word "Rev.," at the top right hand side of each section's first page. Temporary policies or procedures supersede permanent policies and procedures which will remain in the (three-ring) manual binder; they can only be replaced by the issuance of replacement policies and/or procedures. In the event that a policy and/or procedure is to be discontinued, an order will be issued in memo form by the person who originally approved the policy and/or procedure, or by a successor or agent. Requests for temporary or permanent policy and/or procedures will be handled as follows:

A. Any user, management person, information systems person, work group head or manual holder can submit a request for a temporary policy and/or procedure, or for a permanent revision to the *Information Systems Policies & Procedures Manual.*

B. Revision requests will be handled in the following manner:

1. Request a revision in the form of Exhibit 1-1.

2. Submit one copy to the approving authority (or successor) for the policy and/or procedure.

3. The approving authority will review the request and approve or deny in memo form citing a reason for whatever action is taken. The person assigned to investigate the request will be identified in the memo. The person assigned to determine the course of action deemed necessary may also be the approving authority. The recommended course of action can result in a feasibility study if the required undertaking is large or expensive enough.

4. If the request is denied, the person requesting the change may move up the chain of command (as defined in the company's policies and procedures manual) to the level needed for resolution.

C. The revised documentation will be issued in the same manner as the original documentation to all affected manual holders. The person responsible for maintaining the manual or any work group or stand-alone microcomputers policies will keep a current listing of all manual holders who will be identified as having a partial or complete manual. Partial manual holders, who will have identified which sections they receive, will be cross-indexed by those sections. When a particular section is replaced, a list of appropriate manual holders can be provided for distribution. The lists could be best maintained in a computer database, and distribution lists could be printed as needed.

When permanent revisions are issued, all pages for the given section will be reissued. If corrections to current procedures are required, and numbering is not affected, only the affected pages need be distributed. This applies to both temporary and permanent policies and/or procedures. All releases will have a cover memo noting:

1. The person issuing the release.

2. The effective date or dates of the release.

3. The reason for the release.

REVISION REQUEST

NAME/TITLE: _____

DEPARTMENT: _____ DATE:_____

MANUAL AREA:

CHAPTER: _____

SECTION: _____

PAGES: _____

SUGGESTED REVISION:

Write the proposed needed revision. Attach any necessary details, along with supporting documentation.

REVISION RATIONALE:

Describe the problem and how it is affecting the current operation or will affect future operation. How will the proposed revision resolve the problem?

Signed: _____ Date: _____

Approved By: _____ Date: _____

Approved/Disapproved and Date: _____

Date Revision Completed: _____ By Whom: _____

COMMENTS:

Exhibit 1-1. Revision Request

Chapter 2
D OCUMENTATION PROCESS

1. POLICY

2.1 POLICY

Documentation is a formal means of conveying information.

It is a permanent record of operation methods, development techniques, and organizational policies. Documentation provides the media for the recording of procedure development, design, implementation, operation, and revision data. It incorporates policies, rules, and information that must be distributed properly to all users associated with information systems operations so that energies are directed and coordinated correctly.

The documentation detail will depend on the skill levels of users involved who should be able to understand a system or operation through this method. This is especially true when users are non-data processing people. Yet, user documentation is often put off until the last minute, is written hastily by non-professional writers, and most often is considered an after-the-project nicety rather than a requirement of the project itself. For these reasons, company information systems policy requires that documentation be an integral part of any undertaking. This effort will be budgeted for and the assigned funds used for documentation only. Users who do not want poorly written instructions or documentation will not be required to "sign off" on them (i.e., accept them).

User documentation should be written following specific standards defining the content, approach, and objectives. The standards provide a uniform plan for handling every aspect of documentation.

However, information systems policies and procedures are only as good as the effort to correctly maintain and enforce them. User documentation must be kept current or it is useless. Some of its major benefits are a flexibility that allows for changes and an ability to use temporary procedures. The enforcement of the computer policies and procedures provides, in addition, the greater benefit of minimizing cost and confusion, while maximizing the investment in software, hardware, and related items.

Information systems areas requiring policies and procedures documentation are:

- Procedure development.
- Computer management operations.
- Computer users.
- Computer user support.
- Special areas (redefining vendor software, hardware documentation, etc.).

A standard three-ring binder should be used to contain the applicable computer policies and procedures for the corporate, work groups, and stand-alone areas. Work group managers should have all policies and procedures that refer to their jurisdiction. The person responsible for microcomputer administration and control, or an agent, should have a complete information systems policies and procedures manual. If the firm maintains an off-site records backup operation, it too should possess a current copy of all the information systems policies and procedures. If a systems and procedures unit exists, it should maintain an appropriate number of complete manuals.

2.1.1 ISO 9000 Procedure Policy

Firms that are going to be involved with ISO 9000 must have well-documented policies and procedures in place for certification. In this case any portion of user procedures that is part of a ISO 9000 certification should comply with the appropriate format.

2. FEASIBILITY STUDY

2.2 FEASIBILITY STUDY DOCUMENTATION PROCEDURE

A feasibility study is conducted to determine the practicality of changing, developing or acquiring a system or computer program. Such studies can be omitted when a project is mandated by top management and/or outside regulatory agencies. Each feasibility study, which will consist of a small scale systems analysis and a feasibility report, will require a binder to contain documentation such as memos, correspondence, vendor literature, and detail information.

The analysis section is a scaled-down study of a current system and a determination of the practicality of the request. The feasibility report contains documented findings as to the request's feasibility. The final feasibility study report is prepared based on these two sections and any other pertinent information.

2.2.1 Feasibility Study Request Memo

Each feasibility study request will be initiated by an authorized requesting memo or e-mail memo. The individuals authorized to initiate such requests will be identified by the firm. The memo will state:

- The nature of the requested system or software.
- The expected tangible and intangible benefits from the new or revised system or software.
- The date by which a reply to the report is needed.
- The contact person for further information about the request.

2.2.2 Feasibility Study Binder Contents

If the feasibility study request is denied by the approving authority a notification is sent to the person requesting the study, explaining the reason(s) why the request was not approved. Both the requesting and reply memos will be filed in a "feasibility reject file" in the area of the systems and procedures unit. When the request for a feasibility study is approved, a feasibility binder labeled with the title of the study will include the following:

- An accumulated table of contents.
- All memos related to the study.
- Vendor correspondence.
- Vendor literature.
- Accumulated costs data for the study.
- A log listing the calendar days and hours worked on the study.
- Documentation of all meetings.
- A telephone log regarding all phone calls made and attempted.
- A copy of the final report.

2.2.3 The Final Feasibility Study Report

The final feasibility study report will be formatted in the following manner:

- Cover page, containing project title, author, and date.
- Overview of the request.
- Rationale for initiating the information systems project, or for changing an existing system.
- The body of the final report providing the details of the project/program.
- Exhibits.
- Summary, containing recommendations, estimated costs, estimated calendar time needed, and estimated man-hours of all persons involved in the project.

Comment:
Remember calendar time and people time are not interchangeable. If it takes one person 100 hours (12.5 days) to paint a barn, the barn cannot be painted in one hour by 100 people.

3. PROJECT DOCUMENTATION

2.3 PROJECT DOCUMENTATION

Project documentation includes instructions, charts, a copy of the feasibility study, correspondence, and other material dealing with a specific project. It provides a permanent description of the undertaking along with the solutions to problems and the methods used to resolve them.

When starting a project, a project binder is created to provide an ongoing record of information relating to the specific project. It should include all related material and vendor information and correspondence throughout the life of the project. It is important to know which document supersedes another. Therefore, each document should be dated before placing it in the binder.

At no time are the contents to be removed from a project documentation binder. If necessary, a copy can be made of any needed part(s) of the binder contents and both the date and the word "copied" posted on each reproduced page.

2.3.1 Identification and Responsibility

A project number and title are used to identify each project binder. Responsibility for initiating and maintaining the binder rests with the project leader/ manager or other responsible person as designated by the information systems head or systems manager.

2.3.2 Contents of Project Binder

The binder of a proposed project contains:

A. Table of contents

B. Project proposal

The project report may be in the form of a feasibility study or a systems design, or it may specify software requirements. The project proposal should contain:

1. Description of the project

   A brief statement describing the project and its objectives, and a copy of the feasibility study. The responsible person drafts the project description which may be in much more detail than a feasibility study.

2. Major project tasks

   An outline of the steps necessary to complete the project.

3. Estimated costs

   Computed estimated costs for each major task and/or items to be purchased. Costs should be identified as "estimates" obtained at the time the proposal was written and are subject to revision. See Exhibit 2-1 for one format for reporting project proposal costs. Consistency of format, once established, is more essential than individual style and saves time when reviewing the contents.

4. Time estimate for each task

   Estimated dates for inception and completion of each task based on the needed resources being available as scheduled.

DESCRIPTION OF PROJECT
(Brief description. Use a separate sheet if needed.)

MAJOR PROJECT TASKS (Use only those applicable to this project.)

	START DATE	FINISH DATE	ESTIMATED COST
Preliminary Analysis	xx/xx/xx	xx/xx/xx	$xxx,xxx
Systems Analysis/Design	xx/xx/xx	xx/xx/xx	$xxx,xxx
Programming	xx/xx/xx	xx/xx/xx	$xxx,xxx
Data and File Conversion Costs	xx/xx/xx	xx/xx/xx	$xxx,xxx
System and Program Testing			$xxx,xxx
Training Costs			$xxx,xxx
Hardware Purchase			$xxx,xxx
Software Purchase			$xxx,xxx
Administrative Costs			$xxx,xxx
Miscellaneous			$xxx,xxx
TOTAL COST			$xxx,xxx

ESTIMATED ANNUAL OPERATION COST

Data Entry	$xxx,xxx
Processing	$xxx,xxx
System/Program Maintenance	$xxx,xxx
Administrative	$xxx,xxx
Other (specify)	$xxx,xxx
TOTAL ESTIMATED ANNUAL OPERATIONS COST	$xxx,xxx

PROJECT STAFFING
(Name the Project Leader and state the estimated number and competence level of personnel assigned to work on the project.)

PERSONNEL TO CONTACT
(List names of people best able to answer pertinent questions about the various tasks within the project.)

Exhibit 2-1. Format for Project Proposal Costs

5. Project staffing

   The FTE (full time equivalent) personnel assigned to the project by job title and name. Dates of commitment for anyone assigned only for a portion of the project are also listed.

   Competence levels of personnel assigned are identified. This is essential when personnel, such as vendors or consultants, are on loan from user areas and outside sources. The caliber of personnel can determine the success of the project.

6. Project contact personnel

   A list (names and titles) of persons best able to answer pertinent questions about the project. This is most important when dealing with vendors who may be inclined to contact persons in the organization who will benefit them most instead of the project leader or designated person.

C. Systems concept

   A paragraph, or more, written for non-technical, management-level personnel, which provides a detailed overview of the project objectives. For larger projects, the systems concept paragraph(s) specifies the objectives, scope, and methods to be employed. For smaller projects, a short descriptive paragraph suffices.

D. Project resource schedule

   After the Project Proposal worksheet is prepared, a Project Resource Schedule (see Exhibit 2-2) is developed to show the estimated hours per week each task will require. Once the work is completed, actual hours spent on each task are recorded.

2.3.3 Project Progress Folders

Project progress documentation folders, maintained during the life of the project, contain the history of the project and copies of all relevant correspondence filed by date. They also provide a complete historical record, which becomes a source of information when writing a project completion report, and should reflect any agreements between the project group and users or vendors. The folders should include:

A. Correspondence

- Memos and letters.
- Project status reports.
- Minutes of status and problem-solving meetings.

B. Manpower utilization record

The estimated hours per task versus the actual hours per task are posted to the Project Resource Schedule (see Exhibit 2-2). Any line item variations that reflect a cost of over $100 are explained in a memo form at the time of the actual expense posting.

C. Project documentation check sheet

To insure that documentation is being completed, a Project Documentation Check Sheet is used (see Exhibit 2-3). This will be a source for what documentation is to be done.

4. SYSTEMS DOCUMENTATION

2.4 SYSTEMS DOCUMENTATION

Systems documentation is the recording of activities associated with systems analysis and design efforts. It provides proposed system design specifications in a format which management can easily evaluate on merit for approval. It also provides required specifications for software and vendor bidding. Systems documentation and its maintenance are vital to the success of a project and future systems maintenance.

2.4.1 Systems Documentation Binder

A systems documentation binder is maintained for each project but is not intended to replace the project documentation process. Forms in this section (Exhibit 2-4 and Exhibit 2-5) are examples of standard formats to be used as needed. This binder is maintained by the lead systems analyst for the project and contains:

A. Title page

The first or title page contains the project name and identification number, effective dates, and the lead analyst's name and title. Names and responsibilities of all other persons assigned to the project are listed on the second page.

Project Name _____ Project Number _____

DIRECT EXPENSE	Period 1		Period 2		Period 3	
	Est	Act	Est	Act	Est	Act
Project Manager						
Systems Analyst						
Programmer						
Clerk						
Other						
Training						
Total Hours						
Total Dollars						
Cumulative Hours						
Cumulative Dollars						

Project Leader _____ Date _____

Exhibit 2-2. Project Resource Schedule

Project Name _____ Project Number _____

DATE:		Project Manager:	
Required	Actual	ITEM	Responsibility
		Request Evaluation	
		Design Specifications	
		System Definition	
		System Flowcharts	
		System Input	
		System Processing	
		System Output	
		File/Database	
		System Controls	
		System Test Data	
		System Audit	
		System Recovery	
		Nomenclature Glossary	
		Software Description	
		Software Controls	
		Software Tests	
		Help Desk Assignments	
		Operation Instructions	
		System Acceptance	

Exhibit 2-3. Project Documentation Check Sheet

B. Table of contents

This reflects the specific contents in the systems binder and requires updating as changes and/or additions are made.

C. Revision sheet

Included in every systems binder (see Exhibit 2-4), it contains columns for:

1. Number of revisions

   Revisions are numbered sequentially starting with 1.

2. Revision date

   Effective date of the revision.

3. Portion revised

   The specific part of the system under revision, including all areas of documentation such as procedures, flowcharts, reports, etc.

4. Name

   The name of the systems analyst making the revision.

5. Authorization

   The name of the person authorizing the revision.

2.4.2 Systems Concept

The systems concept is prepared by the lead systems analyst from specifications provided by the requesting authority. This section will include copies of correspondence or written requests which outline the requirements of the system. Once approved, it serves as a guide for analysts to design the technical specifications of the system and includes:

A. Approval

The first page lists the project name, the requesting authority's name, and the title of the person approving the project.

B. Project history

This section states the background that justifies the project.

C. Project objectives

The details of project objectives are presented. All functional areas affected by this project are listed, and any problems with crossed lines of authority are noted so that the required coordination can be spelled out. In addition, anticipated results from the successful completion of the project are detailed. To ensure complete understanding of the system by management and users, what will not be accomplished by the system is also noted.

D. Requirements

The documentation requirements necessary for a proper completion of the project are:

- A brief explanation of the work to be done during each phase.
- A schedule for inception and completion dates of each phase and the key tasks within each phase. To help picture the overall schedule, Gantt charting is recommended for key tasks and phases of complex projects.
- Special requirements for project software from vendors and/or for in-house programmed software.
- Special requirements for outside acquisitions such as equipment, consultants, contract personnel and/or vendor services.
- Current in-house equipment resources that will be committed to the systems project.
- Man-hour resources, by names and titles, to be committed to the project.
- Resources expected from the requesting authority including hardware and personnel assistance such as training of extra manpower during conversion of the system.

2.4.3 Systems Specifications

Systems specifications provide a means of communication between the designer and the software providers who can be in-house programming staff or vendors. They provide a record of the structure, functions, flow, documentation and control of the system and include:

A. System narrative

- Current date.
- Descriptive title of the system.
- General requirements with a description of each and with sources cited.
- Source, expected schedule, and volume of input data.

NUMBER	DATE	PART REVISED	REVISED BY	APPROVED BY

Exhibit 2-4. Revision Sheet

- Size and characteristics of the data.

- Sample exhibits of input documents.

- Outputs indicating volume and due dates. This may be a monitor display and/or hard copy.

- Sample exhibits of outputs.

- References to material or organizations that may furnish additional information. This may include vendor supplied information.

B. System flowcharts

Pictorial systems which display flowcharts identifying the processes performed and the sequence of the performances. Each symbol within a flowchart identifies a process as manual or computer. Each system flowchart is contained on one page; if greater detail is required of any given area of the system, a subsystem flowchart is drawn which both non-technical management and computer programmers are able to understand.

C. Program specification requirements

These define the environment within a system in which a subsystem or a single program operates. They describe:

- Inputs and outputs, including source, format, disposition, retention method, and time period.

- Process, controls, functions, and limitations. These specifications, prepared by the systems analyst to be used only by the programming staff, need to be confirmed by the person responsible for programming that they can be accomplished by this staff.

D. File/Database specifications

A complete and detailed specification of the files and/or database used in the system are identified. If a database is employed for storing data elements, a database dictionary is maintained by the database administrator, and the systems project should comply with appropriate procedures. This applies to file specifications if they also fall under the jurisdiction of the database administrator. A reference sheet describes the file layout, field definitions and source references. A sample file layout is shown in Exhibit 2-5. The file layout contains:

- File name.

- File number or label.

- Current date.
- File label.
- Record size.
- Storage medium.
- Record length required.
- Blocking factor (tape only).
- Retention requirements (daily, monthly, etc., and the expected currency is the number of days between the cutoff date and the completion of the update). "Monthly 5 days" means the file is updated monthly with 5 days required to complete the update.
- Security level.
- File sequence.
- Remarks.

E. Input description

The format for all the data going into the system. It provides the following information for each input record:

- Name.
- Date.
- Status (raw data or in computer media form).
- Each field identified within a record, its type and length.
- Number of records per cycle (day, week, etc.)
- Disposition after it is received by the system.

F. Output description

The layout of each output should be displayed in monitor or hard copy format and be part of the systems documentation. Forms designed for this purpose include:

- Name of report.
- Number of report.
- Location and length of each item within a report layout.
- Number of copies.
- Relationship of items in the report to the source of the item information in the input description.

FILE NAME:

FILE NUMBER:	DATE:

FILE LABEL:

RECORD SIZE:	FILE SIZE:

DISK:	CD:	TAPE:	BLOCKING:

RETENTION REQUIREMENTS:

REMARKS:

Exhibit 2-5. File Description

5. SOFTWARE DOCUMENTATION

2.5 SOFTWARE DOCUMENTATION

Software documentation serves various functions. First, program maintenance has become a major expense. The investment and effort required to document software is rewarded by reduced maintenance costs, and possibly management job security. Next, it communicates to the systems analyst or project leader that the programming has been properly done. Program documentation also provides information systems operations and users the information needed to operate the software. It also furnishes the auditors with information about the controls that have been established. Finally, it shows systems management what exactly has been accomplished with the money spent.

2.5.1 Software Binders

Information about developed programs and purchased software is maintained in "software binders," one for each written program or purchased software package. They contain:

A. General information

    This section identifies the software and its objectives. Each program should have a unique identification number. The programs may be grouped together using any of the following categories:

    - Low-level written programs.
    - High-level written programs.
    - Reusable code.
    - CASE tools.
    - Operating software.
    - Database software.
    - Network software.
    - Purchased mainframe programs.
    - Purchased workgroup software.
    - Purchased microcomputer software.

B. General objectives

    The general objectives include a brief narrative statement of each program's purpose or use.

C. Purchased software

Any license agreements connected with the programs, including the number of copies purchased and the last date of purchase. Any "Beta" operating software will be so identified, and its agreement information placed in this section.

D. Program's systems specifications

Vendor-supplied information will also be included.

E. Program flowcharts

Flowcharts will be drawn by hand or flowcharted using available software that employs the ANSI (American National Standards Institute) symbols (refer to the Flowcharting section of this chapter). There are several commercially available software programs which can generate the ANSI symbols and facilitate the drawing of these charts.

F. Written program documentation

- Source code listings.
- Source of input and format.
- Pre-alpha naming conventions. These are needed for the database, inputs, outputs and controls.
- Hard copy layouts.
- Screen display layouts.
- Screen layouts displaying control buttons, text boxes, and screen labels.
- Database layouts, definitions of field items, and naming references.
- Table layouts.
- Data element cross references.
- Subroutines, sources, and listings.
- Table lookup tables.
- Index of table field names (the names that can be found in database, programs, and input/output locations). Useful when programming and doing maintenance later.

2.5.2 Operations Specifications

The programmer or programmer analyst is responsible for preparing operating instructions that can be used by the central computer operations staff, client/server users, work group systems, end user systems, or stand-alone users. This documentation should contain detailed instructions on how to operate the program and handle exceptions that may occur, and will require the signed and dated approval of the highest authority for the unit which they are intended for. LAN, WAN or client/server user instructions will require the approval of the head of information systems or his/her designated representative. The types of information to be included are:

A. Cover page information

- Program number.
- Program description or name.
- Name of programmer or help desk contact.
- Type of program.
- Priority requirements.
- Estimated processing time.
- Date prepared and revision dates.

B. Input/Output requirements

- Keyboard instructions.
- Scanning instrument instructions.
- Removable disk and/or CD instructions.
- External label.
- Internal label.
- Printer(s) required.
- Form number.
- Number of copies required.
- Portrait or landscape printing.
- Report disposition.
- Other input/output devices not listed.

C. Magnetic tape instructions:

- External label.
- Internal label.
- Input or output usage.

- File protection requirements.
- Tape disposition.

D. General operating instructions.

E. Restart procedures.

2.5.3 Program Test Data

Listings of input used for testing and the resulting outputs are kept in the program test file. Monitor displays are screen printed or drawn for documentation.

2.5.4 Backup and Recovery

Procedures are written for both corporate and other operations for each running system. All changes are noted with the date and the name of the person responsible. Each program must have a recovery procedure in the event of a computer failure. Each backup procedure will be tested after it is placed into operation and each time maintenance has been performed. Backup procedures require the following:

- When and how the backup was done.
- The location where backup programs and data are stored.
- The number of backup generations required. If more than one, they should not all be stored in the same location.
- If an outside backup facility is available, a complete written procedure is required for its operation.

6. COMPUTER OPERATIONS DOCUMENTATION

2.6 COMPUTER OPERATIONS DOCUMENTATION

The operating procedures necessary to initiate, schedule, process, control, and restart all phases of the system(s) while it is in operation are maintained in a binder for the operations personnel. All the documentation must be kept current. The project leader is responsible for compiling and validating new systems. Maintenance information systems personnel must update existing manuals.

The computer operations documentation procedures can vary depending on the configuration of the system's hardware. The corporate computer center operation, with hardware in the form of a mainframe, minicomputer, or microcomputer, is under a corporate computer operations head, who is also in charge of client-server operations. This person is part of the corporate information systems and officially accepts the operations documentation. The acceptance of documentation is noted on the upper right hand corner of each procedure section's first page.

The head of corporate computer operations can have responsibility for work group systems manual maintenance or this can be the responsibility of the work group management, whichever best serves the users. The acceptance of documentation is noted on the upper right hand corner of each procedure section's first page by the authorized person.

If microcomputer operations, stand-alone or LAN, have a microcomputer manager, this person will approve operator manuals for his/her area of jurisdiction. If there is none, a user area manager will be assigned the task of approving the operation manuals. This task may be delegated by the manager, and if need be, the help desk person(s) may be consulted or so delegated. The acceptance of documentation is noted on the upper right hand corner of each procedures section's first page by the authorized person.

2.6.1 Corporate Computer Center Operation Procedures

This section details the information systems operations procedures for the corporate system which cover general information pertaining to the overall corporate system(s), backup and recovery, and job procedures.

A. General information

Includes a narrative description of the overall operation, the system hardware, the operating system, the purpose of the system, and the methods used to accomplish the tasks. The users of this documentation are information systems operations personnel.

Gathering and maintaining the following general information, that could apply to all runs, is the responsibility of the corporate information systems head:

- Overview and purpose of operation procedures.
- Names, titles and home telephone numbers of all operations personnel.

- Published shift schedule.
- Contact person for operating system problems.
- Contact person for hardware problems.
- Gantt chart illustrating all scheduled runs.

B. Backup and recovery procedures

Documented by the systems unit in close collaboration with the firm's auditors and the corporate computer center operations management. The ongoing maintenance of these procedures by the systems maintenance people is essential to the organization. Off-site backup and recovery emergency procedures are also maintained. The firm's auditors and corporate computer center management must both approve all changes. Included in these procedures are:

- A list of who has what authority.
- Backup and recovery on-site procedures.
- Backup and recovery off-site procedures.
- Disaster plan and procedures.

C. Computer operation procedures

Job instructions should include the following:

- Job set-up instructions.
- The sources of originating data.
- The media used for inputting data.
- The output media.
- Output forms and their disposition.
- Sample of output forms.
- Sample of monitor displays.
- Corrective action to take for error messages.
- Expected job run time.
- External file label instructions.
- Input and output retention procedures.
- Computer log procedures.
- Contact person's telephone number for run problems.

D. Terminal user procedures

For users who operate terminals and/or client/server microcomputer systems. These users are not always familiar with information systems terms; therefore, operations documentation must be absolutely clear. Possible educational and/or physical limitations of users should be taken into account. User procedures should be simple to read and follow (eighth to tenth grade level for nonprofessional personnel). The monitor screen can also be a source of help instructions. Terminal user's instructions should include:

- Start-up steps, password, etc.
- Corrective action to take for error messages.
- The proper method to sign-off the system.
- Method(s) to obtain hard copy output.
- Help desk contact.

2.6.2 Work Group Computer Systems

A work group (client/server) computer system can be under the information systems or corporate computer center operations head. It can also be a self-contained unit which may or may not rely on the information systems organization for its policies and procedures documentation. This is a management decision.

The design of work group systems will be under the control of the corporate information head to insure that corporate policies are followed. The design and documentation process can be performed by the information systems unit, contracted out, or undertaken by the work group itself. The operational documentation procedures will be continuously monitored by the corporate information unit to insure that maintenance procedures comply with the corporate standards. The work group computer system's communication network will follow policies and procedures laid down by the corporate head of computer networking.

A. Work group general information

Includes a narrative description of the overall work group operation, the system hardware, the operating system, the purpose of the system, and the methods used to accomplish the tasks. The users of this documentation are, most often, more familiar with the efforts of the group than they are with computer technology. The following general information items apply to the work group computer operation and the tasks of the file server computer:

- Overview and purpose of operation procedures.
- Contact person for software problems.
- Contact person for hardware problems.
- Start-up procedures for the system.
- Shut-down procedures for the system.

B. Backup and recovery procedures

When the work group (client/server) system uses and produces financial and/or property information, a close collaboration with the firm's auditors and corporate information systems management is required. Both groups must give their approval to all backup and recovery procedures. The ongoing maintenance of these procedures will also require approval of both groups. If an off-site backup and recovery operation is in place, procedures for this operation are also maintained. Changes to these procedures require the approval of the auditors and/or corporate computer center operations management. Included in these procedures are:

- A list of who has what authority.
- Backup and recovery on-site procedures.
- Backup and recovery off-site procedures.
- Disaster plan and procedures.
- Off-site network access for on-site operations.

C. Work group computer operation procedures

For users of microcomputers that are networked into a work group system. These users are not always familiar with information systems terms; therefore, operations documentation must be absolutely clear. Possible educational and/or physical limitations of users should be taken into account. User operations should be simple to read and follow (eighth to tenth grade level for nonprofessional personnel). The monitor screen can also be a source of help instructions. Operators' instruction procedures can contain the following:

- Turning on the microcomputer, password, etc.
- Accessing program or data from file server.

- Sample of monitor displays.
- Corrective action to take for error messages.
- Expected job run times.
- Input and output retention procedures.
- Help desk's telephone number.
- Turning off procedure.
- How to access tutorial information.

2.6.3 Independent Microcomputer Systems

Stand-alone or networked microcomputers that are not part of a work group or a corporate information system fall into this category. These are microcomputers found throughout a firm and may not have any relationship to other microcomputers. But, to maintain order, consistency, and a higher level of overall efficiency, their documentation process requires a central source. The corporate information systems unit has the responsibility for company-wide "independent" microcomputer documentation, maintenance, policing, and training, as well as help desk operations for the procedures issued.

A. Microcomputer general information

Includes a narrative description of the overall corporate policies and procedures pertaining to the operation of microcomputers. Users of this documentation are, most often, more familiar with the duties of their own jobs than with computer technology. Their educational levels will vary widely, from the factory floor to the CEO's office. Therefore it would be prudent for the writer of this documentation to address more than one reading level.

The general information part of this documentation should apply to all users of independent microcomputers throughout the firm, and should include the following information items:

- Corporate policies governing microcomputers.
- Turning on the microcomputer, password, etc.
- Daily microcomputer housekeeping procedures.
- Overview of the operating system.
- Accessing needed programs or data.
- Getting on the network: LAN, WAN or Internet.

- Turning off procedure.
- How to access tutorial information.
- Contact person for problems.

B. Microcomputer operation procedures

For given kinds of software or special hardware for a particular micro-computer user. This documentation is in module form, one module for each given piece of software or hardware. The microcomputer documentation manual contains the Microcomputer General Information portion and as many Operation Procedures modules as required. Copies of vendor information are included whenever it is considered helpful to the user. The following items should be considered for each documentation module:

- Program or hardware operating instructions.
- Corrective action to take for error messages.
- Backup and retention procedures.
- Help desk's telephone number.
- Turning off procedure.
- How to access tutorial information.

7. FLOWCHARTING STANDARDS

2.7 FLOWCHARTING STANDARDS

Flowcharts perform several functions in the systems investigation, analysis, design, development and installation phases. Traditionally, flowcharts have been hand drawn, but today there are good software flowcharting programs available even for microcomputers. These can be used for drawing organization charts as well.

> **Comment:**
> It might be a good idea to try out a demo program.

Flowchart diagrams range in complexity from global system flowcharts to procedure step detail flowcharts. The levels of flowcharting are:

A. Global systems

 These interrelate with other computer systems outside the organization.

B. Total systems

 These have an interrelationship with more than one system within the internal organization.

C. System

 This is confined to one area of operation (as in a billing system). (See Section 2.7.3.)

D. Subsystems

 Subsystems may appear at more than one level with the first subsystem being part of a system flowchart. (See Section 2.7.3.)

E. Program or procedure flowcharts

 Both depict detail logic or operation steps at their lowest level. Most often, program flowcharts (see Section 2.7.7) are used for programming instructions, while procedure flowcharts (see Section 2.7.4) are used for manual procedure steps.

2.7.1 Global System

A "Global System" is identified here as an interaction of systems, with one or more outside of the organization. An example would be the system of a travel agent interacting with both an airline ticket reservation system and the credit card company system. The reservation information and cost have to be approved by the credit card company for the travel agent to issue a ticket for the airline flight and to add the ticket cost to the customer's credit card account. This is a Global interactive system in operation.

The flowchart exhibit(s) will be all on one page. Since there are no recognized standard symbols for Global system flowcharts, the manner in which the flowchart is illustrated will depend on the IS technical skills of the viewers, that is, the lowest level the whole group can recognize.

2.7.2 Total System

A "Total System" is identified here as an interaction of two or more systems within the organization which require the interaction of all participating systems to function. One example occurs when the production control system interacts with the incentive payroll system of manufacturing, which then interacts with the inventory system for inventory control. The payroll is affected by the worker's scrap rate which affects inventory and scrap rate report counts. The production unit count credits the worker's pay, but also affects the PM (preventive maintenance) schedule, etc.

The flowchart exhibit(s) will be all on one page. Since there are no recognized standard symbols for Total System flowcharts, the manner in which the flowchart is illustrated will depend on the IS technical skills of the viewers, that is, the lowest level the whole group can recognize.

2.7.3 System Flowchart

The system flowchart shows how the information flows through the system. It is all on one page, allowing the system to be viewed in its entirety. If greater detail is required of any given area of the system, a subsystem or lower level flowchart is drawn for that purpose which illustrates only the desired detail.

System flowcharts are not governed by any national standard. Since they are used for a diverse audience of viewers, from top management to programmers, flexibility is needed to be able to target a presentation appropriately. While programmers are able to follow a system flowchart drawn for top management, top management may have a problem with one drawn for a project team of systems analysts and programmers because it will often utilize standard programming flowchart symbols.

Systems flowcharts are often viewed by a whole group of people at one time. There is almost no limit to the size of a flowchart and the symbol size is governed by the viewing distance of the audience. With large groups, it is better to use overhead projection since anything larger than a flip chart becomes a problem to transport and store. Symbols may be used to depict items such as machines and buildings to help top management understand the system, and may, in turn, help sell it. Color is also a good tool to make the system flowchart easier to understand and more interesting to read.

2.7.4 Procedure Flowchart

The procedure flowchart is an excellent method for documenting a manual operation. Placing the flowchart horizontally on a page of quarter-inch graph paper, which comes in rolls of different widths, allows the total procedure to be illustrated on one document. Length presents no problem since the document can be rolled up and stored. The only limitation to length is the space where the chart is displayed for viewing.

Procedure flowcharting is useful for illustrating manual office procedures and is easy to follow, even by people outside the data processing area. It confirms to the operations personnel that the systems analyst has recorded the procedure correctly. It also gives the systems analyst an easy-to-follow source of information when writing or dictating documentation procedures.

Six symbols are used to draw the procedure flowchart. They represent:

- Original information placed on a document.
- Addition of information later to the document.
- The physical handling of the document.
- Document inspection to render a decision.
- Document holding or storage.
- Document leaving the procedure area.

These are illustrated in Exhibit 2-6. A Sample Procedure Flowchart is shown in Exhibit 2-7.

If a new, changed procedure contains manual operations, it too can be drawn as a procedure flowchart. In this case, both the old process flowchart and the proposed process flowchart are drawn on the same page so the two can be compared. When preparing a procedure flowchart, the following must be taken into account:

A. The direction of flow is left to right.

B. Charts are drawn with a number two pencil.

C. The procedure flowchart is identified in the lower left hand corner with the following:

- Project name.
- Project number.
- Date.
- Name of person who produced the flowchart.

D. All input documents have a receiving point, a starting point, and a disposition. Documents may be sent to a file, disposed of (disposal) or sent to someone else.

E. Each line represents a document flow. If a line represents one or more documents, it should be kept at the same level as long as practical.

Process or Element	Symbol
Original operation, the first time information is placed on a document.	
Adding information to a document in a later procedure step.	
Handling the document, such as sorting, matching, separating or stapling.	
Inspection of a document for a decision to be made. Two or more courses of action will follow.	
Storage of document(s) as inactive, delayed, filed, or held. Also used as a destroy symbol.	
Sending or moving the document from one area to another. Also used to show document being sent outside.	

Exhibit 2-6. Procedure Flowchart Symbols

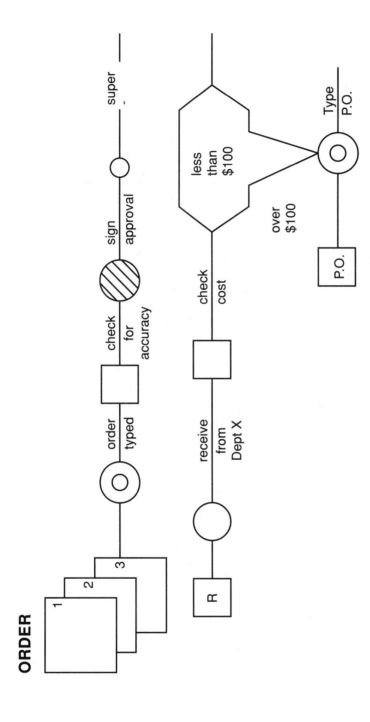

ORDER

1
2
3

order typed

check for accuracy

sign approval

super

receive from Dept X

R

check cost

less than $100

over $100

Type P.O.

P.O.

Exhibit 2-7. Sample Procedure Flowchart

F. Process steps are described briefly by printing the information to the right of the symbol.

G. When a multi-copy form is originated, the parts are illustrated by the inspection symbol and the form title or number is printed inside the square.

H. When the same activity affects two or more documents simultaneously, it is shown by drawing a vertical rectangle around a symbol indicating the activity. The flow lines are drawn to meet the rectangle.

I. The charting of one document affecting or creating other documents is shown on the line of the affected action. A "V" line coming from the original document is dropped or inverted to meet the affected document line. After the action shown by a symbol is completed, the last leg of the "V" returns the document to its original level.

2.7.5 Dataflow Diagram

Dataflow (data flow) diagrams are replacing the more traditional systems flowchart. Like its predecessor, it has not been guided by any one national standard. There is more than one proposed set of symbols, but all share the same concept and objective. The four diagramming symbols used in this text are based on work by C. Gane and T. Sarson. Their book, *Structured Systems Analysis and Design Tools and Techniques,* is the source of the concept and symbols represented here.

Data flow diagrams, which have been around for some time, are familiar in the academic environment. They have many advantages over traditional systems flowcharts when presenting graduated levels of overviews for both current and proposed systems. Because the documentation system is so simple and employs so few rules and symbols, there is little variation between textbooks illustrating its use. Its simplicity provides for a more uniform pictorial presentation of systems that can be followed by systems analysts, programmers, operations personnel, and most users. There are commercially available dataflow diagram templates and microcomputer drawing software. See Exhibit 2-8 for the dataflow symbols. The standard programming flowcharting template may be used with some minor substitutions. The auxiliary operation symbol can replace the dataflow environmental element symbol. The process symbol can replace the dataflow process or procedure symbol. The programming or procedure flowcharting templates can be employed to draw the data storage symbol.

The dataflow diagram illustrates the systems flow and transformation process all on one page, which allows it to be viewed in its entirety. Subsystems requiring greater detail are drawn at the next level, also in their entirety, one per page, and with an identification number linking them to their source. This is illustrated in Exhibits 2-9, 2-10, and 2-11. This procedure can be repeated until the final, lowest subsystem level. The complexity and number of subsystems within the undertaking determine the number of levels that may be "exploded." The dataflow diagram levels may be defined as follows:

A. Context diagram

    The total system concept is drawn as the "large picture," illustrating all data flows into and out of the system. The processes themselves remain unnumbered and are not described in this general overview. The context dataflow diagram would be the one most likely considered for use in a management presentation (see Exhibit 2-9).

B. Level 0 (zero) dataflow diagram

    This level represents the total system, numbering and describing each process. Data storage symbols are used to depict the movement of data to or from storage (see Exhibit 2-10).

C. Level 1 dataflow diagram

    This level represents one of the processes or procedures found at the zero dataflow level that has been exploded into its own subsystem detail (see Exhibit 2-11).

D. Level 2 dataflow diagram

    This level represents the further exploding of a given process found at level 1 into its own subsystem detail.

Comment:
The ease of freehand drawing of this kind of flowchart lends itself well to prototyping. The user working with a systems analyst can easily follow the procedure and the concept of what the four dataflow diagram symbols represent.

Process or Element	Symbol
Entity, an environmental element, can be the source or destination of data to or from the system or subsystems.	
Process system or procedures that act on data being received from an external source or an internal file (hard copy or computer database or file).	
Data storage. This can be a computer file or database, hard copy, microfilm or COM, reference lists or tables, even the back of a tablet.	
Data flow. This can be in many forms, such as LAN or WAN systems, direct computer communications, the US mail, UPS, courier or what have you, between the process system (symbols) and data storage or external source. An arrow will be drawn at the contact point of the receiving symbol to denote the recipient of the data.	

The diagramming symbols used for data flow diagrams are based on work by C. Gane and T. Sarson, *Structured Systems Analysis and Design Tools and Techniques,* Prentice Hall, Englewood Cliffs, NJ, 1979.

Exhibit 2-8. Dataflow Flowchart Diagram Symbols

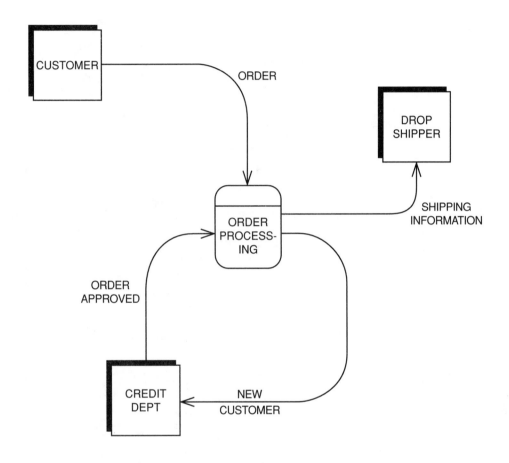

CUSTOMER

ORDER

DROP
SHIPPER

ORDER
PROCESS-
ING

SHIPPING
INFORMATION

ORDER
APPROVED

CREDIT
DEPT

NEW
CUSTOMER

Exhibit 2-9. Context Dataflow Diagram

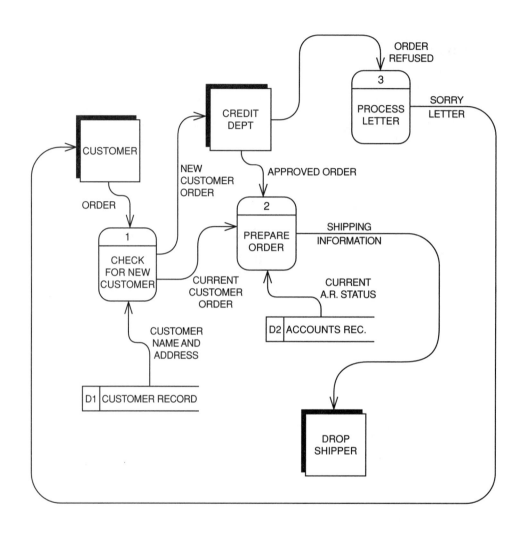

Exhibit 2-10. Level Zero Dataflow Diagram

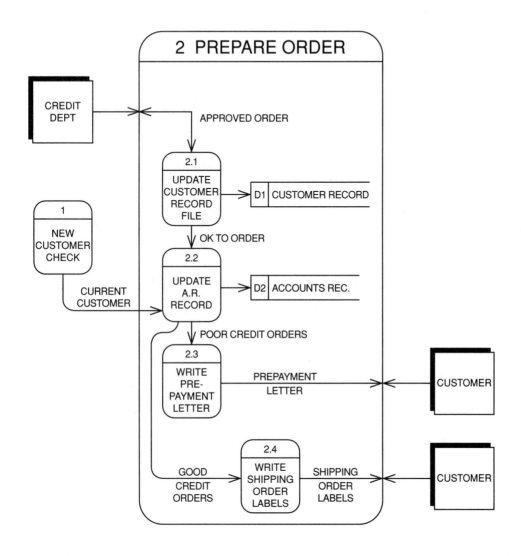

2 PREPARE ORDER

CREDIT DEPT

APPROVED ORDER

2.1 UPDATE CUSTOMER RECORD FILE

D1 | CUSTOMER RECORD

1 NEW CUSTOMER CHECK

OK TO ORDER

2.2 UPDATE A.R. RECORD

D2 | ACCOUNTS REC.

CURRENT CUSTOMER

POOR CREDIT ORDERS

2.3 WRITE PRE-PAYMENT LETTER

PREPAYMENT LETTER

CUSTOMER

GOOD CREDIT ORDERS

2.4 WRITE SHIPPING ORDER LABELS

SHIPPING ORDER LABELS

CUSTOMER

Exhibit 2-11. Level One Dataflow Diagram

2.7.6 Supplemental Dataflow Conventions

The dataflow diagramming procedure can get complex. With successive levels of explosions one may have the equivalent of a bucket of entangled wire coat hangers to deal with. To help clarify the diagram, each of the four symbols employed can utilize supplemental conventions. Their use is illustrated in Exhibit 2-12. Following are additional conventions that may be of help:

- Entity symbols that are duplicated contain a diagonal slash in the bottom right corner. This can reduce the complexity of data flow lines.

- Process symbols contain the process number in the top part of the symbol. When a diagram is exploded, a decimal representing the current level is added to the process number to provide for an audit trail of the related detailed processes (see Exhibit 2-12).

- Data storage symbols have a boxed area on the left side of the symbol in which to write the data storage ID. A vertical line drawn to the left of the ID indicates a duplicate data storage location.

- When data flow lines cross each other, one of the lines may use a small crossover bridge to illustrate that the lines do not intersect.

Dataflow diagrams may be drawn by a single person or as a group effort. If prepared by a group, a black board or white board can be used. Or use a flip chart to keep a record of what was drawn. A board that can reproduce hard copies from the board's display would be the most ideal instrument.

Using dataflow diagrams is good both for documenting a current system or developing a proposed system.

A. Dataflow Diagram Development Procedure

Develop a freehand context diagram. This can start with on-hand user input.

- List the external entities, data flows, and processes.
- Determine the scope of the system being charted.
- Draw the context diagram.

B. Develop a level zero dataflow diagram

- Apply detail to each process or procedure.

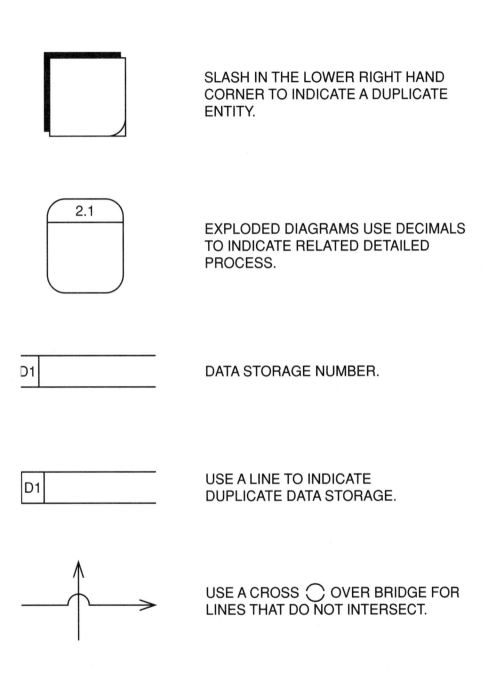

SLASH IN THE LOWER RIGHT HAND
CORNER TO INDICATE A DUPLICATE
ENTITY.

EXPLODED DIAGRAMS USE DECIMALS
TO INDICATE RELATED DETAILED
PROCESS.

DATA STORAGE NUMBER.

USE A LINE TO INDICATE
DUPLICATE DATA STORAGE.

USE A CROSS ⌒ OVER BRIDGE FOR
LINES THAT DO NOT INTERSECT.

Exhibit 2-12. Supplemental Dataflow Conventions

- Identify and post data storage. Note data storage types such as hard drive, floppy disks, file drawer, etc.

- Identify process exceptions and post to the diagram.

C. Draw the diagrams with the aid of a template. Relabel any symbols requiring more meaningful text and clean up the arrangement of the symbols.

D. Explode to the next level and repeat A, B, and C above.

2.7.7 Program Flowcharts

A program flowchart shows operation steps and logic decisions to be followed by the computer for a given program in the processing sequence. All the symbols employed should conform to the ANSI (American National Standards Institute) standards. These symbols are shown in Exhibit 2-13.

Follow these rules in preparing the flowcharts:

A. Draw charts on $8\frac{1}{2}$-by-11-inch or 11-by-17-inch white, 20 pound paper.

B. Draw charts with a number two pencil.

C. The general direction of flow is top to bottom, and left to right.

D. When the flow is not specified or whenever increased clarity is desired, use arrows to indicate the direction of flow.

E. Identify each page with:

- Project name.
- Project number.
- Name of person who produced the flowchart.
- Date.
- Page n of n.

F. The terminal connector to show that a line is carried to a following page is identified with an upper case alphabetic character in the center of the connector symbol. The line being continued on the following page starts with a connector symbol and the same character in its center as the departing connector. In the event that the line does not continue on the following page, post the page number to the right of the connector symbol and post the departing page number to the right of the receiving connector.

G. Describe process steps briefly by printing the description within the symbol. If necessary, print additional information next to the symbol to clarify a step.

H. When changes are made to the flowchart at a later date, the change should be noted, dated, and signed by the person making the change.

Diskette Input/Output This symbol is used for floppy diskettes of all sizes. (Not ANSI standard.)	
Hard Disk This symbol is for hard disk input or output.	
Magnetic Tape This symbol is for magnetic tape cartridge or reels as input or output.	
Auxiliary Operation This symbol is for an off-line operation such as downloading a magnetic tape to microfiche.	
Preparation This symbol represents the modification of an instruction or group of instructions which change the program itself.	
Manual Operation This symbol is used to show a manual operation which is limited to the speed of a human being.	

Exhibit 2-13. ANSI Flowchart Symbols

Process This symbol represents a processing function. It can also represent a system symbol for a central processing unit.	
Decision This symbol represents a decision step, with one or more alternative paths to be followed.	
Input/Output This symbol represents the input or output of data.	
Flow Lines Flow lines are used to connect the symbols and show the process flow.	
Annotation This symbol is used for adding comments to an operation step.	
Connector This symbol is used to exit to or enter from another part of a flowchart, especially when using another page.	
Terminal Point This symbol is used to start or stop a flowchart.	
Communication Link This is used to show data being transmitted over communication channels.	

Exhibit 2-13 (cont'd)

Sort Symbol This is used to represent the arranging of a set of items into a particular sequence.	
Predefined Process This symbol is used to illustrate a sub-routine that is specified elsewhere.	
Document This symbol represents a printed document output.	
Display This is to show output displayed on a CRT.	
Off-line Storage Any storage that is not directly accessible by a computer.	
On-line Storage This symbol is for input or output which uses direct access storage such as hard disk, diskettes and so forth.	
Scanning document This symbol is used for source documents which are to be scanned as input. (Not ANSI standard)	
Manual Input This symbol is used for manual input entered from on-line keyboards.	

Exhibit 2-13 (cont'd)

Chapter 3
SYSTEMS ANALYSIS AND DESIGN

1. INTRODUCTION

3.1 INTRODUCTION

Most projects begin with the initial project planning stage and progress in order through each succeeding phase. However, some projects may begin later in the process. Therefore, it is the responsibility of the project leader or systems analyst to make certain that the project has had the required planning.

A plan is required to manage a project in the most efficient manner. Its purpose is to provide an overall, consistent format to follow when undertaking systems projects. It includes a procedure to keep management informed on the status of each project by periodic progress reports, starting with the first phase and following through to the end. The plan should aim for what results are achievable with the resources allotted by management.

3.1.1 Policy Objectives

The policy governing project development requires the following:

A. An organization of systems projects into major phases.

B. A timetable that specifies both chargeable and calendar time.

C. A directive stipulating the format for the progress report which can be arranged by task phases to be completed or by target date, the date by which each phase is to be completed.

D. An overall plan that ensures the principal features required for an acceptable undertaking. These are:

1. Economic feasibility

   Will the new system pay for itself in its expected lifetime?

2. Organizational feasibility

   Will the system operate within the current organizational structure?

3. Technical feasibility

   Will the proposed system actually work?

4. Operational feasibility

   Can the system work within the environment for which it is designed? If applicable, will it successfully operate outside the firm?

3.1.2 Scope

The scope of a systems project is identified by its constrained elements. First, the relevant activities of the project set up limits. These activities may be confined by time limits, dollar resources, the extent of required changes, and/or organizational or systems boundaries. Second, the subject area identifies and restricts the project scope. If expanded beyond its subject area, the project loses its frame of reference, unallocated resources are likely to be expended, and the objective of the project becomes less clear. Therefore, a policy to contain the scope of a management-approved project is essential to its success.

> **Comment:**
> Many IS or systems managers can attribute late, over-budgeted or uncompleted projects to a wandering into unrelated areas of user needs. Objectives and careers are jeopardized if control over the scope of a project and resources is not retained. This lack of control may help explain some of the management turnover in the information technology profession.

2. DEVELOPMENT AND PLANNING

3.2 SYSTEMS DEVELOPMENT AND PLANNING

The system project's organization requires a standard procedure to ensure that proper planning, control, and status reporting are accomplished. These defined procedures provide standards to (1) assess a project in progress, (2) assess the merits of one project over another, and (3) provide a tool when reviewing employees for merit rewards.

3.2.1 Project Planning

The following tasks are included in project planning:

A. Definition of project goals:

- Systems output.
- Systems throughput process.
- Systems control mechanism.
- Systems requirements.
- Determine calendar time needed to complete project.

If any of these five areas can be subdivided into measurable milestones for reporting, it should be done. (For example, throughput processing, which may entail more than one manual procedure or computer program.)

B. Project plan preparation

A brief plan and a schedule are developed outlining the tasks to be performed (as well as the time necessary to perform them) in order to accomplish the project goals. These include:

- Identifying the work necessary to accomplish project goals. This also includes tasks which are applicable to projects but were not identified as work to be covered in planned goals. These should be divided into measurable units or milestones.
- Developing detailed database, file, report and program specifications.
- Establishing budgets.
- Assigning responsibilities for tasks.
- Preparing work load schedules.

- Preparing appropriate project documentation.
- Developing Gantt charts from project schedules for planning and reporting the status of project tasks.
- Preparing a format and schedule for project status reports.

3.2.2 Analysis of Requirements

The project leader or head systems analyst works closely with the potential user to ensure that the systems requirements are defined and understood, and that the user does not expect the system to be revised in the near future. A number of techniques are available to ensure that all systems requirements are precisely defined. These are:

- Determine the capabilities of the project team to achieve given system objectives.
- Establish operating parameters.
- Organize all pertinent data elements.
- Define processing requirements.
- Determine output requirements.
- Determine required database or file needs.
- Determine required data input requirements and the method of input.

To ensure that all requirements have been defined prior to the systems design phase, use a checklist similar to the one shown in Exhibit 3-1.

3.2.3 Estimating Resource Requirements

A resource estimate, prepared for each project, is used to allocate resources for projects and provide a basis for project financial control. Estimates may also provide a basis for preparing user service charges. The person in charge of planning should do the following:

A. Estimate the man-days required for analysis and programming. This estimate may be revised as programming proceeds. Contingency time is added for each defined task depending on similar past experience and/or the track record of the person assigned the task. Contingencies should also be considered if the project covers an extended calendar time period. This can help avoid a possible late or over-budget project.

A. Data Input Editing

1. Does editing look for missing data?
2. Does editing include verification of format?
3. Does editing include verification of codes?
4. Will editing be completed in a single process?
5. Will editing procedure vary due to external conditions?
6. What will be the bypass procedure?

B. Database and File Updating

1. How frequently are backups done?
2. Are partial updates done?
3. Must source data be corrected prior to update procedures?
4. Are files purged periodically?
5. Are purged data files transferred to inactive files?
6. Will a transaction backup file be on-line?

C. Output Preparation

1. Is the output on a monitor?
2. If the output is hard copy, how many copies are needed?
3. Is the hard copy output a regular report or only provided on demand?
4. Do the reports contain summaries and intermediate summaries?
5. Will output be made available for a LAN or WAN network, for a client/server system, or by MODEM?

D. Error Correction

1. Will the error correction routines require rewriting the source document?
2. Is it possible for uncorrected data to enter the processing system?
3. Can an error be corrected after it has been placed in a file or database? How?

Exhibit 3-1. Systems Development Checklist

A wise project head may plug in an additional amount of time for the whole project and call it the "contingency factor." If a project becomes late or over budget, as most projects do, this budgeted extra time will be welcome. The man-days needed should be converted to dollars. If all the time and/or money allocated is not needed, the project will finish ahead of schedule and/or under budget which can reflect well on the project head.

Prepare Gantt charts for the man-days required, indicating the calendar time personnel will be available since not all project personnel are available full time. Set milestones within each Gantt chart to identify the status of each project task. This status can be plotted against the budgeted allotted time to determine whether the task is on schedule.

B. Gantt chart the budget allotted for each task or phase. When reporting the financial status of the project, plot the actual amount spent on a separate chart. Then compare the amount spent to-date to the amount that should have been spent at any given point in the project. With these two Gantt charts plotted in parallel, financial problems can be recognized.

C. Identify and estimate all equipment, software, and service costs required for the new system. A dollar contingency amount should be added to cover any unforeseen expenses.

3. SYSTEMS ANALYSIS

3.3 SYSTEMS ANALYSIS

The objective of systems analysis is to analyze a system that is operational. Of course, if a new system is to be designed that is not replacing or altering one already in place, there will not be a need for this analysis. In that case only the requirements for the new system are needed for the systems design.

Prototyping a new system may not require a thorough systems analysis on the part of the IS (information systems) design person, but any information he or she can obtain about the user area will be helpful. This information can reduce the time needed for the prototyping development. Also, the user will have more confidence in the systems analyst if he/she "speaks the user's language," and this could enhance the final design.

The process of systems analysis has changed little over the years. Some people new to systems analysis and others who do not want to allocate resources and/or costs to this effort avoid it, or limit its scope. This lack of analysis accounts for a good portion of new system failures. It is a common practice for known consulting firms to relegate this task to their lower-priced help. The consequences are self-evident. There also can be a problem of "paralysis through analysis," that is, spending too much time on this phase. But this is seldom the case.

This section on analysis provides the traditional, proven procedures. The process resembles learning to ride a bicycle: knowing the steps does not guarantee success, but knowing and practicing the procedures can produce the desired results.

3.3.1 Pre-Analysis Survey

Certain pre-analysis information would help before attempting to contact the user for an analysis of the current operating system. Gather as much knowledge about the unit as possible. A feasibility study is a good place to start.

Discover who the unit's head and subordinates are, probably from an organization chart for large units. One Fortune 500 firm employs organizational charts with pictures to go along with the names and titles. Try to remember the names of the unit's personnel and their respective titles. Also, know who works for whom. Any information about personalities that can be discovered beforehand, and also the status of the unit within the rest of the organization, would help. Become aware of the corporate politics with which the unit's people are involved. These hidden power structures can be a mine field, delaying the system's progress.

Examine current procedural documentation. This will provide the systems analyst with the "formal" procedures of the current operation. Later the analyst will have an opportunity to confirm whether the procedures are still valid, and, if not, what has changed. The operating procedures should include forms used. If not, obtain copies. They will help you understand their role in the operation.

3.3.2 Initial Unit Visit

Call the unit's head for a first meeting in his/her office. If the head is not in, leave a voice mail message to return the call.

> **Comment:**
> Prepare for the visit. Dress in a manner consistent with what is expected of a manager in the area. If the area being visited is down in the bowels of the manufacturing operation's spray painting section, do not wear your new $500 outfit.

The first visit with the unit's head may need to be played by ear. Some might be too busy to spend time with you, while others will talk your head off. This is when the art of listening becomes important. It has been said "you cannot be a listener with your mouth open." Ask the unit's head about the operation, the unit's problems, the unit's people. If time and conditions permit, include a little social chatter, along with a cup of coffee. Later, have the person introduce you to the employees. At this time set up "the best time" for the return visit. If this person cannot see you within a reasonable time, ask to speak with someone lower on the organization chart, or start with the first person in the unit working with the current system.

3.3.3 Information Gathering Interviews

It is wise not to spend too much time on the first visit with any one person. Speaking with a person six times for ten minutes each is better for the systems analyst than a single one-hour visit because the analyst will learn more and also develop a closer relationship with that person. Remember when conducting an interview:

- Try to start at the beginning of an operation flow.
- Try to interview the person at his/her place of work. If this cannot be done, find a neutral place to meet.
- If the person is ill or has a problem come back later.
- Develop listening skills.
- Do not repeat rumors.
- Interview all the people in the unit if possible. In that way no one will be seen as a favorite, and more will be learned. Even if several people perform the same job, each may see it from a different perspective. One may come up with something that the others overlooked.

- Be open with your note taking. Shorthand pads work well.
- Do not jump to conclusions.
- Listen carefully for what the person really means.
- Leave your information technology jargon at the door.
- Be aware of the body language of the interviewee.
- Look for the content and not the style of delivery of the information.
- Do not assume anything.
- Avoid playing favorites with workers.
- Define what tools are employed: hardware, software, files accessed, etc.
- Ask questions. (But be aware of who may have a stake in or have developed the current system.)
- Give people time to get the correct answer.
- Collect copies of documents and ask:

  —What is the daily volume of forms, reports, etc.?

  —From what outside places do documents come?

  —Who originates the first inside document?

  —Why is the document used?

  —How is the document completed?

  —Where are the documents filed?

- Other questions:

  —Has the worker come up with his/her own procedures to make things work?

  —How often and when are backups done?

  —What is the security procedure?

  —What problems are there with operating instructions?

  —Whom do you contact for help?

- Conclude the interview by thanking the person.

3.3.4 Document the Interviews

After the interviews are over, you must analyze the information gathered. Draw (freehand) flowcharts from the data collected.

Return to the unit and authenticate the flowchart(s) by observing the actual people doing the jobs. If need be, send a follow-up memo verifying the approval of the documented information by the person or persons interviewed.

Dictate or write the present procedures so they can be included in the final systems report. Prepare the final flowcharts and make necessary copies.

3.3.5 Work Sampling Studies

Work sampling is a tool used by the systems analyst to find out how people are spending their time at work. Since labor costs are a significant part of operating cost, it is essential to know how that time is spent. To justify the cost of new procedures or hardware investments, work sampling is used to study a current operation. It is a simple procedure, and when properly used can reveal what areas require further study.

As a simple example, take the question, "Should the company purchase a second copy machine?" The systems analyst performs random observations of the number of people waiting in line to use the copy machine, then turns that number into hours per day of wait time. These hours represent dollars: the cost of an employee waiting instead of working. This cost plus the price of acquiring a new machine, along with the additional cost of operating a second machine (floor space, etc.), determine the write-off time cost for the acquisition. This information helps management decide to make the purchase or not.

Another facet of this work sampling information for this particular decision might be the travel time of people who use the copy machine. Ask people waiting the location of their work units to help compute this travel time. Perhaps the second machine could be placed better in order to reduce travel time costs.

This is a very simple example. More complex studies can ferret out other kinds of information. One study done under cover revealed that in a department of 16 people, each person was spending 35 percent of the time doing no work at all. The reason was a lack of supervision.

Another study was set up to find out how people in an engineering support unit of a Fortune 500 firm spent their time and what new equipment needed to reduce the heavy overtime. The new manager was at a loss to discover what the problem was. The study discovered that employees were not working as hard or as efficiently as they should have because they enjoyed the overtime too much. These findings enabled the company to eliminate Saturday overtime costs.

Other information can help address specific problems. For example, in one instance discovery of a new government regulation that required a ratio of hours to workers that equalled three persons made it possible to cost justify these three people quickly and cheaply.

A work sampling study involves the following:

A. Observation times

Observations of the work area to be studied are performed at random times and dates. Random numbers can be generated by computer software, taken from a random number table in a math book, or drawn out of a hat. It is suggested that two sets of observation times be drawn: a small sample of 50 or so, a larger sample later. The specific sample size is dependent on the number of items and people observed. About a hundred observations per item type observed is typical. There are formulas available used by industrial engineers to compute the number needed for the required confidence level.

B. Preliminary observations

Compose a list of tasks for the preliminary study of 50 observations. Personal time and miscellaneous should always be included. "Out of the area and available but no work" may in some cases be selected, too. These tasks are posted to the tally sheet for observations (see Exhibits 3-2). The observations are performed only by the systems analyst and no one else, especially not the boss. People are not normally identified by name.

The observations are taken in a split second and tally marked (i.e., a mark is made for each observation, four in a row, with the fifth mark across the other four). The tallies are counted and posted in the total column on the right hand side. After the tallies are posted, each total value is divided by the total number of observations. For example, with a preliminary observation of 50, divide each task total value by 50 to get the percent of time spent with that task. Added together the percent value will total approximately 100 percent.

C. New tally sheet

Using the results of the preliminary observations, add or delete items from the final observation study. Those with less than a five percent tally are normally deleted from the final study. When the miscellaneous category is very high, over 20 percent, try to identify a category or categories to be removed and placed under their own tasks. Then construct a new tally sheet for the final study.

Date(s) _1/10 – 1/20/97_ By _Mary Smith_

Unit observed _Billing Support_ Number of people _4_

Task	Tally	Total	%
Filing	ΙΝΙ ΝΙΙ ΙΝΙ ΙΝΙ ΙΝΙ ΙΝΙ	30	30
Telephone	ΙΝΙ ///	8	8
Reading	ΙΝΙ ΙΝΙ /	11	11
Writing	ΙΝΙ ΙΝΙ ΙΝΙ ΙΝΙ /	21	21
Personal	ΙΝΙ ΙΝΙ	10	10
Misc.	ΙΝΙ ΙΝΙ ΙΝΙ ΙΝΙ	20	20
	TOTAL NUMBER OF OBSERVATIONS	100	100

Exhibit 3-2. Completed Sampling Tally Sheet

D. Final observation study

The final observation study is made at the random times and dates selected. Complete the tally sheet as explained in section B. Then divide each task total by the total number of observations to get the task percentage.

3.3.6 Final Report

Place the procedure text and flowcharts in a binder with a cover sheet titled "Final Analysis Study Report" and a name to identify the study. The cover memo summarizes the study and includes any recommendations as well as any further comments the analyst may wish to make. This memo is not placed in the report binder but is sent to the project leader, along with the feasibility study and the report. The dates and hours expended on the analysis should be reported in the format required by the project leader.

4. SYSTEMS DESIGN

3.4 SYSTEMS DESIGN

The objective of systems design is to take the systems parameters as defined in the development and planning phase and create a system to the degree allowed given the allocated resources and time frame. Resources and time limitations are determined by the defined scope of the project. If a systems analysis final report is available it should serve as an information base in designing the new system.

The systems analyst synthesizes the elements of a number of design alternatives and compares them with the design criteria. They should be compared to each other and to the current system. The one that comes closest to achieving the defined objectives, with the best utilization of resources, is the best choice. This decision is not that of the systems analyst alone; management and/or the user will have an impact on the final selection of the "best" solution. The analyst may be the designer of the alternative systems, but management and the user have to live with the selection long after the analyst has moved on to other projects.

The procedure steps required to achieve optimal design are:

• Establish detailed system design specifications for selected design.

• Determine proper utilization of software, hardware, assigned personnel and contract services.

- Prepare a final systems report supported with documentation and system flowcharts.
- Gain acceptance of the proposed system from requesting authorities and users.

3.4.1 Systems Design Specifications

The development of systems design specifications includes any refinements that can be incorporated into the design as requested by users and the requesting authority. Final design documentation will include input, output, database, and software specifications to meet the design requirements. Above all, backup and recovery procedures, along with security requirements, are a must.

A. System specifications

The details for this phase are determined by what is needed to communicate the system requirements to programmers or software vendors.

Following are guidelines for developing these specifications:

1. Develop output requirements first based on user report or monitor display needs.

2. Develop file specifications.

   An index of table field names (the names which can be found in database, programs, and input/output locations) is developed. The specifications include all data elements required for present or anticipated needs, and a data dictionary to provide their specifications.

3. Define the input layouts.

   This is the format of all data to be captured for use by the system. This input can be source documents coming into the information systems data entry unit or input received as captured data from outside the computer operation. The source of captured data received by the system is input from terminals or other, nonkeyed data, and is of major concern to the systems analyst who must ensure that only the required input gains entry to the system.

4. Develop the processing requirements. Processing operations required by the software are described in detail. In addition, general guidelines may be required for some functions such as:

   - Procedures for entry of corrections.

- Controls to monitor out-of-balance conditions (e.g., a minus payroll check or inventory balance).
- Editing routines for missing or incorrect data entering the system for the first time.
- Proper restart procedures for the user.

B. Manual procedures

Clerical tasks are included to:

- Review data to ensure it can be entered.
- Correct input data.
- Change data already in the system.
- Hold or dispose of input data.
- Distribute printed output.

3.4.2 Utilization of Resources

Essential to preparing the system design specifications is understanding the availability of hardware, software, and personnel resources. Analyze these to determine their adequacy to fulfill the systems objectives. If any of the three is inadequate, changes are required. If the resources cannot be changed, it may be necessary to alter the system's scope or objectives.

3.4.3 Final Systems Report

The proposed system design is documented in the form of a final systems report which defines objectives and states how the proposed system design will meet them. The scope of the undertaking is defined, along with a proposed timetable for installing the new system. It contains proposed costs and return expected, in both tangible and intangible benefits, for the resource investment. Its purpose is to inform and gain acceptance of the proposed system, and the report is hand-carried to the proper individuals one to two weeks before the verbal presentation is to be made.

The report contains the following:

A. A summary of the full systems study.

- An overview of the events leading up to the study.
- The subject of the study.
- The objectives and scope of the proposed system.

- A statement of recommendations and justifications for the proposed system.

B. Body of the report
   1. A description of the current system, including:
      - A brief description of the current system and how it is employed.
      - The purpose of the current system.
      - The problems with the current system (if any) and the rationale for a new system.
   2. A description of the proposed system, including:
      - An overview of the proposed system.
      - The scope of the project.
      - Exhibits of all reports and monitor displays.
      - System flowcharts.
      - Systems documentation of the proposed system and any vendor-supplied material that provides additional information.
      - A summary of proposed recommendations.
      - A list of personnel needs:
         a. Manpower required to install the new system.
         b. Manpower required to maintain the new system.
      - A proposed timetable for installing the suggested system and the work hours required to complete the project.
   3. The financial information section, including:
      - The operating cost of the present system.
      - The operating cost of the proposed system.
      - The installation cost of the new system and its estimated useful life.
      - The tangible and intangible benefits of the proposed system.
   4. Proposed system summary

      A positive statement of the rationale for installing the proposed system. The summary also contains any reservations or apprehensions that may exist about the timetable, funds, software, hardware, outside contractors, or personnel available for the undertaking.

C. Appendix

1. Prior reports

2. Memos and letters

3. Other supporting documents not included in the body of the report:

   - Sample documents and forms.
   - Charts.
   - Graphs.
   - Gantt charts.
   - Tables of data.
   - Vendor literature.

3.4.4 The Acceptance Presentation

Gaining acceptance of the proposed system is the last step before systems implementation. All concerned parties are brought together for a verbal and visual presentation. Everyone attending should have had enough time to read the report. This presentation is used to confirm that the proposed system will meet its objective and stay within the defined scope.

Although not always required, the presentation to gain final acceptance can be just as important as the final written report which serves as a basis for the verbal presentation. But reading the report itself is not enough. Therefore, a different approach must be adopted to resolve any problems, whether political or technical. It is very important that the presenter know the attitudes, political positions, and status of all those attending the presentation. Not everyone present may be supportive; some may object to possible added demands on their areas, loss of present control, or loss of operations.

Here are some suggestions on how to sell your proposal:

- Be relaxed. Otherwise, people may think you are trying to hide something.
- Gain approval by seeking support from people before the meeting.
- Decide whether you want credit for your innovation or acceptance. You may not get both. This is the corporate game of politics.
- Do not expect others to think like you do.
- Do not present any surprises. People do not like them.
- Never expect that people want change or innovation simply because they may have indicated they did in the past.

Well-planned audio and visual aids help to create a positive impression on the audience. Flip charts particularly add visual interest by providing step-by-step information with graphs, flowcharts and text materials. You can write notes on the edge of each page to assist you in making the presentation.

Overhead transparency projections are easy to use, but they require some preparation to look professional. The information to be presented should be readable by all in the audience. A safe rule to follow is: place the material at your feet and stand up. If you can read it, so can your audience. With the computer graphic software now available for making overhead transparencies, presentations can look professional. Always have a replacement projector bulb available.

In-house graphic arts departments may be of help in producing the visual aids you require. They may even have a micro or lap-top computer system that will allow projections of microcomputer visual output, often in color. Vendors may be a source of visuals, too.

Whatever materials you use make sure you are comfortable with them. New, untried hardware or software can spell disaster. Check the room out the day before and have a dry run if you can. The day of the presentation arrive no less than a half hour before to insure everything is ready. Test any equipment to make sure it works. Your high exposure may not spell a promotion, but a disaster is something you may have to live down.

The presentation should help gain as much support for and acceptance of the new system as possible. In some cases, it may even wrap up its sale. Following is a basic presentation outline:

A. Introduction

   The introduction consists only of preliminary descriptions. Introduce yourself and the subject of the presentation. Explain how the system study began and progressed, and how the presentation will be made. Include:

   • A statement about the need for a new system.

   • An explanation about how alternative systems were reviewed before selecting the one being presented.

   • An explanation of the format that will follow the introduction.

B. The body

   The body is the heart of the presentation. Use terminology familiar to those present, especially management and users. Those attending the presentation will be more interested in what is done than how the technology works. Emphasize the benefits of the new system and not its hardware or software. Have a positive attitude about the benefits (such as faster processing or response time, better accuracy and control, and, maybe, reduced costs). Reliable information and honesty about any drawbacks are necessities. The body should:

1. Briefly describe the current operating system.
2. Describe the proposed system and any alternate proposals.
3. Present the economic information:

   • Current system operating costs.
   • Proposed system operating costs.
   • Cost of installing the proposed system. (Be conservative with cost claims.)
   • Intangible benefits and/or requirements imposed by customers, vendors, or the government.

4. Provide recommendations for the proposed selection.

C. Summary of the presentation

All the tangible and intangible benefits of the proposed system should be stressed.

D. Discussion

1. Open the meeting and answer questions.
2. Keep discussion going; call on people who support the proposed system for their input.
3. Be aware of the attitudes of the people who are present and have a strategy ready to handle any negative comments.

E. Conclusion

The object of the conclusion is to end the presentation on a positive note. This is done by:

1. Summarizing the areas of agreement brought up during the open discussion.
2. Making a positive statement as to what will happen with the project and how those involved will be kept informed of its progress.

5. SYSTEM PROTOTYPING

3.5 SYSTEM PROTOTYPING

This section covers ideas and procedures for using prototyping to design a working systems model. Prototyping is an analysis and design technique that involves end users in defining the requirements and developing the system according to their needs and desires. It helps define the end user requirements much more quickly than using the traditional analysis and design approach. The system complexity can involve a number of (modular) prototypes.

Prototypes can be hand drawn (see dataflow diagrams, Chapter Two, Section 6.3) or developed with computer software tools that are available for both Apple and IBM PC hardware. Computer-aided systems and software engineering (CASE) technologies automate the analysis and design process using modeling tools and other techniques. Also, Fourth-Generation Languages (4GLs) can serve as prototyping tools and can be installed easily on today's microcomputers.

The newer kid on the block is JAD (Joint Applications Development). If you plan to try it, start with a "safe" project, one that has very little chance of failure because:

- User is skillful and cooperative.
- The application is a one-user and/or simple application.
- Minimum of hardware/software changes needed.
- Top quality team is assigned to the project.
- Safe pause in computer use to complete the project.
- Adequate budget.

A well-selected user is essential.

The systems analyst working with the user can develop an iterative series of prototypes which can be viewed and revised interactively. This reduces both the calendar and chargeable project time.

Prototyping is best suited for developing systems that are not well defined, or for exceptional, smaller systems applications. It allows for the visualization and conversation required for quick systems development. All too often users will ask for something they cannot define or else they cannot see how changes will satisfy their needs. This type of situation would be a candidate for a prototyping effort.

The characteristics that most systems share when they are likely candidates for prototyping are:

- User requirements are difficult to define.
- The application has few users, often only one.
- The application may be ad hoc or even parochial in nature.
- The application has a low volume input and/or output.
- The application requires a minimum of editing controls.
- User(s) may only require a stand-alone microcomputer using their own files or database.

3.5.1 Prototype Development

The systems analyst will need to consider what kind of system requires development since not all undertakings are suitable for prototyping. A traditional system that cuts across two or more departments would most likely be a poor candidate. Another poor candidate would be an order processing or payroll system. Rather, single user, novel and/or complex applications, and semi-structured or even unstructured applications are all good candidates for this kind of approach.

The systems analysis management must also evaluate the environmental conditions that the systems analyst will be placed in. The political climate and the user's personality play a major role in the success or failure of this kind of undertaking.

The lead systems analyst maintains a prototype project folder, which contains all papers related to the project, and also an activities diary for which a shorthand pad can suffice. The diary should be hand posted while the information is still fresh and should contain information such as: day's activities, how much time is spent on each activity, and any other information the analyst deems worth keeping. The diary is not for publication, but is only a reference record to be placed in the prototype project folder after the effort is completed.

The procedure for prototyping is as follows:

A. Estimate project expense

   Both direct and indirect costs are computed. This includes the system analyst's and programmers' chargeable time, along with other development costs. Software and hardware costs are generally considered indirect costs, but a one-time use software package required for the project is a direct cost.

The calendar time frame is defined, as well as the estimated man-hours to be committed by the information system's personnel. If the costs and time requirements are agreeable to both user and information system's management the project will proceed. The costs may be charged directly to the requesting user's budget or applied to an information systems budget for such projects.

B.   Develop manageable modules.

Module size is reduced to a manageable level so that each module can be built separately from other system or subsystem modules. Each is also designed so as to allow other modules to interact with its features. This development is done in concert with the end user(s) and the systems analyst.

C.   Build the prototype.

As the systems analyst gathers information about the user's requirements for the application, he/she assesses user feedback about the developing prototype in order to better visualize the systems requirements. Successful prototyping depends on early and frequent end user feedback to the developing process. User changes made early in the development process will reduce costs and total project development time.

The systems analyst illustrates to the user(s) as early as possible how parts of the system actually accomplish their objectives. This early construction of an operational prototype will allow early user feedback so that the systems analyst can gain valuable insight into the direction of the prototype construction. To develop the prototype as quickly as possible, the analyst uses whatever special tools are available, such as personal, workgroup or even organizational databases, computer software, and other prototype design tools. Access to databases, other than personal ones, will require the permission of the data administrator and/or the database administrator.

Rapid prototyping development reduces the chance of changes imposed by the user. The longer it takes to develop a system the more the system is susceptible to changes imposed by the user and/or the operational environment. This rapid prototyping development safeguards against overcommitting resources to a project that could eventually become unworkable.

Comment:
The saying "strike while the iron is hot" applies here. The hotter the iron is the easier it is to work. The longer a project is stretched-out the less chance it has to succeed. It could even be turned into a can of worms.

D. Modify the prototype.

The prototype will be exposed to an iteration process. Modifications made with each iteration should move the system closer to what the user(s) says is required. But each modification requires another evaluation by the end user(s).

As with the initial development, revisions must be done as swiftly as possible in order to maintain the project momentum. The duty of the systems analyst is to keep the project moving. The analyst must encourage the user(s) to maintain his/her responsibility to evaluate each revised version for required modifications as soon as possible. The prototyping process requires that the user(s) debug the program as it evolves.

The analyst must also prevent the user(s) from deciding a prototype is operational before it is completed. In this process the systems analyst acts more as a facilitator of iteration than a designer.

This whole process requires good people skills on the part of the systems analyst, who cannot listen to the needs of the user(s) with his/her mouth open. Also, technical vocabulary should be left behind when communicating with the user.

The systems analyst should steer the prototype in a direction that will require a minimum of skill on the part of the user(s), to operate. The completed system must be easy to understand, learn and operate by all users. Today, the trend is to provide the user with an on-line interactive system which uses a monitor as a source of output.

If a chain of interactive prototypes is required for the completed system, the interaction between each prototype module must be operational for the project to be finished. This kind of prototype development could have more than one user, a potential for user disputes which should be resolved as soon as possible.

E. Complete the prototype.

The prototyping is complete when the user has what he/she wants and the systems analyst is willing to sign-off the prototype. The sign-off can take two forms:

1. Scrap the prototype. This action is taken when the user(s) is not satisfied with the finished product or the requirements are beyond what can be reasonably provided.

   The systems analyst is the representative of the systems department, the database administrator, and the data administrator. These areas require limited access by the end users. The systems analyst is required to police the needs of the user so that they do not violate any policies or procedures that are in place for these areas.

2. Accept the prototype. Operationally completed prototypes require sign-off by both the user(s)and the systems analyst. This can take the form of a joint memo from both to the user's management and the head of the systems department. The user(s) by this time will have been trained in the operation of the prototype system, and a operation manual will have been completed and in place. This training and documentation is the responsibility of the lead systems analyst assigned to the project.

   A final project memo is sent by the lead systems analyst to the systems manager within a week after the prototype has been signed-off. This allows for a follow up to confirm that all went as planned. The memo is a summary report on the effective utilization of information systems resources on behalf of the prototype effort. The report may end with an editorialized summary by the analyst responsible for the prototype. The prototype project folder and its diary are sources of information for this report.

3.5.2 Types of Prototyping Methods

Due to different needs, a single "all in one" prototype model is not realistic. However, there are four concepts available to the systems analyst. All four, when applied, follow the same prototype development procedures as outlined in 3.5.1. They are as follows:

A. First-of-a-series prototype

A pilot prototype is developed as a full-scale system, can be made up of subsystems and is a "true" prototype, i.e., one that is developed and debugged at one site. The prototypes that follow are modified to further improve the system. The first-of-a-series is volume tested after it is debugged to insure that the prototype can be replicated at other sites with a minimum of effort and problems.

B. Modular prototype

This is a prototype that does not contain all the attributes that the final system version will have. This method allows for the rapid development of less complex prototypes. After the first has been developed, another similar-featured one is developed and joined to the first to construct a finished product. There can be any number of designated characteristics prototypes connected to complete a final version.

C. One-shot prototype

This is a one-time (or one-shot) prototype for a given one-time need. It could be used at a later time, but seldom is. This type can afford to be very inefficient, as long as the cost to develop it is less than what would be gained from a more efficient operating model. The retrieval, storage, and computation can be primitive, if workable. If this type of prototype is popular, time and effort to develop a "user/request" form would make sense. This form would save time for both the user(s) and systems analyst or programmer analyst.

Comment:
Using such a form for one-shot programs is not a new idea. This writer developed one for a General Electric Engineering department some years ago.

D. Input-output prototype

This is a scale model prototype without an operating program used to save the cost of developing an expensive process program. This prototype has well-defined input and output formats, much like that for a model car. Management may see enough from this to determine that the cost of the process development is worth it. A software tool used for this prototype would be a good word-processing program. Of all the prototypes, this is the one least used.

Comment:
The last time an input-output prototype was observed by this writer was one constructed by a group of students who were working on a systems project. The students were to write a COBOL program which would produce a printed report. But instead of having the program perform the calculations, they hand calculated the results from input test data and then used WordPerfect to print the report. There was no operating program, just an output prototype.

6. SYSTEMS IMPLEMENTATION

3.6 SYSTEMS IMPLEMENTATION

This section covers the procedures governing implementation of the proposed system. This is the most challenging task of any information systems undertaking.

3.6.1 Systems Implementation Prerequisites

The following must be completed before a system is implemented and approved as operational.

A. Systems documentation conforming to the standards defined in Chapter Two.

B. A system walk-through

    1. Purpose

        The purpose of a systems walk-through is to prove the logic of the system with another systems analyst or with users. It must be proven that data records are compatible between operations and/or programs. "Index of Table Field Names" is referenced, updated, and corrected at this point. The walk-through starts with input and is followed through to the required output.

    2. Input requirements

Input requirements for walk-throughs include:

- Raw data or machine usable input.
- Batch or on-line input.
- Control totals or record counts.
- Database elements chosen or generated to provide realistic test data.

3. Anticipated processing

   This includes the process steps required to provide output of data or update of the database or files.

4. Anticipated outputs

   These are normally classified into categories and are followed through to ensure all the data elements are available in the forms required. (Refer to "Index of Table Field Names" to confirm.) The following actions are taken:

   - Total record counts, units, dollars, or other data are checked against expected values.
   - The contents and format of monitor displays and reports are checked against stated requirements and pre-computed results.
   - Errors are identified for those items expected to be rejected by the system.
   - Output data elements that will become input to other systems are checked for compatibility.

3.6.2 Implementation Procedures

The following actions are taken as part of the implementation phase:

- Develop implementation plans, estimates, and conversion procedures.
- Review and update systems specifications to reflect requirements developed during programming.
- Develop test data for program and systems testing.
- Evaluate results from program tests, systems tests, volume tests, and any parallel testing operations. This is done with users to ensure that test specifications and system requirements have been met.
- Update schedule changes.

- Develop training procedures for systems operations and user personnel.
- Confirm that all operational procedures and manuals are in place.
- Confirm that all operational personnel have been trained.
- Request systems operations and/or user sign-off.
- Perform any tests that the auditors have requested.

7. SYSTEMS MAINTENANCE

3.7 SYSTEMS MAINTENANCE

Before a request for any maintenance is approved, the system is examined to determine if it should be modified or redesigned. The presence of the following three factors tends to favor redesign instead of modification:

A. The cost of maintenance of a project exceeds 30 percent of the actual development costs.

B. The existing system has been patched extensively or modified over a period of two to three years.

C. The existing system lacks proper documentation and there is sufficient factual information to justify redesign of the system.

3.7.1 Types of Maintenance Projects

Maintenance efforts may originate from one or more of the following sources:

- Change in policy.
- Change in procedure.
- Change of system flow.
- Change of program instructions.
- Change of operation requirements.
- Change of operating system.
- Hardware changes

3.7.2 Requirements and Responsibility

The systems' head defines the responsibility for coordinating requirements for system maintenance and establishes the tasks to be performed.

A. Review and estimate of work required

The standard task list is reviewed to determine which tasks are necessary to satisfy the maintenance request.

- Identify the problem to be solved by the maintenance project.
- Define the scope and the limitations of the maintenance effort.
- Rewrite operational procedures as required.
- Redesign input/output documents, files or database requirements, and monitor displays or reports as required.
- If needed, correct the Index of Table Field Names.
- Designate programs and procedures which require modification.
- Make needed program changes.
- Test revised programs.

Comment:
The writer recalls a very simple revision that was too "simple" to test and that cost the programmer his job and the firm over one million dollars.

- Document the revisions.
- Perform system tests.

B. Management and/or user approval

Management and users are responsible for the following tasks:

- Approving the intent and objectives of the system modification.
- Helping to develop test data for the system modification.
- Reviewing and approving the test results.
- Making operational personnel available for any retraining required.

3.7.3 Control

Control check-points are established for each maintenance project. Their purpose is two-fold: to ensure the quality and completeness of the maintenance project, and to ensure that the changes made to the system do not alter policy or degrade the system's present performance.

Minimally, controls should be at the following points:

- Completion of program testing.
- Completion of system testing.
- Completion of changed documentation.
- End of maintenance (for confirmation that policies have not been changed).

3.7.4 Revision Conventions

These revision practices are followed:

- All binders for the revision are updated at the same time to avoid any documentation conflicts.
- A revision information cover page is completed for each binder being revised, and is so noted with a revision number and date.
- Obsolete documentation is labeled "obsolete," the date posted, and the documentation filed or destroyed according to the record retention procedure.
- Each procedure or policy affected has the revision number posted at the top right hand side of each new page of documentation.

Chapter 4
Programming Procedures

1. SOFTWARE POLICIES

4.1 Software Policies

Business software must adapt to users' needs for useful information and functionality. This software should model the business in its changing and complex operations. Creating or buying software is much more than a question of resources and cost. It can also be a question of remaining competitive in order to stay in business. There is a need on the policy level to provide some sort of direction for software development, purchase, and maintenance.

Software and programmers have traditionally been free of organizational policies. However, organizations have recently become aware of the costs and risks associated with a lack of such programming and software policy. The move toward interactive processing, client/servers, work group and microcomputer users makes clear the necessity of policy development.

4.1.1 Proprietorship of Computer Software

All programming software developed during work hours by programming personnel paid by the hour is the exclusive property of the employer. Salary-exempt personnel have no proprietary interest in the programs they develop. All programming effort and documentation is the exclusive property of the employer as long as the hardware/software used belongs to the firm.

Additional programs and software policies apply to:

A. Purchased Software

Purchased software and software documentation may only be copied as specified by the vendor. No versions of any purchased software are permitted beyond the number the firm has purchased. This applies to all organization personnel.

B. Unauthorized Software

Personnel may not purchase or write their own software for use in the organization without authorization. They may not bring to the organization any software in any form that is not the property of the organization. The downloading of any unauthorized software to company-owned hardware away from any company site is also not permitted. Any violation of this policy subjects the offender to immediate discharge and/or the reimbursement of all costs associated with such action.

4.1.2 Uniform Programming Practices

The head of computer programming is the authority for both setting standards for computer programming throughout the IS organization and for allocating the resources for new programming development efforts.

Uniform programming practices are maintained throughout the organization as defined in the company policies and procedures manual and only approved documentation procedures are used. Programs are written in a structured manner using sub-sets following the industrial norm. Individual styles of coding are not practiced. Only one style of programming is used for any one authorized computer programming language. The procedure section Software Development (Section 4.2) will be a further extension of the procedure policies that govern program development.

4.1.3 Program Languages

The adoption or discontinuation of any program language can have serious and long-range consequences. Therefore these actions, as well as any upgrades of any given language, must be approved by the head of information systems.

Any purchase or upgrading of operating or network systems software will require the approval of the head of information systems. This policy applies to all corporation systems whether they be corporate, work group, or microcomputers.

4.1.4 Beta Software

Beta acquisition must be a concern at the policy level for the information systems of the entire company. It shall be the responsibility of information systems management to formulate this policy and its required procedures. Top management of the organization will be kept informed about the policy and its rationale. The IS management will be the only party that can approve the involvement of the company in any Beta testing and the degree of that testing. Any employee involved with unauthorized Beta testing can be subject to immediate discharge.

There can be more than one level of involvement in Beta testing at any given time. But the degree of each Beta involvement will be decided by IS management. By the nature of its responsibility management is required to have the essential information needed for such commitments. Beta testing can affect different levels of obligations, from the strategic interest of the company to postponing an upgrade.

4.1.5 Audit Review

The closer an organization comes to computer dependency, the greater the need for systems and programming audits. Audits are necessary to assure that the system is running properly.

Management bears the ultimate responsibility for having an IS audit policy which can assure management of the validity and integrity of financial and reporting programs. The actual audit procedures are the auditors' domain. They are determined and the actual audit performed by either internal or external auditors.

Comment:
Computer-related fraud has become an everyday possibility. IS managers and auditors have learned caution from newspaper accounts regarding computer fraud, mismanagement, and lawsuits. These stories are spectacular because of the growth in unauthorized access to databases.

Auditors are engaged to approve and oversee financial programs but they oversee the data's accuracy. A wise IS manager requires the auditor's stamp of approval to confirm reliability of financially related systems and programs. Audit reviews seek to:

1. Review all corporate computer programs that are under development or in the process of having maintenance performed to assure that adequate and reliable audit controls are built into the system and program software.

2. Determine that specified controls are actually reliable within operational system programs.

3. Confirm that access to operating programs and databases by MODEM or any sort of network access is continually governed by the current state of security to prevent unauthorized access.

4. Confirm that established accounting standards have been met and employed by all information systems using them.

2. PROGRAM DEVELOPMENT

4.2 PROGRAM DEVELOPMENT

The longer it takes to develop software the greater the chance that problems will occur. "Creeping user requirements" can be legitimate. It's simple. User needs do change. Anyone who is responsible for software development or who is an IS head should read Capers Jones' book *Assessment and Control of Software Risks*, Prentice Hall, 1994.

Mr. Jones has done an extensive study of IS projects and has come up with no fewer than 50 major problems that affect software development. He notes that "few projects have more than 15 software risk factors at any time, but many projects have half a dozen simultaneously." He points out that the "five most frequently encountered risk factors for large IS shops" are:

- Creeping user requirements.
- Excessive schedule pressure.
- Low quality.
- Cost overruns.
- Inadequate configuration control.

Application overload and the deterioration of programming quality have played havoc with programmer productivity. The prudent IS head would be wise to not only have effective programming policies and procedures in place but make certain they are adhered to.

4.2.1 Review of Software Specifications

The initial step in program development is a review of the system's software specifications to ensure that there is no misunderstanding of specifications requirements between the systems analyst or user and the programmer(s).

A. General review

With the purpose and scope of the programs understood, the next step is to determine their relationships in the total system. When reviewing each program:

1. Review the program's place in the system.
2. Check the functions of the programs preparing the input for the program under review. Include the sequence of the input elements and contents of the element sets. In addition, check the purposes of the program(s) which will use the output of this program.
3. Resolve any questions regarding the system or programming requirements.

B. Detailed review

In order to ensure a complete understanding of the requirements for the program(s), consider the following items:

1. Data element specifications

   These determine the precise record formats for files and the data dictionary specifications for database systems. For example, are the "year" data elements a four numeric character field, or is there some other solution to resolve the year 2000 problem?

2. Processing specifications

   These determine calculations and comparison tests of data.

3. Systems specifications

   These are reviewed to resolve any ambiguities or problems.

4.2.2 Program Organization

Before the detailed logic of a program is developed, the programmer organizes the major logic functions needed to accommodate the requirements of the programming language or software selected.

A. Program Logic

This is represented using program block diagrams as logical modules for structured programming. These reflect the relationship of the logical modules and the detailed processing that take place within each structured module. By using structured programming, the problem's solution can be divided into logical parts or routines so each may be programmed as soon as possible. This permits complex problems to be broken down into simpler sections. Each module routine becomes a separate entity.

A building block module is created and controlled by a single routine called the main line, which provides the master control that ties all individual processing modules together and coordinates their activity.

Modification of module routines is simplified. Changing or adding new routines is accomplished by changing the main line routine. This transfers control to the new routine.

To design a modular program, determine the program parameters. List the requirements, elements, and functions of the program as they are developed, with no attention to logical order. Once this is done, review and revise them to determine the logical order of the processing routines and design the main line of the program. Then an overall flowchart can be drawn. Since this flowchart can reveal errors in logic, pay careful attention to it.

In preparing and using the "modular" structured programming method, the following criteria are used:

1. Structured flowcharts

A structured system flowchart gives an overall picture of the major component elements of the routine. Program flowcharts then progress to any desired level of detail, depending on the complexity of the routine. The program coding should be referenced throughout. In this way, the programmer can easily compare the chart to the actual coding for the purposes of debugging.

2. Comprehensive narration of each routine

The narration of each structured routine states its purpose, describes data it processes, and generally explains the program logic as portrayed by the structured flowchart.

3. Programming conventions

The use of standardized nomenclature conventions and standardized program documentation techniques permits someone unfamiliar with the program to readily understand its content. This is very helpful for later maintenance programming.

B. Program efficiency

Efficiency comes from proper use of an existing structured routine to build balanced and flexible programs. Efficient programs require the following:

1. Programming so that a minimum of effort is required later for maintenance programming.

2. Taking full advantage of the overlay capabilities of available software and hardware.

3. Using peripheral devices to maximize the capacity of the whole system.

4.2.3 Reusable Component Identification

Reusable components are those having identifiable commonalities across programs of a given project. The project must be large enough or consist of several smaller projects in the same general domain to justify a reuse strategy. For reuse to pay off a specific plan must be developed before program coding starts. Reuse planning prior to coding a new system will help organizations avoid the error of thinking about reuse too late.

There needs to be a taxonomy system developed to identify modules for reuse. No one taxonomy system will apply to all reusable component libraries.

Program module commonalities include common data, common constants, common formula process, common tables and/or reiteration processes.

Because one builds the models prior to coding the actual program modules, potential reuse is greater.

One word of caution: make sure the module works. There is no worse tragedy than having reusable code that has a bug placed into your library. A list should be maintained of the locations of each module in case errors are detected later, as well as for future update requirements.

4.2.4 Procedural Coding

Standard techniques are used to code program instructions. These are the source code instructions whose procedural language the assembler or compiler uses to generate the object program.

A. Source coding

All coding documentation requires the programmer's name, the program name, date and other pertinent information as determined by the project leader or programming supervisor.

B. Coding requirements

- Use techniques identified with the language selected.
- Use clear, descriptive comments for explaining complicated or tricky techniques. (Remember that someone may need to make changes in the program at a later date.)
- Follow standard coding procedures.

C. Desk checking

The next step in program coding is desk checking which is performed after the source program is written but prior to any program compiling. Desk checking includes:

1. Verification of program logic

The programmer traces the flow of the program through each possible path.

2. Construction of decision trees

Decision trees are constructed for both desk checking and object program testing at a later time. These trees represent data points to test for all program exceptions, as well as normal conditions.

4.2.5 Testing

The purpose of testing a coded program is to detect syntax and logic errors. Syntax errors are detected while compiling a source program into an object program and commonly occur when program coding rules for the language being used are not followed. Syntax error messages are produced by the compiler following the statement which contains the error. In some cases, an object coded program is not generated because of syntax errors.

After all syntax errors are corrected, an object program is generated by the compiler for testing program logic.

Use the test data prepared in desk checking to generate input data for testing the program's functions. Several types of errors are often made by programmers and can be detected and corrected with the proper testing procedures. These errors are classified as:

A. Clerical errors

B. Logical errors

C. Interpretation or communication errors

(These occur due to misinterpretation or misunderstanding of the program requirements.) After testing is complete, the auditors may provide test data to be run in order to confirm that auditing standards have been met. Testing is not an afterthought, but should be considered early in the developmental stage of programming.

4.2.6 Documentation

The purpose of program documentation is to allow other programmers to perform maintenance on the program at some later date. It also defines the manner in which the program is to be run, outlines the controls necessary, and provides information for operations personnel. In addition, it provides management with a means of obtaining information about the program's operation, complexity, and costs.

Programming documentation is noted here because it is a by-product of the preceding steps. Details are provided in the Program Documentation section of Chapter 2, Software Documentation (Section 2.5).

4.2.7 Non-Procedural Coding

When using a non-procedural 4GL, one tells the computer what is to be done, not how to do it. Computer-aided software engineering (CASE), one form of 4GL coding, is a very helpful tool for systems development. 4GLs employed in prototyping require a different set of procedures than procedural coding. The time span over which 4GLs are used dictates a different approach for its utilization and documentation. Before and/or during the employment of 4GLs, pay careful attention to the naming conventions, error routines, monitor screen displays and data dictionaries.

The use of RAD (Rapid Application Development) offers a menu of pre-coded samples of monitor screens or hard copy reports to select from. On-screen prompting takes the user and programmer through selecting a database and on to specifying output content. Since this is a shell product, the programmer may need some procedural code or 4GL to custom code the final RAD product. This procedure may also involve pulling reusable modules of code to complete the task.

Both CASE tools and RAD are used to develop programs in a manner totally different from the procedural approach. Testing, although still performed, is less time-consuming. Documentation is a byproduct of most of this effort. The following can be done for the programmer:

- Pull-down screen menus.
- Pop-up screen windows.
- Scrolling "help."
- Screen list boxes.
- Color screen highlighting.
- Dataflow diagrams.
- Data modeling.
- Program specifications.
- Code generation.
- Documentation.

3. PROGRAMMING CONVENTIONS

4.3 PROGRAMMING CONVENTIONS

There may be a different format coding convention for each programming language used. RAD and CASE tools conventions, depending on the vendor, may not be similar to procedure language software. In any case, conventions should be used consistently.

4.3.1 Coding Conventions

A. Program coding

- Coding format is restricted by assembler or compiler language specifications.

- All program coding documents should have the programmer's name, program title, page number, and date on each page, with the total number of pages in the program posted on the first page.
- Pages are numbered in order.
- Four blank lines are left at the bottom of each page for later insertions.

B. Character representation

- All alphabetic characters are written in the uppercase.
- Special care is exercised in coding to distinguish alphabetic O and numeric zero (0).

C. Comments or notes

Comments or notes are used to explain special mathematical or programming techniques at that point in the program where these techniques appear.

D. Names used in programming

- Data element names and variable names are related to the type of data being stored.
- The size of names used is limited by the naming conventions of the language.
- Procedure names used for programming correspond to the names of those procedures used in the program flowcharts.

4.3.2 Controls

It is the responsibility of the programmer to incorporate into the program the controls specified by the program supervisor, systems analyst, or auditor. Programmers may point out any additional controls necessary for proper processing of data through the system. These controls may focus on such details as:

- Specifying the use of standard labels.
- Sequence checking input files.
- Validating vital input elements not checked by a previous program.
- Showing specific control totals to be accumulated within the program.

4. PURCHASING SOFTWARE

4.4 PURCHASING SOFTWARE

The decision to purchase software is arrived at when in-house development cost is prohibitive or when there is a lack of programming talent available in the time frame required for its development. Also, it is totally impractical to write software that is already available as an "off-the-shelf, shrink wrapped" package. One type of packaged software known as "horizontal software" is mostly available for microcomputers. Examples would be word processors, spread sheets, or data storage programs. This software is used universally by all kinds of institutions. The other type of packaged software, "vertical software," has a much more limited market. It is used for specific procedures by organizations that have common needs. An example would be a billing system for hair dressers. This type of software is becoming more available now for microcomputers, minicomputers, and mainframes.

When software cannot be programmed "in-house" it will have to be obtained in one form or the other. If a shrink-wrapped program is not available, you will have to contact outside software contractors for bids. If possible, three bids should be requested. Contractors can perform the work at their facilities or yours. How much control the company wants over product development will govern where the contractors work. A somewhat different procedure for requesting a purchasing order and for payment of the invoice will be required, depending on where the work is done. (See Asset Management, Chapter 7, for more software procedures.)

4.4.1 IS Purchased Software

IS purchased software is requisitioned against the information systems budget for software. Someone will be delegated as the coordinator for requisitioning IS purchased software by the head of information systems who will also furnish the software budget information. Included will be the total dollars budgeted for software, a list of authorized personnel who may request the purchase of software, and the kind of software they may requisition. A dollar limit per order will also be noted. Any request for software which exceeds this limit will require the approving signature of the head of information systems.

A. IS software requisition procedure

The coordinator of IS software purchasing will be sent a memo listing the software requested and the reason for the request. The date by which the software is needed will also be noted. The coordinator will check approved software purchasing lists by name and kind of software. The coordinator will then prepare a purchase requisition. If the requisition can be approved by the coordinator, information will be extracted for the monthly software report before the requisition is sent to purchasing; if not, it will be forwarded to the information systems head for his/her approval.

The information systems head will approve or disapprove the request, note the decision on the requesting memo, sign and date it, and return it to the software coordinator.

The coordinator will take the approved requests and issue purchase requisitions. Information will be extracted for the monthly software report before the purchase requisitions are sent to purchasing. If corporate policy mandates that the information systems head sign the requisitions, that signature will be needed before they are sent on to purchasing. The unapproved requisitioning memos will be answered by the IS head, providing any information as to why the request was turned down. The original requesting memos, requisition copies, and reply memos will be filed in the form of hard copies or scanned into a computer data file.

B. IS monthly software report

The software coordinator will report monthly by memo to the head of information systems the following information:

- The cumulative to-date expenditures for software.
- The remaining dollars left in the budget.
- The name of each kind of software and the amount spent on it.
- The total amount spent to date by kind of software purchased.
- The name of software purchased by each organizational unit and dollars spent.
- The total dollars spent to date by each unit.

C. Payment of invoice

For purchase orders to be paid the IS software coordinator will have to confirm the software has been received. If there are any problems, the coordinator should notify accounts payable to hold up payment to the vendor. If the software is returned, purchasing and/or accounts payable should be notified. If the vendor will not accept the return of the software and there is a problem with it, this information should be given to the systems head. If the vendor requires a rewrapping charge, the original purchase order is cancelled and a new requisition written for the rewrapping charge which will have to be applied to the software expense list and identified as such.

4.4.2 Other Software Requisition Procedures

Other units that have their own budgets to purchase software will use the same procedures as they do for their other purchases. The information systems unit will publish and distribute a list of approved software that they support. Questions will not be answered and help will not be offered by anyone in the information systems unit, including the Help Desk, for any software that is not on the list.

The small print on a package of software lists restrictions that exist unless the vendor guarantees something else in writing. Documentation should be reviewed before the seal is broken on the program disk container since it is easier to return unopened software. If the seal is broken and the software does not provide the expected results, ask the purchasing department to contact the vendor. Also send a memo to accounts payable instructing a hold on payment of the invoice until the problem is resolved.

4.4.3 Contract Programming

The purchase of contract programs or software is governed by the organization's policy for contracting outside services. The purchase order should contain a statement describing an acceptable program as noted in this chapter's section on Software Installation (Section 4.6).

The vendor will provide the source code, as part of the software documentation, which will be converted to object code and tested. These results will be compared with the vendor's test output to insure it is the same. The vendor will be provided with test data that has been approved and/or generated by the user, and a copy will be used for the furnished (in-house) source code test.

Once the software has been paid for, there is little leverage to have corrections made (assuming that the firm is still in business when corrections are needed). Therefore, the wise IS manager sends the contract and/or purchase order specifications to the organization's legal department before signing any commitments.

4.4.4 Contract Programmers

These are programmers who are paid by the hour to work on projects they are assigned to. Their work is paid for by accounts payable checks. They may or may not work at your place of business.

When contract programmers start they should be provided information about the company's established rules of programming and documentation. Giving them samples of previous project efforts to review would be helpful. Contract persons working at the firm's IS site should be provided with a desk and required tools. A short introduction to staff and a tour of employee facilities should be given by the person they are reporting to. Other information about working with contract programmers is provided in the sections Contracting with Vendors and Contract Personnel Acquisition (See Chapter 15, section 3).

The contract person should be monitored closely during the first week or two to assure proper job performance. This monitoring should be in addition to the regular progress reports filed weekly by all programmers. Any personality problems with staff or users should also be noted and addressed promptly.

4.4.5 Evaluation of Packaged Software

There some major issues to address when purchasing packaged software which can apply to almost any type of software supplier. They are:

- Will the vendor be in business next year?
- What warranty will be provided?
- Will the software integrate with other software used by the company?
- Will the software adapt to the company's information systems standards?
- What flexibility will the software package provide?
- Is the current company hardware compatible with the proposed software?
- Will the documentation provided be user friendly?
- What type of training is offered?
- What other expense will be required?
- Can the vendor provide modifications to the software?
- Is there an upgrade planned in the near future?

- Is there a vendor Help Desk?
- Will the vendor supply a copy of the purchase contract?
- What is the vendor's reputation?
- How many users are there of the software?
- Is there a users' support group?
- Will the vendor supply the names of current users? If the answer is yes, contact them and ask them for other users to contact!
- What is the major business focus of the vendor?

To discover how difficult or easy it will be to implement the proposed software, the following issues should be addressed:

- How complex is the installation procedure?
- Will vendor provide installation assistance?
- How easy is the software to maintain?

To evaluate vendor-supplied software ask current or former users the following:

- Would they buy from the same vendor next time?
- Did the software perform as promised?
- Was the training of value?
- Was the documentation easy to follow and complete?
- Were there any implementation problems?
- Did installation or operation have any hidden costs?
- Would the referenced user allow a visit to his/her site to see how the software is working and talk to operations personnel?

New packaged software must be evaluated, whether for new applications or for placement on the "approved purchase list," especially if this purchase will commit the company to buy in volume. Depending on the type of software considered, use the following procedures:

A. General use software evaluation

A person or formal committee will be responsible for general use packaged software evaluation. A request for such evaluation can come from a user, a systems analyst, information systems management, or the party performing the evaluation. The person or committee responsible will be a source for packaged software information consulting services. Exhibit 4-1 is a sample form used for software evaluation.

Whenever possible, more than one vendor should be evaluated for the same kind of software. Computer publications, as well as their advertisements, are a good source of evaluation information. Keep an information folder for each type of packaged software evaluated.

B. Client/server and vertical software evaluation

Client/server and vertical packaged software will require a preliminary operations hands-on test followed by controlled client/server or work group prototype operations testing. A users' evaluation will also be required. The amount of time required for each controlled group prototype test will vary with the complexity of the software operation and the number of planned future users. That is, the more users, the safer the software should be, i.e., free of bugs. The time required for testing will also be limited by the seller of the software: the time limit on returning the software or when the invoice has to be paid.

4.4.6 Beta Software Testing and Evaluation

Any Beta commitments will require the prior approval of the head of information systems or a designated agent. Any commitments to use Beta testing will be limited to pilot operations that are not part of the corporate information systems operation. No Beta operations will be planned beyond the time limit specified by the vendor.

Beta testing will not have access to the corporate system or database at any time but will be limited to client/server, work group or stand-alone micro systems. It will not have contact with any processing or database that is under the domain of the auditors.

All costs associated with a Beta testing operation will be monitored and reported monthly to the head of information systems. In addition, a final report will be submitted after Beta testing is complete. The following will be reported:

A. Personnel time

Personnel time will be kept for IS staff, user employees and other workers. The total time for each group will be reported. If required by the head of IS, the dollar cost by each group, the total cost and any overtime incurred because of Beta testing will be listed and identified in the report.

B. Other costs

Costs, other than personnel, will also be reported. This covers such items as: supplies, postage, long-distance telephone calls, costs of outside services rendered, any charge back services (computer, copies made, etc.), and expense account reimbursements.

C. Beta operating problems

Any Beta testing and/or operating problems occurring during the month will be reported, with the estimated total cost of each occurrence. It should be noted if any problem has occurred before and, if so, how often.

D. Vendors contact documentation

Copies of correspondence sent to vendors, telephone call notes, and e-mail sent or received will be attached to the report. Comments addressing these issues will be summarized by the person writing the report.

E. User reports

Copies of Beta testing memos or e-mail concerning the project will be attached to the report. Comments addressing these issues will be summarized by the person writing the report.

F. Report summary

The person writing the report will summarize the status of the Beta testing. Any changes the vendor plans to make that would benefit the future use of the software should be noted. Any recommendation as to continuing or discontinuing the Beta testing or any other comments worth noting should be included. Also, the question of whether the Beta shut-down date will create any problems should be addressed.

A final report will be submitted after Beta testing has been completed.

- Attached to the final report will be a copy of all completed Software Evaluation Worksheets (see Exhibit 4-1). Benefits derived from the Beta test project should be reported in detail. The report will also include a summarized cost benefit analysis and what final action was taken based on the Beta testing.

Software Title _____   Version _____

Vendor _____   Software Description_____

_____

Vendor Address _____

Contact Person   _____   Phone # _____

Purchase Order #   _____   Date_____

Date(s) Software Tested_____   By _____

Software Copied to Server_____   Date_____

Rights Are Assigned/Flagged (list rights) _____

Software Copied to Other Servers (list) _____

_____

Software Evaluation (attach extra pages and documents)_____

_____

_____

_____

_____

_____

_____

Documentation Evaluation (attach extra pages and documents) _____

_____

_____

_____

_____

_____

_____

_____

_____

_____

_____

Exhibit 4-1. Software Evaluation Worksheet

5. PROGRAM TESTING

4.5 PROGRAM TESTING

Software that was written by IS programming staff, contract programmers or contracted with an outside firm will require program testing according to the procedures presented here.

4.5.1 Test Planning

All new and maintenance programs require testing, the magnitude and complexity of which may be determined by the auditors. User acceptance should not be overlooked. Everyone concerned in the company may be happy with the test results, but unless the user is satisfied, operation problems may occur later. A formal test plan should be composed of the following:

- General information.
- Test plan.
- Approval.
- Test results.

A. General information

   This section contains pertinent information needed to identify program(s) and the project with which it is associated. The following information is included:

   - Project number.
   - Program number(s).
   - Date.
   - Programmer(s).
   - Scheduled completion date.
   - Language the program is written in.

B. Test plan

   This section describes the steps required for testing individual segments of each program's logic. The information includes:

   - Program number.
   - Test number.

- Function to be tested.
- Test priority.

C. Approval

This section contains the signature blocks required to approve the test plan and authorize the testing. The program supervisor or project manager will also use this part of the program test to indicate the type of testing to be conducted.

1. Unlimited

    The programmer may test until completion without additional review and/or approval.

2. Limited

    A specific number of tests are permitted before approval expires and a review to approve further testing is required.

D. Test results

This section reflects the progress of the program during testing including date of the first test, systems tests, and volume test. If tests are to be run for the auditors, the date the auditor's presence is required will be noted.

4.5.2 Test Preparation

To ensure that test data is representative, all conditions shown in the program flowcharts must be included. The flowchart can be reduced to a decision tree by showing only the decision points and the conditions for the decisions. This makes it easy for users or auditors to follow the decision conditions.

Another tool for test preparation is a decision table. (See Exhibit 4-2 for a Decision Table Structure.) The box labeled "title" contains the procedure title. The area labeled "condition stub" lists all possible conditions to be tested. The "action stub" area lists all actions that can take place. Under "decision rules" are listed "condition entries," the actual conditions that determine how the data will be treated, and "action entries," the actions that determine which course to follow predicated on the entry conditions. A sample procedure for credit approval is shown in Exhibit 4-3. A decision table for an "else" rule is shown in Exhibit 4-4.

For best results, someone other than coding personnel should prepare the test data. This does not prevent the coder from doing preliminary testing as long as the final test development is done by someone else. This procedure and use of the decision table enhance the potential for detecting errors.

Test material is retained and kept current for later use in testing systems and program specifications. Following are specifications for preparing test data:

- The requirements outlined in the system specifications must be clearly understood.

- The logic and major routines requiring testing must be reviewed and the findings documented.

- The test data must be filed in the library or project folder. This material is considered part of the documentation and must be maintained during the life of the program.

- All modifications to the system must be reviewed by the responsible analyst or program supervisor to determine if any changes are required in the test data. When a change is made, the programmer or test preparer conducts tests with the pertinent data to ensure that the modifications are correct and have not affected other processing areas.

4.5.3 Test Analysis

The following should be carefully checked to avoid testing errors:

A. Input/output
    - Proper heading format, line spacing, spelling and punctuation of reports.
    - Correct data element size and content.
    - Report output matches expected specifications.
    - Correctly keyed-in data.

B. Problem analysis
    - Original specifications are understood.
    - Flowcharting does not have logic errors.
    - Coding errors are not present.
    - No software revision errors exist.

C. Year 2000 testing

    It is essential that the software handle dates for year 2000 and beyond and be tested with any year/date information.

	DECISION RULES							
TITLE	1	2	3	4	5	6	7	8
CONDITION STUB	CONDITION ENTRY							
ACTION STUB	ACTION ENTRY							

Exhibit 4-2. Decision Table Structure

CREDIT APPROVAL	DECISION TABLE							
	1	2	3	4	5	6	7	8
ON APPROVED LIST	Y	N	N	N	N			
PAST EXPERIENCE OK	—	Y	N	N	N			
APPROVED CO-SIGNER	—	—	Y	N	N			
SPECIAL APPROVAL RECEIVED	—	—	—	Y	N			
APPROVE ORDER	X	X	X	X	—			
RETURN ORDER	—	—	—	—	X			
GO TO TABLE A5	X	X	X	X	—			
END OF PROCEDURE	—	—	—	—	X			

Exhibit 4-3. Decision Table

EMPLOYMENT	DECISION RULES	
	1	ELSE
COLLEGE DEGREE	YES	—
3 YEARS PROGRAMMING EXPERIENCE	COBOL	—
APPLICATION FORM	GET ONE	
INTERVIEW	SCHEDULE	
DISPOSITION	—	REJECT

Exhibit 4-4. Decision Table with "Else" Rule

4.5.4 Operating Program Maintenance

Only maintenance programmers will have access to the software and will only be allowed to copy it for maintenance. The maintenance of running programs is forbidden without the approval of the operations manager, and auditor if required. A violation of this procedure is grounds for dismissal.

After the required maintenance is completed, the program(s) should be tested. The procedures described in section 4.6.1, Review and Acceptance of Test Results, will be repeated in order for the changes to become part of the operating system.

6. SOFTWARE INSTALLATION

4.6 SOFTWARE INSTALLATION

Transferring a software program from developmental to operational status follows standard review and approval procedures. These procedures apply to programs developed by IS programming staff or contract programmers, or contracted with an outside firm. Purchased or completed Beta tested software will follow the same procedures whenever possible. Only after the software or system passes all testing procedures can the conversion begin.

Installation or conversion is placing into operation the tested software or system which either replaces existing programs or is completely new. When discontinued software is being replaced by a new system, the options are:

A. Phased

In a phased installation, the new system is installed in modular fashion or in phases. When one phase is identified as operational and accepted, the next part of the installation can begin.

B. Direct

Direct installation is a complete, one-time conversion or installation. The old system is replaced completely by the new. Operations has to be totally involved with the installation and operation of the new system software.

C. Pilot installation

In a pilot installation, the new system is installed as a prototype operation in one safe location. After this operation is running properly, it may be installed in other locations. This type of installation is ideal for work groups or independent microcomputer operations.

D. Parallel conversion installation

This type of installation is most often used with corporate IS computer operations. It is the safest and most preferred method of installing a new software system, but it is the most costly. If after comparing output results and the database status of both systems, the results are compatible, the new installation is considered complete.

New software installation, when no existing software is being replaced, can occur as phased, direct, or pilot installation. The other procedures for software installation are the same whether a new system is replacing an old one or not.

4.6.1 Review and Acceptance of Test Results

To ensure that the correct results are obtained from extended program testing, a review should be conducted with users, and auditors if they are involved. Acceptance will be confirmed by memo from involved users and/or auditors which will be directed to the system project manager or the program supervisor. A vendor who is involved with the project will receive this information from the system manager and/or programming supervisor.

4.6.2 Review and Acceptance of Documentation

Documentation should be prepared according to established specifications. Any needed changes or additions will be conveyed by e-mail or hard copy memo to the appropriate person in charge of documentation approval. Its acceptance will be conveyed by memo to the heads of programming and systems.

4.6.3 Acceptance of Contracted Software

The installation of contracted software will follow the same installation procedures as in-house developed software programs. Acceptance of purchased software as operational includes informing accounts payable via memo or e-mail that the invoice can be paid. The note should contain the vendor's name, the item name and description, and the purchase order number. If, on the other hand, the software does not meet the standards specified in the purchase order, a memo or e-mail is sent to the purchasing and/or accounts payable departments so informing them; purchasing department will then inform the vendor.

4.6.4 Development Programmer Sign-Off

After the installation of the software is completed and accepted, the development programmers will no longer have access to the operating system software. Their access codes will be removed from the controlled access subroutine in the system software.

7. PROGRAM MAINTENANCE

4.7 PROGRAM MAINTENANCE

Program maintenance tasks, maintenance responsibility, and maintenance conventions are required for program maintenance. In addition, year 2000 maintenance needs to be considered.

4.7.1 Types of Program Maintenance

A. Program revisions

Program revisions are changes made that do not require a major logic change. Examples are:

- Updates of constants and other variables.
- Increases in the dimensions of tables, arrays, or work areas.
- Implementation of hardware features.
- Correction of minor processing deficiencies.
- Conformation to programming standards.

B. Program modification

Program modifications are changes which involve the redesign of program logic or the relationships of the sub-programs. They are required to accommodate changes in input or output specifications.

4.7.2 Responsibilities and Controls

A. The head of computer programming has the authority and responsibility for new programming, while the IS computer operations head has the authority and responsibility for maintenance programming.

B. Testing or program maintenance will not be performed on any operating software under the control of IS computers or work group systems. This will be done off-line with no access to the operating system software.

C. Testing or program maintenance should verify that changes have been made properly and that sections of the program which were not changed are functioning in the correct manner.

D. The programmer and program supervisor will review the final test output and documentation for correctness and completeness.

E. User management or IS computer operations management will require a sign-off before the modified software is placed into operation. Once this occurs, the maintenance programmer will no longer have access to it. However, in case of an emergency the programmer may regain access under supervision and with the permission of user management or IS computer operations management.

4.7.3 Conventions

In addition to the conventions outlined below, those established for program development (as found in 4.3.1 Coding Conventions) are followed in performing program maintenance.

A. Changes to flowcharts

Flowcharts are modified in the following manner:

1. Changes are made to the contents of a symbol by erasing the pencil-drawn symbol, redrawing it, and penciling in the new contents. The correction date is posted next to the symbol and initialed. There is no limit to the number of these changes except that imposed by neatness and legibility.

2. If a flowcharting program is available, a new chart is drawn by that program. The changes are noted on the new chart, dated, and initialed by the programmer. Both old and new charts are filed.

3. Additional pages added to flowcharts because of changes require off-page connectors to direct the flow to the inserted pages.

B. Changes to reports

Always retain one copy of the original report layout in the documentation.

1. Report layouts are to be redrawn if lines are altered.

2. Rubber cemented patches can be used to cover text changes.

3. If reports are generated by report design software, the old design and the new design are to be filed together with changes noted in the new report.

C. Changes in program coding and testing

1. A source program is copied into a new file before extensive changes are made. After testing is complete, and the updated program put into operation, the old source program may be erased after 90 days.

2. When testing program changes, the entire program must be checked, not only the routines which were inserted, deleted, or changed. Those segments which were not changed are tested to insure that the program will continue to function properly. The test data becomes part of the program documentation.

4.7.4 Year 2000 Maintenance

The year 2000 can present problems to any current computer operation because programs or data input with a two-digit year format are heading for a crash. The coming year 2000 presents four major concerns:

1. Data fields that have allowed for two characters will now have to be expanded.

2. The year 2000 will be a millennium year.

3. The year 2000 is also a leap year.

4. The year 2000 contains many zeros.

Comment:
Even before the year 2000 arrives there will be problems. An example can illustrate the problem. You are buying a new sailboat in '97 financed for ten years, the contract ends in '07 but when the program subtracts 97 from 07 you get minus 90.

Depending on the magnitude of the year 2000 problem, a coordinator or a task force will be required to address the problem. The person(s) should be knowledgeable about maintenance programming and review the current program documentation to develop a strategy to resolve the problem. A report diary should be maintained to provide documentation as to what has been done. This diary will come in handy when making activity and status reports.

There are several other things that should be addressed. The approach used to prepare for year 2000 dating will vary depending on the mix of hardware/software, the number of sites, and the number of systems and programs.

For small to more complex operations the following may be done as needed:

A. Check data files for year fields.

   First check and validate the existing files for improper year data fields. Correct where needed.

B. Seek vendor help.

   Contact the firm's hardware and software vendors for assistance. If they cannot be of help, ask if they can recommend someone.

C. Obtain a year 2000 compliant library.

   Purchase or develop a year 2000 compliant subroutine library for all programs used.

D. Develop a program/database listing.

   Develop a listing of which programs access which files and/or databases. From this, correlate the date data with the programs to find programs that will need attention. These can be sort or utility programs, as well as processing software.

E. Review all input/output formats.

   All input and output documents should inspected for required changes. The ones found for correction should be listed. Different lead times may be needed for different items changed. Items reviewed will be: hard copy reports, preprinted forms, and screen displays. Be aware of the current stock of preprinted forms which may need to be changed and the reorder lead times. Be ready to order necessary forms when the corrected software and data files have been updated. The timing of these two activities is essential.

F. Correct programs and data files.

Programs with source code and data files can be addressed in more than one way. Set up a contract programming project effort, do it with current program maintenance personnel, or use both. It is important to set up a sequence of what is to be done in order of priorities and to keep track of what has been done.

For software without source code, contact the maker of the software for information. If it is no longer in business, seek help from other users or user groups. If worse comes to worst, the software may have to be replaced by other, more reliable purchased software.

For more simple operations, such as a one-person shop or simple work group operations, the following may be done:

A. Any programs that have been updated for year 2000 should be listed.

B. For each updated program, the following should be listed, indented under the program name: the database, input/output, and other programs it interacts with. As each item is date corrected, the person making the correction should sign and date the entry.

C. If the total listing becomes unwieldy, the information should be placed in a file management program.

Chapter 5

IS Computer Operations

1. IS COMPUTER OPERATIONS POLICIES

5.1 IS Computer Operations Policies

This section sets down the policies used to govern an information systems computer center operation. The operations area is restricted to operational and identified vendor support personnel; but because of today's distributed data processing and computer networks, access is not limited to persons physically entering the area. It can also be vulnerable to unauthorized access through telecommunications, and every precaution needs to be taken.

5.1.1 Security and Safety

To maintain proper computer room security and safety, the following are good policies to have in place:

A. Restricted access

A system is necessary allowing only authorized personnel to gain entry to the area: those persons needed to operate, supervise, or provide maintenance to the area and its equipment. Moreover, anyone entering or leaving the area must register in a daily sign-in/out log.

B. Restricted on-line access

Access to the system from outside the computer center must be controlled with proper user and ID codes which are to be changed no less than twice a year. To further limit access, codes that are no longer authorized should be deleted as soon as possible.

C. Power supply

1. The computer center area must have its own power supply connected to the main power source for the building.

2. A back-up UPS (uninterrupted power supply) or a fail-safe device is required to prevent a disk crash if the main power fails.

3. A battery or self-starting generator should be available to provide emergency power for worklights, room ventilation, and air conditioning.

D. Air conditioning

The computer center must have its own back-up air conditioning system.

E. Construction hazards

The computer room area must not be adjacent to any natural gas or liquid-transporting pipes, high voltage lines, or magnetic radiation sources.

F. Fire precautions

Fire extinguishers should be the safest possible. All materials used in constructing the computer room area must be fireproof.

G. Smoke detectors

Smoke detection equipment must be installed.

H. Data backup

Database and file backups will be kept as current as is reasonable. Off-site data and software backup will be maintained.

I. Low profile of the computer area

The computer center area must maintain a low profile. No signs directing persons to the center should be displayed.

J. Safe location

The actual site of the IS computer center must not be located on a flood plain or within 50 miles of an earthquake fault.

5.1.2 Housekeeping

Following are policies which apply to housekeeping in the computer center:

A. No smoking, drinking or eating is permitted.

B. Operations personnel are responsible for maintaining a clean working area.

C. Operators are not to attempt to repair any equipment without the specific authorization of the supervisor or maintenance vendor.

D. Operators are not to alter programs without specific authorization of the supervisor.

E. The computer is not to be used for other than assigned operations.

F. Temperature and humidity are to be monitored at all times and kept within the recommended ranges for the equipment.

5.1.3 Disaster and Recovery Plans

A well-organized disaster plan helps ensure the firm's continued operation in the event of such an emergency. Likewise, an effective recovery plan in the event of computer hardware or software failure is a necessity. The company cannot be without an IS computer operation of some sort for more than one hour.

2. GENERAL OPERATIONS

5.2 GENERAL OPERATIONS

This section covers general procedures to be followed by the IS computer center personnel and any visitors. Each center is run as a closed shop with operation areas restricted to only those persons required for the center's operation.

5.2.1 Security and Safety

Following are procedures which apply to the security and safety of computer center operations:

A. The computer operations area is to be locked at all times.

B. Access to the computer center is restricted to operations personnel, approved vendor maintenance personnel, and/or operations management personnel due to report for duty at a specified time. Tours by visitors, employees, vendors, or customers must be authorized and approved by the head of IS computer operations.

C. A record of all who gain entry to the computer area, together with the time of entrance, will be kept using a sign-in/out log or a computer ID card door-opening system.

D. Fire extinguishers and/or their controls are to be easily identifiable. Instructions must be posted next to the instruments.

E. Operations personnel are responsible for knowing:

1. Location of fire alarms, extinguishers, and controls for firefighting systems.

2. Emergency power-off procedures.

3. Emergency procedures for notifying the fire department, the programmer on call, and the appropriate management personnel.

5.2.2 Housekeeping

Standard measures are required to maintain cleanliness and ensure safety in the computer operations area.

A. Eating, drinking and/or smoking are not permitted in the computer center area. Signs to this effect are to be posted in the computer center and on or near the outside door of the computer center area.

B. Operators who are under the influence of prescribed sedatives or similar medication are to be given assignments that will not endanger the operator or the equipment.

C. Operations personnel are responsible for the general cleanliness in their areas. Items removed for use are returned to the area where they belong.

D. Personnel will not place their feet on top of desks or equipment. Shoes must be worn at all times.

E. Personal radios, TVs or audio equipment are not permitted in the computer center area.

F. Personal phone calls are limited to five minutes.

5.2.3 Downtime Procedures

Where there are hardware or software failures, downtime procedures require computer operators to describe and record:

A. General conditions at the time of the failure.

B. Unusual activity observed in any I/O device prior to computer failure.

C. Information received from outside sources for correcting the problem.

5.2.4 Disk Handling

Proper disk handling ensures data availability for jobs and reduces read-write errors.

A. Disks are to be stored in proper containers when not in drives.

B. Disk storage containers are to be filed in place when not in use.

C. Contents of disks are to be identified by external labels placed on the front of the diskette.

5.2.5 Tape Handling

Following are procedures for handling tapes:

A. General tape procedures

- Clean hands are a must for operators handling tapes.
- Read-write heads should be cleaned in accordance with the manufacturer's recommendations.
- Tapes are kept in protective containers when not in use.
- To prevent accidental recording, read-only tape reels should have their write-protect rings in place and tape cartridges should have their record tabs in place.

B. Tape handling procedures

- Tape reels are handled near the hub to avoid crimping tape edges.
- Tape should be mounted squarely and evenly on the tape transport.
- Tape reels should be checked after use to discover irregular rewinding.
- Tape drive doors are closed when tapes are not in the process of being mounted or dismounted.

3. OPERATING PROCEDURES

5.3 Operating Procedures

Computer room operating procedures are a combination of vendor-provided instruction manuals and programmer's instructions peculiar to each application. If any procedure appears to be incorrect, confusing, or contradictory, the problem should be brought to the attention of the appropriate operations supervisor.

5.3.1 Process Flow

The flow of source document input and hard copy output is funneled through a reception area or user input/output counter. This area provides a buffer to the area outside computer center operations.

Source documents are routed to the data entry unit which enters the data and transmits it to the computer room. For purposes of control, the data entry area is separate from the computer room. And, as with any part of the computer center operations area, only authorized personnel may gain entry.

Data being carried into the computer room comes from the data entry area or directly from the receiving input/output counter where it is usually in the form of tapes, disks, and turnaround documents. (Turnaround documents are output documents the computer generates and sends out—for example, utility bills, installment payment documents, factory timecards, etc.) When they are returned, their computer-printed information can be read by both computer input devices and the human eye.

Computer operations keeps off-line data in a storage area called the data library which is controlled by a librarian or computer operator who logs tapes and disks in and out. Entry to the library is through the computer room. In addition to the flow of data between operations and the library, there is a flow of backup data to and from an off-site data storage location.

5.3.2 Computer Operations Procedures

The heart of the computer center is the computer. Operation of the computer equipment is the duty and responsibility of the computer operator, also identified as the console operator. This person's duties and responsibilities vary depending upon the computer, and the policies and procedures of each computer center operation. In a small shop, one individual may be responsible for virtually all activities. Regardless of the size of the computer center operation or the computer system used, some duties or tasks are traditionally performed by the console operator, although the computer operation may at times be run unattended.

A. Daily shift duties

The operator beginning a shift first checks with the one ending the prior shift to ascertain if there are any problems. Then the operator:

1. Checks for system messages on the display monitor or system message log book.

2. Checks the schedule of the previous shift. If there are any priority jobs which have not been completed, the operator rearranges the job schedule. If there is a major problem, he/she contacts the operations supervisor.

3. Performs housekeeping tasks such as cleaning the tape drives, disk drives, etc.

4. Updates the tapes and disks required for the rest of the shift. Sets aside tapes and disks to be taken to the data library. Goes to the data library to exchange tapes and disks.

5. Checks to see if a backup is required and if so, performs it.

6. Monitors the console display screen for the status of jobs being run. If the system does not generate its own processing log, the console operator maintains a written one for each day's operation. The information logged consists of the number of the job completed, the start and finish times, and any remarks.

7. When questions arise about a job being run, the operator checks the operator's manual and related documentation for that particular job. When all else fails, the supervisor may be contacted.

8. If an error causes a job to be terminated prematurely, the operator corrects the problem by following the restart procedure for that job.

B. Other shift responsibilities

In addition to general tasks, some other duties and responsibilities for a console operator are:

1. Power up/power down the system. The console operator may be required to turn the computer system on and perform an IPL (initial program load) procedure.

2. Turn the computer off (power down), if the computer center does not operate 24 hours a day, or for other specified reasons. The operator follows standard power down procedures as listed in the operator's manual.

3. Initiate the processing procedure required if there are any batch jobs to be run. The operator checks, before starting the job, to ensure that all the required data is available.

4. Monitor the batch processing job being run.

5. Check tapes or disks into the computer center from other sources.

6. Check in any turnaround documents using the job procedures for logging in documents.

7. Transmit messages to on-line users of the system including down time and its duration.

8. Change the priority of jobs waiting to be printed by accessing the spooling system.

C. Administrative responsibilities

Administrative responsibilities are performed by the person in charge of the computer operation, which, in a one-person department, can be the operator. These responsibilities include:

1. Ordering supply items.

2. Ordering and maintaining technical manuals.

3. Distributing technical briefs and standards.

4. Scheduling computer maintenance.

5. Designing and maintaining special forms and logs as required for computer center operations.

6. Scheduling operators by shift.

7. Training new operators.

5.3.3 Peripheral Equipment Operation Procedures

Computer systems have a host of on-line and off-line peripheral devices. In a single operator shop, the console operator is responsible both for the mainframe computer and for all these devices. In a one-person computer center operation, the individual responsible for the entire operation functions as the data entry person, the console and peripheral equipment operator, the data librarian, and the center administrator. In a larger operation, these duties are assigned to different people.

The following peripheral devices and their required operation procedures may be handled by one or many operators. These procedures are defined by vendor's manuals or written by a systems analyst. They are defined as duties or tasks required by the operations personnel. Examples are:

A. Printers

Output from printers is controlled by the spooling program in the computer system. The operator determines what kind of paper is required for the scheduled print-outs.

The center may employ more than one kind of printing device, each with its own manufacturer's operations manual. A printer operator might be responsible for any of the following kinds of printers:

- Impact printers
- Wire-matrix printers
- Ink-jet printers
- Laser printers
- Computer output microfilm

Duties required for printer operations include:

1. Changing paper in or adding paper to the printer following the manufacturer's instructions.
2. Checking print alignment before starting the printer when a job changes.
3. Monitoring paper supply and output stacks.
4. Removing paper jams.
5. Changing printer ribbons or replacing toner as required. Output should be checked at the start of each job to determine whether this is necessary.
6. Performing minor preventative maintenance, as designated in the instruction manual, and cleaning the machine when needed.

B. Magnetic tape drives

Tape drives are reel or cartridge. Cartridge drives present less of a handling problem than reel drives, but in either kind, the tape should never be touched. When mounting a reel tape on a drive, care should be taken to avoid letting the tape touch the floor. The following required procedures apply to both types:

1. Tapes are never stacked on top of each other in a flat position.

2. Tapes are never left on top of tape drives.

3. Tapes are always write-protected prior to reading.

4. External labels are checked before mounting tape to ensure that the correct tape is being used.

5. Magnetic tapes are cleaned as needed.

6. A record of all tape read/write errors is maintained: the tape number, drive number, type of error, time and date of the error.

7. A record of scratch tapes is maintained. (Scratch tapes are those that have been previously used for other jobs but the data they contain are no longer needed.) All old external labels are removed.

8. Tape error messages that appear on the monitor or console typewriter are responded to immediately.

C. Direct-access devices

Removable direct-access storage can be in the form of disks or CDs. The operator handling tape drives often handles the direct-access devices, too. On-line computer systems are noted for having many direct-access storage devices. Operating procedures for the devices are defined in the manufacturer's manuals, but some duties and responsibilities are common to almost all devices. Following are duties or procedures associated with direct-access devices:

1. Floppy diskettes are retained in their storage containers when not in use.

2. A felt pen is used when writing on diskette labels.

3. Diskettes are not placed on disk drives or close to telephones.

4. Blank diskettes are formatted in advance and kept, ready for use, in a dust-free container.

5. The insides of disk and CD drives are kept free of foreign objects.

6. Prompt response to console messages is necessary. An operator takes corrective action by following the manufacturer's manual or disk operations manual. If instructions to correct the problem are not available, the operator contacts the lead operator or operations supervisor. Some of the more common problems which transmit error messages are:

- File-label errors.
- Disk drive not ready.
- Duplicate file names.
- Reading errors.
- Writing errors.

D. Other peripheral devices

Computer centers today utilize a large variety of peripheral devices in addition to standard printers, direct-access storage devices, and magnetic tapes. One may also be custom made for a specific computer center application. Some of the more common devices are:

- COM (computer output microfilm).
- Optical readers.
- Magnetic-ink character readers.
- Page scanners.
- Modems.

The degree of operator involvement depends on the device. The manufacturer's manual prescribes the correct operating procedure. Any additional instructions should be available in the operation's procedure manual for the job being run.

In the event of equipment failure, the operations supervisor is notified. Operator requirements of the more common devices follow:

1. COM

The computer output microfilm device is most often a stand-alone off-line device requiring a tape input. Tape handling procedures have been defined in the tape handling duties section (5.3.3.B). The operator follows the manufacturer's operating instructions in running scheduled jobs. Main duties required for the device are to:

a. Perform minor maintenance as required by the instruction manual.

b. Mount tapes for output as scheduled.

c. Maintain a log of start and finish times by job.

d. Clear any jams as prescribed in the instruction manual.

e. Check distribution counts for each job.

f. Make sure supplies are available before output is started.

2. Optical readers

Optical reader input documents can be user-generated documents or the computer center's own turnaround documents. Operation of the device follows the manufacturer's instructions. Input is most often in batch form. The main duties required for operating the device are to:

- Perform minor maintenance as required by the instruction manual.
- Maintain a log for the run times of each batch of input.
- Clear any jams as prescribed in the instruction manual.
- Repair or provide replacement documents for damaged documents.

3. Magnetic-ink character readers

This type of input device receives input from users and may have additional information keyed in at the data entry unit. Operating duties are similar to those for the optical readers.

4. Modems

The modem is a peripheral device that serves as an on-line input/output instrument between outside users and the IS computer. For the most part, it runs unattended. If the modem goes down or is known to be out of service, the console operator provides users with information about the current or pending shut-down. Pending shut-downs can be transmitted as screen displays.

4. REPORT DISTRIBUTION

5.4 REPORT DISTRIBUTION

There are many different types of forms created for printed reports. Forms and reports are not the same. A form is basically a sheet of paper which contains preprinted information and has spaces for additional data. Pre-printed information can be logos, headings, lines, boxes or constant narratives, for example, a payroll check. A report is information printed on blank paper.

Forms can be single sheets, as used by laser printers, or continuous, as used by impact printers. Pre-printed forms are usually purchased, while flat forms can either be purchased or printed in-house. Reports are also produced by COM units in the form of microfiche.

Procedures for generating reports were covered under A. in the Peripheral Equipment Operation Procedures sub-section (5.3.3) of the Operating Procedures section.

The preparation of reports requires knowledge of how these reports are to be distributed; this information provides the basis for control of both reports and forms. Therefore, pre-printed forms inventory and control are part of the preparation of reports operation. Their inventory levels are dictated by quantity discount purchases and delivery times. "Controlled forms" require special care to ensure their availability and security. They contain printed, usually sequential, numbers to help prevent theft. (Payroll checks, bank drafts, and savings bonds are all examples of "controlled forms.")

Discovering that there are not enough checks to meet the payroll is an unnerving experience for any IS manager.

Procedures for forms inventory and control are covered in Forms Management, Chapter 16. The report preparation area should have storage space available for both stock forms and controlled forms, with a fireproof, lockable container provided for controlled forms.

5.4.1 Preparation of Credits

Computer operations personnel are responsible for loading the correct forms or microfiche into the printing device when output reports are generated. When continuous forms are used, pin-feed margins and the pages remain attached until the entire job is complete.

Single sheet laser print-outs and microfiche output require different preparation procedures. COM is usually processed off-line, while impact and laser printing occur on-line.

A. Continuous-forms procedures

If the continuous form is a multi-part form with carbon paper, the carbon paper remains between the copies. When accounts payable and payroll checks are printed, the checks are not yet signed. Continuous form documents are processed as follows:

1. The printed reports are placed in a decollator (procedure for operation in the manufacturer's instruction manual).

2. If pin-feed margins are to be removed, the margin slitter on the decollator is turned on.

3. If multi-part forms with carbon paper are used, the carbon paper is attached to carbon spindles on the decollator.

4. The forms are run through the decollator and stacked.

5. Forms that require bursting are run through the burster. Single sheet copies are stacked after the bursting operation.

6. Imprinting procedure

   Checks that require imprinted signatures have it done with a continuous-form imprinter or during the bursting operation. The procedure used depends on the hardware available.

   • Accounts payable

     Accounts payable checks are imprinted by a stamp provided for the check writing process by that unit. When the checks are delivered to accounts payable, the imprinter stamp is also returned. The beginning and ending check numbers are reported to accounts payable in accordance with its procedure. All damaged checks are marked "VOID" and returned.

   • Payroll

     Payroll checks are imprinted by a stamp provided for the check writing process by the payroll unit. When the checks are returned to that unit, the imprinter stamp is also returned. The beginning and ending check numbers are reported to the payroll department in accordance with its procedure. All the damaged checks are marked "VOID" and returned.

     When running confidential payroll or expense reimbursement checks, only authorized personnel are allowed in the processing area and signs are posted to that effect.

7. When computer-printed reports have been prepared for distribution, they are moved into the distribution area. Confidential reports are placed in sealed cardboard boxes.

B. Laser output procedures

   The preparation of laser-printed reports for distribution is a simple procedure. The documents are processed as follows:

   1. Single-copy reports are moved to the distribution area. Reports of more than one page are stapled together in the upper left-hand corner.

2. If more than one copy of each multipage report is required, the pages are collated and stapled in the upper left-hand corner of each report.

3. The reports are moved to the distribution area.

C. Microfiche Procedures

Microfiche (COM) are processed as follows:

1. The operator checks to see if there is more than one copy of each microfiche document. If so, all copies (up to 20) are placed in one microfiche envelope.

2. When there is more than one microfiche document to each report output, or multiple copies of each, the microfiche are sorted and then placed in their respective envelopes.

3. The report name is posted on the outside of the microfiche envelopes.

4. The envelopes are taken to the distribution area.

5.4.2 Report Distribution

The IS computer operations department produces a variety of reports. Some have no special needs, while others require extensive attention from the time they are printed until they are delivered.

The preparation, processing, and distribution information required for each report is posted to the Distribution Control Form, (see Exhibit 5-1) which is completed by the systems analyst or programmer responsible. Procedures for processing these reports are as follows:

A. Report log maintenance

A report generation listing is provided at the start of each day by the console or computer operator and forwarded to the report distribution area.

1. The operator crosses off the report on the Distribution Control Form with a yellow marker.

2. The operator posts the time the report was received after the name of the report on the Distribution Control Form.

3. At the end of each shift, the operator going off duty notifies the arriving operator as to reports that have not been produced.

B. Distribution procedure

The person processing the reports checks the Distribution Control Form to learn their disposition. If there is any variation from what is expected, that person notifies the computer console operator.

Changes to the Distribution Control Form are only made when a memo is received with instructions from the responsible systems analyst or programmer. The memo is held in a file as long as the report is produced.

When the reports are complete, the operator sets them aside for proper distribution. Those that require maximum security are kept locked until such time as the documents leave the area.

C. Distribution methods

The distribution method for reports depends on the report's security status and the distance between the user and the data processing center. The following options are available:

1. User pickup

Report users come to the computer center, or a satellite pickup area, to obtain their reports. Bins similar to the boxes used by post offices, but larger, are used for this purpose. Areas that require some degree of security will have locked doors on the bins.

2. IS computer operations delivery

Computer operations center personnel deliver reports to recipients located near the computer operations or who require special equipment for large volume delivery.

3. Mail delivery

The reports are picked up or delivered to the mail room. Mailing methods are:

a. Interoffice mail

Interoffice mailing envelopes are used for interoffice delivery.

b. Outside delivery

Some computer-printed reports must be mailed through the United States Postal Service. These are items such as purchase orders, bills, and government reports. Packing or envelope inserting is done in the mail room. Large shipments may be sent by UPS.

Report Title:

Report No: Security:

Effective Date: Supersedes:

Description:

Form No: Copies: Burst: Decollated:

Copy	Department	Title	Method
1			
2			
3			
4			
5			
6			

Special Instructions:

Exhibit 5-1. Distribution Control Form

5. DATA SECURITY

5.5 DATA SECURITY

This section covers procedures to insure data security throughout the computer center operation. These procedures are designed to ensure that the management and systems operations audit policies will be satisfied and to support their enforcement.

5.5.1 Data Security Responsibility

One person selected to be responsible for data security reports to the head of Information Systems and to a security committee of three to five members which authorizes the implementation of its policies. This committee will have a majority representation from the firm's audit area to enable the controller to influence policy and verify that the security responsibility is fulfilled in line with the audit and control policies of the firm. This data security may or may not be a full-time effort. The person may have a title reflecting the status of the position if it is a full-time responsibility. Otherwise, the task will be undertaken in conjunction with other duties. If the latter is the case, the security position should not be subservient to the other responsibility. Suggested titles for the position would be: security officer, security coordinator, supervisor or manager of security, chief of security, data security officer or coordinator, or data administrator.

5.5.2 Span of Data Security

A. Data security begins at the point data is captured for the Information Systems operation. The actual process of receiving and capturing raw data is under the domain of data security.

B. The vehicle used to hold captured data will be returned to sender if required. The return will require a confirmation of time, date, title, and data contents. A record log will be maintained of the returns by item, date and time, with the signature of the receiver. If the return vehicle or raw data documents are to be transported by a third party (U.P.S., U.S. Postal Service, or some other agent), a signed and dated receipt will be required to confirm the transaction. Receipts will be held for one year.

C. Retained hard copy raw data will be held under the jurisdiction of the data security person or delegated authority in a secure area until there is a disposition of the material. The length of time the material is kept will be predicated on policies for the various items.

Retained instruments used to convey data other than on hard copy, such as tapes, disk, etc., will be kept in a secure place as other such records are kept. The length of time the material is kept will be predicated on policies for the various items.

The internal disposition of retained data instruments will depend on their source. Tapes or disks that can be erased will be erased and returned to service. A log will be maintained of the erased items by day, title and control identification. Each batch listing of erased items will contain the signature of the operator doing the erasing. The log will be kept for no less than one year. Raw data documents will be shredded. The level of shredding will depend on the level of security required:

1. Confidential data will be finely shredded.
2. Classified data will be cross-shredded.
3. Unclassified data will need only simple, one-way shredding.

A "destroy log" will be maintained of the shredding operation. The log will contain the name and identification of each batch of raw data. Each batch destroyed will list the level of security and the name of the person performing this duty. The log will be kept for no less then one year.

D. Released data and information hard copy will be duly recorded. ("466-1324" is data; "telephone number: 466-1324" is information.) If Report Distribution procedure (Section 5.4.2) is not employed, a release log will be maintained for the local release of data and information hard copy. Confidential hard copy will be contained in a sealed envelope. The release log will record the signature of the person receiving the envelope, the date, the time, and the item description. The log will be kept for no less than one year. Documents or other storage devices released to outside the organization require a second party verification of the release entered into a log which will contain the item name and identification, date, time, method of shipment, the person releasing the material, and the person receiving the material. Otherwise, procedure 5.4.2.C. is to be followed.

E. Internal data (data on the system) and secondary storage will also be under data security care. If Information Systems employs a person as database administrator, that person will be responsible for the physical security of data and/or information. Required procedures for the safety of captured data and information and the policy enforcement will be the responsibility of the designated data security head.

5.5.3 On-line Processing Data Security

Teleprocessing (LAN and WAN) and on-line IS computer access standards and protocol are the responsibility of the person delegated to data security. This subsection defines how the on-line data security system operates.

A. Access authorization for database data

The data security person in concert with the database administrator will categorize the security access levels. The database administrator will group the records within a given database so that the record elements, as much as possible, will have the same level of security. This is to prevent elements of a higher level from being accessed by a person with a lower level access to the same record.

The database administrator will use the data dictionary to provide the access level of each listed element. A valid security method is to group only like-level security elements into the same record. However, an element of a lessor level may be included to avoid developing other records only for the sake of common security level confirmation.

To enhance security the data dictionary will list the programs authorized to access the data elements. This is to limit authorized program access to specific users, identified by the user's password. If the data dictionary does not provide for a given level of access for the user wanting the higher level data elements, access will be denied. Employing an IS computer terminal may further enhance control by limiting terminals as to program access.

Comment:
This system is to prevent some clerk from getting into highly confidential data that only the controller should have access to. There have been cases of some very interesting data turning up on terminals that should not have had such access.

Gaining access to data is one thing, but unauthorized altering of the data is something else. The data dictionary should allow access to individual data elements based on password level, as follows:

1. Read a data element only.
2. Change the data element.
3. Remove the data element.

In cases of vulnerable data, a procedure can be instituted to off-load the old data element and to record the time, the occurrence, and the password performing the alteration.

B. Access authorization for files data

Files must only be accessed by approved user passwords which should be grouped by access levels. This grouping should be a joint effort of the database administrator and the data security person. If there is no database administrator, the security person alone will classify which files are to be accessed by which password level. Program access to files will be controlled by the level of the password to which elements in the data records can be:

- Read only.
- Changed.
- Removed.

A file access log should be maintained by the computer system to record the time, file identification, and password accessing the files. If files are altered, it would be wise to offload the changes-only records, as they were before the change, as an audit trail. This file should be under the control of the data security person and kept for no less then one year.

C. Control of password file

The vendor-supplied passwords and account numbers should be removed before a system is placed into operation. The password control file is the responsibility of the data security official and access will be through an encrypted authorized password program. To access a listed code the password will first need to be decrypted. This list will be under lock and key. The encryption instrument will be in a different locked location. A log will be maintained for each access of the password file, listing the reason, code, and time and date.

D. Granting of data set access

The data dictionary will list the restrictions level for each data set. Access will be granted only to those authorized for access at the given level or higher.

E. Granting of access levels

The granting of access levels will be authorized by the security officer and database administrator. The level which is assigned can be granted either for a given time period or an indefinite period. The approved access levels will be reviewed by the security officer and database administrator no less than once each year. A random review will also be performed at a time known only to the security officer. The results of the review will be documented and filed.

The access level will be commensurate with the person's need, that is, the level determined by the job description, and changeable if a job requires higher access.

Comment:
It would be wise to run a routine retail credit check on the financial status of a person receiving a highly vulnerable access level before granting the access code. Research has indicated that people who are desperate tend to be much more susceptible to taking advantage of an ill-gotten opportunity than not. Also, a person's credit rating can change for the worse at any time, and it would be wise to be aware of this before it is too late.

Given access levels may require a great deal of protection because of the monetary vulnerability of the data elements. New and transferred personnel will require the appropriate screening for granting of and for determining respective levels of access.

Comment:
There was the story some time ago of a US government data processing clerk who was spending money like a member of Congress on his yearly salary of $23,000. By the time management started wondering just how he could support his new lifestyle, he had cashed millions of dollars in checks made out to his dummy company.

F. Termination of employees with restricted access

The termination of an employee should never take place until the person is denied all access to the system, if at all possible. The employee's password must also be removed from that part of the system which accesses any data or program files.

G. Restricted access after voluntary employee termination

When an employee provides notice that he/she will terminate employment, a review of whether to terminate or restrict access to privileged data should take place and a decision be made within 24 hours of receiving notice.

H. Data entry processing

Data entry processing must be separate from file maintenance processing to protect the integrity of the system. File maintenance procedure is discussed under 5.5.4 File Maintenance Data Security.

I. Security bypass

Bypassing the security restrictions for on-line processing is not permitted; it can only be done by following the file maintenance procedure. See Section 5.5.4 File Maintenance Data Security.

J. Unauthorized access times

Terminal access at other than authorized times or on unauthorized terminals will require supervisory approval. The supervisor authorizing the access will forward a memo requesting permission to the data administrator/data security person. That person will notify computer operations when granting the request, and this unit will initiate the procedure to allow the access after the following information is provided:

1. Person to be authorized access.
2. Information/data to be accessed.
3. Date and start/end time of access.
4. Reason for access, other than normal conditions.

Network messaging, when available, should be employed both to send the requesting memo and to notify computer operations with the messages or memos saved for no less than 30 calendar days.

K. On-line programmer file access

No access will be permitted whatsoever for on-line programming, or accessing and testing of database or files. This means all live database or files access and includes even live archival data. Only copied files can be accessed by programmers for their use. Using copied files will require the approval of the database administrator, with the files provided by computer operations. Any such unauthorized access of live data or files will be grounds for dismissal. Strict operations control procedures should always be in place to prevent such accessing.

L. Data dictionary data protection definition

The data dictionary will contain information about all the data elements and their respective applications. The level of protection granted or not granted will be noted in the data dictionary by element or data sets. Any corrections or changes to this information should be published and disseminated on or before the correction or procedure is performed.

5.5.4 File Maintenance Data Security

The file maintenance operation is under the jurisdiction of the database administrator. This includes the loading and maintenance of files and/or databases. The data administrator/data security person has the responsibility to establish the policy for file maintenance data security, along with its privacy and integrity. File maintenance will be a separate procedure from that of data entry operations and will cover the updating of all files and databases.

- File maintenance.
- Database maintenance.
- File up-loading.
- Generating a work access file or database for a given programmer for access and the testing of programs.

Confidential, classified, and unclassified file maintenance will be performed and documented under supervisory review which will ascertain:

- When the maintenance was done (date and time).
- Who performed the maintenance.
- What files were processed.

- What data elements were affected.
- What transpired in the maintenance process.
- What files were reproduced, if any, and the disposition of the files.
- What audit trails are there to confirm the process, such as transaction files and/or pre-maintenance files or databases.

Very confidential file maintenance procedures will require the review of the data administrator/data security person to identify what, if any, maintenance requirements were performed at the supervisory level. This file maintenance will also record the same documentation as in confidential or unclassified file maintenance.

5.5.5 Password Controls

The password policy will be defined by the data security person and the procedure required will be stipulated by the database administrator. If it is challenged by the data administrator/data security person, the problem is presented to the data security committee whose decision is final.

A. Types of passwords

There may be two kinds of passwords: one that is assigned by the database administrator or an agent, and one that is self-assigned. A person given a self-assigned password receives a temporary assigned password required to be changed after he/she first signs on. The authorization of user-assigned passwords is limited to only those persons approved by the data security person.

B. Changing of passwords

All passwords will be changed from one to twelve times per year by the authority of the data administrator who may call for a password change at any time there is a need for it.

C. Password display

Computer systems will suppress passwords and IDs on the monitor screen and all printed output. Passwords are not to be displayed on or near the monitor. A second notice of a violation of this procedure will require a reprimand by the database administrator/data security person. Any serious problem about this will be referred to the security committee.

Comment:
How many times have you seen a password posted to the monitor?
3M's "Post-it's" were not invented for this purpose!

D. Password coding

Passwords will be limited to no more than 10 alphanumeric characters.
At no time will a person or department/unit name be part of the password. No whole word that may be found in a dictionary will be used.

E. Password files

Password files will be encrypted. The encryption code keys will be
held by the database administrator and the data security person. This
information should be placed in a fireproof and locked container. A
backup copy should be enclosed in a sealed envelope and placed in
an off-site location. When a new encryption code key is required, the
sealed envelope will be inspected by the database administrator or the
data security person to insure that the envelope was not tampered with
before the contents are destroyed.

5.5.6 Terminal Controls

Access to the system by terminals requires both physical and procedural operation controls for direct access to the main system or a network
system. Terminals employing both WAN and LAN systems should require
stricter controls than would be used by terminals employed in the computer operations areas. Required controls are:

A. Physical location

The actual physical location of a terminal is a major consideration.
Remote or secluded areas may invite unauthorized access attempts and
also be more vulnerable to vandalism and theft. When such a location
is unavoidable, the terminal should be in a room that can be and is
locked after normal business hours. If not possible, enclosing the unit
or using a cable lock should be considered.

B. Terminal locks

Terminals that can access any databases or that are in remote or secluded areas must have locks. Personnel assigned such a terminal will be responsible for locking the unit when they are not in the general area for an extended period, such as more than an hour. When more than one person is assigned the use of the machine, the last one to leave the area is responsible for locking the terminal and will be informed by his/her supervisor of any infraction. A supervisor not enforcing this procedure will be informed in writing by the data administrator, with copies of the notice sent to the person's immediate superior and all members of the data security committee. All personnel using terminals should be made aware of this policy both in their training and in the written terminal procedures.

Each lock will be different from the rest. In the event that a group of terminals are to be shared by a work group, a common key may be employed. The person responsible for issuing keys for given areas will hold duplicate keys under locked conditions. The data administrator, members of the data security committee, and the computer center terminal maintenance employees will each be issued a master key. The master terminal keys will never be removed from the firm's premises.

C. Terminal operating system controls

The computer operating system will maintain a log record of each terminal sign-on, consisting of date, time frame, and password for each access. The same software will control the access using the time-of-day frame and automatic time-outs. Any violations will be logged by terminal, password, time, and date. A listing of the violation log, by date, will be forwarded to the data security person and the computer operations manager daily.

The database administration software will ascertain which terminal, along with the allowable password, can access which file. The data dictionary will identify which transactions can be initiated by the user. The final control will be exercised by operations program.

These controls will be confirmed as operational by the database administrator before they are placed in service. A reconfirmation will be required in the event of any program maintenance, regardless of what the maintenance effort entails, before the program is placed back into operation.

D. User ID/password identification

The computer operating system will allow three attempts at entering a user's ID and password identification. If all three attempts are incorrect, it will allow no further access for a given time period which will be determined by the data administrator/security officer.

Passwords will be assigned to given terminals. Any attempt to use a password with an unauthorized terminal will be prevented by the computer operating system. The attempt will be recorded as a violation and reported on the listing noted in 5.5.6 TERMINAL CONTROLS, C. Terminal operating system controls, paragraph one.

E. Modem access controls

The same terminal and user ID/password controls will apply to modem access. The computer dial-up telephone number(s) will be changed periodically, at the discrimination of the data administrator.

The level of control for the dial-access will be determined by the data administrator with level 1 the lowest and level 3 the highest:

1. Standard user ID/password and terminal control.
2. Access confirmed by automatic call-back system or caller ID hardware.
3. Access confirmed by data center personnel by physically calling back the listed authorized number.

A computer record of all unsuccessful attempts to gain automatic access to the system will be maintained. The physical call-back procedure will have a manually maintained log containing the same information. A daily notice of the unsuccessful access attempts will be sent to the data administrator and the computer operations manager by computer operators assigned the task.

5.5.7 Audit Trail Monitoring

An ongoing audit trail monitoring program should be in place to police the access and flow of data and information to and from the central computer system. This program will use the data dictionary, the database administration system, and the operating control systems to accomplish this. It will provide for the report listings noted in 5.5.6 TERMINAL CONTROLS, C. Terminal operating system controls, paragraph one, as well as other information:

A. A transaction detail file

This will contain the transaction detail by terminal and user (ID/password), with the date and time of each access. It can be kept on tape or disk and used to reconstruct the most recent backup file when it is necessary to return the database/file to the point of the last transaction. A computer program will be available to produce a listing of this file which can be reviewed manually by either the database administrator or the data administrator or agent on demand.

B. Exception reports

A file will be maintained of daily exception reports called for by any source. A weekly report will list each exception report requested, grouped by requesting party, as well as the data accessed, the date and time. If the computer system time is charged back to the user, the time and/or dollars will also be posted.

C. Teleprocessing report

A teleprocessing network report will be generated weekly by the computer operations manager. It will outline all access to the system and identify any abnormal occurrences. If needed, an attempt will be made to explain the reported activity. The report will be distributed to: the data administrator, the database administrator, and the IS head.

The data administrator will evaluate it and compile a monthly statistical analysis report from the weekly reports, and from any other sources deemed necessary. This Monthly Statistical Analysis Network Report will be sent to the IS manager, the database administrator, the computer center operations manager, and all members of the data security committee. Each monthly report will be discussed at the data security committee meeting and discussion recorded in the minutes.

5.5.8 Data Entry Controls

User manuals, that users can understand without error, will be available at each terminal. The user's name, ID or password will not be written on the manual which will be put into a locked drawer at the end of each work day.

Training material, such as instruction manuals and tutorials, will be available for any terminal operator in the language that person understands.

An immediate supervisor will be responsible for the operator's proficiency and the data administrator/data security officer for enforcing this procedure. Any supervisor refusing to comply will be reported in writing to his/her superior and the data security committee.

Data entry procedures will be followed to minimize the loading of incorrect data into the database/files:

- Computer program instructions will edit incoming data for errors before the data is uploaded to files or database. The data may be contained in a buffer file before it is edited. The editing parameters will be listed in the data description tables or the data dictionary. Also, they may be developed using data decision tables.

- Any overrides to this procedure will require both the operator's supervisor and the computer operations shift supervisor's approval. The shift supervisor will note the time of the override in the shift log book. Any temporary computer program patching for an override will require the normal procedure for program maintenance to be followed. In the event of an emergency, the computer manager may be contacted to expedite the maintenance programming required.

**The IS Audit Manager's
Ten Requirements of a Security Program
(From a Fortune 500 Oil Company)**

1. Establish and enforce policies on acquiring PCs. Establish network guidelines and enforce them, and enforce disciplinary actions for violators.

2. Preform pre-employment checks.

3. Secure physical access to computer center.

4. Backup all data, JCL and programs and store at an off-site storage facility.

5. Insure adequate power, air conditioning and fire protection.

6. Develop and enforce documentation and approval standards.

7. Establish program change controls.

8. Monitor usage of computer resources.

9. Control the teleprocessing network.

10. Evaluate security and control systems.

5.5.9 Data Communications Backup

The person or group sending data will be responsible for maintaining the data backup until notification that the original data is no longer required. This backup may be in the form of:

- Source document retention.
- Captured digital data in the form of batch tape backup or secondary storage random accessed files.

Data communications hardware backup provisions should also be considered, depending on the size of the operation and/or security dependency, in the form of:

- Backup Modems at critical sites.
- Alternate data lines available for dial-up backup.
- Alternate dedicated lines available.

Comment:

A Fortune 500 company had its alternate dedicated backup line buried in parallel when a backhoe cut them both by accident. This is some sort of message!

The backup provisions should be tested, unannounced, by the data administrator or his/her agent. The tests should be periodically performed no less than once per year. The test results should be documented in a memo and copies sent to the database administrator, IS manager, and all members of the data security committee.

Chapter 6
IS SUPPORT OPERATIONS

1. IS SUPPORT POLICIES

6.1 IS SUPPORT POLICIES

The IS computer center area consists of an IS computer operation and support areas. The support areas are restricted; only authorized personnel may gain entry. The computer room itself requires a higher level of authorization to gain entry. The main purpose in keeping the support areas apart from the computer operation room itself is to insure security.

For better security, and to prevent conflict of interest, personnel responsible for the support areas report to the IS (corporate) Computer Center Manager, not to the head of Corporate Information Systems or the IS Computer Operation Manager/Supervisor.

6.1.1 Support Area Environment

The support area must be a clean and air-conditioned environment. On a daily basis, housekeeping personnel may enter all areas except the data library area and the computer room itself. A fireproof, walk-in vault should house the data library or, if the volume of data does not justify this, a fireproof safe in the data library area. An off-site fireproof vault is also required for backup programs and data.

No smoking, food or beverages are permitted in the support areas. (A separate room may be provided for the storage of personal effects and for smoking and food and beverage consumption.)

6.1.2 Systems Software Support Policies

Operations personnel, systems software support personnel, and Help Desk personnel report to the technical support manager who reports to the IS (corporate) computer center manager. Software support responsibilities include the operating system plus utility and compiler software but do not include maintenance on any programs written by the systems or programming units. Service of both sides of a client/server system is also the IS computer center's responsibility. No one other than operations programmers or maintenance programmers may perform any maintenance on the operating software unless given special permission by the head of the IS computer center.

6.1.3 Tape Storage Policies

The limited life span of magnetic tapes mandates the close monitoring of their age and condition. It will be a policy to copy all tapes to a replacement media and have them confirmed as operational before the old tape drives are removed from service.

2. DATA LIBRARY

6.2 DATA LIBRARY

The data library is perhaps one of the most critical areas of the IS computer center. It contains magnetic tapes and/or disks and is off-line storage for both data and software.

Data libraries are usually enclosed within a fireproof room or large vault. In smaller operations, a fireproof safe may be all that is required. A duplicate off-site data and software library needs to be located a safe distance from the main site.

6.2.1 Purpose of the Data Library

A data library is responsible for several services, including:

A. Database or file security

All the activities associated with the protection of data from fire, nature, misuse, and unauthorized access.

B. Data control

The activities and procedures for backing up, storing, retrieving, and retaining data.

C. Software backup

Maintaining backup copies of all current operating software.

D. Data file maintenance

Activities associated with keeping track of the data and software in storage. (If tapes are stored, they should be monitored for condition and reproduced as needed.)

E. Non-data storage

In some cases the data library houses other items such as:

- Computer-generated reports.
- Policy and procedure manuals.
- Blank checks or other vital forms.

6.2.2 Data Library Operating Procedures

Data library operating procedures are performed by the data librarian. In smaller shops the person responsible for the data library may also have other duties. The primary responsibility is to support the computer center operation. Following are the librarian's duties and responsibilities:

A. Receiving new disks and tapes

Upon receiving new disks or tapes the data librarian:

1. Compares quantity received with original order and billing information. If the quantity is incorrect, notifies the IS Computer Operations Manager/Supervisor.

2. Inspects disks or tapes for signs of damage. If any are damaged, notifies the IS computer operation's head.

3. Logs in new tapes or disks and assigns each a consecutive number. The date received and vendor are also posted to the consecutive number log.

4. Notifies the computer operator that the disks or tapes have been received if a disk/ tape inventory is maintained on the computer system. If there is no such inventory, the data librarian will maintain a card file for disks and tapes.

B. Maintaining a file inventory

The librarian monitors the disk and tape inventory. Computer disk/tape inventory programs are available or, for smaller operations, a manual card inventory is kept.

1. Manual card inventory file

   A 3-by-5-inch file card is used for each disk or tape. Posted to it are the disk or tape number, the file label, date and time created, and the current file name.

2. Computer disk/tape inventory program

   A computer program maintains the status of the disk/tape inventory. A report is available from an on-line file. (See Exhibit 6-1.) The data librarian:

   • Checks the status of all disks/tapes daily.
   • Updates the disk/tape inventory file.
   • Maintains a sign-in/sign-out log for daily movement of disks/tapes to and from the data library. (This log is for updating the disk/tape inventory file.)
   • Updates and checks the status of the off-site data library inventory daily.

C. Maintaining software backup files

The data librarian maintains backup copies of operating software at both on-site and off-site storage locations. The duties performed are:

1. Maintaining a record of all stored software. (A sample form is shown in Exhibit 6-2.)

2. Replacing old versions of programs with new versions. (Authorization to replace programs comes in the form of a memo from the IS computer operation's head.)

D. Other Duties

1. Maintaining and controlling the policies and procedures manual inventory.
2. Maintaining and controlling the "controlled forms" inventory.
3. Maintaining and controlling any vital records.
4. Keeping the data library area clean and neat.
5. Cleaning tapes periodically as needed.

Date: Report No:

Disk No.	File Label	Date	Time	File Name
1	PAYROLL	09/01/96	13:40	Payroll Master
2	ACCT PAY	09/02/96	09:30	Accounts Payable
3	INV	10/30/96	10:15	Plant Inventory
4	A/R	10/01/96	12:45	Accounts Receivable

Tape No.	File Label	Date	Time	File Name
1	MPT	09/01/96	09:40	Master Programs
2	XXX	10/31/96	08:30	Scratch Tape
3	XXX	12/21/95	11:40	Scratch Tape
4	PR-TRAN	10/01/96	14:45	YTD Payroll Transactions

Exhibit 6-1. Disk and Tape Inventory Status

Program #	Name	Language	Source	Date
PR3	Payroll	COBOL	Smith	01/15/94
123	LOTUS 1-2-3		Purchased	01/11/96
INV-6	Finished Goods Inventory	COBOL	Jones	07/04/95
STA	Stress Analysis	QBASIC	Smith	11/14/95

Exhibit 6-2. Program Inventory

3. DATA ENTRY PROCEDURES

6.3 DATA ENTRY PROCEDURES

Operating procedures are a combination of vendor-provided instruction manuals and data entry instructions peculiar to each application. If the procedure appears to be incorrect, confusing or contradictory, the problem is brought to the attention of the Computer Operations head.

6.3.1 Data Entry

Data entry procedures can cover a host of input methods. Processing can be done in "batches" or "on-line."

When raw data is to be converted to "captured" data in machine-readable format, data entry instructions must be provided by the systems analyst or programmer. The instructions should include an example of the raw data source documents from which input information comes. Data entry procedures, with example source documents containing identified data elements for input, are placed in a folder for each job that can be performed in a centralized or decentralized data entry operation.

Both types of operation have advantages and disadvantages. The way an IS computer center handles data entry is somewhat different from a decentralized system.

6.3.2 Centralized Data Entry

A centralized data entry organization requires a unit within the computer center staffed by employees of the IS computer center processing operations. Source documents from any place in the organization (including the mail room) are forwarded to the data entry section for processing. The advantages of centralized data entry over a decentralized system include:

A. Good utilization of machine resources since all data entry equipment is located in one place.

B. Skilled data entry operators who provide efficient use of equipment.

C. A procedure for verifying input data since there is more than one data entry operator.

D. Better controls over the data entry activities. (This is an important consideration since data entry provides an opportunity for dishonest operators to key in unauthorized orders for goods or monies.)

The procedures for data entry processing are:

A. Each batch of source data is date-and-time-stamped upon arrival in the unit. Batch numbers are sequential.

B. Each batch is logged in on the Data Entry Log (see Exhibit 6-3).

C. Each batch is identified for verification (if required) and placed with other batches of the same type for data entry by priority.

D. When a batch is entered, the operator initials and posts the time and date of completion. Source documents are forwarded to one of the following:

    - A verification holding area (if required).
    - A work completed area.

E. Documents that require verification are assigned a priority and made available to a different operator than the one who entered the data.

F. The verification operator re-keys the data to ensure that it is correct. Corrections are made if necessary. The verification operator initials and posts the date and time on the source document with a blue marker after completing the batch. The batch of source documents is forwarded to the work completed area.

G. The batch number, time and date are posted to the "Completed Batch Log" after the documents arrive at the work completed area (see Exhibit 6-4). The batch is then filed or returned to the originating department.

H. Filing is by source document and disposition date. When source documents are to be disposed of, the standard disposition procedure is followed.

I. By the end of each day, the numbers of all entered batches posted to the Data Entry Log will have been crossed off with a yellow marker.

J. After the Data Entry Log is posted to the Completed Batch Log, the Completed Batch Log is filed. Each sheet is held for six months, then discarded. The Data Entry Log is filed after all batch numbers have been crossed off. This sheet is also held for six months, then discarded.

Date _____

Source Document	Batch No.	Time Rec.	Initial

Exhibit 6-3. Data Entry Log

Date _____

Batch Number	Time Completed	Initial

Exhibit 6-4. Completed Batch Log

6.3.3 Decentralized Data Entry

Decentralization indicates that the data entry is not limited to one location. Most often, decentralized data entry activities are located where they originate. In this situation, responsibility for them is placed on personnel other than computer operations personnel.

Those who operate decentralized input devices are usually familiar with the source documents, data, or information associated with the input. There is also less need to convert raw data from a familiar format to a different format for use by a centralized data entry operator because the individual entering the data is accustomed to the information.

The advantages of decentralization over centralized input are:

A. There are fewer content errors because of user familiarity with input data.

B. Data preparation is the only step in the data entry process because decentralized data entry is usually on-line and, at times, non-keyed.

C. Time is frequently saved in the preparation of data for the computer system because it is usually converted to captured data as it is originated.

Many firms employ both centralized and decentralized systems for optimal efficiency. The decentralized data entry procedures for batch processing are the same as defined under centralized data entry procedures.

The instruments providing on-line data to the computer system can come in many different forms; most common is the on-line monitor with a keyboard. Others are bar code readers, optical or magnetic character readers, and voice input. In addition to on-line procedures, keyboard input needs to have special computer operating control procedures provided for the system when in use.

The procedures for on-line monitor/keyboard data entry processing are as follows:

A. All personnel and terminals are identified with the proper codes to ensure that only authorized terminals and personnel enter data. This includes mobile units, too.

B. When the data is displayed on the screen correctly the operator keys in the proper code to send the data to the computer.

C. All data is edited by the computer system to ensure that correct data is being received. If the computer discovers an error in its input editing routine, the computer will not place the information into its database but will hold the data in temporary storage and notify the monitor terminal of the error. The operator can then correct or abort the input.

D. The computer system maintains a log by terminal to identify, by user code, when each user logs on and the type of data entered.

E. At each monitor terminal there should be a binder with general operating instructions, along with procedures for each kind of data to be entered.

6.3.4 External File Downloading

Files can be downloaded from the firm's distributed systems input, commercial databases, commercial on-line services, or even the Internet. Each of these downloading procedures will require a computer operations procedure, to be provided by the programming staff. Except for a firm's distributed system, all downloading will be under operator control.

Except for a firm's distributed system, all downloading will be to an off-loadable secondary storage device. Before this information can be placed into the main system, it will have to be confirmed as "clean;" that is, that it has no embedded virus or distorted data.

A Downloading Log Book will be maintained by the computer operators. It will record by date, time, and operator name, the source of input, amount of input, time required, ID of secondary storage device and any problems incurred.

6.3.5 Data Entry Administrative Duties

Data entry units which employ more than one person have a supervisor or lead operator to keep track of batches and assign data entry jobs. Administrative responsibilities are performed by the supervisor, lead operator, or a designated operator. These duties include:

A. Scheduling each batch that enters the unit. If there is a conflict of schedule and work loads, the IS Computer Center head is to be contacted for permission to use overtime or to change schedules.

B. Maintaining up-to-date operator procedures and documentation for each job.

C. Checking the documentation of new jobs for possible discrepancies, unfinished work, errors, and/or ambiguity. Providing copies for each operator and a file copy of all data entry documentation procedures. Updating procedure modifications on all copies in the department.

D. Maintaining ongoing communications with systems analysts, programmers and users to assure a continued understanding of any new or pending changes. This includes source documents, input procedures, volume by day and hour, and schedules.

E. Maintaining data entry supplies.

F. Maintaining vacation schedules for operators if vacations are not all taken at the same time.

G. Contacting the repair service in the event of equipment malfunction.

4. COMPUTER CENTER TECHNICAL SUPPORT

6.4 COMPUTER CENTER TECHNICAL SUPPORT

The primary purpose of the technical support unit is to provide technical services to the IS computer center area of operations. Its four sections are communications, database administration, systems software support, and the client/server Help Desk.

6.4.1 Communications

The communications section or unit is responsible for the hardware, software, wiring, cabling, maintenance, and leasing of services for the operation of all corporate communications. Also included in this section are LAN and WAN systems. This unit will assist management with any vendor bidding for communication hardware or software. It will keep the IS computer center operations management and users informed of any status changes in communications. Users are responsible for informing communications in the event of transmission problems.

The communications section provides written instructions to the systems analysis and programming units regarding communications. Notice to users of operating procedures is in memo form.

The unit is responsible for the system of wireless data transfer. This includes both the hardware and software systems. The standards developed by the PCCA (Portable Computer and Communications Association) should be followed whenever possible. With the proper standards, processing wireless microcomputer data can be simplified by connecting existing applications to the wireless environment.

This unit is also responsible for telephone communications throughout the firm, from the switchboard operator to the voice mail system. The operation and maintenance of the telephone hardware and software is its responsibility as well. The following reports will be generated:

- Monthly telephone usage by phone number (see Exhibit 6-5).
- Monthly telephone usage by department (see Exhibit 6-6).
- Monthly telephone usage by the company (see Exhibit 6-7).

The usage by phone number report will be sent to the person assigned the telephone or, in the case of multiple users, to the unit's head. The usage by department report will be sent to the department manager to which the telephone users report. The usage by company report will be sent to:

- IS computer center head.
- Corporate controller.
- IS computer operations head.

6.4.2 Database Administration

The database administration section is headed by a database administrator who is responsible for maintaining and controlling the data processing databases. Duties are to:

A. Select and maintain the database software.

B. Identify personnel and control access to the database as to who can:

- Read specific information.
- Change information.
- Add information.
- Delete information.

Not only will the access be controlled by a person's ID code, but also by which terminal will be allowed access. Terminal access will be limited to given "windows of time." (This is to prevent the cleaning person from accessing data at 10:00 P.M., a common problem nationwide.)

C. Control and maintain the database data dictionary.

D. Maintain procedures for file and database backups.

E. Provide consulting service to data processing departments and users.

F.   Provide disaster planning procedures, and test them from time to time.

G.   Locate and set up off-site data and software backup system.

H.   Maintain directory services.

Depending on the size of the database administration, this segment can be part of the database administrator's duties or delegated to a directory services manager.

A directory is a collection of information for given applications. It holds all the information relating to each application, such as user-access and user-log-on IDs. Its services make it possible for all applications to share the same database of user and network information, reducing the need to replicate the same information throughout the network. Directory services can be used to find numerous objects on a given network and, therefore, is a LAN-based key to information tracking needed by developers of software systems.

Software to drive this system is made available by several firms, such as Novel, Microsoft and Banyan Systems, both for network and non-network operations.

Directory services is responsible for evaluating software best suited to the firm's current needs. It will install the system and maintain it, and will also provide user instruction and procedures for the software's proper usage.

6.4.3 Systems Software Support

This section covers the software support of the operating system. The applications programs, in-house and purchased software, are the responsibility of the systems software support programmers. Maintenance of operating programs is the responsibility of the programming department. But the maintenance of the operating system software is the responsibility of the systems software support programmers who:

A.   Make changes to operating system software when informed by memo from the head of the systems software support section.

B.   Inform by memo computer operations, programming, and affected users of any changes to the operating system software.

C.   Test new operating system software before it is put into use. Also, test for changes to the operating software.

D.   Assist the database administrator with programming needs.

E. Write and maintain console operators' procedures in the standard procedure format for operating software.

F. Review for approval the operators' instructions provided for operations programs.

G. Assist in volume program testing and auditors' studies.

H. Maintain system controls for accessing the computer system.

I. Assist with console operators' training when putting new systems into operation or making changes to the current operating system.

6.4.4 Client/Server Help Desk

There are three basic forms of client/server Help Desks: a computer operator for very small operations; a full-time staffed, in-house Help Desk; and an outsourced Help Desk. Which you choose depends on the given situation. A computer operator or in-house Help Desk is generally for client/server systems while an outsourcing Help Desk is more often used by microcomputer users. But whatever approach is employed, some one person must be responsible for the Help Desk's existence and maintenance. Following are basic considerations for implementing and maintaining a client/server Help Desk.

A. Determine requirements for such an operation, for example:

- What current and future use is to be.
- How to evaluate user requirements.
- How to communicate user requirements to system development or vendors.

B. Seek out available vendor systems

- Look at complete packages.
- Look for diagnostic and monitoring tools.
- Look at Internet services available.
- Look at distributive support technology available.

C. Consider user services, such as:

- Directory of services.
- On-site education and training programs.
- On-line tutorials.

D. Develop Help Desk staff

- Develop job descriptions.
- Determine staff requirements.
- Prepare Help Desk orientation procedure.
- Provide a comprehensive training program.
- Instill a proper service attitude.
- Provide a safety net for stress and burnout.
- Provide for performance evaluation and feedback.
- Monitor performance and provide feedback.
- Introduce Help Desk staff to users.

E. Management considerations for Help Desk operations

- Develop budget requirements.
- Utilize technology to enhance productivity.
- Maintain on-going user communication.
- Seek out user information and training needs.
- Create and publish a monthly and annual report.
- Create an informative monthly user newsletter.

The day-to-day operation of a client/server Help Desk is routine, but often unexpected events occur. The required procedure for day-to-day operation is as follows:

A. Log-in incoming contacts on a microcomputer.

1. Ask user for user ID number and name.

2. Enter ID number to screen prompt.

3. When the name of the user comes up on screen, the computer begins keeping track of the time the user is in contact. If user's name on screen is different, ask for the correct name. If this is not provided, hang up.

4. Provide user with help needed.

5. When contact with user ends, press enter key on keyboard. Choose kind of service from menu. (Menu may vary from one company location to another.) Type short, one sentence description, if needed, on monitor display. Press designated "log key." Help Desk operator is now ready for next inquiry.

B. Prevent fatigue

Help Desk personnel should not be on the system for more than two hours at a time without time off for lunch or a personal break.

C. Compile monthly report

The data collected for each contact will be included in a monthly report prepared by each Help Desk employee. One copy will be sent to the IS computer operations manager, one copy retained by the Help Desk operator, and one copy sent to user management. If there is more than one Help Desk worker, a combined report will be sent to both user management and the IS computer operations manager. The report will list:

• The number of contacts made by users.

• Time range of all the contacts made.

• The total time used by user, sorted in descending order by amount of time spent.

• Total time spent with users.

• The count by type of service rendered.

The basic pricing options to consider are:

A. Per-solution price

With per-solution pricing, users pay a fixed fee for each call answered and problem solved. This fee may have to be adjusted from time to time.

B. Per-desk price

This a common option selected. The fee is based on the number of users. The price may range from $20 to over $300 per user served.

C. Call-block pricing

This Help Desk service comes in fixed blocks of calls (a given number) at fixed prices. This allows user management to place a usage cap on Help Desk outsourced calls.

Vendor-provided Help Desk service most often comes from the vendor's site. This remote service is generally less expensive than on-site service, and creates very few problems.

NOVEMBER 1996 TELEPHONE USAGE REPORT

FOR: John Smith

Phone number: 456-3321   Department: Accounts Payable #4311

DATE	TIME MADE	MIN TIME	NUMBER CALLED	COST
10/23	9:21	23	800-431-7708	00.00
10/23	10:03	4	513-4141	00.10
10/23	14:19	27	422-313-7931	11.22
10/23	16:33	11	456-5362	00.10
10/26	8:46	2	481-6116	00.10

TOTAL TIME 1 Hour and 7 Min   TOTAL COST 11.52

Exhibit 6-5. Usage by Phone Number

NOVEMBER 1996 DEPARTMENT USAGE REPORT
FOR: Accounts Payable #4311

PHONE NUMBER	USER'S NAME	TOTAL TIME USED	TOTAL COST
456-3321	John Smith	14 Hours 22 Min	47.63
456-3322	Mary Brown	11 Hours 14 Min	48.21
456-3347	Phil Montros	22 Hours 4 Min	67.83
	DEPT. TOTALS	47 Hours 40 Min	$163.67

Exhibit 6-6. Usage by Department

MONTHLY TELEPHONE USAGE REPORT
FOR: November 1996

DEPARTMENT	ID NO.	HOURS	DEPT. COST	YTD COST	BUDGETED
Accounts Payable	4311	48	164	1741	2000
Payroll	4321	27	43	421	600
Shipping	3741	63	221	2643	2500
COMPANY-WIDE TOTAL		138	438	4805	5100

Exhibit 6-7. Usage by Company

Chapter 7
A SSET MANAGEMENT

1. ASSET MANAGEMENT POLICES

7.1 ASSET MANAGEMENT POLICIES

Asset management policies address both hardware and software assets. Well-defined and maintained asset management policies and procedures will be financially rewarding, will fine-tune the company-wide microcomputer information systems operations, and will help avoid embarrassing litigation.

Top management must formally direct the asset management policies and procedures to be the duty of the Information Systems organization. To be successful IS should be required to:

- Inform all employees of the directives.
- Explain the need for the policies and procedures.
- Mandate that only company-owned hardware and software be used by employees in the performance of their duties.
- State that no downloading of company-owned software will be permitted to privately owned computers or secondary storage in any form.
- Permit infractions to be noted in the employees' records.
- Emphasize that serious or repeated violations of Asset Management policies will be grounds for dismissal.

Comment:

The bygone mainframe days seldom had asset management problems. The hardware was purchased under capital expense budgets and the software was developed in house. All this activity came under the domain of the data processing department. But today, computer hardware is found throughout the company, and often there are no controls over purchase, standardization or utilization. Software is even more of a mixed bag. It can originate from legitimate in-house development or purchase or from questionable or illegal sources. This anarchy can appear insignificant because of undocumented direct expense, but the indirect repercussions can be great and the cost astronomical.

The burden of asset management for microcomputer hardware and software assets is often placed on the doorstep of corporate information systems. This is, however, too often through default rather than proper planning.

This writer installed an asset management program some years ago to determine what additional investment was required to "bring the resources level up to satisfy the demand." After the program was completed, it was found that there was already more invested than what was required.

The policy objective of resource management, in the simplest terms, is to reduce cost while increasing overall efficiency, and to avoid possible litigation. The department management cannot see the forest for the trees, and top management cannot see the trees for the forest. The asset management people should be able to see both.

The second most likely candidate today for the responsibility of computer asset management would be the purchasing unit since it controls the purchase order system. For example, use of purchase orders makes controlling the purchase of office furniture a simple process. There is seldom the problem of people making their own furniture, buying it with petty cash funds, having a "free trial," or even stealing it. Although microcomputer hardware and software are no longer controllable through a purchase order system, the purchasing unit can still play a role in information systems control.

2. CONTRACT ASSET MANAGEMENT

7.2 CONTRACTING ASSET MANAGEMENT SERVICE

One route for installing an asset management system is to contract out the effort for the entire firm, a given area, or an entire corporate division. This does not remove the responsibility IS has for this function. The established asset management policies will be maintained by any such service. The contract can cover the hardware or software, or both. It can also provide for a system which either the customer or the contractor (or vendor) will install and operate. For the acquisition procedure see Chapter 15, Vendor Contracting.

The output reports as described in this section are generic. Do not expect all vendors to offer the same reports or output formats, although each product will contain common features. In vendor selection the last thing to consider is the output format of the reports; it should be based on which service best meets the needs of IS management.

7.2.1 Outsourcing Full Service

The terms of the contract with the vendor will be negotiated by the management of information systems with final approval of the legal representative of the company. The needs will be determined and specified so as to fulfill the management policy for asset management of microcomputer hardware and software.

When contracting for full service, the vendor will develop, install, and operate the system. The major issue here is to be certain the corporate cultures of both firms are compatible. Then it is advisable to look at other operations the vendor has developed, installed, and operated. Are their users pleased with the system? How different are the user firms from yours?

Some one person from the information systems organization will have to be assigned the coordinator's duties. The title for this position is computer asset manager. If not full-time, it can be combined with the responsibilities of the microcomputer coordinator, and/or the software coordinator. This one person's work load will depend on the firm's microcomputer size and complexity.

The computer asset manager should also be involved with the vendor selection because he/she will be the major contact person with the vendor, who will have been provided with the needs (requirements) specifications. Establishing an asset management service should be treated as a project. Project control and reporting will be normal for this undertaking.

The tools and procedures to be employed by a vendor should be defined in the "Bid Proposal." In addition, the calendar time needed to accomplish each of the following must also be included:

A. Inventory of hardware

The inventory should be taken in the shortest calendar time possible. After it has been completed by unit, an update procedure should be put in place to maintain a current unit hardware inventory. This procedure will be augmented by random inventory spot checks.

Each hardware item inventoried will be tagged with a scannable inventory tag placed on the equipment in the same location for each type of hardware.

Each new acquisition of hardware will be tagged. The purchase price, department, and employee-assigned responsibility for the hardware will be input to the microcomputer inventory system.

B. Physical inventory of software

The inventory of microcomputer software can be taken either at the same time as the hardware inventory or later. This will depend on the vendor's system. The software of each microcomputer and file server will be identified and logged in; unauthorized software will be purged and recorded to identify to what degree, for each area and user, software violation has occurred.

This software data, by each microcomputer (desktop, laptop and notebook system) and person responsible for that computer, will be input to the microcomputer inventory system. Purchase price, department, and employee-assigned responsibility information relating to new microcomputer software added later will be input to the microcomputer inventory system.

C. Microcomputer inventory system

The microcomputer inventory system will be used by departments and employees within departments to maintain an ongoing microcomputer hardware and software inventory. It will generate a physical report by department after each inventory (first and subsequent inventories). The physical inventory report will also be run at the end of each fiscal year and upon demand by the software coordinator. A copy of the Department Software Report will be sent to the department head and to the software coordinator listing the following:

- The department name.
- The date the physical inventory was taken.
- The name, total quantity, and total cost of each software type.
- The total cost of the department's software inventory.
- The kind of software removed and the number of each kind that was removed.

A detailed listing of each employee and his/her assigned microcomputers will also be produced. A copy of this Department Users Report, indicating the department name and the date of the inventory, will be sent to the department head and will be available for the software coordinator, if requested. It will also list the following by employee:

- Hardware assigned to the employee.
- Software on each computer after inventory.
- Unauthorized software removed, by computer.
- Total cost of hardware by employee.
- Total cost of software by employee.
- Total cost of both hardware and software.

A Department Hardware Inventory Report will be run, after the Department Users Report, for each department. A copy listing the following will be sent to the department head and to the microcomputer coordinator.

- The department name.
- The date the report was run.
- The hardware type, quantity, and total cost of each type.
- The total cost of the department's hardware inventory.

A Total Hardware/Software Asset Report will be run, listing the hardware/software assets by department. There will be four columns across each page: department name, number of PCs, total original investment for hardware/software, and average age of department PCs. The bottom line will indicate totals of the same information for the whole company. This report, to be run at the end of the fiscal year and upon demand, will be sent to the head of information systems, the controller, and the computer asset manager.

The vendor is expected to maintain full service of the asset management system for the life of the contract. Any changes to the system during the contract period will be negotiable with the vendor. Any intent not to renew the service, by vendor or customer, must be given in writing three months before the expiration of the contract.

7.2.2 Outsourcing for a Turnkey Operation

The terms of the contract with the vendor will be determined by the management of information systems. The needs will be determined and specified so as to fulfill the management policy for asset management of microcomputer hardware and software. In this case the needs will determine the asset management system to be developed and provided by the vendor but operated by information systems. The information systems head will delegate the responsibility for the turnkey operation to the software coordinator or the microcomputer coordinator, or a new position of computer asset manager can be created. Which of these options is chosen will depend on the size of the firm and the physical location of the microcomputer systems.

The vendor who contracts to provide a turnkey computer asset management system will develop and install it. The vendor will also furnish documentation and training for its operation which will be the responsibility of the firm. The contract with the vendor should include a help desk and maintenance provision.

Before the contract is signed it is advisable to look at other operations the vendor has developed and installed. Are the users pleased with the system? How different are the users' firms from yours?

The person who will manage the system should also be involved with the vendor selection. He/she will work with the vendor, who will have been provided with needs (requirements) specifications, and will be the major contact person. Establishing an asset management service should be treated as a project. Project control and reporting will be normal for this undertaking. The person appointed to manage the system will be responsible for all reporting.

The tools and procedures to be employed by a vendor should be defined in the "Bid Proposal." In addition, the calendar time needed to accomplish each of the following must also be included:

A. Inventory of hardware

   The inventory should be taken in the shortest calendar time possible. After completion by unit, an inventory update procedure should be put in place to maintain a current accounting. The update procedure will be augmented by random inventory spot checks.

Each hardware item inventoried will be tagged with a scannable inventory tag which will be placed on the equipment in the same location for each type of hardware.

Each new acquisition of hardware, before the system is operational, will be tagged. The purchase price, department, and employee-assigned responsibility for the hardware will be input to the microcomputer inventory system.

B. Physical inventory of software

The inventory of microcomputer software can be taken at the same time as the hardware inventory or later. This will depend on the vendor's system. The software of each microcomputer and file server will be identified and logged in. Unauthorized software will be purged and recorded to identify to what degree, for each area and user, software violation has occurred.

This software data will be input to the microcomputer inventory system by each microcomputer (desktop, laptop and notebook system) and person responsible for that computer. Purchase price, department, and employee-assigned responsibility information relating to new microcomputer software added later will be input to the microcomputer inventory system.

C. Microcomputer inventory system

The microcomputer inventory system will be used by departments and employees within departments to maintain an ongoing microcomputer hardware and software inventory. The software system will generate a physical inventory report by department after each of the first and subsequent inventories. The physical inventory report will also be run at the end of each fiscal year and upon demand by the software coordinator. A copy of the department report will be sent to the department head and to the software coordinator and/or computer asset manager. The Department Software Report will list the following:

- The department name.
- The date the physical inventory was taken.
- The name, total quantity, and total cost of each software type.
- The total cost of the department's software inventory.
- The number of each kind of software removed.

A detailed listing of each employee and his/her assigned microcomputers will also be produced. A copy of this Department Users Report will be sent to the department head and will be available for the software coordinator and/or computer asset manager, if requested. It will contain the department name and the date of the inventory. This Department Users Report will also list the following for each employee:

- Hardware assigned.
- Software on each computer after inventory.
- Unauthorized software removed, by computer.
- Total cost of hardware.
- Total cost of software.
- Total cost of both hardware and software.

A Department Hardware Inventory Report will be run, after the Department Users Report, for each department. A copy will be sent to the department head, the microcomputer coordinator and the computer asset manager. This report will list the following:

- The department name.
- The date the report was run.
- The hardware type, quantity, and total cost of each type.
- The total cost of the department's hardware inventory.

The vendor is expected to produce "clean" printouts of all reports contracted for before the system is considered operational. After the system has been accepted by IS management, it will be maintained by the person appointed to service the asset management system. When the contract has been completed, further assistance or any changes to the system will be negotiable with the vendor.

7.2.3 Contracting for Consulting Service

The terms of the contract with the vendor will be decided by the management of information systems. Needs will be determined and specified so as to fulfill the management policy for asset management of microcomputer hardware and software. In this case, the needs will determine the asset management system to be developed and provided by an in-house team, with assistance from the vendor. But it will be operated by information systems whose head will delegate the development responsibility for the asset management system to a project team. The responsibility of project manager can be delegated to the software coordinator or the microcomputer coordinator; a computer asset manager, a new position, can even be created to manage the project. Which option is chosen will depend on the size of the firm and the physical location of the microcomputer systems.

The vendor who contracts to work on a computer asset management system will provide software and consulting services to help develop and install the system. He/she will also furnish documentation and training for the operation of the system which will be the responsibility of the firm. The contract with the vendor should include a maintenance and upgrade provision.

Before the contract is signed it is advisable to look at other operations the vendor has developed and installed. Are the users pleased with the system? How different are the users' firms from yours?

The person selected to operate the system should also be involved with the vendor selection. He/she will work with the vendor, who will have been provided with needs (requirements) specifications, and will be the major contact person. Establishing an asset management service should be treated as a project. Project control and reporting will be normal for this undertaking. The person appointed to the project and designated to operate the system will be responsible for all reporting.

The tools and procedures to be employed by a vendor should be defined in the "Bid Proposal." In addition the calendar time needed to accomplish each of the following must be included:

A. Inventory of hardware

   The inventory should be taken in the shortest calendar time possible. After it has been completed by unit, an update procedure should be put in place to maintain a current inventory. The update procedure will be augmented by random inventory spot checks.

   Each hardware item inventoried will be tagged with a scannable inventory tag placed on the equipment in the same location for each type.

   Each new acquisition of hardware, before the system is operational, will be tagged. The purchase price, department, and employee-assigned responsibility for the hardware will be input to the microcomputer inventory system.

B. Physical inventory of software

   The inventory of microcomputer software can be taken at the same time as that of the hardware or later, depending on the vendor's system. The software of each microcomputer and file server will be identified and logged in. Unauthorized software will be purged and recorded to identify to what degree, for each area and user, software violation has occurred.

This information will be input to the microcomputer inventory system for each microcomputer (desktop, laptop and notebook system) and person responsible for that computer. Purchase price, department, and employee-assigned responsibility information relating to new micro-computer software added later will be input to the microcomputer inventory system.

C. Microcomputer inventory system

The microcomputer inventory system will be used by departments and employees within departments to maintain an ongoing microcomputer hardware and software inventory. The software system will generate a physical inventory report by department after the first and subsequent inventories. The physical inventory report will also be run at the end of each fiscal year and upon demand by the software coordinator.

A copy of the department report will be sent to the department head and to the software coordinator listing the following:

- The department name.
- The date the physical inventory was taken.
- The name, total quantity, and total cost of each software type.
- The total cost of the department's software inventory.
- The number of each kind of software removed.

A detailed listing of each employee and his/her assigned microcomputers will also be produced. A copy of this Department Users Report, containing the department name and the date of the inventory, will be sent to the department head and will be available for the software coordinator, if requested. It will also list the following by each employee:

- Hardware assigned.
- Software on each computer after inventory.
- Unauthorized software removed, by computer.
- Total cost of hardware.
- Total cost of software.
- Total cost of both hardware and software.

A Department Hardware Inventory Report will be run, after the Department Users Report, for each department. A copy will be sent to the department head and to the microcomputer coordinator and/or computer asset manager. It will list the following:

- The department name.
- The date the report was run.
- The hardware type, quantity, and total cost of each type.
- The total cost of the department's hardware inventory.

A Total Hardware/Software Asset Report will be run, listing the hardware/software assets by department. There will be four columns across each page: department name, number of PCs, total original investment for hardware/software, and average age of department PCs. The bottom line will indicate totals of the same information for the whole company. This report, run at the end of the fiscal year and upon demand, will be sent to the head of information systems, the controller, and the computer asset manager.

The vendor is expected to produce "clean" printouts of all reports contracted for before the system is considered operational. After the system has been accepted by IS management, it will be maintained by the person appointed to service the asset management system. After the contract has been completed, further assistance or any changes to the system will be negotiable with the vendor.

3. ASSET MANAGEMENT PROJECT

7.3 ASSET MANAGEMENT PROJECT (IN-HOUSE)

Developing, installing, and operating an asset management system is a complex effort. The development and installation should be handled as a project, and the installation should provide a well-documented, operating asset management system.

A project manager should be appointed to head up this project. A computer asset manager should be appointed to serve on the project and later to administer the firm's system. This person, in addition to having the qualities and skills of a good project manager, should also be familiar with microcomputer hardware and software and understand software licenses and copyrights.

Comment:

The computer asset manager should contact the Software Publishers Association at 1730 M St. NW, Suite 700, Washington, DC 20036-4510, or call (800) 388-7478 for current microcomputer and client/server information. A copy of the Association's latest newsletter is available on the Internet at *www.sta.org*, and anti-piracy information is available through its home page. It can provide information, courses, and membership opportunities. It would be advisable to have both the project manager and computer asset manager attend one of its seminars.

7.3.1 Developing the Asset Management Plan

The project manager and computer asset manager develop the Asset Management Plan, with the approval of the head of Information Systems. The plan should contain the following:

A. Asset management project team

An asset management project team will be formed, the size to be determined by the head of Information Systems.

B. Preplanning survey

The project team will develop a hardware and software asset management plan. Before its completion, a survey will be conducted as to current

- Internal hardware controls.
- Internal software controls.
- Acquisition procedures for hardware and software.
- Microcomputer data and software protection.
- Software license compliance.
- Unauthorized microcomputer hardware.
- Unauthorized microcomputer software.

This information will define the current status to be used as a control. It will also provide information as to how the asset management system can be installed with a minimum of conflict and effort.

C. Asset management plan

The plan will utilize the information from the preplanning survey to:

- Define components of the proposed asset management system.
- Draft a project timetable.
- Plan the selection of standard software.
- Plan for communication of the implementation.
- Plan for the needed controls.
- Select a user test area for the system.
- Determine project and operation costs.

7.3.2 Plan Implementation

The implementation of the plan will be a major part of the asset management project. Following are the major areas:

- Selecting and obtaining delivery of software.
- Installing the software.
- Testing the software.
- Training operational personnel.
- Setting up the help desk.
- Preparing for a system audit.
- Asset tagging the hardware and making inventory of the software.
- Establishing proof of purchase for the software.
- Taking corrective actions.
- Developing continual audit program.
- Putting in place an operating hardware/software acquisition system.
- Maintaining a microcomputer users' education program.
- Installing and maintaining a disaster recovery system.
- Providing a network security and virus system.

7.3.3 Implementation and Operation

The implementation will start in a prototype area, preferably one that will offer the best opportunity to debug the system. After that area is operational, the system can be implemented in additional areas. Following are steps to be followed to implement and operate the new asset management system:

A. Inventory of hardware

The inventory should taken in the shortest calendar time possible. After it has been completed by unit, an update procedure should be put in place to maintain a current inventory. This update will be augmented by random inventory spot checks.

Each hardware item inventoried will be tagged with a scannable inventory tag placed on the equipment in the same location for each type of hardware. Each new acquisition of hardware must be tagged before the system is operational. The purchase price, department, and employee-assigned responsibility for the hardware will be input to the microcomputer inventory system.

B. Physical inventory of software

The inventory of microcomputer software can be taken at the same time as that of the hardware or later, depending on the system software selected. The software of each microcomputer and file server will be identified and logged in. Unauthorized software will be purged and recorded in order to identify to what degree, for each area and user, software violations have occurred.

This software data, by each microcomputer (desktop, laptop and notebook system) and person responsible for that computer, will be input to the microcomputer inventory system. Purchase price, department, and employee-assigned responsibility information relating to new microcomputer software added later will be input to the microcomputer inventory system.

C. Microcomputer inventory system

The microcomputer inventory system will be used by departments and employees within departments to maintain an ongoing microcomputer hardware and software inventory. The software system will generate a physical inventory report by department after the first and subsequent inventories. The physical report will also be run at the end of each fiscal year and upon demand by the software coordinator.

A copy of the department report will be sent to the department head and to the software coordinator. The Department Software Report will list:

- The department name.
- The date the physical inventory was taken.

- The name, total quantity, and total cost of each software type.
- The total cost of the department's software inventory.
- The number of each kind of software removed.

A detailed listing of each employee and his/her assigned microcomputers will also be produced. A copy of this Department Users Report, containing the department name and the date of the inventory, will be sent to the department head and will be available for the software coordinator, if requested. This report will also list the following by each employee:

- Hardware assigned.
- Software on each computer after inventory.
- Unauthorized software removed, by computer.
- Total cost of hardware.
- Total cost of software.
- Total cost of both hardware and software.

A Department Hardware Inventory Report will be run, after the Department Users Report, for each department. A copy will be sent to the department head, to the microcomputer coordinator, and to the computer asset manager. It will list:

- The department name.
- The date the report was run.
- The hardware type, quantity, and total cost of each type.
- The total cost of the department's hardware inventory.

A Total Hardware/Software Asset Report will be run, listing the hardware/software assets by department. There will be four columns across each page: department name, number of PCs, total original investment for hardware/software, and average age of department PCs. The bottom line will indicate totals of the same information for the whole company. This report, run at the end of the fiscal year and upon demand, will be sent to the head of information systems, the controller, and the computer asset manager.

Chapter 8
WORK GROUP OPERATIONS

1. WORK GROUP POLICIES

8.1 WORK GROUP POLICIES

Computer work groups that are part of information systems can be to some extent autonomous. However, the more the group relies on information systems for assistance the less autonomy it will have. Even with "total" autonomy it will need to comply with universal standards for hardware and software utilization. It will not have any more autonomy than that found with any free-standing microcomputer operation.

A work group system can be a client/server operation employing an information systems server, or an autonomous work group with its own server system. It can be a closed system or can be provided with a gateway for external network access. There is no restriction as to the hardware configuration of the group, as long as the equipment is justifiable.

The company is responsible for complying with certain practices found in the industry. The responsibility for assuring that these practices are being followed should be delegated by management of the corporation to information systems management.

2. WORK GROUP COMPLIANCE PROCEDURES

8.2 WORK GROUP COMPLIANCE PROCEDURES

Work group computer systems can vary, in configuration and process, from one area to another within the same corporation. However, the work group compliance procedures applicable to "common procedures" are to be followed by all work groups within the corporation. When operation needs are expanded beyond the common procedures, procedure documentation will conform to the requirements set by information systems.

8.2.1 General Operations

This subsection covers general operations to be followed by the work group when operating its computer system. Each will have a person appointed as the unit's work group computer coordinator (full or part-time duty).

A. Work group computer coordinator's responsibilities

Following are the responsibilities of the coordinator:

- Anticipate possible hardware needs.
- Anticipate new software.
- Provide information and service for users.
- Provide for informal and formal training.
- Oversee operation policies.
- Be a source for operation documentation.
- Disseminate new operating information.
- Provide for needed backup hardware.
- Be the liaison between the work group computer operation and corporate information systems.
- Be a knowledge source for user applications.
- Perform hardware maintenance.
- Perform software updates.
- Perform backup of files and database.
- Maintain a supply inventory.
- Be the facilitator for disaster recovery.
- Be on call for after-hours problems.
- Maintain computer security procedures.
- Police system for unauthorized software.
- Maintain an operation performance problem log.
- Write a monthly exception report to the unit manager and IS computer operations manager.

B. Terminal operations

Each terminal will be provided with a current operations manual. This may be supplemented by other manuals which are vendor-supplied or written in-house.

There are standard terminal operating procedures that apply to all terminals:

- Turning on the terminal.
- Daily housekeeping operations.
- Weekly housekeeping.
- Turning off the terminal.

C. Operation rules and procedures

When providing the rules and procedures to be followed by all system users, the work group computer coordinator will explain the rationale behind them.

- No food or beverages close to the terminal area.
- No smoking near software or hardware.
- No telephones near computer disks.
- No illegal copying of software.
- No personal software allowed.
- No personal use of computer system.
- No personal disks allowed.
- No hardware may be removed from the department.

Operators should inform the work group computer coordinator of any need for ergonomic devices. Those available are:

- Keyboard wrist rest.
- Mouse wrist rest.
- Foot rest.
- Ergonomic keyboard.
- Arm support.
- Ergonomic adjustable chair.
- Adjustable workstations for special employees.
- Radiation and/or glare monitor screen cover.

3. IS CLIENT/SERVER PROCEDURES

8.3 INFORMATION SYSTEMS CLIENT/SERVER PROCEDURES

In a work group client/server operation, information systems computer operations provides the server. The following procedures for this type of work group computer system operation are to help insure safety. There could be more than one such work group computer system within the corporation.

8.3.1 IS Client/Server Support

The IS Computer Operations help desk will provide support for general computer client/server operations and will be available for work group users with operation problems. If it cannot handle a problem, it will contact a person who can.

The work group's particular technical operation concerns will be addressed by someone from its work area who will be appointed by the work group management and will be identified as the work group computer coordinator. This person, who will also be responsible for communicating the group's needs to IS computer operations and/or the systems unit, will have the following responsibilities:

- Assist the IS trainer with work group training needs.
- Provide informal training to computer terminal users.
- Be a knowledge source for user applications.
- Be the Information Systems work group contact.
- Maintain a reference library of publications for the work group.

8.3.2 Work Group User Education

The work group will receive information about and training for the use of its hardware and software. This will be the responsibility of the project management group installing the new system.

After the new system is operational, provisions must be made for instructions for subsequent system changes. The work group computer coordinator will assist with this task.

Provisions should be made for new employees utilizing the work group system; suggestions are self-paced learning instruments, such as:

- Computer tutorials.
- Program learning manuals.
- Audio instruction tapes.
- VCR tapes.
- Operation manuals.

The work group computer coordinator will assist with the training of new work group computer terminal users and will, in addition, be responsible for instructing the new user regarding the work group's utilization of the computer system. The coordinator will also inform users of pending operational changes and assist them once the changes are in place.

8.3.3 Terminal Operations

There are standard procedures for operators of terminals or work stations which are:

A. Turning on the System

To turn on the system, the operator follows the operating manual's prescribed procedures. The operator checks to see that the monitor display and all peripheral equipment are operating properly. If not, the operator consults the manual and proceeds when the system is ready. If the terminal is not working properly he/she will contact the help desk whose telephone number should be on the first page of the operating manual.

Before contacting anyone for assistance, the operator will:

- Write down the details of what happened.
- Make a list of what corrective measures were tried.
- When assistance is available, bring the computer system up to the place where the problem occurred.

B. Turning off the System

Turn off the system in the following sequence:

1. Exit from the operating system.
2. Turn off peripheral equipment.
3. Turn off the terminal.
4. Remove all floppy disks.

C. Daily Operations

Check hardware daily for:

1. Quality of the monitor display. Adjust as needed.
2. Cleanliness of the equipment. Cleaning the equipment as needed may be done at the start or end of each work day, and at other times during the day when there is high volume use.

If work station has a printer:

1. Check paper supply in printer. Add paper as needed.
2. Check quality of printing. Replace ribbons or printer cartridges as needed.

These actions may be taken at the start or end of each work day, and some may need to be performed more than once a day.

D. Weekly housekeeping

The key operator/user will vacuum or dust off the keyboard and wipe clean the monitor glass once a week. High-use diskette heads will also be cleaned weekly. If the heads are not often used, a once per month cleaning will suffice.

E. Dust covers

In areas that have a higher than normal amount of airborne dust, dust covers should be used for microcomputers, keyboards, monitors, and other attached devices when not in use. For very dusty areas there are special keyboard covers that can be employed while using the keyboard. Since these special covers will require periodic replacement, a supply should be maintained by the microcomputer coordinator/key operator.

F. Floppy disk backup

When data is kept on floppy disks and not on a hard disk, it must be copied for backup. The two floppy disks, original and backup, must not be stored together. The backup copy must be write protected.

8.3.4 Operation Rules

The following rules apply to all persons utilizing the computer system:

- No food or beverages are to be placed on or near the hardware or software.
- No smoking is permitted near the hardware or software.
- The computer and disks must be at least two feet from telephones. Other magnetic devices should be kept away from the computer, disks, and tapes.
- No illegal copying of software is permitted.
- No hardware or software may be removed from the firm's premises without written permission.
- No personal hardware, software, or disks are permitted on the premises.
- No down- or up-loading of any non-company software or data will be permitted.
- No personal hardware or software will be allowed on the premises.

8.3.6 Accessories

Accessories are classified into two groups, ergonomic devices and productivity devices which are to be purchased and coordinated by the work group computer coordinator. (The following items are not identified by brand name.)

A. Ergonomic devices

   Terminal ergonomic devices are to help the human body interact with the computer system and function with the least amount of fatigue, error, and bodily harm. The following types are available:

   - Keyboard wrist rest.
   - Mouse wrist rest.
   - Foot rest.
   - Ergonomic keyboard.
   - Arm support.
   - Ergonomic adjustable chair.

- Adjustable workstations for special employees.
- Radiation and/or glare monitor screen cover.

Comment:

REMEMBER THE REQUIREMENTS FOR THE AMERICANS WITH DISABILITIES ACT!

B. Productivity aids

The following, if used properly, have been known to increase productivity:

- Tilt'n turn monitor stand.
- Copy holders.
- Copy holder and light.
- Diskette storage devices.
- Desktop print stand and/or organizer
- PC roll-out keyboard system.
- Keyboard with mouse.
- Mouse pad.
- Mouse holder.
- Keyboard labels for F keys and/or other keys.
- Wastepaper container and paper shredder.
- Workstations (that include a drawer for personal items that can be locked).
- Speaker telephone.

Chapter 9
FREESTANDING MICROCOMPUTER

---

1. FREESTANDING MICROCOMPUTER POLICIES

9.1 FREESTANDING MICROCOMPUTER POLICIES

Some firms today do not consider microcomputers to be capital assets, while other firms lease this hardware. This reduces the accounting activity required for capital asset accounting. But because microcomputers are so inexpensive and accessible, proprietorship rights are not controlled. This equipment will, in total, cost more, produce less, and jeopardize the firm's operation and security if not properly organized and controlled. The IS organization is the most qualified to perform this function.

9.1.1 Acquisition of Microcomputers

Information Systems management sets the standards for microcomputer hardware acquisitions. These cover:

A. The lease, purchase, or rental of microcomputer equipment.

B. The brand of computers acquired.

C. The brand of peripheral equipment acquired.

D. Maintenance contracts.

9.1.2 Acquisition of Software

Information Systems management controls site-licensed software whose charges are based on quantity. The cost of software is paid by the user.

Departments may purchase their own software as long as it is on the list which the information systems department supports.

9.1.3 Personal Hardware and Software

No personal hardware or software is allowed. All hardware and software of any kind, including in-house developed programs, are the sole property of the firm. This policy is enforced to reduce problems with equipment, software failure, damage to data files, and the introduction of viruses. To restrict access to the firm's data and/or programs and prevent virus transmission, disks or tapes belonging to the firm are not to be used in personal home computers.

9.1.4 Microcomputer Management

The Information Systems department is expected to be involved in strategic planning for the microcomputer needs of the firm which include hardware, software, maintenance, and support and training for users of this technology. The degree of involvement will vary, dependent on the operation requirements of each department.

An advisory panel, consisting of management level staff and line operations personnel, guides Information Systems management and settles disputes concerning the current and strategic needs of the firm.

9.1.5 Backup Hardware and Software

The information systems department is responsible for maintaining backup hardware and software which are available as needed, on a loan basis, to users.

9.1.6 User Training

The information systems department is responsible for coordinating and providing microcomputer user training. This consists of both formal classes and individual, self-paced instruction.

Comment:
The firm's management has the responsibility of providing current policies to insure that microcomputers are providing the best possible service to the firm. Microcomputer anarchy has caused the demise of more than one senior executive.

2. MICROCOMPUTER COORDINATOR

9.2 MICROCOMPUTER COORDINATOR

The microcomputer coordinator's duties and responsibilities will vary from one location to another, depending on needs. The actual title may also vary, but whatever the title, the objective of the position is to ensure that the microcomputer policies are enforced.

9.2.1 Responsibilities

Following are responsibilities of the person assigned the position of microcomputer coordinator:

A. Process requests for new hardware and software.

B. Keep abreast of user hardware and software needs.

C. Provide an on-going hardware and software troubleshooting service for users to handle day-to-day operating problems.

D. Provide informal and formal training assistance for microcomputer users.

E. Enforce policies regarding microcomputer hardware and software operations.

F. Disseminate new hardware/software information.

G. Provide backup service for microcomputer hardware and software.

H. Provide microcomputer LAN service and/or supervision.

I. Maintain a microcomputer electronic bulletin board for user's concerns.

J. Maintain a microcomputer store.

K. Publish a microcomputer newsletter.

9.2.2 In-House Consulting Service

The microcomputer coordinator acts as an in-house consultant for users of sanctioned microcomputer equipment and software. They can be in desktop, transportable, laptop, or notebook machines form. Assessing present and future needs of these machines is one of the services provided. The consulting service also covers the areas of microcomputer communications and networking. The coordinator is responsible for maintaining a compatible standard for microcomputer and LAN or WAN communications.

The coordinator works with user personnel responsible for communications to ensure continuity and compatibility of the microcomputer systems.

Microcomputer access to mainframe databases requires approval by the coordinator before any contact is made with the database administrator and/or data manager.

The coordinator will maintain a daily log which is the data source for monthly reports of his/her activities. Depending on cost accounting practices, users may be charged for the time they use. The daily log will record, by user charge code, time spent on the following items (travel time will be also be included):

- Microcomputer hardware troubleshooting.
- Microcomputer software troubleshooting.
- Informal and formal training assistance.
- User consulting service.

The coordinator's indirect (administrative cost) time will be kept in the following categories:

- Reading and other education methods used to keep up with current technology.
- Communication network services.
- Electronic bulletin board usage and maintenance.
- Maintaining the microcomputer store.
- Publishing newsletter and other information.
- User education and training preparation (when not charged to a given department).
- General administration duties, etc.

9.2.3 Microcomputer Training

The coordinator is the training provider for microcomputer and computer terminal users. The coordinator may enlist the services of the IS training unit or the firm's training department in carrying out this responsibility. Training may be provided on a group or individual basis. Charges for this service will follow established cost accounting practices. There is no service charge for the loan of text material, the use of self-paced instruction programs, or the loan of instructional hardware.

The coordinator will maintain an up-to-date library of reading material and self-instruction programs available for users. The latest versions of operating hardware and software manuals will be included.

Instructional programs will be developed in-house, contracted for with outside developers, and purchased "off-the-shelf." Unless developed or purchased for given departments, the cost will be applied to the indirect administrative training budget.

The coordinator will require a work area next to or part of the microcomputer store to house his/her office and training development effort. This area will be:

- Secured when not in use.
- Air conditioned and air purified.
- Equipped with furniture and storage facilities.
- Soundproof enough in a given part of the area to record voice or other sound.
- Equipped with a classroom that can double as a studio if no other is provided. This classroom is not required to be in the same area as the computer store facilities.

A required minimum of capital equipment is needed for a microcomputer training operation. Most of the items will be stationary, but some may be portable and loaned to users. There should be on hand more than one of each item to be loaned. The following microcomputer training equipment is considered the minimum needed:

- White board.

Comment:
This is much more practical than a blackboard and can double as a projector screen.

- Table-top lectern.
- Portable overhead projector.

- Flip chart (floor model).

- 35mm slide projector.

- 35mm camera with flash attachment.

- Camera copy stand with lights. If daylight film is used, blue (daylight rendering) photo flood lights should be used to provide the correct color balance.

- VCR and color monitor.

- Supply items: non-permanent color markers, overhead transparencies (both write-on and laser printable), spare projection bulbs, flipchart paper, 35mm daylight slide film (film speed of 200 or more), slide trays, and erasers.

9.2.4 Microcomputer Newsletter

The newsletter may be published monthly, but not less than quarterly. It should announce forthcoming training programs, tell who completed what programs, give new hardware or software availability, list hardware and software available for hands-on experience in the computer store, and list contact telephone numbers for microcomputer or network assistance.

An information systems newsletter may take the place of a separate microcomputer newsletter if it incorporates the information needs of the microcomputer users.

The size of a newsletter should be $8\,1/_2$-by-11-inch: printed on 11-by-17-inch paper and folded into an $8\,1/_2$-by-11-inch document. If this is not possible, stapled $8\,1/_2$-by-11-inch paper will do. Using desktop publishing software to produce the newsletter would be ideal, but high-end word processing software can also generate a professional looking newsletter. Graphics will enhance its appearance, and photos even more.

Comment:
Remember, a late newsletter may not be called a "news letter" by its readers.

3. MICROCOMPUTER ACQUISITION PROCEDURES

9.3 MICROCOMPUTER ACQUISITION PROCEDURES

The microcomputer coordinator will be responsible for the inventory control of all microcomputer hardware (desktop, transportable, laptop, and notebook) and software acquisitions. He/she will also assist users with any future hardware and software requirements, and should be attuned to microcomputer users' expected needs.

Purchase requisitions for microcomputer hardware, software, and service or consulting contracts are forwarded to the information systems department's microcomputer coordinator who approves the purchase requisitions and forwards them to the purchasing department. Purchase requisitions are used only for approved budgeted expenditures.

9.3.1 Hardware Acquisition

The procedures for hardware acquisition are:

A. Approved hardware purchases

Departments with budget approval for hardware expenditures complete a purchase requisition and forward it to the microcomputer coordinator who will check the capital expense budget listing and confirm that the purchase can be approved.

If it is not on the approved list, the purchase requisition is returned with a memo explaining the problem. If it is in order, the coordinator dates and signs the purchase requisition and forwards it to the purchasing department.

B. Hardware loans

Departments requesting a loan of hardware from the microcomputer store send a memo/e-mail to the coordinator with the following information: (In the event of an emergency, a telephone call will do.)

- What is to be loaned.
- Expected length of time for the loan.
- Reason for the loan.
- The department and person requesting the loan.
- Where the equipment will be used.
- The person who will be using the equipment.

When the equipment is released, an "out card" will be completed by the person receiving the equipment. The card will contain the date, time, equipment loaned, serial number, and to whom it is loaned, and will be signed by the receiving person. The card will be filed, by date, under the requesting department until the item is returned, when the card will be signed and dated by the person returning the item.

The "out card" file will be reviewed once per month. Delinquent borrowers will be contacted about returning the equipment. Cards for returned items will be held on file for one year.

If any damage is observed to the item it will be so noted on the card which will become the source for a damage memo report to be completed by the coordinator. This memo will be sent to the department head of the borrower. Arrangements will be made to repair or replace the piece of equipment. The coordinator will decide the amount of money, if any, that will be charged to the borrower's account for the repair or replacement.

C. New hardware acquisition

The coordinator serves as an information source for future hardware acquisitions by maintaining a published list of "approved" hardware (hardware sanctioned for purchase). If the desired hardware is listed, the user need only provide budgeted funds to acquire the equipment.

However, the purchase of hardware that is not sanctioned will require a request either for a one-time purchase, or for the item to be placed on the approved list. The procedure for either action is to write an explanatory memo to the coordinator containing the following information:

- Item's name, and vendor's name and address.
- Cost of the item.
- Quantity required.
- Reason special item is required.
- What happens if item is not approved.
- Personnel responsible for item's maintenance.
- Personnel responsible for training and operation support.

If required, the coordinator will hold a meeting with the party interested in the new hardware. If an alternate piece of approved hardware is not acceptable to the user, and the request is not resolved, the coordinator will contact the head of information systems for disposition of the problem.

The information systems manager will inform the requesting party by memo of his/her decision. If the equipment acquisition is still not approved, the user may appeal in writing to the Microcomputer Advisory Panel whose decision is final.

9.3.2 Software Acquisition

Software may be developed in-house or be acquired from an outside source. In-house software development will only be pursued if no commercially available software can be found for less than the in-house cost. The availability of in-house programming personnel is also a consideration. Arrangements for any in-house developed software will be made by the coordinator who will decide whether the actual programming effort may be done in-house or contracted out. The cost of this effort will be charged to the requesting user's department budget.

Software can be purchased for multi-users or a single user. Most is purchased from vendors, while some is only available for an annual fee. Also, up-grades are generally available for a single user or multi-users. Purchased "off-the-shelf" software is available in two forms. One type is for the "horizontal" market, that is, for widespread use across many different kinds of firms. Examples of these would be word processing or spreadsheet software. The other type is for the "vertical" market, that is, for applications pertaining to given industries. This kind of software may be more flexible, because in some cases the source program is available making it possible to alter the program to meet the user's own needs.

It is the duty of the coordinator to continually seek newer and better software. He/she will maintain a published list of approved software which will be continually up-dated with equipment newly approved to respond to new needs. Only approved software may be used. In the event that the coordinator does not approve requested software, the requesting party may appeal in writing to the Microcomputer Advisory Panel, whose decision is final.

Software acquisition procedures are as follows:

A. Specially developed software

    A user who requires software that is not available by purchase works with the coordinator to define the needs. The coordinator then submits a memo to the person responsible for microcomputer programming systems and provides enough information so that a project proposal can be developed and the cost estimated. (In some cases, the microcomputer systems programmer and the coordinator may be the same person.) Project proposal information is reviewed with the user requesting the program. If time and money are available, a formal request in writing is issued by the user management.

Program development is handled using the standard procedures for information systems program development. As long as no security problem exists, the new software will be made available to other microcomputer users.

B. Purchased software

The user sends a memo requesting the approved software to the coordinator who reviews the request and, if it is in order, sends the software to the requesting party. An internal charge will be made to the requesting department's account.

If the software is not in stock, the coordinator will issue a purchase requisition on behalf of the requesting department which will be copied, while another copy will be forwarded to the purchasing unit.

C. Software registration

All software registration will be handled, completed and mailed by the coordinator in the name of the company.

D. Software library

Copies of all in-house developed microcomputer programs and the original licensed software, as well as backup copies of other purchased software, are maintained in a software library. Users with one-of-a-kind software are encouraged to have backup copies housed here as well. All software will be the most current version in use. The library will be part of the computer store, and under the control of the microcomputer coordinator.

E. Software demo disks

Software demo disks will be provided to users requesting them. These can be provided by vendors or developed in-house, and will not be charged to the user's account.

Comment:

The software library may provide an opportunity for potential users to try software before obtaining their own copies. The library also contains proper documentation and user instructions so that software can be tested. The microcomputer coordinator may be called on to demonstrate software or demo programs to potential users.

9.3.3 The Microcomputer Store

The "microcomputer store" is a hardware and software display area. Hours will be indicated next to or on the door and listed in the microcomputer/information systems newsletter; it will be secured when closed.

The coordinator maintains the microcomputer store for:

- Useable hardware displays.
- Storage of backup hardware for loan to users.
- Microcomputer hardware accessories.
- Useable software running on company hard drives or floppies.
- Packaged software.
- Microcomputer supply items.
- Microcomputer furniture.

Comment:

A picture is worth a thousand words and the "real thing" is worth a thousand pictures. The store displays useable items that are on the "approved list" so that they can be seen and tried. Users are given an opportunity for "hands-on" experience with sanctioned hardware, software, and accessories. Computer furniture and ergonomic devices are also available to be seen and utilized.

9.3.4 Communications Acquisition

Microcomputer communication systems require some planning on the part of the potential user and the coordinator who acts as a resource person for acquisitions. The coordinator must maintain an information file of LAN (and lesser degree of WAN) hardware and software to be used when considering future acquisitions or upgrading. There are a variety of LAN systems today, including wired or wireless. There is even one that employs power supply lines as the transmitting media. Remote network users (mobile or home offices) utilize modems to link with LAN systems.

For modem acquisitions a user-request memo, signed by the user's superior and defining the modem needs, is sent to the coordinator. The user will be supplied with an "approved" modem hardware and software with the required (or a higher) transmission rate and installed by the coordinator.

Comment:

Fax-modems are now available, which allow for double duty and convenience. Microcomputer network communication acquisitions may require approval of the person responsible for corporate communications. This is especially true with WAN system interfacing or when linking two or more LAN systems. The gateway and modem selection will also require the approval of the organizational communication person. If this is not required, the coordinator will be fully responsible for installing the micro-LAN communication hookup and for providing the users with the required instructions and operation manuals for the on-line communication systems.

Comment:

LAN-based e-mail has started to replace information systems host-based systems. The pros, so far, outweigh the cons for this trend. Some of the major reasons for the move to e-mail are: lower prices, availability of Windows support of LAN-based e-mail, and emerging mail-enabled applications.

Acquisitions of LAN-based e-mail systems fall under the domain of the coordinator who also is responsible for its maintenance, upgrading, and support.

9.3.5 Database Access Acquisition

Microcomputer users requiring access to a mainframe database will consult with the microcomputer manager regarding their needs. He/she reviews the user's needs and contacts the database administrator, and the data administrator, if there is one, for user access. Both the database and data administrators' approvals are required for the user to access the information system's database. If it is that of another user (in the same work group), or part of a network of microcomputers, the coordinator contacts the data administrator for written approval. If there is none, the coordinator resolves the problem with the user, and sends a requesting memo to the database administrator for access.

The coordinator also makes arrangements for new microcomputer users to access the database and provides them with training and an operation manual.

4. MICROCOMPUTER OPERATIONS

9.4 MICROCOMPUTER OPERATIONS

Microcomputer (desktop, transportable, laptop, and notebook) operations utilize recommended manufacturers' standards as outlined in the manufacturers' manuals. These manuals are to be supplemented with those provided by the information system's microcomputer coordinator which are both purchased and written in-house.

Comment:

Because manufacturers' manuals are often written to meet deadlines and need to be corrected after use, publishers have filled the need with some that are easier to understand.

Today's technology has encouraged the use of the microcomputer as a user information and learning instrument with the aid of self-paced tutorials or even the "help" key. This technology should not be overlooked by the person responsible for the organization's microcomputers.

Various operations within the company may have differing degrees of autonomy, but the microcomputer policies, enforced by the coordinator, apply to all microcomputer users.

9.4.1 Microcomputer Security

Desktop microcomputers or any stationary microcomputer should be located in a safe environment. The person assigned nonstationary equipment assumes full responsibility for the safekeeping of both the hardware and the software. Preventing unauthorized access of any microcomputer system should be of utmost concern to all employees. The following items address this issue:

A. Physical location

The room in which the computers are kept should be locked when not in use. If this is not possible, serious consideration should be given to employing a cable lock to deter any removal of the desktop computer hardware. Any transportable computers should be kept in a safe place at all times; this includes the time the hardware is in transit. All portable computers must be handled as "carry-on luggage" while in public transit. When microcomputers are being transported for a special event that does not permit them to be carried individually, permission must be requested in writing from the coordinator. Approval will be granted in writing, along with the special one-time procedures to be followed for the event.

If a desktop microcomputer is moved to a new permanent location within an area under the jurisdiction of the coordinator, the coordinator will be informed in writing within 24 hours of the move. If the new area is not under the jurisdiction of the current coordinator, he/she must approve the move before it takes place and inform the asset manager and the new area's coordinator.

B. Access security

Stationary microcomputers with a modem or network and/or hard drives with any restricted information will be required to have one of the following:

- A lock.
- An access security board.
- An access security board with a lock-slot, so the board can utilize a cable security system.
- Personal access code software (in the event the microcomputer does not have an available slot for an access security board).

- An access security board with a motion alarm. In the event that a building alarm is available, and the situation warrants, an external connection to the building alarm system should be made. The alarm may be set to notify IS operations, and the firm's own security force, or an outside security service.

C. Software and data security

Software disks will be stored in a locked place. Data disks and back-up tapes and disks will be stored in a PC media safe or other such comparable device if so warranted by the data administrator or coordinator.

9.4.2 Daily Operating Procedures

There are standard operating procedures that apply to all microcomputer operations:

A. Turning on the system

To turn on the system, the operator follows the manufacturer's prescribed procedures.

Comment:
Approved power backup hardware is highly recommended in the event of a power failure. If there is no such device, care should be taken not to use the machines when a power failure is likely.

The operator checks to see that the monitor display and all peripheral equipment are operating properly. If not, the operating manual is consulted. The operator proceeds when the system is ready.

Portable computers that have access to AC power supply will be checked for the status of their batteries. If the batteries require recharging (or to prolong battery life), the available AC power supply will be used. If the power supplied is outside of the U.S., be sure that it is compatible with the hardware requirements.

B. Turning off the system

When turning off the system:

- Exit from the operating system.
- Turn off peripheral equipment.
- Turn off the computer.
- Remove floppy disks.
- Turn off the surge protect switch.
- Check battery-powered microcomputers for recharging needs, and when necessary, recharged batteries as soon as possible.

C. Daily operations

Systems are checked daily (by the Key Operator/user) for:

- Paper supply in printer. Add paper as needed.
- Quality of printing. Replace ribbons or printer cartridges as needed.
- Quality of monitor display. Adjust as needed.
- Cleanliness of the computer equipment. Cleaning the equipment as needed may be done at the start or end of each work day, and at other times during the day when there is high volume use.

D. Weekly housekeeping

The key operator/user will vacuum or dust off the keyboard and wipe clean the monitor glass once a week. High-use diskette heads will also be cleaned weekly. If the heads are not often used, a once per month cleaning will suffice.

E. Dust covers

In areas that have a higher than normal amount of airborne dust, dust covers should be used for microcomputers, keyboards, monitors, and other attached devices when not in use. For very dusty areas there are special keyboard covers that can be employed while using the keyboard which require periodic replacement. Therefore, the coordinator/key operator must maintain a supply.

9.4.3 Operation Rules and Procedures

The following rules and procedures apply to the operation of all microcomputers:

A. No food or beverage is to be placed on or near the hardware or software.

B. No smoking is permitted near the hardware or software.

C. A clean and cool and dry air working environment is recommended for the computer.

D. The computer disks and reading heads must be at least two feet from telephones. Other magnetic devices should be kept away from the computer, disks and tapes.

Comment:

This writer demagnetized some videotapes, a while back, over some just-purchased software that was hidden under some papers. The new software disks were demagnetized, too.

E. All computers and peripheral equipment must be plugged into a surge protection unit. Non-computer electric devices should not be plugged into the surge protection outlet or into the same wall plug with the surge protection device. Only grounded electrical outlets are to be used.

F. No illegal copying of software is permitted.

G. No hardware or software may be removed from the firm's premises without written permission, for each occasion, from the coordinator. Portable computer systems that are used away from the workplace will require a permission letter or ID card signed by the manager to be kept with the system at all times. The permission letter/ID card will identify who has permission to use and carry the authorized equipment and software. It will also contain the serial numbers of the units authorized and will identify the software contained in the system.

H. No personal hardware, software, or disks are allowed on the premises.

I. No hardware or software (including portable equipment) will be loaned to non-company persons.

J. Floppy disk labels will be written with a permanent marker before they are applied to the disks.

K. Floppy disks will be kept in their disk containers or storage unit when not in use.

9.4.4 Backup Procedures

Depending on the area of use within the company, backup procedures may vary. Not all data and software have the same value (although it is better to be safe if not sure). The following procedures are recommended:

A. New software

New purchased software is backed up in accordance with the software manufacturer's specifications. If only one copy can be made, the backed up copy is sent to the coordinator for the software library. After being copied, the new software is tested. If a problem is found, the coordinator is contacted. All copied software disks and tapes will be write-protected.

B. Hard drive backup procedures

1. At the end of each work day, all new data should be backed up onto disks or tape. Some active transactions (such as word processing, billing, etc.) will need to be backed up more often.

2. A backup copy of the hard drive software should be maintained on disk or tape.

Comment:
There is the story of a small company in Florida that had its microcomputer system stolen along with the AR file, and no backup. It placed an ad in the newspaper that promised it would not press charges and that offered a reward if the microcomputer was returned undamaged. The company did not get a response.

C. Floppy disk data

When data is kept on floppy disks and not on a hard drive, the floppy disk is copied for backup. The two copies of the floppy disks are not stored together. It is recommended that the backup copy be write-protected.

9.4.5 Microcomputer System Crash

In the event of a microcomputer system crash, the operator turns off the power, writes down what occurred just prior to the crash, as well as the time of the crash, and calls the coordinator/key operator for assistance. A sign should be posted on the computer stating that the system has crashed and it is not to be used. Portable computers should be taken to the coordinator.

9.4.6 Hardware Problems

For hardware problems, the operator refers to the operating manual. If the problem cannot be corrected, the problem and its effect on the hardware are noted, and the microcomputer manager/key operator is contacted. A sign is placed on the (desktop) microcomputer indicating that it is not working and is not to be used. If a peripheral device does not work, a sign is placed on the device noting that it is out of order and indicating whether or not the computer is useable without the device.

9.4.7 Software Problems

For software problems, the operator contacts the Help Desk. If the Help Desk cannot resolve the problem, the operator contacts the coordinator.

Before contacting anyone for assistance, the operator will:

- Write down the details of what happened.
- Make a list of what corrective measures were tried.
- When assistance becomes available, bring the software up on the computer at the place where the problem occurred.

9.4.8 Accessories and Supplies

Microcomputer accessories can improve productivity, reduce fatigue, and improve morale. These accessories and supply items will be on a "recommended or approved list" provided by the coordinator. A list of items will be carried by the computer store; other items not stocked will be listed, with their vendors, in the store. This information helps when ordering through the purchasing department. The approved list will be published, updated, and distributed by the coordinator.

Comment:

If the volume justifies it, a purchasing agent or unit should be responsible for these items. This would not only help with standardization, but would insure good vendors at competitive prices. The purchasing people are much better at this than the IS people, and they have no problem saying no.

The items can be purchased from the user's department petty cash fund or with a budget requisition. Supply items will be requisitioned from the unit responsible for office or computer supplies according to standard operating procedure.

Accessories are classified in two groups: ergonomic devices and productivity aids. (The following items are not identified by brand name.)

A. Ergonomic devices

Microcomputer ergonomic devices are to help the human body interact with the microcomputer system and function with the least amount of fatigue, error, and bodily harm. The following types of ergonomic devices are available on the "recommended list" provided by the microcomputer store:

- Keyboard wrist rest.
- Mouse wrist rest.
- Foot rest.
- Ergonomic keyboard.
- Arm support.
- Ergonomic adjustable chair.
- Adjustable workstations for special employees.
- Radiation and/or glare monitor screen.

Comment:

REMEMBER THE REQUIREMENTS FOR THE AMERICANS WITH DISABILITIES ACT!

B. Productivity aids

The following, if used properly, have been known to increase productivity:

- Tilt'n turn monitor stand.
- Copy holders (flex arm, attachable or standard).
- Copy holder light.
- Diskette storage devices.
- Cartridge storage devices.
- Desktop print stand and/or organizer.
- PC roll-out keyboard system.
- Keyboard with mouse.
- Mouse pad.
- Mouse holder.
- Keyboard labels for F keys and/or other keys.
- Wastepaper container and paper shredder.
- Workstations that include a drawer that can be locked for personal items.
- Speaker telephone.

Chapter 10
IS MANAGEMENT AND AUDIT

1. MANAGEMENT AND AUDIT POLICIES

10.1 MANAGEMENT AND AUDIT POLICIES

This section presents the policies needed to ensure that professional information systems management objectives are maintained. These policies direct management so resources can be properly utilized and monitored.

10.1.1 Management Objectives

Actions to take to identify and implement both specific and comprehensive IS organization objectives include the following:

- Develop departmental policies and standards for systems, programming, operations and users.
- Ensure the prompt and continuous implementation of those policies and standards.
- Ensure that projects are completed on schedule and within budget.
- Develop a cooperative attitude among IS personnel concerning user's needs.
- Develop and maintain priorities.
- Develop and maintain ongoing IS planning.
- Inform top management of the current and potential benefits of information systems.
- Maintain optimal budgeting for personnel, hardware, and software.
- Develop a department-wide drive for accuracy.

10.1.2 Performance Monitoring

IS management is responsible for the constant monitoring of the performance and output of areas under its direct control. This covers IS systems, software development, and operating systems.

10.1.3 Management Resource Planning

This section defines IS management's responsibilities for planning and directing the use of proposed resources, including personnel, hardware, and software.

- Personnel requirements are a major element of resource planning. IS managers are responsible for having the number and caliber of personnel required for current and planned needs.

- Hardware and software planning is influenced by user justification, selection, and utilization of equipment resources. Requirements for change, replacement and additions to current hardware and software are determined by the interplay of various factors. Continuous monitoring of hardware and software performance is necessary to determine the most effective course of action.

- Network resource planning is required so that different computer systems can interact. The development of technology in this area is ever changing and needs the attention of a proactive IS management to remain current.

- A database is a volatile resource that requires constant attention to avoid misuse and to provide for the ever expanding demand for data.

10.1.4 Strategic Planning

IS management should use either the firm's strategic plan as a guide or its own long-range planning, taking into account long-term user needs. In addition, short-range planning must take into consideration long-range strategic plans.

IS management must also be prepared to downsize or expand the information systems areas that may be affected by strategic planning needs.

10.1.5 Audit Policies

The information systems operation must be able to satisfy the requirements of an IS audit which comes in two forms: the management audit and the systems audit. The systems audit is one which a firm's inside or outside auditors perform and is mostly concerned with the system controls and audit trails. A management audit can be a self-evaluation or can be performed by an outside audit firm with IS management skills.

> **Comment:**
> An IS operation can pass a systems audit and yet fail a management audit, in which case the firm is paying for more than it is getting. Unfortunately, not as many management audits are performed as systems audits or the turnover of IS management personnel would be greater than it is now.

It is common practice for a CPA firm to run a systems audit of the IS operations when it conducts an audit program. An audit policy should be in place to ensure that IS will be able to have both systems and management audits.

10.1.6 Systems Audit Requirement Policy

An IS operation contains controls that should minimize undesirable events and also alert system users to potential problems. The system controls should contain an audit trail that is maintained at all times.

10.1.7 Management Audit Requirements Policy

Management audit policy should contain provisions that will enable the system to satisfy a systems audit. They should cover the following:

A. Management control

Comparison of IS costs with the sum budgeted. The amount budgeted must be within reason for the service provided.

B. Resource allocation

  1. Maintenance of priorities in line with needs.
  2. Assurance that talent is available for required projects.

C. Project management audits

    1. Proper project controls in place.

    2. Contingency planning in place for unforeseen problems.

    3. Project post-implementation audit procedures in place.

D. Technology audit

    1. Verification of the quality of the hardware and software.

    2. Verification of technical skills of staff.

    3. Verification that application systems have:

- Proper documentation.
- Backup procedures.
- Acceptable programming quality.
- Standards for maintenance procedures.

E. Operations management audit to assure:

    1. Proper machine utilization.

    2. Acceptable recovery and security procedures.

    3. Acceptable employee skills levels.

    4. Maintenance of low rerun time.

    5. Downtime minimums for system.

    6. Cost-justified operations expenses.

10.1.8 The Systems Development Cycle Audit

Correct methodologies must be used so that audit standards can be met. The following needs to be assured:

A. Preliminary analysis

The investigatory work and analysis required for a proposed system have been done.

B. User service request evaluation

The current system operation, including cost to user, has been assessed. Potential tangible and intangible benefits are detailed and the ultimate objectives of requested services have been assessed.

C. Requirements and objectives

Detailed definitions have been assembled and descriptions of the requirements and objectives have been identified by the users.

D. System design

The design is being approached in a standard manner, to satisfy the user's needs.

E. User nomenclature

User terminology has been defined at the lowest level of required detail for the project.

F. Manual procedure specifications

The proper level of detail is present in all manual operation specifications that will interface with the computer system.

G. Computer programming

Programs are prepared to process data to meet specifications of output and control. The inputs and outputs that are manual should be able to interact with system programs.

H. Documentation

Operations and user manuals are current and easily understood.

I. Implementation

1. Program testing is required.
2. User and operations training will be conducted.
3. A plan is developed for the conversion with contingency backups.
4. A self post-implementation plan is established for final project evaluation.

2. MANAGEMENT PLANNING

10.2 MANAGEMENT PLANNING

IS planning is becoming more important because of the popularity of strategic planning. The need for joint user and IS operations planning also has increased, because the more complex systems become, the more vulnerable they are to obsolescence.

A rapidly changing outside environment increases the need for planning. State and federal regulations can impose program changes, and customer or market demands may require the employment of new technology. The wise IS manager is attuned to pending changes.

In small IS departments, the IS manager may be responsible for all management planning. Large departments may have a staff assistant or a planning staff unit to carry out most of the work.

10.2.1 Procedure for Plan Development

A. Assign responsibility.

Planning responsibility is considered a staff level function. The personnel responsible report to the IS manager and should have the following qualities:

1. A good knowledge of existing and planned applications.
2. A good knowledge of IS operations.
3. A good knowledge of the firm's operations, which requires ongoing contacts (both formal and informal) with users and users' management.
4. Good organizational, budgeting, and cost accounting skills.
5. A good knowledge of the currently used software and hardware and an awareness of pending releases by manufacturers and vendors.
6. Good technical writing skills.
7. Credibility within the firm.

B. Prepare a plan context.

1. Obtain a written record of the past history and success record of the IS department.
2. Maintain an ongoing record of current activities and commitments—how projects have fared in terms of keeping to time schedules.
3. Know the current constraints of the IS department, such as:

   • Budgeting status.
   • Status of current hardware and software.

- Status of IS personnel, including good and bad points.
- Users' management skill levels.

C. Identify organizational goals.

Maintain a list of organizational goals along with users' goals. Beware of goal conflicts. Benchmarks are required to determine if progress is being made toward achieving goals.

D. Identify organizational goals for IS planning.

These goals should ensure that planning is done and the budget can be justified.

E. Identify planning priorities.

Select first those applications that will help gain IS credibility.

F. Identify resources required.

- Personnel
- Hardware
- Software
- Vendors with credibility

10.2.2 Planning Maintenance

Because of changing needs and the availability of new technology, periodic updating of IS plans is required. A formal review should be performed twice a year, but this does not preclude updating in the event of a major change.

Along with the review of plan status, a risk analysis should be performed to review the probability of risk for all planned projects.

Comment:
It is not wise to be overburdened with too many risky projects at any one time.

3. RESOURCE MANAGEMENT

10.3 RESOURCE MANAGEMENT

This section defines management's responsibilities for directing the use of IS resources, both expense and capital investment items. To properly manage resources, projected requirements are made for personnel, supplies, outside services, purchased software, and hardware.

10.3.1 Inventory of Resources

IS management maintains an ongoing inventory of its resources. Personnel, software, and hardware are monitored with short-term and strategic planning requirements in view. An asset management system should be in place for the control of company-wide computer hardware and software resources.

A. IS personnel organization

An organizational chart of the IS department, containing portraits of management personnel in position boxes, should be maintained.

Comment:
Marathon Oil Company, with its large computer services organization, has found this picture-at-a-glance of who is in charge of what to be helpful.

The talent available within each unit of the IS department is listed in a personnel inventory.

In addition, a personnel profile needs analysis of each unit is required to make it possible to fill current and projected needs.

B. Software inventory

A listing of currently active (in-house developed and purchased) software is maintained. The software coordinator will be responsible for making and keeping this list up-to-date.

1. Purchased software information includes:
   - Dates of purchases.
   - Vendor.
   - Purchase price.
   - Record of user problems.
   - Type of vendor support.
   - Future software needs.

2. In-house programmed software information consists of:
   - Dates programs were written.
   - Revision dates for programs.
   - Author(s) of program(s).
   - Program revisor (if any).
   - A record of user problems.
   - Future programming needs.

C. Hardware inventory

A listing of current hardware is maintained and grouped as follows:

1. Mainframe computers.
2. Peripheral devices.
3. Microcomputers owned by the IS department.
4. Microcomputers owned by other users.
5. Peripheral devices owned by users.
6. Expected future purchases of hardware.

10.3.2 Organizational Structure of IS

The organizational structure of IS is more or less governed by the size of the IS operation and its complexity. Its distribution, whether centralized or decentralized, also affects its organizational structure.

Standardization is used throughout IS, and benefits all information systems whether centralized, decentralized, or distributed. Its organization is structured so that corresponding user levels can be identified. The three levels, with increasingly detailed procedures, are:

A. Policy level

This level involves IS and user management working mostly with long-range planning. It is at this level that policies are refined. Procedures can then be written at lower levels to execute the defined policies and agreements. The relationships at this management level are both formal and informal.

B. Supervisory level

This level makes possible the enforcement of policies by ensuring that proper procedures are developed by IS. The user supervisory level works with IS to ensure that user policies are defined in written procedures. Both user and IS supervisors work on a day-to-day basis with the procedures.

Procedures may be altered as long as both the supervisors and managers agree that policies are still being maintained. The relationships at this management level are both formal and informal.

C. Operation level

The operations, or working, level relationships of IS personnel and users are both formal and informal. It is at this level that IS develops the procedures which user operating personnel execute. The process steps are documented, while day-to-day contacts are less formal.

4. IS SYSTEMS AUDIT

10.4 IS SYSTEMS AUDIT

The following are IS audit procedures used to ensure that minimum standards have been set.

10.4.1 Systems and Programming

Systems and programming procedures adequately meet auditing standards when the following have been accomplished:

A. The company's application development/acquisition methodology is formalized.

B. Written programming standards covering coding techniques, documentation, testing, acceptance, and conversion are satisfactory.

C. The segregation of duties into application program development, cataloguing of programs for production, and operating systems programming activities have been established.

D. Control of program changes is maintained.

E. Program documentation library procedures have been employed to ensure adherence to systems/programming standards.

F. Controls of on-line programming terminals are maintained.

G. Program documentation, including program changes, is complete.

10.4.2 Computer Operations

Computer operations procedures adequately meet auditing standards when the following have been accomplished:

A. There is compliance with computer operations standards and procedures.

B. Reporting mechanisms are used by management to monitor IS operations.

C. Equipment maintenance is performed and records of equipment problems are maintained.

D. The computer center has proper physical and data security.

E. Controls are maintained over information systems hardware, files, and production program libraries.

F. Proper separation of duties is maintained between input, computer operations, and output.

G. A disaster prevention plan is documented and in effect.

H. Emergency power supply is adequate.

I. Recovery procedures and contingency plans are in place.

J. Operating systems procedures are in effect.

   1. Duties are separated between production data file maintenance and operating system maintenance.

   2. Documentation of the operating systems is complete.

   3. Controls are in place for changes to the operating system.

   4. Controls are in place for utility programs, primarily those with production data or program file-altering capabilities.

K. Data controls are adequate.

1. Control points are evaluated for audit trails.

2. There is compliance with written procedures.

3. Control totals generated at input are reconciled at each turnover point.

4. There is control of negotiable or sensitive documents generated by the computer.

5. There is compliance with data security policies for on-line terminals.

10.4.3 Teleprocessing and Networks

When teleprocessing or networks are employed, audit procedures ascertain that the following have been complied with:

A. A written data security policy is in effect covering all applications employing teleprocessing and/or network systems.

B. Data security activities are independent from systems and programming, computer operations, output, and data input.

C. Access to systems is restricted by user identification and passwords.

D. Access codes are properly protected and changed with reasonable frequency.

E. Transaction files are maintained for all messages entered by terminal input.

F. Unauthorized attempts to gain access to the system are monitored and recorded.

G. User manuals adequately describe processing requirements.

H. Alternate processing procedures are incorporated into disaster recovery plans.

10.4.4 Database Management

The database management system adequately meets audit standards when the following have been accomplished:

A. There is an appointed database administrator.

B. Written procedures are employed for maintaining a data dictionary file.

C. Transaction logs and procedures effectively allow for recovery of the database.

D. Data security measures are employed to prevent unauthorized access of data and/or changes to it.

10.4.5 Microcomputers

Microcomputers employed outside of the IS operation adequately meet auditing standards when the following have been accomplished:

A. There exists a formal institution-wide microcomputer policy and it is followed.

B. An individual is assigned and carries out the function of enforcing microcomputer policies, maintaining an inventory of hardware and software, and assisting users in the use of the system.

C. Physical and data security is maintained.

D. A disaster recovery plan exists for microcomputer operations.

10.4.6 Work Group Computer Systems

The client/server work group computer systems employed outside of the IS operation adequately meet auditing standards when the following have been accomplished:

A. There exists a formal institution-wide work group computer policy and it is followed.

B. An individual is assigned and carries out the function of overseeing client/server work group policies, and assisting users in the use of their system.

C. Physical and IS data security is maintained.

D. A disaster recovery plan exists for client/server work group computer operations.

10.4.7 Contracting for Vendor Services

Vendor service contracts adequately meet auditing standards when the following have been accomplished:

A. Contracts are approved by the firm's legal authority.

B. Vendor(s) fulfill contract requirements.

C. Applicable backup and contingency plans are in effect.

D. Vendor is on solid financial footing.

E. Vendor's staff has confirmed credentials.

10.4.8 IS Management Post-Implementation Reviews

Determine whether the IS management maintains post-implementation reviews and continued reviews of existing systems. Reviews should adequately determine that:

A. System designs are consistent with original objectives.

B. Computer programs are in compliance with standards.

C. Audit trails and controls are satisfactory.

D. Program and system testing plans are satisfactory.

E. Test results are satisfactory.

F. System and program documentation is adequate.

G. Program changes are properly reviewed and authorized.

H. Program changes are properly author identified and documented.

I. Users are duly informed of changes and provided with revised user operation manuals.

J. User training has been adequate and timely.

K. Source and object programs are in parity with each other.

L. User management is satisfied with the system.

5. IS MANAGEMENT AUDIT

10.5 IS MANAGEMENT AUDIT

This section provides an overview of the quality of management and supervision desirable for information systems. (The IS management function is no longer foreign to outside auditing firms. To prevent being replaced by a facilities management service, IS managers should give particular attention to this section.)

10.5.1 IS Organization

This section covers IS organizational structure and the procedures required to foster an effective management operation.

A. Organization

1. The IS and corporate organizational charts should identify:

   - The organizational structure.
   - IS management reporting directly to senior level management.
   - Appropriate segregation of duties.

2. Key personnel biographical data should be recorded and requirements for the positions held should be documented.

   - Qualifications required for the position and credentials of individual holding the position.
   - Staffing level requirements.
   - Provision for management and technical successions.

3. Detailed job descriptions should be written for each type of position. The job description should represent the actual required work.

4. Adequate continuing management and technical education should be in place.

5. An adequate compensation program should be in place for attraction of qualified personnel and staff retention.

B. Planning

1. An active planning group, which includes members of the user community, should exist.

2. Minutes must be maintained of planning meetings for senior management support.

3. The planning meeting minutes will contain:

   - Dates, times, and personnel in attendance.
   - Status of short- and long-range information systems plans.
   - Current operating standards, including security and backup procedures.
   - The status of current major projects.
   - The status of IS budgets and the current operating cost.

- Corrective actions to be taken for any present or future IS deficiencies.
- Reports or development studies that should be noted.

4. Strategic planning
   - Documentation of current corporate strategic planning is maintained.
   - Documentation of IS strategic planning activities is maintained.
   - Future staffing level requirements by position are maintained and include positions to be created.
   - Any significant changes that will affect the institution's organizational structure, hardware/software configuration, and overall IS goals are documented.

10.5.2 IS Control

IS management requires controls to ensure that the operation maintains adequate safeguards at all times.

A. Management standards and procedure controls
   1. Personnel administration has adequate segregation of duties.
   2. Systems development has sufficient audit trails.
   3. Computer operations has an adequate segregation of duties and a limited access to file information. Activities are performed only by authorized personnel.
   4. Telecommunications operations has proper access, with assurance that only authorized personnel access the system.
   5. Computer-stored information has limited access, only by authorized personnel.
   6. Contingency planning procedures are current and enforced.
   7. Disaster recovery procedures are current, published, enforced, and tested. Documentation of test efforts should be available for examination.

B. Effectiveness of IS reports

Reports for senior management about IS activities indicate the effectiveness of the IS operation. These reports, also furnished to the IS steering committee, include:

1. Management reports providing current status on software activities.
2. Performance and problem reports prepared by user groups.
3. Reports of systems utilization and planning prepared by operating managers.
4. Internal and external audit reports of IS activities.
5. Management audit reports.
6. Comparable performance norms available from firms in the same industry.

C. Project performance reports

To ensure control of projects, performance reports are written for management of selected projects. These reports compare actual performance with project plans. Reasons for any variance are determined and reported.

D. Follow-up documentation

Documentation of management follow-up is kept for the IS control operation. This is to determine whether or not management has taken positive action towards correcting the exceptions reported.

10.5.3 IS Financial Analysis

IS operating costs are analyzed and compared to those considered standard for the same size and type of institution. This is very important when IS has a lump sum budget.

> **Comment:**
> When users are charged for services these services can be compared to charges considered normal by outside vendors. Competitive bids can be solicited to get an idea of how the costs compare.

In analyzing financial statements and IS operating costs one must:

A. Consider cost allocation methods used.
B. Assure cost allocation methods applied are similar for both lump sum budgets and user chargeback systems.

C. Confirm that units of processing are within industrial norms.

D. Assure that programs are within industrial norms.

E. Make certain telecommunication costs of service are competitive.

F. Affirm that vendor services meet financial requirements:

1. Obtain the name, location, and Dun & Bradstreet rating of vendor.

2. Determine that services are covered by a formal written contract.

3. Determine that there is no conflict of interest between any IS employee and vendor.

4. Check vendor invoices against work done to ensure that the service was rendered as billed.

Comment:

Operating costs is an area of major concern to an IS manager. When top management looks at growing IS costs, members may want to know what the same service would cost if furnished by a vendor or, in some cases, by users performing the same procedures on their own systems.

With the decreasing prices and growing capabilities of microcomputers, many users, more than ever before, are considering having their own systems. This also applies to client/server work group systems, too.

10.5.4 IS Insurance Coverage

Insurance coverage for information systems must be designed with attention to its special needs. The insurance should cover:

- Employee fidelity.
- IS hardware and facilities.
- Loss resulting from business interruption.
- Cost of transaction errors or omissions.

- Extra expense, including backup site expenses.
- Reprogramming and software expense.
- Transportation and living expense costs when employees must work out of town.
- Water damage from firefighting.
- Acts of God.
- Other probable risks.

10.5.5 Public Laws

IS management has to comply with a whole host of public laws. Its main concern is compliance with laws governing employees. These rules come mostly under EEO, OSHA or the Wage and Hour Administration. The Human Resource office is consulted from time to time or when new rulings are known.

With the use of purchased software and "off-the-shelf" systems, copyright law is now an important consideration.

Remember—the company is responsible and liable for the actions of its employees.

> **Comment:**
> One case involved a large IS operation in Indiana that was cited by the Wage and Hour Administration for not paying overtime to 27 group leaders over a five-year period. The overtime was ordered to be paid. In another case, the Equal Employment Opportunity Commission would not permit IS management to force a data entry operator to work on Sunday.

Another concern of IS management is that the IS computer operation be in compliance with all laws and copyrights. Computer operations management is responsible for this and should keep the head of information systems informed.

Chapter 11
SYSTEMS AND OPERATIONS AUDIT

1. AUDIT POLICIES

11.1 SYSTEMS AND OPERATIONS AUDIT POLICIES

Systems and operations audit policies are more technical than IS management policies. A frequent problem is that, when no policy is established, technicians make decisions they are not qualified to make.

11.1.1 Systems Development and Programming

This section covers standards and procedures applicable to the firm's systems development and programming activities. Services purchased from vendors must meet these in-house standards as well as the business standards the firm requires.

The procedures set forth in this chapter follow recommended standards for policies, determined by industrial norms.

11.1.2 Operations Audit Policies

Operations policies cover teleprocessing, data controls, and all computer operations, including user services. The procedures set forth here in the operations sections are governed by industrial norms. When policies affect the audit concerns of operations (data control, user services, and teleprocessing), it is best to strongly recommend that industrial norms be followed.

The size of information systems operations does not alter operations standards. Procedures should guarantee uniformity in all IS operations, even if there is more than one within the firm; this is corporate IS's responsibility.

Microcomputers and work group computer systems must also comply with the audit policies. Corporate IS has a dual responsibility: to inform users of the policies and to ensure that the policies are followed.

2. SYSTEMS DEVELOPMENT AND PROGRAMMING

11.2 SYSTEMS DEVELOPMENT AND PROGRAMMING

To ensure that systems development and programming meet audit norms, the procedures set down in this section are presented in more detail than those in other sections. Systems development and programming involvement may range in complexity from purchasing off-the-shelf software systems to developing in-house systems to purchasing turnkey systems.

11.2.1 Standards

Standards for systems development, programming functions, systems development methodology, and program and system documentation are to be adequately defined and followed. There should also be controls for application programs and software changes.

A. Written standards are to be developed for:
1. Systems design and development.
2. Software package selection.
3. Application programming.
4. Operating systems programming.
5. Program testing.
6. Systems implementation.
7. Systems and programming documentation.
8. Program change controls.
9. Quality assurance and cataloging.

B. Application systems design development standards require:
1. Project feasibility studies.
2. Project cost benefit analysis.
3. Predetermined progress milestones and follow-up review of progress reports.
4. Documented user approval of proposed systems design.

5. Documented user approval of program tests, user documentation, and user's final acceptance.

6. Documented post-implementation studies.

C. Programming standards require:

1. The use of control totals, programmed audits, and validation checks of input before processing is done.

2. Audit trails and exception reports of uncommon transactions.

3. Standardized routines and modular coding.

4. Standards for reusable coding practices.

5. Proper involvement of users in major decisions affecting input, logic flow, and output.

6. Test plans, including testing for all conceivable error conditions. Tests are never performed with live database files.

7. Completed documentation and user training before systems implementation.

8. CASE tools standards used.

D. Documentation standards include:

1. Systems narratives.

2. Program narratives.

3. Record layout schematics and output formats.

4. Database dictionary listings.

5. Descriptions of edit checking and programmed controls.

6. Current source program listings.

7. User or operator instructions.

8. User manuals.

9. A chronological listing of program changes.

10. Documentation of maintenance changes.

11. Prealpha naming conventions.

12. Screen display layouts.

13. Data element cross-references.

14. Index of table field names.

E. Current user manuals are to be distributed to all appropriate user departments in the quantity required.

11.2.2 Programming Activities Control

To control programming activities and to ensure uniformity and conformity, the following guidelines are to be followed:

A. Documents that are generated for new programs and after-program changes are reviewed to ensure that documentation contains the following:

   1. Pre-numbered program change control forms.
   2. A description of the problem or reasons for change.
   3. Approval of change request by the affected user management.
   4. Name of programmer and date of change.
   5. Signature and date of supervisor who reviewed and approved the actual program change.
   6. Signature and date of program librarian or quality assurance person cataloguing the program changes.
   7. Confirmation that a copy of the approval was sent to the audit department.
   8. Any supporting documents, as well as source listings of codes affected by a change and object listing of programs covered by the documentation, are held in the program library.

B. All program modifications are reviewed and approved by the user department prior to any implementation.

C. The program documentation update must reflect that program changes are being done as soon as practical.

D. Changes to the operating system are subject to the same control procedures as application programs.

E. Sufficient numbers of persons with training and experience should be available to provide backup for major systems and programming functions.

F. Systems programmers have restricted access to application program libraries and documentation to assure security. (These restrictions reduce the possibility of embezzlement by the programmer.)

G. Application programmers are denied access to:

   1. Documentation and source listings for the operating system.
   2. Production program libraries.
   3. Live data files.

H. Records of temporary program changes using patches or system utilities are maintained and reviewed by supervisory personnel.

I. All temporary program changes are replaced by properly authorized program changes as soon as is practical.

J. The documentation librarian's duties include:

   1. Review of documentation during system development to ensure adherence to standards and appropriate authorization of exceptions.
   2. Control and safeguard of documentation.
   3. Confirmation that the revised documentation reflects actual changes.
   4. Distribution of documentation to authorized parties.
   5. Maintenance of all documentation and standards manuals to ensure they are current.

3. COMPUTER OPERATIONS

11.3 COMPUTER OPERATIONS

The objective of this section is to provide a base of established industrial norms for computer operations. This chapter also covers the procedures for contingency and recovery planning, applicable to a wide scope of IS operation sizes, along with physical and internal controls.

11.3.1 Computer Room Controls

The computer room environment must be controlled to ensure safe computer operation. The following safeguards are appropriate for a wide range of room sizes:

A. Adequate procedures are in place to ensure that only authorized persons are permitted in the computer room.

B. The operation of computer hardware is restricted to authorized personnel only.

C. The repair of computer hardware is restricted to authorized personnel.

D. The computer room facility is adequately protected with:

   1. Procedures to minimize the accumulation of paper and other flammables in and around the computer room.

2. Heat, smoke and water detectors.

3. Proper portable fire extinguishers.

4. A suitable fire control system.

5. Waterproof equipment covers.

6. Temperature and humidity control equipment.

7. Intrusion detection devices.

8. Alternate power supply.

9. Emergency lighting.

E. Smoking, eating, and drinking are prohibited in the computer room.

F. Adequate on-call personnel are available, and maintenance agreements covering all equipment are up to date.

G. Preventive maintenance is performed on a regularly scheduled basis.

11.3.2 Computer Operations Management Reporting

Computer operations reporting is needed by IS management for feedback and control. This reporting must be timely, and IS management must examine it closely.

Reports include, but are not limited to:

A. Detailed hardware problem logs

B. Computer generated reports that include:

1. Proper program identification.

2. Job processing times.

3. Rerun times.

4. Down times.

5. Operator identification.

C. Machine utilization and performance reports

D. Console logs or automated summaries of such logs which are reviewed for any unusual activity such as reruns, halts, unauthorized use, etc.

Reports must be produced at sufficient intervals to allow proper control and IS management review.

11.3.3 Computer Operation Controls

Computer operation controls govern the personnel running the computer system. Operators should be aware of these procedures which must be enforced.

A. Operators are cross-trained to provide backup and reduce dependence on key personnel.

B. Operators are prevented from:

1. Originating entries for processing.
2. Correcting data exceptions, such as unposted or rejected items.
3. Preparing any general ledger and/or subsidiary ledger entries.
4. Performing any balancing function (reconciliation) other than run-to-run control.
5. Running test programs against live or backup files.
6. Executing programs from the test library during production runs.
7. Copying source or object programs without prior approval.
8. Controlling report generation and distribution.

C. Operators are denied access to source programs, program listings, and other documentation that is unnecessary for the processing of applications.

D. Operators' run instructions must be adequate and current.

E. The computer center must utilize a formal scheduling procedure.

F. Supervisory approval is necessary to add jobs or modify the schedule.

11.3.4 Program/Data Library Controls

The computer program and data library requires its own audit readiness procedures. Site requirements may vary from location to location; therefore the following are only core duties/procedures required for any library unit:

A. The librarian's responsibilities are not to be assigned to anyone who may have conflicting duties.

B. Standard library procedures are enforced on all work shifts.

C. Only authorized personnel have library access.

D. A program and data file is maintained for all items under the jurisdiction of the library.

E. Data files are issued from the library only on the basis of established run schedules or other evidence of proper authorization.

F. External labels are used to identify tapes and disks.

G. An inventory record of tapes and disks is maintained to identify:

   1. Storage location.
   2. Volume serial number.
   3. Creation and expiration dates.

H. Current copies of the operating system and application programs are maintained in the library vault for immediate backup. Second backup copies are maintained offsite.

I. A machine readable source program is maintained for each application program listed in the production object library.

J. If backup copies of operating systems, application programs, transaction files or master files are used, duplicates must be in the library or in the off-site storage location before being put into production.

K. Backup operating system and application programs in the library are periodically tested.

L. Magnetic tapes and disk packs are stored in a closed, fire resistant, and limited access vault.

M. Controlled storage areas (on and offsite) are provided for work group programs, files, and data.

N. Controlled storage is provided for blank payroll and accounts payable checks. A beginning and ending control number log is kept.

O. The program/data library area contains the following devices:

   1. A suitable fire extinguisher system.
   2. An adequate air conditioning system.
   3. An adequate fire alarm system.
   4. An adequate intrusion alarm system.
   5. A temperature and humidity recording device.

4. DATA CONTROL

11.4 DATA CONTROL

The objective of this section is to provide adequate control procedures to maintain accuracy and integrity of data, which includes input, output, and storage of data files and databases.

11.4.1 Input Controls

Inputs to any computer operation must be controlled to some degree. However, since it comes in various forms, these controls will vary. The procedures are as follows:

A. Reference input manuals, which include examples (copies) and illustrations (drawings) of source documents, are made available for each data entry operator.

B. All data received by the data entry unit is accompanied by pre-numbered transmittal batch forms and posted control totals.

C. A log is maintained of input received, by source.

D. Batch control documents that are received with the input data are retained in an orderly and logical manner for final balancing.

E. Non-dollar transactions, such as item counts, are subject to similar controls used for dollar transactions.

F. Master file change requests require the following:

1. The request in writing.

2. Identification of originating personnel.

3. Required approval from document supervisor.

G. All required procedures must be in place and known by each data entry operator to ensure appropriate processing.

H. If the data entry service is a distance from the sending area, source documents should be sent through a backup procedure.

I. To ensure accuracy of critical control fields, input must be verified by a second data entry operator.

J. Monetary totals and item counts are required for key-to-disk and key-to-tape systems.

K. Input transactions are retained for a minimum of 24 hours in the IS computer area.

L. Data entry personnel are prohibited from originating entries for processing.

Comment:
Allowing IS originated entries may be an open invitation for theft.

M. Supervisory approval is required for correcting entries that are:

1. Entries received by, but not charged to, the data center.
2. Entries charged to, but not received by, the data center.

N. Supervisory personnel regularly review exception and reconciliation items.

11.4.2 Output Controls

Output controls cover both printed and microfiche output. The following procedures are to be enforced:

A. All reports are to be reviewed for quality prior to distribution.

B. Control procedures must be in place to ensure that all reports are produced and delivered as scheduled.

C. A systematic and orderly plan must be in place for pickup and processing of data and the delivery of data output.

D. All distribution procedures should be sufficiently organized and controlled to provide for the delivery of reports to the proper users.

E. Procedures should be in place for the control of signature stamps.

11.4.3 Database Management Controls

A database administrator, responsible for coordinating and controlling the database, follows established standards and procedures for controlling data records and files that are used by programmers. The following procedures apply:

A. To maintain security, the database administrator's access to live data, applications source listings, and other application program documentation is appropriately restricted.

B. The data dictionary contains detailed definitions of all data elements.

C. All changes made to the data dictionary require authorization of the database administrator.

D. All required procedures are in place to assure that the data dictionary remains current and accurate.

E. All procedures are in place to cover database recovery in the event of a hardware or software failure.

F. A transaction log providing for audit trail entries is in place at all times.

G. Any attempts to violate database security are reported to the IS manager in writing by the database administrator.

H. Client/server access controls are in place, and any violation is investigated and reported to IS management.

5. DISASTER RECOVERY/CONTINGENCY PLANNING

11.5 DISASTER RECOVERY/CONTINGENCY PLANNING

Disaster recovery audit procedures also contain the contingency planning procedures. Proof that these are in place, combined with periodic testing, is required to ensure proper system functioning.

11.5.1 Disaster Recovery

Effective disaster recovery and contingency plans require that proper on-site and off-site storage facilities be maintained.

A. An off-site storage location should contain adequate storage space for:

   1. Source and object production programs.
   2. Master files and transaction files to recreate the current master files.
   3. System and program documentation.
   4. Operating systems and utility programs.
   5. Other vital records.

B. The remote storage facility must contain the proper access control procedures.

C. A written emergency plan addresses:

1. The physical security of the computer installation.

2. The actions to be taken in specific emergency situations.

3. The contingency procedures required to recover from a disaster or computer failure.

D. A suitable backup procedure can:

1. Provide backup processing for required processing in volume.

2. Provide sufficient processing time for as long as is required.

3. Provide the documentation required so that management can adequately respond to a disaster.

11.5.2 Data Center Contingency Planning

The data center disaster and recovery contingency plans should include:

A. Data files and program file backups in place.

B. Computer system backup in place.

C. A remote storage location for emergency procedures manuals.

D. An alternate input and output distribution system ready to operate.

E. An on-line network system ready for a backup if required.

F. A complete assignment of duties for reconstruction and off-site processing in the possession of all trusted personnel.

G. A complete contingency procedure in place to recover from a disaster or computer failure.

11.5.3 Systems Assurance

Following procedures provide for systems assurance:

A. Data files, program libraries, and utilities are protected by passwords and other means.

B. Passwords are changed periodically.

C. Utility programs with data files or program-altering capabilities are adequately controlled.

D. Written procedures that cover the acceptance and cataloguing of production programs are in place and up-to-date.

E. All object code production programs are generated from the most current source code versions.

F. All obsolete or unused programs are deleted from current production libraries.

G. Data center management periodically reviews and updates controls and security relating to data files and program libraries.

H. Proper information is promptly made available to all concerned about any hardware or software system changes.

I. Database management critical records are dumped and stored on a sufficiently frequent basis for needed backup and timely restoration purposes.

J. A procedure is maintained to provide information relative to the hardware and software configuration of the backup site.

K. All outside facilities backup arrangements maintain up-to-date written agreements at all times.

L. Client/server operations that employ mirrored systems are in agreement. This should be reconfirmed at random intervals.

6. MICROCOMPUTER SYSTEMS AND OPERATIONS AUDIT POLICIES

11.6 MICROCOMPUTER SYSTEMS AND OPERATIONS AUDIT POLICIES

The objective of this section is to establish adequate controls over the use of microcomputers in an institution. The degree of control necessary depends on the degree of sensitive information handled or the value of processing done by respective microcomputers.

11.6.1 Microcomputer Standards

The standards required for the operational use of microcomputers, including software and hardware acquisition, apply to all microcomputers used in an organization.

A. These standards include:

1. Use of the output data.
2. Restrictions of access to microcomputers.
3. Control of the movement of software and hardware.
4. Removal from the institution of any software or hardware.
5. Restriction on use of software and hardware to that sanctioned by the organization.
6. Restriction on personal use of microcomputers.
7. Modification of hardware or software.
8. Piracy of purchased software.
9. Backup for all data files.
10. Policy that approved games are to be allowed on microcomputers.
11. Restriction of network access to Internet and e-mail to business use only.
12. Review of local area networks (LAN) procedures and controls.

B. Standards covering software and hardware acquisition should include the following:

1. Acquisition will follow standards developed for the institution.
2. Each microcomputer site will possess the required documentation.
3. In-house software development will be performed only by sanctioned personnel.
4. Software developed on the firm's time and/or hardware/software will be the property of the institution.

11.6.2 Microcomputer Environment

Environments in which microcomputers are used do not require the same degree of control needed by IS computer operations. However, their users are usually unfamiliar with IS operation requirements and should be made aware of those that are applicable. The following are standard environment requirements:

A. Microcomputer Security

  1. Physical security required:

  - Key locks on hardware.
  - Backup data files secured in fireproof files or safes.
  - Access areas restricted.
  - Critical information backed up by IS computer operations.

  2. Access controls required:

  - The use of dial-up equipment.
  - Read-only attributes attached to the files.
  - Passwords for access.
  - Inscription of classified data on disks.

B. Housekeeping Environment

  1. Foods and liquids are not to be placed on the same desk or table tops containing computer hardware.
  2. Telephones or magnetic devices are to be no closer than two feet from any hardware or software.
  3. Smoking is not permitted in the general area of microcomputer operations.
  4. The area will be kept dust free.

C. Power Supply

  1. Computer hardware must not share its power outlets with any other devices.
  2. All hardware should be plugged into surge protectors.
  3. Areas that may have power supply problems must have backup supply units capable of providing power for the full time required to bring down the system.

11.6.3 Inventory Control of Hardware and Software

An asset management system is maintained for all microcomputer hardware and software. Records are kept both by the computer asset manager and also by each user area's highest level of administration. The asset manager is responsible for keeping the various inventory records in balance.

7. WORK GROUP SYSTEMS AND OPERATIONS AUDIT POLICIES

11.7 Work Group Systems and Operations Audit Policies

The objective of this section is to establish adequate controls over the use of the work group and client/server systems in an institution. The degree of control necessary depends on the degree of sensitive information handled or the value of processing done by the respective operations.

11.7.1 Work Group Standards

Standards applicable to all work groups and client/server systems in an organization are required for their operational use and include those for software and hardware acquisition.

A. These standards include:
   1. Use of the output data.
   2. Restrictions of access to work stations and terminals.
   3. Control of the movement of software and hardware.
   4. Removal from the institution of any software or hardware.
   5. Restriction on use of software and hardware to that sanctioned by the organization.
   6. Restriction on personal use of work stations and/or terminals.
   7. Modification of hardware or software.
   8. Piracy of purchased software.
   9. Backup for all data files.
   10. Backup of server files and programs.
   11. Policy that games are not to be allowed on the client/server systems.
   12. Restriction of network access to Internet and e-mail to business use only.

B. Standards covering software and hardware acquisition include the following:
   1. Acquisition will follow standards developed for the institution.

2. Each work station and/or terminal site will possess the required operation documentation.

3. In-house software development will be performed only by sanctioned personnel.

4. Software developed on the firm's time and/or hardware/software will be the property of the institution.

11.7.2 Work Group Environment

Environments of work group or client/server systems will not receive the same degree of control by IS computer operations as information system's own client/server systems. The users of work stations and terminals are not expected to be familiar with IS operation requirements but should be made aware of those that apply to them. The following are standard environment requirements:

A. Work group Security

    1. Physical security required:

- Key locks on hardware (optional).
- Backup data files maintained.
- Access areas restricted.
- Critical information backed up by IS computer operations.

    2. Access controls required:

- Read-only attributes attached to the information systems files and database.
- Passwords for access.

B. Housekeeping Environment

    1. Foods and liquids are not to be placed on the same desk or table tops containing computer hardware.

    2. Telephones or magnetic devices are to be no closer than two feet from any hardware or software.

    3. Smoking is not permitted in the general area of microcomputer operations.

    4. The area will be kept dust-free.

C. Power Supply

1. Work stations or terminals do not share power outlets with any other devices.

2. Areas that may have power supply problems require UPS (uninterrupted power supply) units for continuous power supply.

11.7.3 Inventory Control of Hardware and Software

An asset management system is maintained for all computer hardware and software. Records are kept by the computer asset manager and also by each user area's highest level of administration. The asset manager is responsible for keeping the various inventory records in balance.

Chapter 12

IS HUMAN RESOURCE MANAGEMENT

1. IS PERSONNEL POLICIES

12.1 IS PERSONNEL POLICIES

The policies which govern IS personnel may differ from those used in other departments because the nature of IS operations requires some stringency. Therefore, we discuss specific IS personnel policies here only to augment corporate personnel policies.

> **Comment:**
> Computer personnel require special treatment. *Business Week's* article, "Computer People: Yes, They Really Are Different," notes that IS people are motivated more by personal fulfillment and growth than money or job titles. Other research indicates that these persons tend to be more loyal to their profession than to their firm.
>
> The fact that qualified IS personnel are very much in demand and that job turnover is above the norm indicates that retention may require some extra effort. Time is required to replace a competent employee and the replacement cannot be expected to function as well as the previous employee for some time. New personnel may also cost about 15 percent more than current employees; moreover, there may be a time delay if a project is involved.

Comment:

IS employees *are* different from others in the corporation, and IS personnel policies and procedures must accommodate these differences if the department is to function at the level which is normal for the profession and if the turnover rate is to be minimized.

Unless the human resource department considers as normal a turnover of 100% per year, which an IS operation in Michigan experienced, the particular needs of IS must be taken into account.

12.1.1 IS Management Objectives

The broad objectives for IS human resources management include the following:

- Develop IS personnel through training and outside education.

- Maintain an active recruitment policy.

- Develop a cooperative attitude among IS personnel concerning users' needs.

- Develop and maintain an ongoing IS personnel promotion planning system.

- Maintain a comprehensive compensation plan for each job position.

- Provide guidance for employee development.

12.1.2 Recruiting and Selection Policies

Recruiting and selection procedures are limited to "long-term" employment. Personnel should not be hired unless they are to be permanent. Temporary personnel are considered contract workers.

Comment:

Firms have been known to hire regular personnel for a project and then terminate them when the project was completed in order to secure "low-priced consulting services." Feeling abused, these unhappy former employees often spread the word about the firms' unfair employment practices and some have even sued.

The ideal policy is to recruit and select the best people for the job and hire them on a full-time basis. It is a wise institution that can attract and pay for qualified personnel. The selection process is also a major issue. It is better not to fill a position than to hire the wrong person.

12.1.3 IS Performance Evaluation Policy

A policy requiring an effective IS performance evaluation system is needed. Evaluations provide both the employee and the firm with valuable information: employees are interested in feedback about their performance, and the firm wants to know how well employees perform and which of them have promotion potential.

12.1.4 Discipline and Termination Policy

The policy for discipline and termination fills a special need in information systems. Discipline should not jeopardize any future relations the employee may have with the firm but should be fair and acceptable.

Termination of an IS employee requires careful handling. Procedures must be clearly in place and followed precisely to insure that the firm does not become a victim of a departing employee.

Comment:

More than one "fired" information systems employee has had the news services' attention because of departing misdeeds. To keep a firm's name out of the headlines requires some special termination procedures. (See 12.7.1 Termination Procedures.)

2. RECRUITING AND JOB SEARCH

12.2 RECRUITING AND JOB SEARCH

Recruiting and job search procedures are traditionally performed by the Human Resource Department but most of these units need help in recruiting the specific kind of personnel required by Information Systems. Therefore, involvement of IS management is crucial.

> **Comment:**
> Even the U.S. Government is aware of these special requirements with supplemental job application forms for IS positions.

The growth of IS personnel placement firms is a testimony to the need for specialized information systems recruiting. The firms earn their employer-paid fees by delivering the IS personnel needed for the job. However, some care must be used in choosing a placement firm. One personnel manager expected a candidate with 10 years of IS experience to be capable of filling a systems analyst position. When the IS manager interviewed the candidate, it was discovered that this person had been a key-punch supervisor for almost all of the 10 years. The better IS personnel placement firm can be expected to weed out such candidates.

12.2.1 Methods of Recruiting

To obtain experienced personnel the following procedures for recruiting IS candidates have been very successful when combined with more traditional forms:

A. Pay a bonus to present employees for recruiting and hiring qualified personnel. The benefits of this approach are:

  1. Proven personnel will tend to recommend qualified persons like themselves who would fit into the organization.

  2. The cost for the Human Resource office to screen job candidates or the fee to pay a recruiting firm is more than the bounty paid to an employee (which should be no less than $1,000).

3. Current personnel have a vested interest in getting the right person for the job that is open. Employees know what is needed more than Human Resources or the recruiting firm.

B. Consult the person leaving a position, who knows what is needed for the job better than anyone else and often makes an excellent recruiter.

C. Take the time to locate a quality recruiting firm.

Comment:
Find a good firm and work with it. Be careful that it does not start placing your "better" people with other firms. If it does, find another recruiting firm fast. Have the firm work with IS management, not the Human Resource Department.

D. When the right candidates are found, have their corporate job applications sent to the Human Resource Department to confirm their credentials and work experience. Operations personnel applicants by the nature of their job will also require a retail credit check.

E. Avoid nepotism at all costs. Because of the controls needed for an IS operation, hiring relatives will cause nothing but problems. Relatives tend not to abide by the same rules as nonrelatives. They tend to cover up more errors and have higher rates of orchestrated thefts.

12.2.2 College Recruiting

Job applicants must be interviewed carefully. Colleges are an excellent source for entry level IS employees, but some special effort is required to ensure the correct candidates are recruited. Often graduates are trained in the IS area; however, a degree in computer science does not guarantee that a person can fit into an entry level position. Many are well-trained at coding but may lack business knowledge or expertise in the particular languages used in your firm.

Comment:

One noted Midwest university computer science department does not offer any COBOL courses in its program. Unless the company is willing to change to PASCAL, some retraining will be necessary if that university's graduates are hired.

The teaching staff at some universities leaves a lot to be desired. Some teachers have little, if any, background in applications programming and the applications they do use are mostly math oriented. Other schools or universities have teaching staffs with industrial experience so students graduate ready to fit into the industrial environment.

The two-year programs at technical schools usually focus on applied industrial needs, but students receive only a limited number of liberal arts courses. Also, two-year graduates most often cannot be placed directly into salaried positions. The Wage and Hour regulations are very restrictive about this. These regulations should be confirmed with Human Resources before making any kind of offer to a job candidate from one of these programs.

No matter what level of school recruiting takes place, an effort should be made to learn something about the faculty and the programs offered. When a school is found that offers the necessary training, inform its placement office of the company's needs. It will ordinarily try to place the "better" students first. The school may even use the corporations's guidelines to assist with the planning of future programs.

One program that has proven successful for many firms is the internship. With this program, those in the company get to know the prospective candidate. The student not only has to be able to perform, but also has to fit in.

An intern from a well-known university who was smart, but obnoxious, was not hired by the company where he served his internship. The IS manager also contacted every other division in the company to insure that this intern was not hired. A candidate must mesh with the corporate culture and, more importantly, with the firm's IS culture. One misfit on an IS project is worse than having one less person to do the work.

12.2.3 Environmental Influences

In employee recruitment, there are environmental factors to be considered. The IS working environments of a programmer, a data entry operator, and a systems analyst are all different. A prospective employee is being recruited to fit in with the working climate.

Current economic conditions and the present nature of the labor market affect recruiting. Recruiting becomes difficult when the economy is overheated because unemployed, experienced IS people become scarce.

Another environmental factor which influences recruiting is governmental regulation, both federal and employment opportunity (EEO) legislation. Company personnel offices are acquainted with EEO laws and should be used as a resource, but these regulations should not have a major influence on hiring.

Comment:

There are some very good minority IS members who would like to feel they were hired because of their skills and not because of EEO requirements. The second and third computer programmers to work in the state of Indiana were women hired by General Electric. Columbia Record Club's Information Systems department hired available Afro-Americans because they were competent. Both companies did this before EEO laws existed. One does not need to be a liberal to hire qualified women, the handicapped, or minorities, just a smart business person.

3. SELECTION OF IS PERSONNEL

12.3 SELECTION OF IS PERSONNEL

Personnel for a position in IS can come from inside or outside the firm as long as the same hiring criteria are used. The decision to promote or transfer a person to information systems should be based on the person's qualifications for the specific job. If the outside and inside talents are equal, the inside person may be a better choice, since this encourages greater firm loyalty. But promotion or transfer of poorly qualified personnel based on company politics can create problems for the IS manager.

12.3.1 A Diagnostic Approach to Selection

IS management has to choose personnel from a list of candidates who best meet the selection criteria, while considering current environmental conditions. The size and complexity of the IS operation, its status within the firm, and technological volatility will all affect the selection of personnel.

A second circumstance affecting the selection decision for IS is the current labor market. If there are many applicants, the selection decision can be complicated. If there is but one applicant, selection is relatively easy, but there is a danger if this person does not fit the position. It is better to continue recruiting than select the wrong candidate.

> **Comment:**
>
> "Computer World" publishes an annual salary survey that is one of the best around. How competitive is the firm within its industry and national location by job type?
>
> Government regulations often influence selection. For instance, one data entry operator was hired, then terminated, because the person's religious beliefs would not permit working on Sunday. When the terminated employee filed for unemployment compensation, the government brought an EEO suit against the firm. The person was reinstated with back pay. To avoid this kind of problem, the Human Resource Department should be asked to help when anything out of the ordinary arises in the candidate selection process.

12.3.2 Selection Criteria

If a selection procedure is to be successful, the personal characteristics required for effective job performance should be specified by the prospective employee's immediate supervisor. Selection techniques can be suggested and used by the experts in a firm's Human Resource Department to uncover these defined characteristics.

Selection criteria can be summarized under the following categories: education, experience, personal characteristics, and future growth potential. Basically, they should reflect characteristics of present employees who are happy and successful in the same position.

A selection can be made by rating the different candidates on specified criteria, each of which is weighted according to its importance and then totaled. Candidates are then ranked by these scores.

The following are part of the selection procedure:

A. IS Application Form

   A separate application form (either in place of or in addition to the general company application form) should be used to glean information required for filling an IS position. It should be developed by the IS manager, and requested technical information approved by the IS supervisors. Before use, the form should be sent to the Human Resource Department to insure that no illegal questions are included.

B. Formal Education

   The educational criteria must be validated against job performance. The amount and kind of education that correlate with job effectiveness are determined for use in the selection procedure. Formal education can indicate ability, or skills, and the level of accomplishment of the applicant.

   IS managers should examine:

   1. An official transcript sent by the school. Courses and grades should be evaluated.
   2. A copy of the school's catalog describing the relevant courses.
   3. The kind of hardware and software used by the school.
   4. The applied or theoretical orientation of the school's IS teaching staff.

C. Experience

   Another criterion for selecting IS personnel is experience. First choice in a new employee might likely be a person who has formerly held the same type of job successfully. The more experience the better, up to a point. Someone who has done only programming for ten years would not be suitable for a project leader analyst position. What the job applicant did while gaining experience should be considered. A person working for a demanding employer doing several projects in four years is usually a much better selection than someone doing only payroll maintenance programming for ten years (unless program maintenance is all that is required). Ways to confirm experience are:

1. Have more than one interviewer talk with the candidate. It is best to use interviewers with opposing technical views so the candidate is forced to be honest.

2. Have the candidate bring samples of written documentation. Then talk about it to confirm originality of the work.

3. To validate the experience of the candidate, contact former co-workers and employers. A phone call to each of them will produce better results than a written request.

4. TESTING FOR IS PERSONNEL

12.4 TESTING FOR IS PERSONNEL

Tests are used to measure skill levels, aptitude, personality, and should be administered by the Human Resource Department. Because of EEO laws, tests are required to be job related and validated, i.e., that the way people perform on the job correlates with the test. There are tests in print that measure programming or data entry aptitude. Manual dexterity tests can also be used for data entry positions. For systems analysts, the desired criteria should be analyzed by more than one test.

Testing should not be limited to entry level personnel. A person who has been a programmer for five years could have been a poor programmer for five years. Well-organized firms recognize this. One source of tests available is the book *Tests in Print.*

> *Comment:*
>
> For example, a COBOL teacher with two years teaching experience and six years industrial experience applied for a job as a COBOL programmer with a national company in St. Louis. She was required to take a programming aptitude test, which she did pass. However, not all experienced programmers can, and their work may reflect this.

12.4.1 Test Selection

Whatever test is selected, pre-test it with current employees first. Scores which correlate with the known performance records of employees can give you confidence in the tests. No one choice will be 100% dependable, but use of validated tests is one of the best objective methods to select the best person for the job. Some tests are not skill tests but measure what might be expected from a person after training. Time and money can be saved by training the right person and not simply hiring someone who knows all the right buzz words.

5. EMPLOYMENT INTERVIEW

12.5 EMPLOYMENT INTERVIEW

Employment interviews are part of the selection procedure. They begin after candidates have passed the preliminary screening and testing. There are three general types: the structured, semi-structured, and unstructured. All three involve interaction between two or more parties, the applicant and one or more representatives of the potential employer. There is no reason to limit the process to only one method of interviewing.

12.5.1 The Structured Interview

This form helps interviewers with little training; indeed, it is suitable for peer and working supervisors to use. A list of questions to ask each candidate is prepared in advance. The questions can be divided between the interviewers or repeated using different versions. This is an effective tool to help determine the candidate's truthfulness and knowledge of the IS area.

The questions should be forced choice in nature, i.e., yes or no, so the interviewer need only indicate the applicant's response on a printed form. This approach is very restricted and narrow, but it provides an opportunity to analyze an individual's technical position.

12.5.2 The Semi-Structured Interview

In a semi-structured interview, only major questions are prepared in advance. Conducting this form of interview requires greater skill and preparation, but does allow for more flexibility than the structured approach. The interviewer who is skillful can probe freely into those areas that seem to merit further detail. This approach combines enough structure to insure important information is collected (for comparison with other applications) and at the same time facilitates the exchange of information in a freer manner than the strictly structured interview.

12.5.3 The Unstructured Interview

The unstructured interview is best left to IS management and experienced interviewers. The interviewer may prepare a list of topics to be covered but retains the freedom to adapt to the individual candidates. The reliability of the unstructured interview may be questioned, but it does provide the manager with subjective information about each person.

12.5.4 Interview Review

As soon as an interview is concluded, each interviewer should put his/her objective analysis of the applicant into writing. This information should be forwarded to the manager who will be making the hiring decision. If the decision is close, the manager may call a meeting of all interviewers to discuss the merits of each applicant.

When interviewers range widely, the analysis tends to be objective. Each level, from peer to management, will have its own analysis of the applicant. All peer interviewers will not only want to have someone who can carry their own workload, but someone who can fit into the work group.

6. PERFORMANCE REVIEW

12.6 PERFORMANCE REVIEW

While most firms have performance review procedures in place, information systems may require additional reviews because performance is a function of ability as well as skill and effort. For example, a programmer who works late, comes in on weekends and exerts great effort receives a good performance review and a raise. However, this same programmer and ten more much like him/her could possibly be replaced by one highly skilled person who does not have to exert the same effort.

This creates a major problem in reviewing the performance of programmers and systems analysts. The systems analyst may be one of the most difficult people to rate on performance. On the other hand, the measurement of data entry operators presents very few problems. The output less the error rate is considered the performance. Therefore, the IS performance determination can be very subjective, depending on the specific job.

12.6.1 Computer Operations Performance Review

The operations area is a simple one in which to do a performance review. In addition to the standard procedures, the following are also recommended:

A. Data Entry

    The data entry operator's performance is ordinarily measured by the volume of data input less the error rate. However, it would be unfair to judge all data entry operators alike. The kind of source documents an operator processes affects performance. Hand-written documents that have to be coded or words requiring abbreviations slow the input rate and increase the error rate. Therefore, standard keystrokes per minute is not a fair method of measurement and comparison.

    One efficient method is to employ a tool from the industrial engineer's domain, that is, MTM (Motion Time Measurement). This method analyzes the source document and the human effort required to input the data into computer digital form, and therefore determines a realistic standard. Some older systems and procedures analysts, and even some younger, have been trained in this technology. If no one in IS has this skill, contact the industrial engineering department.

B. Computer Operations

    The computer operator's performance can best be judged by efficiency in running the computer system. The control logs and system monitoring software allow evaluation of performance. In addition, the appearance of the IS area provides some idea of housekeeping skills. Surprise visits by management on the night and weekend shifts also provide information. The fact that operators never know when to expect a visit helps increase efficiency.

    The evaluation of some operations personnel can be subjective. Personalities become a factor when evaluating personnel such as the data librarian or the data output and distribution operators. Because these evaluations are subjective, two or more supervisors should conduct them. If the operation is large enough, rotation of supervisors and/or personnel (for cross training as well as employee evaluation) should be considered.

12.6.2 Programmers Performance Review

Program productivity is not easy to measure and can result in primarily subjective performance reviews. But productivity of programmers goes up when they are aware they are being observed. (This increased production is called the "Hawthorn effect.")

Programming productivity can be affected by:

- Program design changes originated by the customer.
- The kind of language used.
- The detail level of the documentation.
- The quality of the information furnished for the program(s).
- The soundness of the test data.
- The working environment.
- The quality of supervision.

Items from this list which may affect the programmer's productivity must be taken into consideration when reviewing performance. It is best to avoid assessments based on lines of code per given time period or pages of documentation per month. Performance reviews may be enhanced by the following:

A. Peer Review

Have IS peers anonymously rank each other's performance. Include programmers, the systems analysts, and computer operations personnel.

B. Time by Program Function

A function is an action or activity, usually at the lowest definable level of structured programming.

- A function has less than 55 coding statements.
- A function has one entry point and one exit point. The time it takes to complete a function is a much better gauge of productivity than the time it takes to write a specific number of lines of code. The number of functions that are completed in given time intervals provides information about the programming skill level of the person coding.

12.6.3 Systems Analysts Performance Review

Systems Analysts are some of the most difficult people to review objectively for performance. All too often appraisal is affected by the person's body language and personality. Another problem is that it takes so long to see the fruits of a systems analyst's efforts that appraisals may be distorted.

The number of procedures that might be added to the firm's own performance review for analysts is limited. However, the following may help:

A. Have programmers provide an anonymous appraisal of each systems analyst.

B. Have user managers appraise analysts who worked on their projects, preferably completed projects.

C. Use peer evaluation.

D. Evaluate project assignments. How the systems analyst works with others and how the systems users rate him/her are valuable sources of performance information. The project manager should provide a project evaluation of each member during and at the completion of the project.

E. Examine the status of the project at its termination. The system's project manager or leader will find no better evidence for evaluation.

7. EMPLOYEE TERMINATION

12.7 EMPLOYEE TERMINATION

To protect the company, information systems managers use special termination procedures. Departing IS employees have many opportunities to vent animosity with destructive activities.

Employees who leave on good terms have an exit interview. If the firm does not have provisions for this, the interview should be taken care of in information systems.

12.7.1 Termination Procedure

Employees who are to be terminated for any reason require the following additional IS termination procedures:

A. The employee is notified of termination away from the work area.

B. The employee's password is removed from the system before the notice is given.

C. The employee turns in his/her IS identification and any keys or magnetic cards.

D. The employee is escorted outside the building. If the employee needs transportation to get home, it is provided.

E. The employee's personal items are collected and boxed and may be picked up in the lobby or sent to the terminated employee within one day.

12.7.2 Exit Interview

All employees are interviewed as soon as possible after having given notice by someone other than the person's own supervisor. This interview is to learn exactly why the employee is leaving. The data collected from departing employees may indicate that an undesirable situation exists and may give management an opportunity to make corrections for the future.

If the exit interview reveals that the departing employee is upset, for any reason, this information should be reviewed by the IS manager as soon as possible to determine if procedure 12.7.1 is necessary to guard the operation from retaliation by the departing employee.

8. EMPLOYEE DEVELOPMENT

12.8 EMPLOYEE DEVELOPMENT

The information systems department is unique in that its employees are attuned to the need to keep up with ever-changing technology. To earn a promotion requires even more effort. The better employees, if not provided an opportunity to learn by the firm, will pay for it themselves. They will also be less loyal to the firm because of it. They will depart at the first advantageous opportunity and leave the firm with lesser quality employees. This education and training necessary for IS employees may have to be provided to IS employees beyond what is available to the rest of the firm.

12.8.1 IS Skills Inventory

A skills inventory will be maintained for each employee of the IS operation. It should be kept as current as any other file and should consist of the following:

A. Person's name and ID number.

B. Date the person started with IS.

C. Starting salary.

D. Formal education received.

E. Other training received.

F. Certifications received.

G. Current job title.

H. Current supervisor.

I. Starting date of the current position.

J. Current salary and benefits.

K. The promotion potential of the employee:

    1. Ready for a promotion.
    2. Will be ready with more training.
    3. Will be ready with more experience.
    4. Will be ready with more training and experience.
    5. Is not ready and may never be ready.
    6. Will never be ready.

L. Foreign languages spoken.

M. Future education plans.

N. Future training plans.

O. Hobbies or interests that could benefit IS or the firm.

P. Next goal/promotion within the firm.

Q. Status when hired by IS:

    1. If transfer employee,
       - Date started with firm.
       - Title and department of last position before joining IS.

2. Previous employer

- Name of firm.
- Position held.
- How long position held.
- Why he/she left former firm.

3. Student.

The skills inventory file should be on-line, with very limited access, since the person accessing the file will be able to generate a hard copy of selected employees' records.

12.8.2 Replacement Order

The replacement or promotability order is depicted on an organizational chart as an inverted tree with the head or CIO of the IS organization at the top.

Below each position's box and connected to it is another box listing the three most likely candidates for the position ranked in order of promotability. With each name is the person's title, length of time in the current position and the code found in 12.8.1 K above, which represents his/her promotability status.

Before this chart can be produced, the IS organization must have a well-defined organizational chart with positions properly titled. For security reasons this might need to be a manual chart, produced and kept up-to-date by the IS head or a delegated employee.

12.8.3 Continuing Education and Training

The IS operation will have its own person coordinating the education and training pursuits of IS personnel. It is recommended that this person also maintain the skills inventory, since the two responsibilities are clearly related. The person should write a yearly report, before each budget request time, as to the success of the continuing education and training program.

This person should maintain records of the effectiveness of different programs. The person should be an advisor to and an information source for those seeking education or training. An inventory of forms will be maintained for employees to apply for monies for their education or training, and for expense reports. Reimbursements to employees are permitted for:

- Seminars.
- Vendor courses.
- College tuition.
- Subscriptions to publications not currently available at the firm.
- Professional dues.
- Attending professional events.

Comment:
Some firms curve the tuition reimbursement to grades received, while others pay a given percentage, from one-half to full tuition expense. Those that curve the reimbursement to the grade pay 100% for a B, and books and mileage for an A. When this writer was with General Electric the training was on company time if it directly applied to your job. If not, the training still could be taken, with half of the time at company expense.

9. EMPLOYEE COMMUNICATIONS

12.9 EMPLOYEE COMMUNICATIONS

There are many avenues for employee communications: e-mail, memos, newsletters, rumor boards, telephone, information meetings, and work meetings. (The newsletter has been covered in Section 9.2.4. Meetings will be covered in the chapter on Project Management.) More than one method should be used to communicate important employee information.

12.9.1 E-Mail and Memos

E-mail and memos should be brief and to the point. Avoid personal comments and local color. Where possible the memo should be written so that, to save time, no answer is needed. "If no response is provided, so and so will be permitted, not permitted or admitted by you."

12.9.2 Rumor Board

When rumors circulate, they need to be addressed right away. One way is through the use of the "Rumor Board":

A. A person concerned about a rumor writes about it on a slip of paper and places it in a locked box attached to the department bulletin board.

B. Management reads the slip of paper and places a response on the bulletin board.

With today's technology, this same idea may be used on a computer network, which would speed up the whole process.

12.9.3 Telephone Communications

Speak normally and clearly. Answer the phone by the name under which it is listed: by person ("Sam Jones speaking") or by department or unit ("mail room").

Speak at a normal speed. If you are to provide information that the other person is to record, ask if a pencil is handy. When reading a list of numbers go slowly and read the numbers in groups. For example, with the number 2379446193, repeat it as 23-79-44-61 and 93. Unlike a memo, on the telephone it is OK to break the ice with other than business conversation. In fact it is better to mix the two.

Chapter 13
IT TRAINING

1. TRAINING POLICIES

13.1 IT TRAINING POLICIES

Information technology training begins with the orientation of new personnel and continues to help employees meet the changing technology skills required for their jobs. Computer personnel realize that skills can quickly become obsolete, and this is one of the reasons they move on to jobs which provide the opportunity to learn new ones.

The training policy of IT is to provide an opportunity for the ongoing education and training of IS employees and information systems users. An IS department will only function effectively if its personnel and users are properly trained. The Japanese are a living testimonial to this.

An evaluation is to be conducted after each training course or program is completed. A second evaluation will follow three to six months after the training has been applied to the work environment.

2. MANAGING IT TRAINING

13.2 MANAGING IT TRAINING

Traditionally, training responsibility has come under the jurisdiction of computer operations managers. However, because of its emerging importance and because today's IT training is not limited to information systems personnel, but extends to all users of the system, it is recommended that the training head for IT control the training function and report to the head of IS.

The scope of IT training is vast, covering many areas, from new employee orientation to the retraining of current employees. There is no one device which serves all needs, so employees should be able to draw on a whole host of training opportunities.

> **Comment:**
> IT training costs exceed ten billion dollars a year in the United States. But in fact, direct training expense is normally far less than the cost of the employee's time during the training.

13.2.1 Keeping Records of Training

Each IS employee file contains education and training information, including that which the employee brings to the department and any needs assessments recommending future training. See Chapter 12 Human Resource Management, Section 8 Employee Development for more procedure information. All training received is posted to a file which is part of the IS skill inventory noted in Section 8 of Chapter 12. Starting a file is simple, but keeping it up-to-date is more of a task. However, this should not be neglected.

IS employee training files contain the following information:

A. Education and training before joining the IS department:

   1. Degrees received, courses taken, dates, and grades.
   2. Dates of non-credit courses taken.
   3. Type of work-related material read.
   4. Dates of certifications received.
   5. Listing of professional memberships and any offices held.
   6. If the employee owns a personal computer, the brand name and software used.

B. Future education and training that would benefit the employee. Training needs information will be collected to know the number of people needing each type. This information can be used to justify a training program and to give the people on record first choice. Priority is as follows:

1. Training or education that would help develop personnel for current positions.
   - Areas of weakness.
   - Areas that require training to stay current with new technology.

2. Training or education needed for promotion.

C. New education or training received

1. Upon completion of training not provided by the IT training department, each employee must forward to the IT department a memo containing the following information to be included in the employee's file.
   - What training was received.
   - Who provided the training.
   - What grade was received, if any.
   - When the training was received.

2. Upon completion of in-house programs, the overseer of IT training programs forwards the necessary information for inclusion in the training record files. For non-IS people a memo will be sent to each supervisor listing which of their employees have completed the training and indicating the following:
   - What training was received.
   - When the training was conducted.
   - Personnel who are to receive credit for completing the program.

13.2.2 Employee Recognition

Employee recognition for completing an in-house course should not be limited to posting the information in the file; a certificate for course completion should be presented by his or her supervisor. Certificate forms are available from most office supply firms and should be completed and signed by the head of training and also the IS manager.

13.2.3 Education Information Booklet

The IT education unit should provide an "education information booklet" to all new IS employees as part of an orientation package. Revised editions should be distributed to all IS employees. It should contain the following information:

A. IS outside education policy and procedures

This information indicates the type of support an employee can expect from the firm for outside education and training. It outlines the procedures required to apply for sanctioned education outside the firm.

B. Scheduled courses offered by the training unit

This data contains information about the courses to be offered, including dates and times, requirements for admission, and procedure for enrolling in courses and/or programs.

C. A list of self-paced training packages available

This list is available from the IS training unit and includes a wide range of instruments such as videotapes, self-teaching texts, and computer learning programs.

D. Publications available

A list of books and journals available in the IT Training department and/or computer store.

13.2.4 Non-IS Employee Training

The need for IT training is not limited to the IS department. Company-wide training should be made available to all client/server and microcomputer users. This not only provides needed training but also helps create good will relationships between IS and the rest of the firm. The charge-back for these services depends on corporate cost accounting procedures.

Request for training may be initiated by a user or an IS project leader. A user's request should be in the form of a memo from the user's management directed to the IT trainer. If a project leader desires the service, it should be part of the formal project effort.

A list of users who complete each course is furnished to the employee's supervisor(s) in the form of a memo from the head of the IT training unit. All persons completing the program are furnished certificates of completion which are forwarded to the employee's supervisor for presentation.

13.2.5 Outsource Training

Because not all IS departments have the resources available for in-house IT training, there is a growing trend to use outsourcing firms to provide professional IT training at your location. See Chapter 15, Vendor Contracting for more information.

Record keeping of outsourcing personnel training will still be done by the IS department for IS personnel. User training will be provided as noted in Section 13.2.4 by a person delegated by the head of IS. Costs will be paid out of the IS training budget. User training can be charged back to the user's budget and prorated if need be. This is all dependent on the internal accounting practice of the company.

The evaluation of this training will be performed by a person from the IS department at the end of the course or program. Payment for the training may be governed by the results of the evaluation. If so, accounts payable must be informed of this procedure before the outside firm is billed for the service. The follow-up three-to-six month evaluation, also performed by the IS department, is particularly important so that future training may be altered if needed. The evaluation is also an effective way to judge the provider of the outsource training.

13.2.6 Annual Reporting

The IT training unit should submit an annual report of activities, including cost.

Comment:
Cost justification of training dollars spent can be a problem, relating dollars to return on the investment, because most of the returns are intangible. Any input from user management can help. However, intangible items do contribute to the company's bottom line and should be listed in the annual report.

The time required to produce instruction packages is often much more than anticipated. Preparation time rule of thumb for a lecture presentation with simple overheads for support can be as much as 15 hours for each hour of lecture. Production of a half-hour sound slide show can take up to 200 hours. General paper work, planning, reporting and equipment repair also consume time. All these hours are reported. Each new program should be treated as a project with its individual cost of materials and time cost reported. Time cost should be computed as hourly cost plus benefits.

The trainer's time is a cost factor, and so is the student's. With today's new technology, training and preparation time can be reduced. Therefore, the training department should house an arsenal of software and hardware tools to be effective. Ineffective resources should be dropped. Plans for the coming year, as well as current year results, should be included in the annual report.

It should also contain the activities of the training unit for the year. The following items are reported:

A. The number of classes conducted.

B. The number of self-study programs completed.

C. The number of new programs developed and for what purpose.

D. The total number of people served by the training unit.

Comment:

Be aware that training and education evaluations can be subjective. People tend to give higher appraisals when they are entertained.

A list of participant evaluation comments should be made. Any supervisor's comments or memo information should also be included.

3. NEW EMPLOYEE ORIENTATION

13.3 NEW EMPLOYEE ORIENTATION

First impressions are lasting, and in time, those employees who react negatively may depart for another firm. To create a positive, lasting impression during an employee's first few days with the firm, the IT department should follow two simple procedures. First, designate a mentor. Second, give the employee a welcome education package.

Comment:

The Central (insurance) Companies of Ohio think so highly of this sort of training that they have developed a detailed procedure for new employee indoctrination and education that is carefully followed.

13.3.1 IS Orientation Package

This package is a compilation of useful information for the new IS employee. It should contain the following information:

A. Organization description

At a minimum, the organization description should include an explanation of how each unit functions and should identify those persons in charge. An organizational chart would be useful for large departments.

> **Comment:**
> The one that Marathon Petroleum Company uses even contains pictures of management.

A short chronological history of the IS operation is recommended. This provides the new employee with information about routes people took when moving up in the organization, areas of vested interest, and fast-track employees. The position that IS has within the organization should also be noted.

B. Equipment and facilities

This section lists all the hardware in use and its locations. Personnel authorized to use the equipment should also be noted.

A facilities map should include the locations of the rest rooms, dining areas and restricted facility areas.

C. Phone numbers

An up-to-date phone directory of the firm should be provided. A supplementary list of numbers for frequently called IS units, personnel, and services should be included.

D. E-mail listing

This listing should indicate the proper way to address e-mail to other employees.

E. Mail

When and how the employee will receive his or her mail is noted. This information should cover both interoffice and outside mail (U.S. Postal Service, U.P.S., FedEx, etc.).

F. Forms

A section of the package should contain a listing of all important forms required by IS personnel providing the name and number of each form, its source and type of destination(s), its purpose, and any other special information.

Samples used by the unit for which the new employee will work should also be included.

Comment:

Remember that the needs of computer operators are not the same as those of systems analysts, so packages for new employees will contain different forms.

G. Schedules

The procedure package should include schedules of operations. They can be daily, weekly, or monthly. For daily schedules, include when normal activities, such as breaks and lunch hours, begin and end.

The weekly, monthly, and annual schedules should contain such items as pay days, holidays, vacation scheduling, and meetings. Some IS departments even publish monthly lists of their employees' birthdays.

H. Glossary and Practices

This section of the procedure package contains a list of common terms and acronyms used by IS and the firm. Practices that are extremely important or different from the industrial norm should be noted.

Comment:

A firm in Michigan, for good reasons of its own, does not run a slash through the character zero. They place the slash through the alpha character O. Because a new programmer was not told of this practice, there were problems. Unusual practices in each department need to be emphasized to minimize difficulties.

I.   Unit procedures

This section contains a listing of all IS procedures and where they are explained. A check-off list is used for each type of IS position and is checked-off and dated as new employees read the material.

J.   IS Project Descriptions

New programmers, systems analysts, and other staff personnel should be provided a list of current and pending IS projects. A short description of the objective as well as target dates are noted, along with the project managers' names.

13.3.2 Mentor Assignment

Sometimes IS orientation requires a "personal touch," and the new employee is assigned a mentor, someone to give a permanent positive impression of the firm. The selected mentor should be personable, someone who can make sure that the new employee will feel comfortable about asking questions concerning what should or should not be done. The mentor must also have patience. Often a simple question answered calmly by a mentor is critical for a new employee. The mentor should not be condescending, an attitude which only makes the new IS employee nervous and doubtful about his/her future with the firm.

It is important to remember that first impressions are lasting. A new IS employee joins the department with high hopes, and a mentor's positive attitude can become infectious, reinforcing these high expectations.

4. EMPLOYEE TRAINING

13.4 EMPLOYEE TRAINING

This section does not attempt to address the detailed, day-to-day procedures of running a training unit, which are up to the head of training. But an IS manager should have a grasp of what to expect.

13.4.1 Determining Training Needs and Objectives

The first step in conducting training is to determine what is actually needed to meet a given objective. Next, an instructional assessment should be made of each person involved in the learning project. What does each person need to learn? All IT training or educational projects should contain this information in their "training project" documentation.

The kind of learning to be accomplished has to be determined. There are three basic classifications of learning, each of which requires different training instruments. They are:

A. Cognitive domain

   Cognitive learning requires intellectual activity of some sort, such as making judgments, synthesizing information, applying learned information, interpreting information, and being able to recall information. This form of learning is the most common in IT training.

B. Psychomotor domain

   Psychomotor learning requires muscle coordination and includes hearing and eye movement. Traditionally this has been associated with IS keyboard data entry, but with the advent of microcomputers, the need for these skills has expanded somewhat.

C. Affective domain

   Affective learning involves values and attitudes. It includes changing undesirable personal attitudes and may be required in training users whose values or attitudes affect productivity or the success of projects and operations.

After determining the instructional needs of the learners, the training instrument is selected. At the same time, evaluation criteria need to be developed to determine when the learning objective has been met. This evaluation may take the form of an exam—written answers to questions, performance of a task or procedure, or even execution of a response to a given condition.

Exams can be written to confirm that the desirable learning level has been met. This is called criterion-referenced testing. People who can master a test at the level required by the learning criteria pass. If a whole group does not meet this level of learning, the learning project has failed. This is a better evaluation of training than a subjective evaluation by employees after they complete training.

13.4.2 Types of IT Training

Training can be provided in a formal manner for groups or informally for individuals. Formal IT training can be divided into two types: instructor-based and self-paced. Instructor-based training includes seminars, classroom workshops and one-on-one instruction.

One-on-one instruction may be the best type of training, but it is the most expensive. Classroom instruction is less expensive, but the cost of the student's time must also be considered. Sending learners away for vendor class instruction can be expensive when the employees are required to be out-of-town overnight.

There can be a problem with classroom workshops and seminars. All personnel involved may not be able to be off at the same time. More than one group may have to be scheduled, and even then, there can be scheduling conflicts.

For these reasons, self-paced instruction has gained popularity in information technology. The training is available when people are free to take it, and they can work at their own pace.

Self-paced instruction does not consist only of reading manuals and other vendor-furnished materials. It can utilize two or more learning tools which can include microcomputers, audio cassettes, and video. The microcomputer utilizes program instruction technology (tutorials) with software in the form of floppy disks and CDs.

When selecting a training approach, the trainer needs to make sure it will work for the learning domain needed. The hardware and/or software should be tried out before any commitment is made to buy or lease it.

For informal education/training of both user and IS personnel, it is important to have reading material available. Computer journals and magazines are a good source of up-to-date information. The average systems analyst should spend seven to eight hours a week just reading, and IS management personnel have been known to do even more.

5. PRESENTATION METHODOLOGIES

13.5 PRESENTATION METHODOLOGIES

Successful training presentations require a capable training presenter, supported with instructional tools and a proper learning environment. It is management's responsibility to supply these. But it is the presenting instructor who has the final responsibility for the learning presentation. Preparation should average 15 hours for each hour of delivery. The more often the delivery is to be made the more the preparation can be justified. A good one-half hour sound slide production can take 200 or more hours to produce. Learners today are very much attuned to what a good media production is, thanks to television. The presentation product can run from a few minutes to an extended program of many hours.

There are several good publications covering industrial instruction and presentations, and some of the better ones are even free. One that does an excellent job of providing information in the form of articles and advertisements is "Presentations," published monthly by Lakewood Publications, 50 South Ninth St., Minneapolis, MN 55402. The subscription information telephone number is 1-800-328-4329. Computer or training professionals may even qualify for a free subscription to the magazine. In addition there are national organizations, including Toastmasters International and industrial training groups, that can help a person develop presentation skills. Reference material for both organizations and publications may be found in the public library.

One of the best, if not the best, training facility in the world is McDonald's Hamburger University in the Chicago area. McDonald's would not be where it is today without its training program. Not only is its training supplied using top-of-the-line technology, but it is cost-justified and administered by qualified management. This training is not limited to Hamburger University but can be found at every level of McDonald's operations.

13.5.1 Presentation Room

The presentation should be conducted in a room that is adequate for presenting instructional materials. It should be large enough to comfortably house the learners without distractions, with enough light for note taking. The temperature should be between 68 and 72 degrees.

Rooms can be rented away from the company, if need be, when adequate rooms are not available or to get the people away from work distractions. The instructor should be familiar with the room before he/she is committed to using it.

Conveniences that would enhance the presentation are:

- Lights controllable by the presenter.
- Power outlets in locations needed.
- A white board for writing or projection.
- A lectern.
- Restrooms close by.
- Place for learners to hang their coats.
- Tables with comfortable chairs.

- A ceiling mounted screen that can be tilted to be perpendicular to the projector.

13.5.2 Presentation Devices

The trainer can select from a whole host of presentation aids, limited only by his/her budget. Information on the following devices may be augmented by the vendor and by demonstrations. The company's own training department may also be of assistance. Before any new device is used, the trainer should be sure he/she can operate it well enough to concentrate on the presentation and not the device.

Before preparing a media presentation, the prospective audience should be considered for both its size and composition. The time allotted will determine the amount of information that can be presented and consumed. The place the presentation is to be made, the importance of the presentation, and the time available will all influence the choice of presentation materials.

- The importance of the presentation will determine how much money may be spent, how much time devoted to it, and how much effort to expend. Will the presentation require several types of visuals to get the message across, and can the cost be justified?
- The purpose of the presentation determines the types of visual materials to be employed. If it is mainly to inform in a general way and to be entertaining, 35 mm color slides might be the visual chosen. If it is to explain complicated information, such as new procedures, systems, or concepts, or numerical information, chart and graph overheads would be better.
- The audience education level and its status in the organization should be considered when making the visuals.

Comment:
Do not assume you know the level of the audience's technical knowledge. If possible, do some research. It is better to understate technical complication than to overstate it.

- It is important to remember that the visuals used in a presentation are to enhance what you are saying, not to replace or detract from it.

Effective visuals employ simplicity, clarity and visibility in their design. The following suggestions should be helpful when constructing these aids:

- Proofread before presenting. Look for misspelling and information errors. Get someone else to verify the materials for you. Set the presentation aside for a day or two, then give it a final look.
- If there is too much information to fit on the visuals, make handouts.
- Never have more than six to eight words per line on a projection or flip chart.
- Use only key words or phrases in the visual. This gives you something to say.
- Never read the visual information for the audience.
- Add color for impact: colored backgrounds and colored lettering.
- Do not show a mass of numbers. Information in this form cannot be visualized like graphs or charts.
- Use computer-generated clip art sparingly. A little will help, but too much can be distracting.
- Remember KISS: Keep It Simple and Short. Each visual should be shown briefly, less than a minute, so do not overload it with information.

A. Flip charts

Flip charts have been around a long time because they are simple to use, quick to prepare, and inexpensive. They tend to be bulky to carry from place to place, but many conference rooms still have them. There are portable versions that are easier to carry in their cases. The smaller ones may be used for up to 15 or 20 people, while the larger ones are good for groups of 30 or more. Following are recommendations that can improve the presentation when using this instrument:

1. The easel

- Consider the use of more than one easel.
- When using more than one, position each so that it can be seen by everyone in the audience.
- Make sure the easel is tall enough so that all can see the bottom of pads.
- Use sturdy easels with a lip to hold different colored marking pens.

2. Easel pads

   - Not all pads have same spaced mounting. Make sure all easels and pad holes match up.
   - Use perforated pads because it is easier to remove pages from them.
   - Writing on white pad paper shows up more clearly than on colored paper.
   - Using lined pads will make writing before an audience neater.
   - If more than one easel is used, try different colored pads. They may help the delivery.
   - Use paper heavy enough that the audience cannot see pages under the one being used or shown.

3. Marking Pens

   - Use wide felt-tip watercolor markers. Permanent ones tend to bleed through the sheets of paper and cannot be used on the white boards.
   - Multicolored markers can add variety to the presentation.
   - Have a systematic method for employing colors, such as using green for page headings and items needing attention, and black for other items.
   - When not using the pen, place it on the easel lip.
   - When the pen starts to squeak, it is running out of ink. Discard it.
   - Have a good supply of colored pens.
   - Avoid using light red pens as red is difficult to read from a distance. Also, about 12 percent of men are color blind, and the most common color they have a problem with is red.

4. Prepared pages

   There are advantages in preparing the flip charts in advance. For one, the printing will be neater and more legible. Class time will not be wasted writing. In addition, notes can be prewritten in pencil on the pages, unseen by the audience until the presenter goes over them with a felt-tip pen. If some pages are prepared in advance, a second easel is recommended for writing on during the presentation. The following are suggested to enhance the prepared pages presentation:

- Have a computer printer produce the flip charts in color. If your firm does not have a printer for the size needed, seek out a graphics firm or large copy shop that can do it for you.
- When traveling place the charts rolled up in a large cardboard mailing tube.
- Insert blank pages between thin pages so that the audience cannot read what is coming next.
- If using a large number of prepared pages, more than your easel can hold, use extra easels.

5. The use of flip charts

    The presenter should first visualize and then write an outline (on $8^1/_2$-by-11-inch lined paper) of the presentation. After the outline is complete, highlight the key points that are to be printed on the flip charts. The outline and any other notes can later be penciled on the edges of the flip chart pages. This should be done after the pages have been lettered.

    If there is but one easel available, place blank pages between the lettered ones for writing on. Notes can still be written on these blank pages. The following are suggestions which should help improve the presentation:

    - Print the block letters one to one-and-a-half inch high.
    - Use wide felt-tip markers.
    - Use the colors in some consistent fashion.
    - Limit the number of lines of information to 10 if the audience is small, and to 8 if the group is large (over 25 feet away).
    - Write key points in a shortened form. Abbreviations and acronyms are O.K.
    - When writing during the presentation have the words penciled in beforehand.
    - Allow 20 to 30 seconds after any writing before flipping the page. Give audience members time for any note taking and thinking.
    - Never stand in front of the easel after you have just completed writing.
    - Minimize loss of audience eye contact except when writing.

- Practice your presentation a few days before in the room where you are going to give it. If presentations are new to you and/or if this is a presentation important for your career, run through it a week in advance in the room where you plan to give it and have it videotaped.

Comment:
You do not need anyone to run the camcorder. Just put it on a tripod.

B. Overhead projectors

Overhead projectors have been very popular for presentations for some time. Its low price makes it attractive, and laser printers can produce some very appealing colored overheads.

Today's computer technology makes this device even more popular. One type of projector allows computer output to be projected through a LCD overhead panel.

There have been other improvements to the old design. Compact overhead projectors that are easy to carry are available, although they cannot employ the LCD overhead panel. Automatic transparency feeders are also available. The continuous roll-feeding device provides a source of blank film to write on, and the presenter is no longer required to stand next to the projector.

Additional information and advice about this device follows:

1. Overhead projectors

   - Always have a spare bulb.
   - Make sure the screen is useable.
   - Lower the room light level to enhance the projected image, but keep it high enough so that people can take notes.
   - Make sure heavy duty extension cords are available when needed.

2. Ways to produce transparencies.

   - Color inkjet printers.
   - Laser printer.
   - Copy machine.
   - Heat transfer.
   - Write-on.
   - Continuous write on transparencies rolls.

3. Markers

   - Overhead color projection pens.
   - Permanent color markers.

4. The use of overhead projectors

   - Have extra markers or pens.
   - Write on the white board with erasable projection pens. This allows the presenter to add to what is being projected on the board.
   - Look at the audience while reading any copy to them.
   - The size of the printing should be large enough to read when it is lying at your feet while you are standing.
   - Allow 20 to 30 seconds at the end of each overhead for note taking and thinking time.
   - Do not crowd the overhead with copy.
   - Use color pens and transparencies to enhance the presentation.
   - Face the audience while operating the computer keyboard and/or overhead projector.
   - Never leave the light on the screen for any length of time with no transparency in the projector.
   - Use graphics to enhance a presentation. Computer presentation software is available with alternatives to the use of a bullet chart. (A bullet chart is what you are reading now.)
   - The use of transparency overlays will add impact to the over-head presentation. Overlays allow the presenter to build and reveal concepts to focus the audience's attention on the evolving subject. As an example, a bullet chart can be built by super-imposing lines of information, adding one bulleted line or sec-

tion at a time, from succeeding layers of transparencies. In this instance, the pages are hinged so they will be in the proper position when laid one over the other and projected on to the screen.

- Carrying the transparencies can become a problem, as static electricity can stick them together. A simple solution is to place them in transparency frames which make handling them easier and also protect them. A frame will also block out any unwanted light from around the edge during the projection. In addition, the edge of the frame provides space for presentation notes.

5. The LCD overhead panel

This device used with the overhead projector allows microcomputer-generated information to be presented on the screen. With the proper hardware and software tools it can greatly enhance the overhead presentation.

Visual information can be imported from other sources. Digital still cameras can photograph artwork which can be inputed to the system for display on the screen. Live photos, in black and white or color, can be taken of flat subjects or even of people in the audience and projected on the screen during the presentation.

With the availability of digital video cameras, even motion pictures can be inputed to the microcomputer and displayed on the screen. This requires more hard drive memory than is normally found with microcomputers at present. But the price of new hardware, including high capacity hard drives, keeps coming down. If digital video is being seriously considered, an LCD projector would be an item worth looking into. It simplifies the hardware requirements for projecting moving images. If this type of presentation material is to be often used, a microcomputer multimedia system might be something to consider.

C. Slide projectors

The 35 mm slide projector is still in use today. For large groups it provides better quality presentations than the overhead digital images. Slide projectors can be with sound added for excellent, large-scale multimedia presentations.

For small groups the easy-to-carry Caramte in its self-contained box can be placed at the end of a conference table, and the slides projected either on the wall or on a pull-down screen, or rear projected onto its own 12-by-12 screen. With its self-contained sound tape system, it is an excellent teaching instrument and can be used for a self-paced learning program.

Photographs of subjects and copy material can be made with a 35 mm camera. A 35 mm single lens reflex camera with a micro lens should be used, with a Kodak gray scale card for correct light meter readings. It is also recommended that Kodak 35 mm Ektachrome day light slide film be used, since the film can also be used for electronic flash or daylight. For the correct light color balance use 250 Watt BLUE light bulbs available from a commercial photo store.

Use a photo copy stand if much material is to be copied. Place the gray scale card over the flat copy work, and take a reading for the exposure. If the item is not flat, place it on the background and focus. Remove the item, replace it with gray scale card, and take a light meter reading. Return the item to its proper position.

Both the Kodak slide projector and the Caramte unit will use Kodak's 80 and 120 slide trays. Any one slide should not be shown for more than 30 seconds. Therefore a presentation with only one tray will be limited to less than an hour. For both units (Kodak and Caramte) a cassette tape is used for the sound. With a stereo system, one track is used for the sound and the other track is used for slide changing marks. Slide sound productions will require some justification inasmuch as it will take over a month's time to produce a half-hour program.

D. Other devices

1. Sound presentation is useful for instruction. An example is walking a person through a set of instructions for a particular procedure. The person can hear the instructions and, with hands and eyes free, take notes or perform the indicated actions.

2. Video (digital and analog) productions are even more involved than slide sound productions. Video can be used by any presenter for some limited applications, but any major effort should be left up to people with the skill and editing equipment needed.

Showing VCR tapes for information and instruction is a good way and an increasingly available way of presenting programs. Some computer vendors have training videos. There are also videos for all kinds of microcomputer instruction. But, if you can, preview before you buy.

3. The computer can deliver a program via floppy disk, CD or network which can be available for a group to view at its convenience or for a single-person tutorial. The program can employ text, graphics, stills and motion pictures. See the library for further information.

Chapter 14
PROJECT MANAGEMENT

1. PROJECT MANAGEMENT POLICIES

14.1 PROJECT MANAGEMENT POLICIES

Project management is the marriage of different technologies in an organized, cooperative fashion for a given undertaking. To coordinate a project requires both technical and managerial skills. The basic policy of each project manager is to allocate personnel to maximize the performance of project activities. This means personnel must be selected on the basis of language skills, analytical capabilities, and hardware knowledge so as to make significant contributions to the project.

Most technical professionals lack the administrative and interpersonal skills needed to function effectively in this position. However, project management responsibility is usually their first step up the management ladder. This chapter places some basic management procedural guidelines into perspective for the project manager. It also establishes a uniform format for managerial procedures to be followed by all project managers.

The IS organization will not be limited to one project operating at a time. Therefore, there needs to be a central authority in the information systems organization to act as the focal point for all IS project activities. This authority will be the IS systems department manager or an appointed coordinator who will settle disputes over resource allocations and monitor the progress of each project, as well as attend all project presentations. All project reporting will be directed to this person.

2. PROJECT MANAGEMENT DEFINITION

14.2 PROJECT MANAGEMENT DEFINITION

Each project must have objectives that are defined by management and achievable. The success of a project assignment must also be measurable; the objectives must cover a limited number of activities. Under the coordinating efforts of the project manager the combination of personnel, administrative, technical, and financial resources is optimized to achieve a definable goal within a given calendar time period. A project will have a starting point defined by time and place. It will also have an ending point: when the project can be defined as complete.

It will have a defined budget allocation. The personnel assigned to it will also have their time and commitments defined because knowing exactly when and for how long such an assignment will be is required for proper project management.

A schedule must be prepared within which work must be performed in measurable milestone units so progress can be reported. Feedback requirements must be defined to meet the needs of the firm's management and the nature of the project.

14.2.1 The Nature of Project Management

What differentiates project management from general management is that project management has a starting point and a completion point. The calendar time period is predetermined before the project starts, and it only exists between these points.

The other main difference between project management and general management is in the way each utilizes personnel resources. All members of a project are associated with it only for its lifetime or less. Their primary obligations are elsewhere; they may be assigned to the project for given calendar days, and even allotted specific times during those days. Their loyalty can only be short lived because all projects have a termination point by definition.

Material resources assigned to the project are expended for the project. Any left over at the project's completion will have a predetermined disposition. They may be purchased during the project's existence or loaned to the project. They can be money, and capital or noncapital items.

An IS project is committed to operate within certain boundaries, to have a specific scope of operation, and resources must be utilized within this committed scope. Any expansion of the scope by the project manager will dilute the effective use of the resources provided.

> **Comment:**
> Lifeboats on ships have two sets of numbers painted on them. One is the identification number and the other is the lifeboat capacity. Lifeboats are resources that are designed for the project of saving lives, but only for a given scope or number of people. If too many people board the lifeboat, all can be lost. That's why side arms are issued to the ship's officers when orders are given to abandon ship.

The nature of project management requires that three important variables be in control: cost, quality, and calendar time. The project manager must ensure project completion, keeping all three within the planned expected limits. Altering any one of the three can affect the others. In general, to improve quality, higher cost and possibly more time would be required. For example, to deliver better, more effective user operation manuals and training than were planned and budgeted for could cost the project more dollars. It would also cost more time if extra resources could not be commandeered to meet the calendar time deadline for the originally planned quality.

The project manager has one other option open. He/she can reduce the scope of the project. However, this action cannot be taken without the approval of IS and user management.

14.2.2 IS Project Types

There are two kinds of projects with different purposes: a feasibility study and a project. The feasibility study is a mini project, used to determine the justification for a full-length project. Not all projects require this: some are mandated by top management or by forces external to the company.

A feasibility study, as its name implies, informs management whether the proposed project is workable. It also provides an estimate of the resources and the calendar time required to undertake the project, all essential to planning. The person who is responsible for this study is a good candidate for the position of its project manager. The contacts made and familiarity with the area gained through doing the study provide a solid base when the actual project is undertaken. The skills needed to do it are gained from being involved in an actual project. Therefore, an experienced project manager is a logical choice.

IS projects can run from a few days to years, while feasibility studies can be accomplished in from one day to a few weeks. IS projects include:

- Microcomputer conversion.
- Main frame conversion.
- Developing a prototype.
- Software implementation (for a wide range of systems).
- Implementation of new operating system.
- System development and implementation of an operation.
- Work group system development and implementation.
- End user system development and implementation.
- A Rapid Application Development (RAD) employing Computer Aided Software Engineering.
- IT projects involving installation of new database, e-mail, Internet, LAN or WAN system.
- Business re-engineering projects which entail discovering and implementing better ways of performing business operations with or without computers.

14.2.3 IS Project Components

The project (feasibility study or project) does not exist in a vacuum. Other components interact with it and permit its existence. One such component is the Steering Committee, which represents management and is attuned to the strategical goals of the company. This committee prioritizes the projects and is also interested in the progress of each one. It will require a report of each project's status monthly. Other components in this scenario are:

A. IS management

   The success of the project will require the support of IS management which controls the IS technical resources loaned to the project. It is interested in the success of the project as well as in its assigned personnel.

B. Project advocate

This person or group is a party to the request. It could also be the one bringing attention to the need for such an undertaking because of a government mandate.

C. User management

The user management who will utilize the end result of the project plays a role, too, and it can also be the project advocate.

D. Other projects

Other projects will compete for resources. The shared resources will require queuing and prioritizing to gain the most overall benefit.

E. Consultants and contractors

Outside resources that have been budgeted for a specific project, they can also be involved with more than one project for the firm. It is their responsibility to deliver what they have been contracted for by the time specified. The advantage of using consultants is that they can provide expertise not available at the company. The advantage of using contractors is that the manpower is available when needed and only then. (See Chapter 15 Vendor Contracting for more information.)

F. Corporate technical experts

These are experts on loan from other areas of the company to the project for given days in the project calendar. If these people were not available, someone with their expertise would have to be hired from the outside. They not only bring the benefit of their experience to the project but a knowledge of and loyalty to the company.

G. The project team

The project team itself is made up of two parts: the project manager and the team members. These two parts must work well together for the project to be successful.

1. Project manager

The project manager must possess certain attributes required for success. (See Section 14.3 Project Management for more information.)

2. Project team members

These are people with skills needed for the project to be successful. They may be available full time or part time for the duration of the project. They can also be scheduled to work on the project for specific, given times. They could hold the following titles:

- Systems analysts.
- Systems and procedure analysts.
- Analyst programmers.
- Programmers.
- Coders.
- Project librarian.
- Forms designers.
- Database designers.
- Network specialists.
- Industrial engineers.
- Project secretary.

14.2.4 Project Lifecycle

A project lifecycle is made up of segments or phases. With the many different types of projects one lifecycle size does not fit all. Besides, not all systems analysts would come up with the same number of segments for a given project. But there is somewhat of a consensus on the elements required, although some can be present for one kind of project but not for another.

The segments can be further defined by the elements that are contained within them. A project lifecycle is identified by its segments or phases. Following is a generic list of possibilities:

- Recognition of a need.
- Request for a feasibility study.
- Feasibility study.
- Report of feasibility findings.
- Request for systems analysis and design.
- Systems analysis.
- Systems design.
- Acquire software (buy or write).
- Test software.
- Install database and/or network.

- Complete procedures.
- System test.
- Complete training.
- Install system.
- User acceptance.
- System follow up.

To aid in reporting project status, the major milestones are the identifiable and measurable segments, and they can be reported as completed or not.

3. MANAGING PROJECTS

14.3 Managing Projects

The management of IS projects starts with the Steering Committee, on which upper level management is heavily represented. The committee members oversee the priorities to determine which projects are to be selected. They also influence which resources are to be allocated to the projects, and have the final say as to the completion date required for each project.

The Steering Committee follows the progress of all projects in process. Members of the committee have the right to change the priorities and the completion date of projects under consideration and in process. They also have the authority to cancel a project.

It is the court of final resort for user and project management appeals. To make these decisions, the committee has access to information that is restricted to the higher levels of management. It is not required to explain or justify its actions to the project or user management.

14.3.1 Projects Director

The projects director oversees all projects assigned to the IS organization, coordinating resources and the efforts of project managers and their staffs. He/she also works very closely with and receives directives from the Steering Committee. This person could be the manager of systems or the head of information systems or his/her appointed coordinator, depending on the IS organizational structure. This is the person that the project managers report to.

When priorities change, project calendar day slippage occurs or personnel available for assignments shift, the projects director has to resolve the resulting problems with the big picture in mind. He/she has limited power to create resources. This is mainly under the control of the Steering Committee. But a wise projects director includes in planning some allowances for slippage, the unavailability of people, wasted project efforts, vendor delays, etc.

If the projects director reports to the head of IS, he/she is responsible for keeping that person informed and will have to work with him or her in planning for staffing and budgeting of future project needs.

This projects director will utilize project management software to oversee all projects. Gantt charts will be used to display the resources assigned to given projects. If people are not needed to work on one project, the projects director will reassign them. This assignment and reassignment is best done using project management tools. (See 14.7 Project Resources.)

If the projects director is also the manager of systems he/she will be responsible for acquiring new systems personnel. If not, the systems manager (if there is one) will be responsible. If there is no systems head, the head of IS will be responsible for obtaining new systems personnel and any other IS personnel needed for projects. Whoever is in charge of obtaining new personnel will work with the Human Resources department which will have to specify the job requirements, set up the interviews, and help select the new people. It will also select the mentor for the new employees when assigning their duties.

The projects director will be instrumental in acquiring consultants and contractors for the projects. He/she, and not the project manager, has the authority to negotiate and sign contracts. This person will follow the procedures spelled out in Chapter 15, Vendor Contracting.

The projects director will write a monthly status report for all projects assigned. These reports will be sent to the Steering Committee and to the head of IS (the projects director can also be the systems manager). Each project will be reported even if there is no activity. If there should have been activity but there was none, the reasons must be reported.

An annual report will be prepared at the end of each fiscal year by the projects director which will provide a narrative of each project, including its successes and problems. It will recap the performance of each project manager. It will identify problems arising from a project manager's weakness and a recommendation for improving the situation. The report will note the responsibility of each project manager after the project is completed. The annual report will recommend future projects for consideration, including resource acquisitions. The systems manager will forward a copy of this report to the head of the IS.

14.3.2 Project Manager

The success of a project depends upon many factors. For one, dynamic and well-rounded people are required. Since all participants are "on loan" to a project, they are aware that it is a one-time thing and they will have vested interests in some other area. The project manager's position may be debased to that of a coordinator, a person with responsibility but limited authority.

Selecting a project manager is the job of either the systems manager alone or the systems manager with input from the projects director. Choosing requires knowledge of certain attributes that have been known to be universally successful. The only testimonial a person really needs is a successful track record with the company. However, a person being selected as project manager for the first time requires special consideration.

New candidates should have demonstrated their abilities by contributing to a successfully completed project in which they were given increasing responsibilities. The first project a person is given as a project manager should be of limited scope and duration. After he/ she has been tested, then longer and more complex projects can be assigned.

Keeping the position of project manager a temporary one is a face-saving decision made for both the project manager and the firm. If the person does not prove to be successful, it is much less a problem than if he/she had been placed into a regular (permanent) position. It also provides excellent training for becoming a manager in the IS organization or elsewhere in the firm.

The selection criteria for a project manager are:

A. Maturity

The person must display an air of maturity. This is required when dealing with senior management and user management. It also lends credibility to the project team.

B. Administrator

The person must be able to routinely perform day-to-day administrative activities, such as reporting, requisitioning, memo writing, etc. This also includes the ability to follow schedules, meet deadlines, and handle resources and budgets. A proactive, rather than a reactive, administrator is much more desirable.

C. IT skills

Because of IT's vastness today, no one person can be expected to be an expert in all its areas, but the project manager candidate must have the technical skill necessary to gain the respect of the IT assigned staff.

D. Company knowledge

The person must have knowledge of the company to insure that the project follows the corporate culture and does not "rock the boat" of senior and user management. The candidate should know the formal organization chart, but also the informal organization to help the project progress smoothly.

E. Delegator

The person must be able to delegate and recognize that when a project team member is successful, that member gets all the credit. When the member fails, this failure is shared with the project manager.

F. Communicator

The project manager must keep the project team management, and others with vested interests in the project, well informed. This includes informal day-to-day oral communication, written communication, formal presentations, teaching, and chairing meetings.

When chairing idea and work meetings an effective project manager will urge all present to contribute, because some good thinkers are often on the quiet side. In addition, since the project manager does not want to discourage communication, he/she does not label ideas "bad."

G. Innovator

The project manager must not be limited to traditional solutions. He/she must be innovative and encourage others to be the same.

H. Leader

The project team must be led through the most trying times. The project manager must be able to work under pressure, remain calm, keep the project objective in focus, and still be sensitive to the team, users, and the corporate culture.

Comment:

Many new project managers mistakenly believe that merely because they are managers, they can automatically rally the support of all those assigned to them. Most seasoned managers readily subscribe to the adage that respect is earned and not bestowed by title. All too often, the respect of those being led is forfeited because of the lack of basic interpersonal or management skills.

Following is a list of practices through which project managers can establish and retain the respect of the team:

A. Have others participate in decision making.

Get the whole team involved in contributing ideas to the project. Though the final decision is not theirs, people value the opportunity to comment because it increases their feeling of worth. An environment of participation garners respect for the project manager who creates it.

B. Be honest.

The project leader who is open and honest with the project team creates an example for the team members to follow and creates respect for his/her opinion.

C. Keep promises.

An effective project manager does not make commitments that cannot be kept. Failure to keep promises, especially without a justified explanation, will quickly lead to a lack of confidence and respect; the project manager's word should have credibility with the project team.

D. Practice strong work ethic.

Project management must display a work ethic similar to, or stronger than, that which is expected from the project team. This work must be visible because employees simply will not feel obliged to do more than the leader does.

E. Be consistent.

Consistency in the treatment of all members of the project team is a must to maintain total team harmony and loyalty. Showing preference only alienates others.

F. Recognize contributions.

Recognition of contributions by acknowledging the ideas of all project team members promotes good will and loyalty. An effective project manager never takes credit for an idea that originated with someone else.

Comment:
Recognition of a job well done shows your appreciation. It costs nothing but can be more valued than money at times. A show of appreciation for the efforts of team members not only improves their output, it also increases their appreciation and respect for you as a project manager.

14.3.3 Project Variables

Project variables include the following activities:

A. Project Inputs

1. Human attributes

    a. User attitude toward computer systems.
    b. User attitude toward other units involved in the new system.
    c. User attitude toward the firm and willingness to participate.
    d. Educational level of users.
    e. Value system of project team and users.
    f. Experience level of user's management.
    g. Age of users and user management.
    h. Top management's commitment.
    i. User's experience with current system.

2. Project team's attributes

    a. Respect for project manager.
    b. Social skills of project manager and group.
    c. Communication skills of project group.
    d. Experience level of project group.

e. Credibility level of project group.

3. Project variables

a. Size of project and project group.
b. Length of project.
c. Value of project.
d. Measurable milestones.
e. Budget allocation.
f. State of the technology involved in the project.
g. Computer program languages to be used.
h. Reliability of purchased hardware and software.

4. Organization variables

a. Size of the firm.
b. Type of industry of the firm.
c. Experience with computer systems.
d. Span of management control.
e. Centralization of operations.
f. Financial status of firm.
g. Progressiveness of firm.
h. Levels of management.
i. Level of management skill.

B. Throughput process of project group

1. Information gathering.
2. Information analysis.
3. Comparisons with objectives.
4. Economic analysis.
5. Using systems analysis tools.
6. Technical writing.

C. Negative entropy

1. Team effort of group.
2. Goodwill.
3. System capability.

D. Project feedback

    1. Cybernetic capabilities.

    2. Reaction to various designs.

E. Project outputs

    1. Goal of the designed and installed running system.

    2. Timeliness of the project.

    3. Maintenance of budget limits.

    4. Minimum of personnel turnover.

4. PROJECT INITIATION

14.4 PROJECT INITIATION

After the feasibility study has been completed, and if its findings are positive, a report is written and forwarded to the Steering Committee for its evaluation. When it approves the project, the project initiation phase begins. The Steering Committee defines the scope and specifies the completion date of the project. It will assign non-IS personnel to the project, approve the use of any outside vendor support, and also at this time provide for a project budget.

From this point IS management takes over to complete the details of the project initiation and appoints a project manager. He/she works with IS management in selecting the full- and part-time IS personnel for the duration of the project. If any outside labor is to be used, these people are also chosen. The assigned project manager is given the task of determining the project's lifecycle so that a schedule for tasks and resources can be drawn up.

14.4.1 Project Lifecycle

The project manager lays out the project lifecycle in the form of a CPM chart. PERT and CPM charts look very much alike. The advantage in using CPM charting is that fewer estimated times are required for each leg (task). The charts can be drawn by hand or constructed using one of the many microcomputer programs available.

After the tasks are organized into a CPM chart the estimated calendar time needed to complete each task is entered. Starting with the finish date and working backwards the calendar start date for the project is determined.

It's important to remember to count holidays and any plant shut-down days. If this results in a start date that has already passed, the CPM chart is reviewed for any tasks that can be run in parallel. If there is manpower available to do this, the chart is reconfigured and the project calendar start time is recomputed. If there is still a problem the project manager immediately contacts the projects director, or, if he/she is not available, the IS head.

If necessary the Steering Committee must resolve the problem. It can change the finish date or provide for resources to reduce the project time.

> **Comment:**
> It is not recommended to count on overtime to meet the finish date. That is like starting a football game without reserve players to fall back on. More than likely, when the people are needed the most they may no longer be available. In fact, any normal IT person knows it is wise to start looking for another job if a lengthy project is going to be shortened by overtime. And this writer does not blame anyone for it.

14.4.2 Personnel Resource Scheduling

The context diagram further defines the tasks to be performed (see Chapter 2 Documentation Process, Subsection 2.7.3 Dataflow Diagram). The time to complete these tasks is estimated in "man days" and inputted into the project management program (see this chapter section 14.7 Project Resources). This can be done manually for simple and small projects involving fewer than 4 people and 12 tasks. Before the project tasks can be assigned, they must be identified and detailed, and the needed skill levels for each must be determined so that they can be matched to tasks.

To a certain extent, skill levels can be determined by job title. But within each job title competency levels will need to be defined. Example, using the basic programmer job title: programmer trainee, junior programmer, programmer, senior programmer and lead programmer. Each has a level of competency that can be matched to a specific task. Assigning a task to an unqualified person can create problems, while assigning the same task to an overqualified person wastes resources. When time permits, personnel development should be considered, too, by using a project task to teach a person a new skill.

The task schedule in man days will be illustrated by a Gantt chart. This can be drawn by hand or by using a project management program. The Gantt charts are to be duplicated as part of the project documentation. If this information is not in a project management program that is networked, copies should be posted and provided to the projects director and IS manager. If there are more than a few projects in process, they need not be provided to the IS head unless specifically asked for.

When allocating task man-hours the project manager should take into account the worker's past record for finishing in the time allowed. He/she should check with the project worker to confirm the time allowed is reasonable. If it is not, a different time allowance should be negotiated. In addition, contingency time should be added, based on worker's past record. If there is no record to go by, time allowed should be conservative. Ten percent above the original estimate is not unreasonable. The project manager then recomputes the project time in light of this new information, rearranging the schedule as needed. If a problem still persists, the projects director should be contacted who will, if necessary, assign additional manpower to the new project, possibly with personnel previously assigned to other projects. When this data has been analyzed by the computer project management program or manually, the project manager will receive the final staffing plan for the project.

14.4.3 Hardware and Software Delivery

The required dates for software and hardware delivery for the project must be identified. Orders should be placed in time to have the items in house when needed. Delays, which should be allowed for, can be caused by the following:

- Custom fabricated hardware.
- Custom written software.
- Items being shipped from a distance. Delays are even more likely when items are shipped from abroad.
- Items that have to be scheduled for processing, such as custom printed forms.
- Pending plant shut-down for vacation or because of a strike.

At the same time, items should not be delivered too far in advance. If items come in before needed, there could be a storage problem, and in addition, the company would be spending money before it has to. Also, items ordered for IT too far in advance could become obsolete before being placed into service or could even have their prices lowered.

5. PROJECT OBJECTIVES

14.5 PROJECT OBJECTIVES

One main project objective is to deliver a particular result or end product within the scope and time frame originally established by the Steering Committee in a form accepted by the user as operational. The final product may be in the form of a new complex system, a report, a manual operation, etc., and the end result may be tangible or intangible.

A second objective is to utilize the resources of the project team in the most effective manner. These resources, under the control of the project manager, should be expended in an optimal manner during the project lifecycle.

> **Comment:**
> Over the years information systems has had a justifiable record of project cost overruns and delays. The longer it takes to deliver a product the less likely it will be acceptable by the users since needs change over time. Projects are delayed by changes which add to the scope which adds to the delay and debases the final product objective, causing the project to run over budget.

14.5.1 Project Lifecycle Objective

The project lifecycle is comprised of tasks that are accomplished by the prudent use of resources available. The effort to complete these tasks requires certain managerial, technical and/or political skills:

A. Managerial

The managerial skill of the project manager plays a major role in achieving the project objective. However, the Steering Committee, systems manager, projects director, and user management can assist or undermine the project manager's effectiveness.

B. Technical

The technical skill of the people assigned to the project, as well as their number, directly affects IT results.

C. Political

The project team should minimize its political "campaigning" activities. But relationships between people are not devoid of political overtones. Almost all project tasks require contact with people outside the project team. The results of these contacts can assist or hinder the project objective.

The tasks identified within the systems lifecycle are divided into sub-tasks so that, if necessary, more than one person can work on a task. Even if one person completes the sub-tasks, this division provides for more convenient milestones with which to report progress.

14.5.2 Project Product Objective

To confirm that the product of the project effort meets the product objective, standards must be set. Tangible objective product standards are easier to define and recognize than intangible ones.

The criteria required for considering a project to be successfully completed must be defined in the feasibility study or in the project approval statement made by the Steering Committee. All involved management parties will have agreed to these criteria, including user management and the project manager. The project should not start the design phase until the acceptance criteria have been defined and accepted. These should include:

- The structure of the product.
- The validation criteria.
- The scope of the product.

The validation criteria should include the following:

- User documentation and training required are specified and in place.
- Follow up procedures are specified and in place.
- Technical documentation for maintenance of software is complete.
- System and volume tests meet standards set.
- System downtime is not more than agreed-to limits.
- Data content of the database meets agreement.
- User support is in place and operational.

6. PROJECT FORMULATION

14.6 PROJECT FORMULATION

Project formulation begins with the feasibility study. Next, the Steering Committee (or whatever authority makes these decisions) sets the project scope and finish date. Finally, project design considerations are added.

The actual finish date and final project cost are based on factors that are not under the control of the project manager. The design estimate is also affected by these same essential estimating factors.

14.6.1 Essential Estimating Factors

Estimating completion dates and work hours needed becomes more accurate as the project advances. Unfortunately this accuracy is needed earlier, as close to the beginning of the project as possible, when it can help the most. Even the best project management software needs accurate estimates.

Estimating performed by the people who are going to do the work is not as accurate as that done by other, unbiased people. Research has shown that project members who estimate their own performance for completion times are consistently optimistic. For this reason, an independent group should be used on an ongoing basis to do the estimating for far more accurate results. The advantages of using an independent estimator, whether an individual or a group, are:

A. Unbiased opinion

An independent party, with no stake in the outcome, will be unbiased.

B. Estimate consistency

The estimates will be consistent. Any discovered errors can be corrected for the person or group.

C. Performance database provided

The performance of employees can be monitored. This also provides a source of employee information for staffing projects.

Factors that can affect the estimate accuracy and ways to minimize this distortion are:

A. Project size

The project size can affect the time and effort needed for completion. This in turn affects the amount of calendar time needed and the final cost.

The longer the project takes the more the user can justify additional changes. These changes that will be required for a useable product also will take additional time to install, which can justifiably lead to more changes. This is called the "Size Snowball Effect."

To reduce this the project undertaking should be as small as possible. In this way, changes made later will be maintenance changes to a system that has been operating, preferable to making the same changes to a yet untested system.

B. Project complexity

The more variables a project has the more time and effort it will take to complete. The size of a forecasting project may be relatively small but very complex.

A complex project can call for more development and more testing time than estimated. The complexity can be reduced if the project can be broken into modules, which also permits additional people to work on the effort.

> *Comment:*
> This author wrote an artificial intelligence program years ago for a General Electric engineering department that took 18 months. It should have taken six to eight months. The debugging of 45,000 machine instructions led to the discovery that there was a bug in the original formulas provided to the programmer.

C. Personnel productivity

This is a universal problem with system and programming departments. In the IS data entry unit the output minus the errors defines the person's productivity. If the source documents are rotated for input, the system for judging a worker's productivity is accurate because the work effort is accurate enough for estimating. This is not the case with the systems and programming production estimates.

A systems analyst's past performance can be a gauge for estimating future performance for similar tasks. The difference in output of programmers has been estimated to be as high as 20 to 1 between the best and the worst.

All too often programmers are judged by how hard they work. The lengthy hours spent and lines of code produced all too often are used to determine a programmer's contribution to the company. Yet the hardest working data entry operator, for example, may be the least productive and rewarded as such.

If the project is in need of one or more programmers, it would be better to bring in proven contract programmers than to utilize those of lower caliber in-house. Management is often willing to pay for good contract programmers, while at the same time is not willing to pay competitive wages for better in-house programmers. A poorly performing programmer can reduce the group total output.

Comment:

There is an IS manager in Ohio who has two systems employees who are paid more than he is. When asked why, he answers, "They are worth it."

D. Resources available

Resources must have quality, but they must be available in quantity, too. There is no assurance that people promised will be available when needed. The longer the duration of the project the greater this problem can become. People leave, retire, get promoted, or get reassigned to other higher priority projects.

If this is a possibility, it would be best to make sure monies are budgeted to obtain contract help. It is better to have this money in reserve than to have to ask for it when it is needed and take a chance on not getting it.

E. Resource technology

The physical and technical resources available to the project team also affect the estimate. These items can include:

1. Work area

The final work area can affect the productivity estimate. Is the project team housed together in a private area, or spread out into different locations without privacy?

2. Programming tools

   Are the programming tools those the staff has worked with? If the tools are new, will training be available in time to be effective?

3. Computer hardware

   The microcomputers available can affect the project team's performance. Are laptop computers needed? What kind of networking is there? What about e-mail and voice mail?

4. Project management software

   If the project warrants it a project management software package should be used. It can help save on the time and effort needed to control the project. Project management tools are covered in Section 14.7.

14.6.2 Factors Affecting Finish Date

There are factors other than incorrect time and cost estimates that affect the finish date, depending on the nature of the project, the user, corporate culture, etc. These factors, including suggestions for resolving problems they can cause, are:

A. Adding programmer help

   If the project develops a need for one more programmer, it would be better to do without the help if the person being considered is not a high producer or performs poorly. In addition, the "communication factor," which will slow down each of the other programmers, along with the new programmer's learning curve productivity loss would most likely reduce the total programming output. Therefore, it is much better to work overtime for more output than to bring in a new person late in a project.

B. Project delays

   Project delays that extend the finish date can cause further delays. This is the "Snowball Delay Effect." One delay creates other delays which in turn create more delays, etc. A delay moves ahead calendar workdays for each succeeding task. This means people may be needed later than scheduled and may not be available. A new schedule must then be drawn up, based on the availability of key people. This can set a project back far enough that the user may now want to make changes.

When there is a delay pending, an effective project manager will look ahead, to anticipate what problems might occur. A project management software package can be helpful. Only as a last resort should the project team work overtime.

There should be plenty of money budgeted for overtime. The law requires overtime pay for hourly people and most programmers. But when an hourly person is making more money than a salaried worker who is working the same number of hours, or more, there will be problems. In this case, the salaried worker should be rewarded with "comp" days off after the project is over, or a money bonus. A better reward would include both.

C. Staff turnover

The loss of project members can have a significant impact on the project. The effect will vary with the role each member plays. When new people replace the ones leaving there is a learning curve to be expected. Therefore, there will be a loss of work effort from the time a project member departs until the new person becomes fully productive. A problem can occur when a key user employee leaves, too. When anyone closely connected with the project leaves, the morale of the rest of the project members is affected. This may become a catalyst, causing others to quit, especially if problems exist with the project.

When effort is applied because of project slippage there is an increase in employee turnover. The pressure and overtime create greater turnover in what is a distinct correlation between the two.

Comment:

It is within the realm of reason that a two-year project with 20 people could have over a 100 percent turnover before the project is completed. That is, if it is ever completed.

However, staff turnover is a normal thing, and it should be expected and planned for. If there is a 10 percent turnover in personnel, and a two-year project has twenty people, no fewer than four people will leave at one time or another. This does not count company transfers or promotions.

One solution is to ask for more people to start the project. Another is to have key players under contract. Overtime bonus pay and time off at the project end will also encourage salaried people to stay.

If CEOs can get million dollar bonuses with firms that are losing money in the U.S., why cannot all project members who complete a project be paid a bonus? It could be prorated to the finish date. This is done every day with contracts for outside construction projects. It certainly could be cost justified. Though there is a lack of research for this theory, the author is willing to assist any firm willing to try it, on a first-come basis.

D. New technology introduced

When new technology is introduced to an ongoing project it steals man-hours of time from the project, which in turn can result in calendar time lost. Training time is needed and there is always a learning curve.

For these reasons, it is best not to introduce any new technology to a project after it is past the analysis phase. If it is to be added, then it would help to have a new person join the project who has already mastered the new technology skills.

E. Administrative paperwork

With the current trend to downsize secretarial staff, the project manager is now expected to perform these duties which include word processing, filing, inputting data to spread sheets and program management software, contacting people, etc. This steals from the time the project manager can spend managing and helping other members of the project.

A clerk typist should be assigned to the project and expected to stay until it is completed or abandoned. This person may expand his/her duties to also be of help to other members of the project. If such a person is not available within the firm, contract outside help. This position should be listed on the staffing request for the project when the budget is planned.

14.6.3 Project Design

The last phase in the project formulation is the design phase. At this point the feasibility study and project estimation and analysis are complete. In the design phase, details are formulated out of which the program or operation will be constructed. The design can provide the criteria for writing or purchasing a computer program, or it can be a scheme for a manual procedure operation or a new report, etc.

After the design phase the actual construction can begin. It is sometimes feasible for the construction to start even before the design is complete, which can reduce the calendar time when there is a need.

Tools are now available that can accelerate the design function. They can be used alone or in combinations. The following is a sample of what is available:

- Prototyping.
- Joint application development.
- Phased delivery.
- Simulation.

Systems maintenance requires about two-thirds of all programming effort at most IS installations. Effort expended in design, construction, and documentation can reduce this time. This planning can help formulate a much more successful system which will open up more time for new project efforts.

7. PROJECT RESOURCES

14.7 PROJECT RESOURCES

IS project resources are comprised of people, tools, techniques, and education. These are assets that have a profound effect on the success of an IS project. IS organizations that have continuous ongoing projects should have a source of project resource information. Depending on the size of the system, this could be the systems manager or projects director who has the added duties of being a resource person for project tools, techniques, and education.

14.7.1 People Resources

People are by far the major expenditure for IS project efforts and a record of their activities must be maintained. A project file and also a project management file must be maintained on a project management microcomputer system of all current projects and their assigned personnel, as well as contract personnel and all assigned personnel. In addition, active personnel will be entered on a personnel project display chart.

After a project is completed data from the project file will be entered in a personnel project history file which will contain data records of each completed project such as:

- Name.
- Job title.
- Project ID.
- Planned start and finish date of project.
- Actual start and finish date.
- Hours committed to each project task.
- Hours required to finish each project task.
- Duties involved for each assigned task.
- Time ratio, hours required divided by assigned hours.
- Total project time ratio.

The project file of all current projects and the project management file will be maintained by the projects director who is responsible for allocating personnel resources for the projects. These files are part of the project management microcomputer system used for controlling people for projects.

The projects director allocates human resources by job title. All consultants and contract personnel will be given the same standard internal job titles assigned to IS personnel. A descriptive narration following the job title will be used when needed. The titles are:

- Projects director.
- Project manager.
- Assistant project manager.
- Systems manager.
- Project secretary.
- Project librarian.
- Systems analyst.

- Systems and procedure analyst.
- Industrial engineer.
- Analyst programmer.
- Senior programmer
- Programmer.
- Junior programmer.
- JAD facilitator.
- JAD recorder.
- Business systems analyst.
- Data manager.
- Database administrator.
- Database specialist.
- Network specialist.
- Quality assurance auditor.

14.7.2 Project Management Tools

There have been over 700 computer software packages produced for computers, mainframes, mini- and microcomputers. The prices start at shareware levels and go into the thousands. Today there are some effective packages for PC's Windows and DOS, Macintosh, and Unix systems.

Comment:

There have been some very good reports about Timeline and Microsoft Project 4.0. Also, there are some excellent self-paced instructional packages to help a user learn the system. According to various studies, no significant correlation has been shown between price and the package rating.

When selecting a project management package, one should first look for software that will run on the hardware that already is installed. Secondly, one should choose the least complex package that will do the job. Other features that must be considered are:

- User support.
- User friendliness.
- Reliability.

The package should contain:

- Work breakdown structure (WBS).
- Single source data entry.
- Calendar support.
- PERT and CPM charting.
- On-line tutorials.
- A database information repository for multi-projects.

It should be able to:

- Perform "what if" scenarios.
- Identify critical path and compute slack time.
- Produce graphics.
- Support capture of resources for allocation to tasks.
- Compare planned to actual Gantt charts.
- Plot milestones.

Other features worth considering:

- Can be networked.
- Can handle multiple projects.
- Has resource leveling.
- Training is available.
- Has individual resource calendars for vacation and training times.
- Can show work completed versus budgeted milestones.

14.7.3 Project Techniques

There is a wide range of project planning techniques. Some require a computer with its supporting software, while others can be applied using manual methods. No one technique resolves all project management needs.

A. PERT charts

PERT charts can display the total project with all scheduled tasks shown in sequence. These can be produced manually or by using computer project management software. The displayed tasks show which ones are in parallel, that can be performed at the same time.

PERT and CPM charts look alike. The only difference is how the task times are computed. The CPM method uses one value (most likely time) for determining the time each task will take. PERT requires a calculation as follows:

$$\text{TASK TIME} = \frac{\text{To} + \text{Tp} + 4\text{Tn}}{6}$$

To = optimistic time

Tp = pessimistic time

Tn = most likely time

The critical path of the PERT/CPM chart computes the project duration. This can be done manually or by using a project management program. The critical path can be worked backwards from a finish date or forward from a start date.

The PERT/CPM chart will show the slack times. Slack time occurs when a task takes less time to do than a parallel critical path task. This information can be valuable. For example, suppose the critical path needs to be reduced in total time by two days. And assume a critical path task of 12 days is found which has a parallel slack task of 10 or fewer days. Simply have the critical path task work overtime two Saturdays, and the total project time is reduced by two days. This is a very simple illustration; more complex solutions for reducing the total project time can be found by using a project management program.

The PERT/CPM chart can be the input for the Gantt charts. Each leg of the PERT/CPM chart can become a Gantt chart which will display the scheduled calendar days. The chart can be available on a monitor screen from a project software package, and/or placed on the office wall.

B. Gantt Charts

Gantt charts are used to show calendar time task assignments in days, weeks or months. As the task progresses and reaches a milestone these can be shown on the chart. The number of days required to complete a task that reaches a milestone can be compared with the planned number. The actual work days, from actual start to actual finish, are plotted below the scheduled days. This information can give a fore-warning that the person is not meeting the estimated time schedule, and adjustments can be made.

Gantt charts can also be used to show dollars allocated versus dollars spent information. This can be compared to the status of task work completed.

Tasks can also be broken down into subtasks, and both can be used to identify the persons assigned. These charts can be produced to show a person's task type assignment by projects. The overall project status displayed allows the project manager to assign or reassign personnel as needed. It also shows him/her when there is a need for shifting project schedules and can warn of problems yet to arrive.

Gantt charts can be produced on graph paper or magnetic boards, or by computer project management software. If the latter, the charts can be displayed on computer monitors and the screen display can also be networked.

14.7.4 Project Management Education

There is a wide range of project education sources today varying from informal self-education to more formal presentations. Sources are available in the following forms:

A. Reading material

   Many books and articles have been printed on this subject. The local library will have a periodical index and books-in-print text. Look under "project management" for the most current source selection. Most larger towns now have computer access to this information. If the library does not have what is needed, it can copy periodical articles and obtain books through interlibrary loan.

B. Seminars

   Seminars are offered by professional organizations as well as others such as: American Management Association, Education Services Department, 135 West 50th Street, New York, NY 10020 (1-800-225-3215); SkillPath Seminars, 6900 Squibb Road, Mission, KS 66201-2768, and Project Management Institute, 130 South State Road, Upper Darby, PA 19082, (215-734-3330). Check the library for more names and addresses.

C. Videotapes

   There are commercially available videotapes on project management.

D. College classes

College project management classes are offered by both engineering and business programs. These classes are more often found at the graduate level, most with no prerequisite.

E. Project management professional organization

The Project Management Institute, 130 South State Road, Upper Darby, PA 19082, (215-734-3330) publishes a monthly "Project Management Journal" and holds seminars.

8. PROJECT PROGRESS

14.8 PROJECT PROGRESS

The project progress is tracked in three ways: task completion, progress measurement, and reporting. This tracking begins when the project starts and ends after it is terminated. Not all projects are completed but all are terminated. Those that are not completed but terminated are the ones most often noted as failures.

14.8.1 Task Completion

As task milestones are reached, this information will be entered into the project management program. As tasks are completed, they are assessed for quality, completion effort required, and effect on the project schedule. The hours estimated to complete the task effort will be compared with the actual hours, and this information will be retained for correcting future estimates.

This task completion information will be utilized to identify the state of the project at different points in time. It will be discussed in status meetings. If the projects start to fall behind schedule, solutions will be sought. The following are some of the solutions that can be used to take care of project slippage.

A. Overtime

Overtime should be used only for completing critical path tasks and only in the short-term. If the need for overtime becomes routine it can affect the personnel turnover rate. The best time for paid overtime is after Christmas, and the worst time is during the summer months.

B. Assign more people

Assigning people at the start of a project is less of a problem than having to add more later on. The worst time is at the end. As more people are added the communication required between project members reduces the output per worker, and the learning curve becomes a factor, too. As a result, the project effort could end up less effectively completed than if no further people had been added.

C.   Farm out a task to a vendor

This action has merit if the vendor has reliable skills in the appropriate area. However, the more the vendor knows ahead of time that the task is coming the better the results will be.

D.   Reduce the project scope

If the user management is willing to reduce the project scope, this may be an effective solution to project slippage, helping to keep the quality of the remaining project tasks intact.

E.   Reschedule module delivery

Modules that may not be required for the finish date could be delayed. This is a better solution than reducing the project scope.

F.   Request additional funds

When funds start to run out before the project completion date, extra money will have to be requested. The sooner this is done the better, because as the end of the fiscal year approaches, there is less money available. If the dollars represent people cost, this is not as much of a problem. Salaried people do not require overtime pay. And both hourly and salaried people are budgeted for, whether they are working on a project or at their regular jobs.

14.8.2 Progress Measurement

Items that must be controlled and managed should be monitored for both quantity and quality. It is harder to measure the quality of output than quantity at the time the work is being done, since the quality of the programming effort starts to show up only when the programs are tested and debugged. Therefore the testing should not be delayed.

Time spent by employees is the greatest cost of the project and it should be closely monitored to provide information with which to gauge the results in terms of the effort exerted. Everyone must complete a time sheet, including the project manager and contract workers and/or consultants. Some of the project management packages collect this data online and summarize it in a weekly report, automatically applying the time and dollar values to relevant project tasks.

So as not to intimidate the employees or have them spend too much time collecting this data, do the following:

A. Explain why the data is needed

   Demonstrate the process used to record the time and explain why it is used. Encourage the use of real numbers, not made up ones or estimates. Stress the fact that the information is for their benefit too.

B. Simplify the recording

   Do not require too much detail. Let it be known that they can receive a telephone call from a spouse or go to the rest room. According to the time measurement people, workers are normally allowed ten percent of their work time for personal time.

   Have the time sheets turned in or inputted to the computer daily. It is a problem to remember on Friday afternoon the efforts expended on Monday morning. For forms inputted to the computer, use a scannable document. It would be desirable to have the worker input the data from his/her own workstation.

   Do not insist that the time utilized agree with the required time.

C. Use continuous work sampling

   Note that this alternative to having the employees keep track of work time would relieve them of this effort and most likely would be more accurate. (However, it would be more costly.)

D. Confirmation of estimates

   Inform employees that the time estimates on which the project is constructed need to be confirmed. Estimates are just approximations and need to be corrected if wrong. This cannot be done without keeping track of the actual time spent.

   As a byproduct, workers will be more productive if monitored.

14.8.3 Project Reporting

Project members should submit weekly and monthly project reports to their respective projects manager, who will then forward copies to the project director. He/she will in turn compile a monthly report of all the projects for the head of information systems and the Steering Committee.

The project team should have a status meeting late Friday afternoon to summarize the week's work; it should not take too much time. Any catching up required can be done on Saturday, if need be. From this meeting and the project management program information, the Monday status report will be produced and issued by the project manager to the project team and the projects director. This status report will note what progress is being made, what tasks are behind schedule, and what effort is being made to catch up. The tasks that are still to be begun will also be reported.

The monthly report will recap the weekly reports and forecast the project's status for the next month. If the current month's status does not agree with last month's forecast the reasons will be given. The monthly report will provide the percent probabilities that the project will meet the finish date and the budget provided. Dollar variances of over five percent, or more than $500, must be explained. Any future items that may affect the project should be reported (such as people going on vacation, or leaving, etc.)

A final report, written by the project manager, will be sent to the projects director recapping the major issues of the project. Problems encountered and how to avoid them in the future will be presented. People who did outstanding work will be noted. This report is only for the projects director who will write a completed project report and submit it to the head of information systems and the Steering Committee.

9. PROJECT COMMUNICATIONS

14.9 PROJECT COMMUNICATIONS

The flow of information concerning a project comes in the form of written communications, e-mail, and meetings. Each has its advantages and limitations.

A. Written communications

These are letters, memos, and e-mail. Letters are used for communications that go outside the firm. Memos and e-mail are preferred for written internal communications. A standard format is used for both types.

B. Meetings

Meetings are very important but costly. Project managers can spend over 50 percent of their time using this form of communication. There are two types of meetings: the one-way communications meeting and the two-way meeting. The one-way meeting is a meeting to inform. The two-way meeting is used to resolve an issue.

Following are procedure steps to use as a guide for conducting a meeting:

1. Write an agenda with time limits for each item.
2. Send out copies of the agenda to all personnel invited to attend.
3. Begin and end the meeting on time.
4. Keep minutes of the meeting and include the names of those present.
5. Limit the number of people for two-way communication meetings to 10 to 12.
6. Arrange the seating for the best communication and control.
7. Place important subjects first on the agenda.
8. Discussion procedures:
   - Keep to the agenda.
   - Be aware of supervisor and subordinate relationships.
   - Draw out shy participants.
   - Give everyone an opportunity to be involved in the discussion.

10. MULTIPLE PROJECTS MANAGEMENT

14.10 MULTIPLE PROJECTS MANAGEMENT

It is seldom that an information systems operation has only one project in process. Therefore, the management of multiple projects must be considered. The systems manager is responsible for the effort but may delegate this responsibility to a projects director.

All projects must utilize the methodology of reporting, operation, naming conventions, etc. This standard must be universal so that resources shared will present no problem when being exchanged. The reports received must also be consistent because of the need to combine them when reporting to the IS head and the Steering Committee.

14.10.1 Resource Sharing

The person responsible for overseeing the multiple projects must be the one to assign the IS people to the different projects. This person will also be responsible for contract personnel and consultants. Arrangements for others, who can be on loan from other parts of the company, is the sole responsibility of the projects director.

The weekly reports will indicate the status of each project and its tasks. The coordination of the people resources by the projects director makes it possible for resources to be commandeered from one project for another when necessary. Coordination duties also include the authorization to place priorities on projects and tasks within projects.

14.10.2 Backup Personnel

When a large number of people are engaged in project activities (over 30) it would be prudent to have extra key workers reporting to the person coordinating the projects to provide for a needed manpower buffer. The type of personnel that would most likely be needed in the buffer pool would be:

- Project secretaries.
- Programmers.
- Systems analysts.
- Network personnel.
- Database personnel.
- IS trainers.
- Documentation writers.
- Systems and procedure analysts.
- Project librarians.

14.10.3 Scope Management

With more than one project in process there can be problems of boundary management with users. To avoid this kind of problem the projects director must be aware of projects that have overlapping scopes. This not only can cause wasted effort if not policed, but can create company political problems. Projects must be viewed in a proactive light to prevent this from happening.

The projects director will have at his/her disposal the repository plans of all projects in process, as well as planned projects. This information should be kept on a database provided by the microcomputer program management system.

Chapter 15
VENDOR CONTRACTING

1. VENDOR POLICIES

15.1 VENDOR POLICIES

The size of Information Systems operations and the uneven demand for IS services influence the type and amount of outside services required. In addition, available funds must be balanced with need: the two are seldom in accord. Outside service vendors can come in the form of management consultants, service bureaus, and outsourcing and contract personnel.

The best policy in dealing with outside vendors is to exercise good business practices based on sound moral and ethical codes. The firm's manner of dealing with vendors can lose or gain respect for it from other vendors, employees and the industry at large.

15.1.1 Vendor Selection

The question is, how does one select a firm that will actually deliver what is wanted, when it is wanted, at the agreed upon price? The two major participants in this scenario are the firm providing the service and the firm purchasing the service.

Comment:
Unfortunately, there are some charlatans who are only in business to make a fast buck, and some firms who overrate their services. Steering the company through the mine fields of vendor

incompetence is only half of this major challenge; the other is understanding one's own firm. An unrealistic internal cultural assessment can spell disaster for any undertaking even when the most competent service organization is employed.

Vendor service contracts should be signed based on the optimal solution for the IS department, not just on price. To avoid any form of possible collusion, there must not be any family or close personal relationships between a vendor and personnel with selection authority in a firm.

In addition all agreements between a firm and the vendor must be in writing. The contract agent of each organization should be the person signing, or else a designated person should be specified in the written agreement. Both parties signing must have the authority to represent their respective firms. Each contract should have a cancellation and a performance clause included.

Comment:

Take care not to develop enemies when sitting in a volatile interactive position as head of an information systems organization. Information systems personnel are mobile, and their paths cross in unexpected ways. Interaction with someone from the past may be required in job searches. An attempt should be made to steer clear of problem situations but, in business as in marriage, many discoveries are made after the contract is signed.

15.1.2 Outside Services

The computer field is too complex to master all of its facets, let alone all the technology necessary to deal effectively with outside services. For this reason, the services of the firm's purchasing unit and/or legal staff might be requested. If the firm is too small to have such in-house experts, it may rely on an outside service for this expertise.

The purchasing department can provide information about vendors with which the company deals. For instance, it is advisable to know when possible if a vendor will still be in business next year. Part of the purchasing department's responsibility is to know the financial status and reputation of vendors as well as the quality of their merchandise. This is information an IS department head should have before beginning negotiations.

The legal department should review any contract with a vendor before large sums of the firm's capital are committed. There are a growing number of attorneys with this type of expertise who may be of assistance. The firm's attorneys should include a penalty clause in the event the vendor does not perform according to the agreement.

Most firms have a procedure to confirm at the receiving dock that an item meets purchase order requirements and to start the payment process for the invoice or bill received for that item. This is usually not the case when purchasing outside services. Therefore, the IS manager must contact the accounts payable department before the bill arrives to insure that only the services stipulated in the contract are paid. In addition, a delay of payment can be used to force an obstinate vendor to be cooperative in meeting contract obligations.

15.1.3 IT Outsourcing Policies

IT outsourcing is not the same as out-tasking. Out-tasking is traditional supplemental staffing for peak activity periods, while outsourcing is identified as a non-core function, or one that is not directly involved with the major money-making areas of the firm.

The area for the outsourcing operation(s) will be budgeted for annually. Vendor contracts that will expire within the next budget year will require a new contract proposal one month before the cut-off for budget considerations. If the current vendor's performance or new proposal is not satisfactory, an RFP (Request for Proposal) will be sent to no fewer than two other vendors.

IS management must have a clear set of long-term goals and objectives for outsourcing efforts. Outsourcing should be used:

- For operations that are difficult to manage and staff.
- To supply talent/resources not available in the organization.
- To reduce internal operation costs.
- To free resources for other efforts.
- To bring improvements and benefits on board faster.

> **Comment:**
> To assist in the refinement of policy and strategy for outsourcing acquisition, The Outsourcing Institute may be contacted at (800) 421-6767 or at 353 Lexington Avenue, Eighth floor, New York, NY 10016. Ask about its free *Outsourcing Information Kit* and a free copy of its quarterly management brief, *The Source.*

2. CONSULTING SERVICES

15.2 Consulting Service Contracting

Consulting services are often justified because in-house skills are not available, extra manpower is required, or the firm is seeking an unbiased objective. Consulting firms have a variety of specially talented personnel who justifiably may not be employed in IS operation. Because work is usually divided into projects and accomplished at that level, these specialists are valuable for specific undertakings. Many of these personnel are well paid, ambitious individuals who enjoy the variety of challenging assignments that only a consulting firm can offer.

Projects and conversions can require more manpower than is normally available. Hiring extra people for such undertakings, then terminating them after completion of a task, creates morale problems. Because consultants are temporary, they are ideal for these situations.

Outside consultants can be totally objective because they are not embroiled in the organization's political struggles. Therefore, they should be able to render excellent professional judgments. Unfortunately, whoever hired the consultant may sometimes have influenced the selection of a "cooperative" consultant, thereby losing objectivity.

15.2.1 Kinds of Consulting Organizations

Consulting firms have a wide array of skills for sale. Some are an appendage of an accounting firm while others are separate entities; therefore the services can and do vary widely.

Some firms are computer related. Feasibility studies and/or total systems design and implementation may be specialties. They may also provide very special skills in the areas of database systems, communication networks, IS audits, and related functions. These consultants are only used on a temporary basis for a specific project or to troubleshoot a given problem.

Other firms may provide software developing services and programming talent. These services require a great range of skills from coding to systems analysis and have a wide range of prices. There must be assurance that skill levels are commensurate with the price being paid and that the promises made are kept. Some firms have been known to indicate what should be received, while delivering much less experience and/or skill than was expected.

Accounting firms that offer IS consulting services are very expensive because of their interest in high revenue contracts. The area of expertise tends to be centered on financial and accounting systems. If there is a need for assistance in this area, it is best to contact a firm's own CPA first.

In the final analysis, the area of the country and metropolitan density determine what is available. A good source of information is other IS management in the area who have needed such services. There is nothing wrong with trying out a new firm; however, performance is best tested with small "safe" projects before entrusting a major undertaking and a critical completion date. It is wise to include a time contingency when establishing due dates. Time needed will vary based on proven skills of the consultant and the importance of the finish date.

Comment:
The wise IS manager uses caution when hiring because consulting can be an avenue for gaining instant professional status with very little money or education. For instance, in one case a student who failed a systems analysis course and dropped out of college later became a computer systems analysis consultant with a record of failures. No official board certifies or regulates computer consultants, and no codification of standard skills and procedures exists.

15.2.2 Consultant Relationship Procedures

Consultants can be a valuable asset if a proper relationship is present. They can be effectively employed or can be acquired for all the wrong reasons. Therefore, it is imperative that the proper conditions are maintained to maximize the benefits a consultant provides while minimizing the cost.

There are several procedures that should be followed when acquiring the services of an outside consultant.

A. Have defined goals

The more nebulous the goal, the more time and money are spent on the project. Since consultants charge by the hour, the more defined the goal the less cost in time and money. The area should be well defined to make the scope of the project as narrow as possible. In addition, do not acquire a consultant for any of the wrong reasons such as:

1. To let the consultant be the bearer of bad news for projects in trouble.

2. To have the consultant as a political ally, the outside "expert" with a level of credibility to justify decisions already made. This is an expensive practice.

3. Being impressed with the out-of-town expert. At times there seems to be a correlation between price, the distance traveled, and perception of the expert's skills. Management may be unduly impressed with a consultant's title, especially one who travels from afar and has "Ph.D." after his/her name.

   Consultants often can come up with solutions gleaned from present employees. There is really nothing wrong with this because a good consultant explores all possible solutions. But it does irritate competent in-house personnel.

4. To be a surrogate. A weak project manager may require a consultant to make decisions. However, a consultant serves at the staff level and should never take on-line responsibility. If this is what is needed, a "facilities management" service should be contracted. It is the less expensive route to take and creates fewer problems.

B. Define specifications and scope

This will give the consultant a clear understanding of what is to be done and what to avoid. Make very clear what is expected as far as specifications and have this confirmed in writing.

Any wasted effort will be included in the bill even if the firm does not get what it wanted.

Because of the high turnover in the computer field, personnel may be here today and gone tomorrow. This also applies to new small consulting firms.

C. Required documentation

The documentation that is left behind after the completion of a project may be the only source of reference when the job is finished. Proper documentation must also be provided for the consultant to insure that the consultant knows what is expected. Documentation is expensive and is all too often debased to save time or money. But saving in this way will create more expenses later. When defining documentation requirements, make sure the consultant's and firm's standards are indistinguishable using the firm's format.

D. Monitoring the consultant's progress

A monitoring procedure for the consultant must be agreed to, in writing, before a contract is signed. Feedback on the status of the consultant's work must be obtained at predetermined time intervals by defining efforts in the smallest measurable units and relating them to percentages of the total. As progress is reported, the cumulated percent of progress completed can be compared to the cumulated dollars spent. These two values should be in accord to assure dollars budgeted will not be depleted before the project is completed. The effectiveness, or lack thereof, of the consultant's performance should not come as a surprise at the end. A visual monitor could be a Gantt chart comparing the percent of units completed to the percent of funds billed by the consultant to date.

Consultants are self-directed persons; they must be to survive in the profession. However, they may be sidetracked by extending their scope or misinterpret directions received from more than one source. As with any newly employed personnel, consultants should not be left alone for long periods of time. Nor should there be any misunderstanding as to the status of an in-process project. This should be well documented in clear and understandably written, dated, and signed reports.

3. CONTRACT PERSONNEL

15.3 CONTRACT PERSONNEL

There may be reasons for using additional manpower for a project or for conversion to a new system. In these cases talented temporary personnel, not consultants, working in-house for the firm are needed. These individuals vary in terms of skills and include data entry personnel, clerks, trainers, coders, programmers, and systems analysts. The length of their stay may vary depending on when they are needed for a project. These people will be paid through the accounts payable system like any other outside service.

This talent can be obtained in a number of ways. Although consultants might provide some of these services, they can be an expensive choice.

Some vendors may also provide systems and/or programming services. Smaller firms tend to make this choice when acquiring a new computer system. Even mainframe vendors may have personnel available at an hourly rate which may also be negotiable depending on the competitive climate.

15.3.1 Justifying Contract Personnel

Many of the reasons for acquiring contract personnel are the same as for contracting a consultant. However, contract personnel are less expensive than consultants, and there may be other benefits to the company. Consider the following when deciding to go with this arrangement:

A. Contract personnel staffing

Other than being paid through the accounts payable unit, contract personnel are treated very much like the firm's own personnel. They should be assigned work like regular employees, with the understanding that there is no long-range commitment. Their assignments can run from a few hours to an almost on-going basis. Some years ago contract workers were thought of as semi-skilled people at best. Today they are found at the technical or management level.

B. Adjunct status

Employees on a contract basis are "adjunct" to the project. Their connection is to the project or task for which they are contracted and not the firm. A set sum of money is budgeted for a project with a given number of billable hours. To avoid the assumption of an on-going employment status, it is advisable to inform contract personnel of the given number of hours that have been budgeted for the project. If their work is monitored, poor performance can be detected before it is too late and an inadequate person can be replaced by someone more competent before the money runs out.

C. Monitoring performance

When a contract person is finished with a project, his/her performance level should be established and recorded. If the same person is to be used in the future, that performance level can be used to compute a reasonably accurate schedule. It is a good practice to try out personnel on small tasks before making long-range commitments.

D. Specialization availability

For a one-time effort, it is often cheaper to hire a contract person than to incur the expense of in-house training (even assuming that in-house personnel are available to concentrate their energies on acquiring a new skill). A specialist who constantly uses a talent, continually honing it, can perform at a higher skill level than anyone trained in-house for just one project.

E. Maintaining employer reputation

When large projects or parallel operations occur without contract personnel, the question arises as to what will happen to surplus personnel after the demand is over. Whether job security doubts are justified or not, employees will begin to notice other job opportunities. The most valuable among them are the candidates who can most easily find opportunities elsewhere. This can leave the firm with less qualified employees to run the operation after conversion.

Because employers compete in a market for skilled talents, it is best not to develop the reputation of hiring, then firing, skilled personnel. As the firm compares job candidates when hiring, people seeking employment compare the merits of different firms. One of the major reasons for job candidates not to accept a firm's offer is its unstable employment profile. This is one reason it has become a good practice to contract skilled workers when there are fluctuating demands.

On the other hand, there are some valid reasons for not contracting personnel. One involves the learning curve, the time needed to master the job or learn about a firm. With lower level jobs this is not much of a problem.

Another reason is that a lower level of loyalty is received from a part-timer. While this is a valid concern, many contract workers are comfortable with temporary employment and can be committed to the task at hand.

It is generally accepted that the more professional the responsibility, the greater the loyalty of the person to the profession rather than to the firm. This may account, in part, for the turnover of skilled personnel who feel their firms are not giving them opportunities to gain professional maturity.

There is also the problem that contract people might make work for themselves to extend their employment, another reason for monitoring their work effort.

15.3.2 Contract Personnel Source Procedures

Vendors may be a good, but not the only, source for obtaining contract personnel. Often the hardware vendor does not have the staff or the price it charges is too high.

The Yellow Pages is a good place to start when looking for contract personnel. If an area has limited resources, the local library can provide the Yellow Pages from cities in the general area. These services may be listed under more than one category. Check "computer services" or "information systems contracting firms." Computer service firms will usually limit the available talent to programming and computer systems personnel.

Data entry firms may have a wide selection of data entry or clerical personnel available. For training needs, look under "training" or "education services" and see what computer service firms have to offer.

There are also self-employed and third-party-employed contracting personnel. Their skills and dependability vary widely. Care should be taken when using a new firm that has not established a track record. There have been reported cases of contract programmers planting "time bombs" in their programs to insure they are fairly paid. Delay of payment to confirm that all goes well might also be a problem because many new firms are undercapitalized. Dealing with these firms is the same as sailing totally uncharted waters and may yield surprises.

Much thought needs to be given to the situation before hiring any contract personnel. When there are delays in finding temporary people, managers tend to lower their standards. Therefore, time is required to prove the worth of contract people on the job. More caution is necessary than for regular personnel because contract people are not loyal to the firm and can create havoc when working with a firm's regular employees in established departments.

With all this in mind, the following procedures for contract acquisition should be followed:

A. Referral contacts

   Try to find a contracting service firm through contacts with other firms. Their referrals are the best way to find a proven personnel contractor. Maintain memberships in IS professional organizations to provide these contacts.

B. Yellow Pages

   If referrals do not provide the necessary results, the Yellow Pages are always a last resort. Check those of your area first. If there are not more than three or four contracting services listed, check the local library which should have out-of-town telephone books. Be sure to contact no fewer than three or four firms to allow for comparison.

C. Competency verification

   When the selection has been narrowed down to no fewer than three vendors, verify their past performance. Ask each vendor for three or more customer references who can be contacted by telephone and to whom you can ask the following questions:

   1. Would you seek the firm's services in the future?
   2. Did the vendor complete the project in the agreed time?
   3. Was the cost of the service within the bounds expected?
   4. Did the talent offered come up to expectations?
   5. Did the vendor leave behind sufficient documentation?
   6. Did the vendor's employee get along with your firm's users and IS people?
   7. Were the contract employees available after the project for clearing up any problems?
   8. Did the contract employees follow your standards for procedures and documentation?

D. Purchasing department's role

   After selecting possible contract candidates, contact the purchasing department which should be involved with the request for bids. Many will lack experience in this area; however, they have the resources to help avoid selecting the wrong firm. Purchasing should, as a minimum, do the following:

   1. Confirm the Dun and Bradstreet ratings of each of the firms selected.
   2. Have the firms "checked out" as to their business status in their community.
   3. Submit the requests for bids.
   4. Establish contacts with the bidding firms.
   5. Play their usual role in purchasing. They are trained to say no to vendors.
   6. Submit in writing the status and ranking of firms asked for bids.
   7. Assist in drawing up the contract. Depending on its nature it would be wise to have purchasing ask the legal department to review anything that is to be signed, before legally committing the firm.

E. Reviewing bid offers

All bid offers should be reviewed, with the help of the legal and purchasing departments. After everything is approved, inform all parties in writing as soon as possible, including those not getting an offer. They may be needed in the future.

F. Contract outline

The contract should contain no less than the following:

1. The start and finish date.
2. The names of people who will be assigned to the project. A copy of each person's resume should be included if not previously received.
3. Number of hours that will be expected for each person assigned to the project.
4. The ground rules:
   - Contract employees' office space.
   - Tools that will be made available.
   - Vendor contact person.
   - Contact person for contract employees.
   - What procedure is required to remove a contract person from a project.
   - The hours of the day they are expected to be present.
   - How they will be paid.
   - What penalty fees will be charged for being late with a project.
   - What rewards will be allowed for completing the project early.
   - What constitutes a completed job.

4. OPERATION SERVICES

15.4 IS Operation Services

Information Systems may need expertise that can best be provided by outside operation services. These can be in the form of hardware or technical or management skills and can be provided on-line or in batch mode.

15.4.1 Hardware/Software Needs

Outside computer services may be appropriate when an application is too large or too specialized for in-house IS operation. A service bureau would be an economical alternative if the application is not performed frequently enough to justify a hardware purchase. If on-site I/O is preferred, a time-sharing service would be a reasonably priced alternative. For one-of-a-kind or seldom-used complex applications, time-sharing would be appropriate.

There are also turnkey services available which can be designed for specific applications. These provide the hardware and operating systems software, along with the applications software.

In either case, the company would be billed for hardware, running time, and any special software rentals.

The company can supplement its computer services through the use of full-service bureaus, public databases, and backup system services.

A. Service bureaus

Service bureaus solve a number of problems by providing data entry services, various computer services, or machine-time rental. Full-service bureaus provide a wide range of services which can be tailored to the specific needs of a customer. These can range from providing a turnkey operation at the customer's site to performing functions that are part of a systems operation at the service bureau's location. Subscription service bureaus provide an opportunity to share a computer application system with other subscribers. The reports produced can be specialized, but the programs and the basic system are the same.

This shared computer application system has very specialized applications and is often used for a specific system or procedure. The reasons for considering this kind of service are twofold. First, the specialized service has a much higher level of expertise than what can be expected from an in-house computer operation. Second, the cost would be substantially lower than performing the same procedure in-house. Billing or providing mailing labels is a sample of what may be offered.

Following are some major reasons for seeking assistance from a service bureau:

• To add capacity to an overtaxed in-house computer system.

• To reduce in-house computer demands by farming out some computer applications during peak load periods.

• To convert a mass of hard copy data to a captured computer form, or convert one kind of computer data file to another.

• To provide a reliable source of computer hardware backup.

• To assist with parallel testing of a new system before the actual acquisition of the new hardware.

The procedure for acquiring the services of service bureau firms is fairly simple. Most of these firms have a price list for what they provide. However, the business is very competitive, and should your company require anything other than normal procedures, you should receive several bids.

Following is the procedure in seeking the services of an IS service bureau:

1. Seek someone in the IS profession able to provide referrals.

2. If unable to locate three or more firms by referrals, use the local Yellow Pages. If these provide fewer than three firms, consult the local library for out-of-town phone books.

3. Confirm competency by asking for current customer referrals, and ask those customers the following questions:

   • Would they recommend the service firm to others?
   • Did the service firm complete their work as promised?
   • Did the cost of the services match the agreed upon cost?
   • What kind of relations did their employees have with the firm?
   • What is the best thing about their service?
   • What is the worst thing about their service?

4. Contact the purchasing department after selecting two or more firms. It should:

   • Confirm the Dun and Bradstreet ratings of each firm.
   • Have the firms "checked out" as to the business status in their community.
   • Have the firms submit requests for bids.
   • Establish a contact person to deal directly with the bidding firms.
   • Have the contractor submit bids in writing.

5. Review received bids and issue a purchase requisition to the purchasing department for the company selected. Notify the chosen firm. Also, notify the firms not chosen, explain why, and thank them.

6. Set up a method of payment and notify accounts payable about the forthcoming billings. Invoices will need approval prior to payment.

B. Public databases

Public database services are much less expensive than having this same service provided in-house. Neither public database nor time-sharing systems are commonly provided in-house because furnishing these types of services is beyond the financial limits of most firms.

Public database information systems are available to the general public, and the types of customers who utilize these services are diverse, from large firms to single persons working in home offices. The service may be thought of as a dial-up computerized reference library.

The basic hardware required is a terminal or a microcomputer and a modem. The faster the modem the better, but local phone lines should be checked to confirm they can transmit the information at the desired speed. If some degree of printed output is required, find software to quickly download information to save line time. Printers will not run at the speed of modem transmission rates. Check on the possibility of dialing into the public database service by using a local phone number. This is a money saver.

There are four major types of vendors of public database services:

1. Commercial services containing one or more databases. The Dow-Jones and *The New York Times* are two examples.

2. Commercial services offering access to numerous databases which are produced by other firms or publishers but which may also contain vendor-produced databases. The information provided can range widely from scientific to business and financial. The hourly access rate usually varies from one database to another within the same vendor's service. Dialog, Nexus and VU/TEXT are some of the more common firms providing such services.

3. Government and non-profit organizations. IRIC is a non-profit public database service providing an educational research database. The federal government offers several services, including the National Library of Medicine with on-line medical data.

4. The Internet, which provides for a host of world-wide accessible databases.

C. Backup system services

If one of today's interactive on-line computer systems goes down, severe problems can occur. A large, multi-site IS operation can provide its own backup. A UPS ("Uninterrupted Power Supply") will be required to insure that the service is accessible in the advent of a power failure.

However, small companies often cannot afford to own backup hardware. Luckily, backup services are available to be used only in the event that a system fails or if the backup system needs to be tested. It is not a service that provides extra computer power for peak load periods. This service is an expensive off-site backup with a monthly standby fee plus additional utilization charges. The switch-over can be performed so that no interruption in service is detected by on-line users.

15.4.2 Outsource Management

Traditionally facilities management services have been contracted to replace the management of IS computer operations. Today outsourcing is often used instead. Outsourcing services are contracted for a wide range of IS operations, including:

- Help Desk services.
- Maintenance.
- Training.
- Programming.
- Systems analysis.
- Database operations.
- Network operations.
- Home page operations.
- IS computer operations.
- End-user computing.

Comment:
One large, well-known corporation contracted for all of its IS responsibilities. Accounting-oriented people were sent in to develop a multi-million dollar manufacturing system which turned into a multi-million dollar disaster. Make sure the outsourcing organization has the skills needed for the area in question. Also, beware of the bait-and-switch routine. Some well-known consulting accounting firms have been known to pull this. Remember the saying "caveat emptor," or "buyer beware."

Facilities management/outsourcing of computer operations does not provide new hardware or software; it utilizes what is in place. This does not mean that an existing operation will not be changed at a later date. Existing operating personnel may also be replaced with more competent people if necessary. In addition, personnel may be terminated if there is an overstaffing problem.

Facilities management/outsourcing of computer operations might be considered for the following reasons:

1. To reduce operating cost through better management. Outside management with no internal loyalties may be needed to make necessary staffing changes.
2. To start-up an operation. Once a professional facilities management service starts up an operation, the department can be turned over to internal operations management. The outside service can stay on for a given time period to make sure everything is up and running, while permanent personnel have a chance to develop skills necessary to run the department.
3. To avoid unionization of personnel, or even get rid of a union shop. Using an outside management service or outsourcing converts the facilities to a nonunion operation without going through a difficult decertification process.
4. To provide services when there is no in-house talent available for a given area.

There are some problems with using a facilities management/outsourcing service operation: the operating responsibility is shifted away from the firm's own controlled management, and the outside management may not understand the firm's needs peculiar to its industry.

There is also a morale issue involved when acquiring a facilities management/outsourcing service. Information systems personnel may resent reporting to an "outsider." This can be a greater problem when there is an expected reduction in the work force. The problem could escalate to such a level that it results in sabotage.

Comment:
In the final analysis, computer operations has to do the job that is asked of it. And it has to do it while being price competitive. Often a facilities management arrangement can provide the fastest route for accomplishing these goals.

5. SELECTION PROCESS

15.5 SELECTION PROCESS

Selecting vendors for outside services and hardware requires the application of stringent evaluation procedures. Note that off-the-shelf software selection does not require this same procedure. This software may be evaluated before vendor selection is made. In this case the item selected determines the vendor.

15.5.1 Request for Proposal

When IS management is ready to receive vendor proposals a formal request for proposal (RFP) letter will be sent to all possible candidates. The RFP will define the format of the proposal to insure that a responding vendor can be evaluated and compared with others.

Such a request for service will be different from that for hardware. (Service RFPs include outsource RFPs.)

A. Proposal for specific hardware/system

  This request approach specifies the hardware or hardware configuration. The item is clearly identified, and the RFP basically asks for a price quotation. The RFP can be open-ended, allowing the vendor to offer newer or different technology for a given price.

B. Proposal for system operation

  This request approach defines the desired system and asks the vendor to translate the performance objective into a hardware configuration. The system operation requirements must be well defined, including:

  • System design defining documentation.
  • Security required.
  • Types of user access.
  • I/O volume.
  • Network requirements.
  • Method of system installation.
  • Evaluation criteria/benchmarks for measurement.
  • Vendor maintenance, training and operation support.

- Reliability level required.
- System expandability.
- Current and future database requirements.
- Computational and process time requirements.
- Off-line data storage requirements.
- Hard copy output requirements.
- Price/budget constraints.
- Current installations running with proposed system.
- Current users of vendor's systems.
- IS contact person.
- Vendor contact person.

C. Proposal for outsourcing/service

This request for proposal is for an ongoing service contract, with a given time limit. Three months before the end of the contract either party not wanting to renew will give written notice to the other party. Any renegotiation should be done before this three-month period.

The service will be billed monthly at a flat rate or prorated by volume. A method for recording what service was provided and what is being paid for should be in place. No invoice should be paid until this information is confirmed.

A detailed description of the service to be provided is required for the RFP. Any terms that are not used by the information technology industry will be identified in the RFP. The following items should be considered:

- System operation documentation.
- Security required.
- Service volume.
- Reliability level required.
- Performance evaluation criteria.
- Service volume expandability.
- Hours and days of service.
- Facilities required by vendor.

- Identification of vendor's employees.
- IS contact person.
- Vendor contact person.
- Clients of vendor's service.
- Contacts for confirming vendor's credibility.
- Length of time vendor has been performing this kind of service.
- Principal owners/officers of vendor's firm.

D. Proposal for one-time service

This request for proposal is for a one-time service contract. This can be for a project that will run over a given time or an operational task. The service may be billed monthly or at the end of the effort. Benchmarks are required to ensure that service billed was what was rendered. The invoice should not be paid until this is confirmed.

A detailed description of the service to be provided is required for the RFP. Any terms that are not used by the IT industry will be identified in the RFP. The following items should be considered:

- System operation documentation.
- Security required.
- Service volume.
- Reliability level required.
- Performance evaluation criteria.
- Service expendability.
- Hours and days of service.
- Facilities required by vendor.
- Identification of vendor's employees by task.
- One-page résumé for each consulting employee.
- Amount of time to be spent on tasks by each employee.
- IS contact person.
- Vendor contact person.
- Former clients of vendor's service.
- Contacts for confirming vendor's credibility.
- Length of time vendor has been performing this kind of service.
- Principal owners/officers of vendor's firm.

15.5.2 Evaluating Vendor's Proposals

All proposals received should be analyzed. The elements to be compared should be in the same sequence on each proposal. Copies will be given to each evaluator, and a date and time selected to meet and discuss them.

Vendors who provide clear and complete information asked for in the RFP and who meet preliminary evaluation standards are selected for more detailed analysis. Those that do not or that indicate pushy vendors will be removed from further consideration.

The vendors' proposals should address the specification elements noted in the RFP. Clear statements should be made by the vendor about the items addressed, including:

A. Hardware

- Hardware configuration.
- Size of primary memory.
- Execution time.
- Cache memory.
- Transfer rates.
- Disk capacity and access time.
- Maximum I/O channels.
- Brand and model numbers.
- Functional descriptions.
- Performance measurements.
- Mean time between failures.
- Maintenance provisions.
- Parts availability.
- Backup system options.
- UPS provisions.
- Operation manuals quality.
- Published evaluation information.
- Benchmark by actual workload samples.

B. Software

This covers contract programming, custom software service, source code of available software, and "off-the-shelf" software.

- Documentation clarity and completeness.
- Program maintenance or updates availability.
- Customer support available.
- Software guaranteed virus-free.
- Customer training resources available.
- Next expected release.
- Compatible operating systems.
- Language software was written in.
- Amount of primary memory required.
- Best operation is at determined level of primary memory.
- Published evaluation information.
- Benchmark by actual workload samples.

C. Service/outsourcing

Evaluation of service or outsourcing is based very heavily on the reputation of the chosen firm. Its past and current service quality should be investigated carefully.

Comment:
It is a common practice for some firms to parade their best people to get the contract signed, and afterwards send in their third string. What is even worse, you are then charged for the first-rate talent.

This practice is not limited to unknown firms. Some of the "better" nationally known firms do it, too.

Some things that can assist in the selection of a service firm are:

- Confirm their credentials.
- Make certain the names of the specific people and the amount of time they will spend on the project are in the contract.
- Ask for former and current customer references.

D. Contact with vendor's customers

A final evaluation should be made before signing any contract. Make telephone calls to a vendor's customers with a similar operation. Ask if they would recommend the vendor's product or service. If they do, set up a site visit.

Visit the operation and observe anything that would reflect the vendor's accomplishment. Since most people are reluctant to offer negative information, ask the following:

1. Would you go with the same vendor again? If so, why? What has been the major problem with the vendor? Do you know of other users of the vendor's product? Are they generally happy? If so, why so? Who are the other users? What are their names and telephone numbers?

2. How long does it take for a vendor's response? Are the people who respond knowledgeable and friendly? Has the vendor ever lied? Has the vendor had the resources to resolve your problem(s)?

3. Does the hardware/software satisfy your needs? Follow up with questions about how long they have had the system and how often it has gone down. Ask about its expandability and up-grading possibilities.

4. Do the users like the system or service? Ask to talk to users and confirm this. Ask users what they liked and disliked about the system or service and why.

5. Ask how long it took to put the hardware/software into operation. Did they receive adequate training? Are the operator's manuals easy to understand and follow?

6. Is the operation or service they are being provided better than what they could do themselves, and why? Is the service worth the cost?

7. Were there any unexpected or hidden costs? What was the nature of these costs? Were the costs reasonable? Was the vendor confronted about this? If so, what was the reaction?

8. Were the vendor's employees easy to work with? Did their salesperson follow up after the sale was made? Does the vendor seem to have a genuine interest in the success of service or product?

9. If they were starting all over, what would they do differently?

15.5.3 Vendor Selection

The final selection of a vendor is based on more than one factor. To make the process more objective, a weighted matrix can be set up to compare vendors by selection factors, with the weight of any one factor a percentage of the whole. An example may be seen in Exhibit 15-1. The nature of the item being requested by an RFP will determine the factors and their weights. The factors should be determined and the matrix parameters prepared before the request for proposal is mailed out to avoid a subjectively weighted matrix.

In the sample presented in Exhibit 15-1, a consultant is being chosen to install a client/server database. Exhibit 15-2 presents selection factors for a firm that manufactures secondary storage devices. Note that each chart contains different weighted factors, chosen for the particular need.

The compilation of the weighted factors is best done using the Delphi method. Have seven or nine people who are familiar with the proposal needs, on their own with no discussion, list those factors and their corresponding weights that each considers important for the vendor to possess. Send the lists to a person not involved with the selection to compile. This person will make a list of all the factors and return this new list to the participants. They will once more go through these factors, choosing and weighting their choices. Again, the papers will be sent to the person not involved with the selection who will group together the factors (together with their weights) that are the most prevalent. He/she will discard the ones that have been assigned low weight values or that have been mentioned only once. The possible combinations are then placed on one sheet of paper and copies are distributed to all contributors for re-selection. This process is repeated until a general consensus is reached.

The vendors that have passed the preliminary selection process are rated from one to ten by the same seven- or nine-person panel or by a new panel. An example of this rating system is shown in Exhibit 15-3. Each rating (from one to ten) is then multiplied by its weighted factor to get a vendor rating value. These values are then totaled by vendor. The one with the highest total is rated first, as shown in Exhibit 15-4.

The vendor rated number one is chosen to receive the contract and will then submit, usually, a standard contract, which of course will be in his/her favor. So, the vendor's representative will be invited to discuss this offered contract in the information systems head's office.

Comment:

At this meeting the IS head could be drinking coffee out of the vendor's competitor's cup. This, believe it or not, has had a track record for helping negotiate a more favorable contract. If not a coffee cup, some other sign of a competitor's presence can give the same message.

The contract terms will be negotiated by the vendor's representative and IS management. Training, documentation, conversion, performance, and acceptance are all included in the bargaining process. Some items in general to consider are:

- Delivery or start dates.
- Finish or completion dates.
- Vendor vs. customer responsibilities.
- Pricing methods for purchase, lease, or rent.
- How and when vendor will bill.
- Removing vendor's disclaimers.
- Provisions for equipment, software, and personnel backup.
- Emergency and preventive maintenance.
- Provision for detailed specifications for hardware, software, or service performance.
- Contract for outsourcing on a job-by-job basis.
- Realistic launch dates for implementations.
- Use only one vendor at a time to avoid conflict in the working environment.
- Avoid long-term contracts with new or unproven vendors.

Any contract should include performance clauses and penalties for nonperformance or late delivery times. After the negotiation the final contract must be examined by the legal representative of the company before it is signed.

Date 11/28/1996

Consultant to Install a Client/Server Database

Factor and Weight	Vendor A	Vendor B	Vendor C
How long in business .1			
Quality of staff .4			
Track record .4			
D and B rating .1			

Exhibit 15-1. Vendor Selection Matrix 1

Date 11/28/1996

Manufacture Secondary Storage Devices

Factor and Weight	Vendor A	Vendor B	Vendor C
How long in business .2			
Sales personnel .2			
Track record .4			
D and B rating .2			

Exhibit 15-2. Vendor Selection Matrix 2

Date 11/28/1996

Manufacture Secondary Storage Devices

Factor and Weight	Vendor A	Vendor B	Vendor C
How long in business .2	10	5	1
Sales personnel .2	3	5	9
Track record .4	2	6	8
D and B rating .2	8	9	7

Exhibit 15-3. Vendor Selection Matrix 3

Date 11/28/1996

Manufacture Secondary Storage Devices

Factor and Weight	Vendor A	Vendor B	Vendor C
How long in business .2	10 × .2 = 2.0	5 × .2 = 1.0	1 × .2 = 0.2
Sales personnel .2	3 × .2 = 0.6	5 × .2 = 1.0	9 × .2 = 1.8
Track record .4	2 × .4 = 0.8	6 × .4 = 2.4	8 × .4 = 3.2
D and B rating .2	8 × .2 = 1.6	9 × .2 = 1.8	7 × .2 = 1.7
VENDOR TOTAL RATINGS	5.0	6.2	6.9
VENDOR RANKING	3	2	1

Exhibit 15-4. Vendor Selection Matrix 4

Chapter 16
Forms Management

1. FORMS MANAGEMENT POLICY

16.1 Forms Management Policy

Top management at the policy-making level must be concerned about forms management policy and must supply the impetus for its development and implementation. In addition, for management to be effective, forms' originators must accept responsibility for improving procedures through a forms review. The responsibility for executing a sound policy must be accompanied by the authority necessary to do the job.

16.1.1 Scope of Forms Management Policy

All forms used internally and externally are covered by a forms policy. A form is defined as any paper document, other than drawings, art work, or text material, which is used to convey information or data.

The control of all aspects of forms design, generation, and disposition comes under the designated head of forms management. External forms are subject to approval by the legal department before being printed. All externally printed forms come under standard purchasing acquisition policies.

16.1.2 Objectives of Forms Management

The objectives of a forms management program are:

- All forms meet design standards.
- All externally used forms maintain the firm's image.
- Forms are designed to minimize the effort required to complete them.

- Forms are printed, distributed, replenished, and destroyed in the most economical and environmentally correct manner.

- A program mission is established for forms management to cover its purpose, responsibilities, and authority at the highest level necessary to achieve the forms management objectives.

16.1.3 Forms Analysis and Design Policy

A sound policy of forms analysis and design practices helps to integrate forms easily into a firm's daily routine and improve its operations. Forms that provide accurate, dependable, and precise information, readily accessible for the operating requirements of the company, help maintain a smoothly running firm.

- Forms have to be economical and cost effective in presentation and use in terms of time, equipment use, and printing costs.

- Forms that go outside the firm represent it, so its image is maintained, in part, by their design. Therefore, the analysis and design of forms require the guidance of management policies. The firm's public relations department may request approval of design on forms which are released to the general public.

- Forms that are used in connection with contractual commitments should be approved by the legal authority of the firm.

- The same standards of forms analysis and design should be used by the forms management unit as well as all other units within the firm. Accepted standards have been defined by the forms industry. In the event that a problem develops in using a standard for a given item because of changing technology, consult federal government standards. The federal government is up-to-date with state-of-the-art technology in the area of forms design because of its vast volume use.

- Responsibility for the design of forms lies with the forms management unit, a part of IS.

2. PROGRAM ORGANIZATION

16.2 PROGRAM ORGANIZATION

Forms management is a staff activity at a level high enough to provide the broad perspective needed for across-the-board improvements and to provide technical guidance. Because forms flow across organizational lines, forms management should represent the highest level of authority within an IS unit.

16.2.1 Program Mission

The mission of the forms program organization is complex. At the least, nine major elements need to be covered.

A. Planning and training

You must sell the services, that is, the importance, of a forms management program. This can be accomplished by establishing guidelines, which must be approved by upper management, building acceptance of the program by related IS staff, and developing understanding by operational users.

Training, which ties in closely with planning, can permit broader participation in the forms management process. Technical guidance should be provided to forms originators both inside and outside the IS operation.

B. Coordination and liaison

Program leadership calls for teamwork to create coordination in such related service facilities as reproduction, forms storage, and distribution. The program also requires a well-selected and thoroughly oriented forms liaison representative in each of the company divisions served.

C. Procedural analysis

Most proposals for a new, revised, or reprinted form are analyzed carefully. The procedure which gives the form credence is considered. The content of the form and its effect upon work methods and procedures is evaluated. Every item of every document is scrutinized. The greater its usage and its cost, the more intense the analysis.

D. Design standardization

Standards for layout and construction are prerequisites for good forms design. Content is translated into a format that insures easy reading, then spaced and arranged to accommodate the desired entries and writing, transmitting and filing methods. The form's size, typography, and construction, including color and type of paper, is determined with these same objectives in mind.

E. Registration and identification

Each request for new, revised, or reprinted forms is channeled to a central authority within IS to be recorded and assigned for analysis. Essential data on numbering and identification, previous or proposed forms revisions, volume, use, production, and distribution are furnished at this control point.

Title and number and, where appropriate, revision number and approved date are assigned for a positive identification. The title links the form to its function. The form number and edition date indicate that the form has been authorized.

F. Procurement and production

Specifications for efficient and economical outside procurement and in-house printing are developed and coordinated with units performing these functions. Outside procurement follows standard operating procedures of the purchasing department. Appropriate justification is required for specialty forms and special bindery operations such as punching, stapling, perforating, folding, and padding.

G. Distribution and storage

The specifications for effective storage and distribution are developed and coordinated by both originating users and supply facilities. Methods are provided for determining current supply levels and designating minimum order packing, setting distribution patterns and controls, and purging obsolete forms.

Comment:
Obsolete forms create untold problems for a data entry system! It's vital to get rid of them immediately. Old forms do not match the forms example in the data entry procedure manual, and can leave out something or ask for data no longer used.

H. Follow-up

After a specified time in use, the more complex forms are followed up on. Spot checks are made at origination and use points. This process is useful in promoting the program, maintaining proper liaison with users, and obtaining data for reporting purposes on benefits and savings.

I.   Program reporting

A continual record of the results is kept as the program progresses, before-and-after data are gathered, and changes in forms and procedures are made. This information, along with any recommendations, is reported to upper management, which determines if the forms management program conforms to management's policy.

16.2.2 Operational Relationships

Many different kinds of employees have a stake in different phases of a firm's forms management. Personnel with the following job titles have varying degrees of involvement with forms flowing through the firm:

- Forms designers.
- Administrative management personnel.
- Systems analysts.
- Programmer analysts.
- Computer programmers.
- Management analysts.
- Filing equipment specialists.
- Records disposal personnel.
- Information systems technicians.
- Methods analysts.
- Systems and procedure analysts.
- Printing procurement staff.
- Forms supply and distribution personnel.
- Customers.
- Vendors.
- File clerks.
- Users who read and act on the forms.
- Government agencies.

Successful operational relationships involving one or more of the groups above require forms management.

A body of knowledge and a set of practical techniques which are fully formulated assure coordination of various interests.

A. Top management

No matter how well conceived the forms management program may be, the operation requires consideration by top management. The direction taken by the program should reflect its views.

Top management requires reports of the benefits to justify the operations of a forms management program. In addition, management is to be kept informed about plans for new forms that will be used by customers, vendors, and the general public. This is to insure that the organizational image is correctly portrayed.

B. The originator

When an employee of the organization has a need to insert data or information to be passed on or collected for which no form exists, that employee can become the starting point for or the originator of a new form. The input and output of the work should be considered, as well as the processing that takes place in between. When the form leaves the desk of the originator, it will have an influence on the other workers. This is when forms management comes into play.

The originator should be sure that he/she has up-to-date facts and information about the procedure for which the form is to be used. This will be vital for the forms designer assigned to the new form and will insure that it conveys proper information when placed in the system. The originator needs to be aware that the forms analyst is concerned with the following questions:

1. Is a new form necessary? Can an existing form be adapted to suit the need? Can an existing "Standard Form" be employed, and revised if need be?

2. Should there be an entirely new concept of the use of this form? Can several forms used in a particular operation be combined into a multi-purpose document?

3. How much can the needs of those completing this form influence its design? Every attention should be given to design factors which reduce work effort. (As a rule of thumb, the labor cost for completing a form is twenty to one for each dollar of forms cost.)

4. How will working conditions at the location(s) where the form will be completed influence design? What limitations in terms of office equipment are imposed on data placement and spacing of the forms?

5. Are there any costly features required by the first draft of the form, such as "carbon spotting," or other unusual construction, which could be replaced by less costly alternatives?

Until these questions have been addressed, the originator should not proceed too far with a draft. Knowing how a forms analyst will approach the design allows the originator to fully participate in the analysis phase of forms improvement which must precede the finish of "his/her form."

C. The initiating user

The initiating user is the person who first fills in the form using the spaces which are provided for that purpose. He/she is interested in having sufficient writing space for the entry of data, captions which are easily understood, and the items to be completed arranged in a logical sequence. The role of the user in forms improvement is to convey any problems promptly to the forms manager.

The forms management staff should review the filled-in forms in the files to see if they provide the user with enough space. The initiating user does not have enough space if he/she handwrites notes in the margin. Boxes repeatedly left blank may not be needed. A "remarks" area may be needed if information is written on the back of a form.

D. The processing user

The next step, after a form has been filled in, usually consists of reading the posted information. The reader may be a data entry operator, a clerk, or a white collar worker, etc. The usefulness of the information supplied on the form is the final measure of its worth. If the information supplied presents processing problems, the form cannot be considered a good one regardless of how easy it is to enter the information.

The processing user is especially interested in orderly organization of the information and in uniform design of related forms. His/her role in forms improvement is to tell the forms management staff promptly of any processing difficulties a form generates.

E. The reports management staff

So many forms are used for reports that there can be conflict about who does this analysis, especially if both the forms management unit and reports management unit contain systems analysts or systems and procedures analysts. Since the mission of most reports management units is focused on content, this conflict can be avoided if procedures clearly assign information verification to that unit. Reports management personnel ask three important questions: Do the reports require information already available? Do the reports require information that is available from an on-line computer information system? Do the reports fail to require information that is needed?

The reports management staff should review a report form first. Since they approve the information aspects of the form, the forms management staff will not have to duplicate their work. A forms clearance document may also be used as a reports clearance document for those forms which are reports.

When the reports management unit undertakes a procedural study, it should always inform the forms management unit, and vice versa. The two units should compare notes to determine if overlapping data are being gathered by an organizational segment. There should be no conflict between reports management and forms management on the design of forms: the forms management unit holds the higher priority.

F. The directive specialist

Most forms used should be prescribed in an appropriate directive. Such directives provide information that cannot be placed on the face of the form itself, but that is needed to complete the form, such as:

- Unambiguous instructions as to who prepares forms, the number of copies prepared, and where and when copies are submitted.
- An illustration of the form with sample entries when this would help insure accurate completion.
- A description of the filing system to be used if the records are to be maintained in a specific way.
- Unusual information about the source and date of supply.

A prescribing directive should not be distributed until the appropriate forms are also distributed, unless the effective date for their use is set far enough in advance to assure availability. Purchasing should follow up the directive to confirm this availability by the effective date, especially with vendor-supplied forms.

Clearing directives related to forms with the forms management unit will often prevent erroneous references to titles, obsolete editions of forms, etc. Also, clearance serves to correct instructions, such as calling for use of typed formats of columnar worksheets when printed forms would be more appropriate. Such clearance will also help to alert the forms management unit to increase the usefulness of hard-to-understand written procedures by providing illustrative filled-in samples.

It is important that users of forms be notified by a directive that a form has been discontinued. It is appropriate that the unit originating a form or the unit responsible for its continuing use should also be the unit to discontinue it.

G. Supply personnel

Supplying forms involves procurement, reproduction, reordering from vendors, storage, and distribution. These are tasks normally assigned to publication and supply, or similar units. Forms management can be very helpful to units performing these tasks by preparing accurate specifications.

An important part of the relationship between supply and forms management is the method used for handling stock replacement orders. A "Stock Replenishment Notice" is usually prepared by the supply unit when the stock level of any form reaches the established minimum, which should be set to give ample lead time for the delivery of the forms.

H. Employee suggestion system

The forms management unit should encourage and promote an employee suggestion program. Employees who give suggestions pertaining to forms improvement should be considered originators. The same should apply to customer, vendor, or public complaints about forms in use. All contributors should receive a positive letter of acknowledgement from the forms management's unit head.

I. Outsourcing operations forms requirements

Any outsourcing of forms management operations will follow the policies and procedures set forth in this chapter. This covers computer-generated as well as standard forms.

3. PROGRAM PROCEDURES

16.3 PROGRAM PROCEDURES

The procedures required to operate a forms management program are devised to insure that the policies set down are followed. They should be consistent with other IS procedures in guidance and format.

16.3.1 Forms Program Procedures

The procedures described in this section are those essential to the support of the primary functions of procedural analysis, forms development, and forms replenishment. They govern the operational control of the forms management function, not the detail analysis and forms design.

A. Establishing major files

A forms management program must rely heavily on its control files. There are usually three: the numeric history file, the current form file, and the functional classification file. (Technology is now available to store the graphic current form files in a computer database so they can be downloaded to users as needed.)

B. Numeric history file

This set of folders provides a complete picture of each form from its development to its current status. To provide the most useful working tool, each numeric folder should eventually contain:

1. A copy of the current edition of the form and any previous editions, each marked "Permanent Copy." Many files may contain several current copies for samples.

2. Rough drafts or work papers showing significant stages of development and pertinent correspondence.

3. A copy of, or reference to, the procedure or other document authorizing use of the form.

4. The original request for approval of the form and any requests for revisions, indicating the names of all using units, and the manner and rate of use.

5. Correspondence received from other sources regarding suggestions for changes to the form. A copy of the acknowledging letter from the unit is filed with the correspondence.

6. Documentation relating to the official final approval for printing or reproduction and issuance of the form.

7. A copy of the registered copyright form, if one exists.

8. The form history record on which is kept a running record of all actions taken on a particular form, including a cross reference to the functional file.

The numeric file must be dependable at all times. Folders on discontinued or obsolete forms must be promptly withdrawn, appropriately annotated, and placed in a separate discontinued numeric file for the length of time required by the records retention schedule.

C. Functional classification file

This set of folders groups together forms dealing with related subject matter. One copy of each collected form is classified by purpose and placed in a subject-titled folder. The main purposes of the functional classification files are to:

1. Avoid the creation of a new form which duplicates an existing form or which is similar to an existing form that can be used or readily revised to serve the need.

2. Detect those forms which might be eliminated because a duplicate already exists, or which might be consolidated with similar forms.

3. Detect those forms which should be standardized for company-wide use, or which should be analyzed and redesigned for simplification and uniformity of format, nomenclature, item sequence, spacing, size, and application of other technology of forms design.

4. Generate studies of particular forms in relation to their governing systems and procedures and in relation to functional and organizational areas, which can result in improvements far beyond the form itself.

D. Assigning identification and control numbers

The assignment of form numbers is a necessary control device. Straight numeric order is the simplest and most flexible system. Avoid elaborate numbering patterns with alphabetic or number prefixes or suffixes to identify special uses. Temporary forms should have an uppercase T prefix added to the number to signify that the form is a temporary document.

It may be desirable, in some cases, to print the old form number in parentheses following a newly issued number, such as "Form 711 (formerly Form 512)." This may prevent copies of both forms being sent to the data entry unit or other areas of the firm.

Supersession notices placed next to the new form number can be helpful and are used regularly by some forms management units. An example would be, "Replaces Form 512, June 1991, which will not be used." These notices have proven particularly advantageous during a time when many forms are being updated at once.

E. Forms catalog

The forms catalog should be made available to any department that needs it. In fact, since this catalog can be on a computer system, it could be set up to be viewed on a monitor or printed on demand.

The following conditions should be considered when determining the content of the catalog:

1. Whether it is needed primarily by originators or by various users in a decentralized IS organization.

2. Degree to which procedures prescribing the use of forms are well-organized and coded and contain needed illustrations of the forms involved.

3. Cost of preparing and updating the catalog measured against its value in promoting standardization and efficiency.

4. The number of forms. The catalog should be housed in standard three-ring binders or a computer database. If the number of forms is excessive for a one-inch binder, multiple binders should be used.

5. Temporary forms used which should be copied on yellow paper as a flag to its nature.

F. Forms review and revision

Reviewing new or revised forms is a major part of forms management. This review will be prioritized based on external usage, volume processed, and the complexity of required procedures. A record of the procedures involved in the processing of the form provides an information base for its review and analysis. A process flowchart may be required to fully understand the complexity of its manual processing.

Quantitative information can also be collected simultaneously with the review and analysis. The following information would help:

- The volume of usage.
- The number of operations required to complete the form.
- The volume of work in arrears at selected points in time.

- The actual time required to complete each form.
- The total actual costs of each stage of form completion.
- The number and nature of errors, queries, or ineffectively completed forms.

G. Initiating forms analysis

The forms management unit should not be confined to forms from originators. There should be an ongoing effort to originate new or revised forms in the unit itself.

To formalize effort, the forms management unit's work would best be divided into projects. Evidence for the need for project analysis may be obtained from the following sources:

1. Suggestions made by employees, vendors, customers, or the general public.

2. Suggestions provided by the systems analysis, programming, or operations units of IS.

3. Suggestions provided by the operating personnel through day-to-day contacts. These may concern both forms and procedures. In the event that a procedure is involved, the systems and procedures or systems analysis units should be contacted.

4. Areas suggested by top management for improvement.

5. Operational areas which are known to have problems with backlogs, to have numerous errors, or to have unusual time logs. These problem areas can be identified from systems analyst or forms analyst observations of operations activity, information in procedural or organizational surveys, work sampling studies, contacts with key or other activity personnel, or other sources.

6. Review of forms and information collected for the forms management files. In performing forms research, the forms management unit has two tools the originator does not have: the numeric and the functional files. However, a forms management unit that is unable to keep these files up-to-date will gradually weaken its position until it finally loses control over the forms of the organization.

A well-balanced project schedule should include short-term projects that can be quickly completed and that will show immediately the benefits of forms management. It should also include long-term projects on more complicated or well-entrenched operations which involve a considerable expenditure of time but which will pay back substantial dividends in man-hours and improved operations.

If managing forms is to be one means of ensuring continuous attention to procedural problems, then the forms management group should not be kept so busy by over-the-counter business that its analysts cannot be spared to follow through on the procedural improvement clues previously noted.

A variation on the use of projects is to set up special task forces to study specific segments of a firm's forms. Under this plan, members of the forms management staff join with other members of IS and/or members of other company units to review all of the forms used in a given activity. For example, the systems analysis or systems and procedures unit might join the forms management unit in a joint study of all forms used for data entry. The task force method of employing more than one unit has the benefit of assuring that a whole group of related forms will be considered at one time rather than piecemeal. A disadvantage is that a task force is not a continuing entity.

H. Preparing specifications

Very few originators have technical knowledge about designing a form, knowing to arrange for pre-numbering, perforating, spot carbons, folding, collating, padding, and scoring. Therefore, the desirability or undesirability of these features should be developed during the analysis of the form and written into the specifications for the completed job prepared by the forms analyst.

I. Establishing standards

Standards must be established to guarantee that all forms have the graphic and physical features required for:

- Simplicity and efficiency of completion.
- Visibility in reading, including filing and finding.
- Acceptability of appearance.
- Economy of reproduction.

Such yardsticks or guides are called standards because they provide for the best practice based on current knowledge. Thus, standards play a large role in any forms management program. There is a tendency, however, to think of them as useful only to the forms analyst.

Actually, they are required at two levels: those standards which can be applied by originators, generally known throughout the firm; and those standards which will be generally applied only by the professional forms analyst. The latter need to be published only for use within IS.

Standards for originators should not only be published but also explained at any training sessions held, demonstrating how the standards:

- Make it easy to insert information on the form.
- Make it possible to use the information after its entry on the form.
- Reduce the error rate of entering and using data on forms.
- Minimize the cost of using and printing the forms.

In order to keep expenses to a minimum, the forms analyst, in cooperation with printing and reproduction, must develop construction standards for such items as:

- Pre-numbering forms for control.
- Punching for standard binders.
- Standard size of documents.
- Type and weight of paper.

16.3.2 Forms Design Standards

The following standards should be applied by the initiating authority or IS designing analysts. The forms analyst assigned confirms that the specifications have been met before forwarding the requisition to duplicating or to the purchasing department.

A. Form size

Flat forms should be 5 $1/2$-by-8 $1/2$ or 8 $1/2$-by-11 inches. Normal file card sizes are 3-by-5, 4-by-6 and 5-by-8 inches. Postcards are 3 $1/4$-by-5 $1/2$ inches.

B. Paper weight and grade

Card stock should be 180 lb. Report covers should be sulphite 32 lb. Flat forms should be 20 lb. sulphite or bond.

C. Color of paper

Specify color only when needed for emphasis or for more efficient filing, routing, or sorting. Red paper is not used. (It will not copy or microfilm.) Reduce the need for colored paper by use of sorting symbols, bold headings, heavy ruled lines, or other devices when possible. Exceptions are permissible for specific organization or operating requirements.

D. Color of ink

Specify other than black ink only when fully justified by volume and increased efficiency in use of the form and when the more economical possibilities of colored paper are inadequate. More than one color should be avoided except with extreme justification.

E. Identification and heading

Heading may run across the entire top of the form or be centered in the space to the left of any entry boxes that have been placed in the upper right-hand corner. Upper right should be designed for file or other ready-reference entries if needed. Within the space decided upon, arrange information generally as follows:

- Form number and issuance or revision date in the upper left-hand corner.
- Form title. Use conspicuous type.

F. Instructions

Well-designed forms require few instructions other than captions and item headings. When required, instructions should:

1. Be set in two or more narrow columns rather than full-width lines.
2. Be listed as numbered items rather than in paragraph style.
3. Be placed as near items to which they apply as possible (unless length detracts from effective layout).

When instructions are segregated on a form, they should be placed:

1. At the top right or center, if concise and applicable to the whole form.
2. At the bottom, if this makes possible a more economical use of space.
3. On the reverse side if no space is available on the face.

G. Address

The position of the name and address, if placed on a form for mailing, should be appropriate for window-envelope use. Forms intended for such use must conform to postal regulations, which in general provide that nothing other than name and address should appear in the window. The form must fit the envelope to avoid shifting of the address. Only standard-size envelopes should be used.

H. Preprinted names

If the form is to be stocked for continuing use, the name or signature of a person may be preprinted, but only with special justification or if legally required. Preprinting of titles only and the use of rubber stamps or automatic signature inscribers are alternatives to be considered.

I. Form arrangement

The following will apply to the arrangement of forms:

1. Align the beginning of each writing space vertically on the form for a minimal number of tabular stops.
2. If a box design is used:
   a. Serially number each box in its upper left-hand corner.
   b. Start the caption in the upper left-hand corner, to the right of number, leaving fill-in space below the caption.
   c. Draw box size to provide sufficient space for fill-in.
3. Place essential information where it will not be obscured by stamps, punches, or staples, or be torn off with detachable stubs.
4. Group related items.
5. Include "to" and "from" spaces for any necessary routing.
6. Provide for use of window envelopes, when appropriate, to save additional addressing.
7. To the extent practical, list items in the same sequence as on other forms from which or to which the same information is to be transferred.
8. Arrange information for ease in tabulating or data entry if either is involved.

J. Check boxes

Use check boxes when practical.

1. Place check boxes either before or after items, but all in the same positions within any line series.
2. Avoid columnar grouping of check boxes if possible because of the potential for registration errors when carbon copies are required. Place check boxes before the first column and after the second column when there are two adjacent columns of questions.

K. Margins

Borders should not be printed on all four sides since this tends to increase production problems and costs. In any event, a margin of $1/_2$ inch from the edge of the paper should be allowed on all four sides for gripping requirements in printing and as a safety margin for cutting.

When ring binders are to contain the forms, one inch should be allowed on that edge for binder ring space. When the form is to be used in a typewriter, the first line should be at least $1\ 1/_3$ inches from the top of the form, and the last line to be typed should be no less than $3/_4$ inch from the bottom. Hand fill-in is permissible above and below these limits.

L. Space requirements for fill-in

To accommodate either elite or pica typewriters, allow space based on ten characters per inch horizontally. (Most computer printers are ten characters per inch.) Vertically, allow six lines per inch for single spacing.

For handwritten information, allow 1/3 more space horizontally than for typewriter fill-in and allow three lines per inch for vertical spacing. In some cases, more space may be required for posting the information, depending on the user.

M. Rulings

The following procedures are to be followed:

1. Use heavy $1/_2$ point or parallel $1/_2$ point rulings as first and last horizontal lines, between major divisions, and across column headings.
2. Use $3/_4$ point rulings across the bottom of column headings and above a total or balance at the foot of a column.
3. Use hairline rulings for regular lines and box lines when no emphasis is required.
4. Use $3/_4$ point rulings for vertical subdivision of major sections or columns.
5. Use leaders as needed to guide the eye in tabular or semi-tabular items.

N. Signature and approval date

Single, handwritten signatures go at the bottom right of the last page. Allow $1/_2$ inch vertically and three inches horizontally. Two handwritten signatures, normally, are placed left and right at the bottom of the last page. Space below the $3/_4$-inch bottom typewriter margin is generally reserved for handwritten signatures and dates.

O. Two-sided forms

The following procedures should be followed for two-sided forms:

1. Two-sided forms should be printed head to foot, especially if top-punched for binder use.

2. If punched in left margin for binder, two-sided forms should be head to head.

3. Three- or four-page forms (one sheet folded once) should be head to head throughout if open-side style, and head to foot if open-end (so that, when opened for use, head of third page follows foot of second page).

4. Head-to-foot open-end forms are preferable for machine fill-in.

5. For multi-page forms, separate sheets of proper page size should be used instead of larger sheets folded to page size, unless the larger sheets can be cut economically from standard paper size and run on standard printing or duplicating equipment.

P. Pre-numbering

Use pre-numbered forms only if accounting or control is required for each form or document. Place the number in the extreme upper right corner.

Q. Punching

For standard press-type and three-hole ring binders:

- Distance from edges of the paper to the center of the hole should measure $3/_8$ inch.

- If three holes are punched, distance from center to center of adjacent holes should be $4 \ 1/_4$ inches.

- If two holes are punched, for press-type fastener, the distance between centers should be $2 \ 3/_4$ inches.

16.3.3 Electronic Forms

Hard copy text and forms are being rapidly replaced by electronic forms processing. Most senior management still prefers hard copy (paper) documents to work with. But, as managers become aware of the new technology, the benefits of using electronic forms become clear. Users are increasingly replacing paper-based processing with electronic forms routed and tracked over Microsoft's Mail and Lotus' CC:Mail.

Some of the benefits include the following:

- Reduces mailing costs.
- Eliminates printing paper forms.
- Increases data-entry accuracy.
- Reduces labor costs.
- Provides document tracking and routing.
- Provides front-end operation for e-mail systems.
- Can utilize the Internet service.
- Supports digital signatures.
- Provides for electronic billing.
- Allows storage and retrieval of documents at remote locations with electronic speeds.
- Provides e-mail distribution of documents.
- Reduces the need for file clerks and secretaries.
- Allows filing by scanning documents at disk side.
- Reduces filing space needed for hard copy.
- Allows archive documents to be downloaded to secondary storage and stored in more than one location.

The forms management organization can begin using electronic forms by employing appropriate design software and hardware. There are several good off-the-shelf forms software systems available. It would be best to research what is available so as to choose the one that best suits the forms analyst and the needs of the firm.

Hardware needs for one of these systems, aside from the microcomputer, are few: a good scanner and a quality printer.

IS would need to closely oversee this technology, following the microcomputer controls noted in Chapter 7, Asset Management. Use of electronic forms will expand forms management's role in the organization.

4. DESIGN CONCEPTS

16.4 DESIGN CONCEPTS

A form is a fixed arrangement of captioned spaces designed for entering and obtaining prescribed information. In the past, forms have been more or less limited to "flat form" printed documents, but today's IS technology has changed this traditional format. Today, forms may be stored on disk, called up on the monitor as needed for completion, and then printed. (With the availability of color printers color type is now simple to produce.)

An effective form is easy to complete, to use, to store, to retrieve information from quickly, and in the end, to dispose of. Forms analysis, coupled with sound design practices, can be used to create such effective forms.

Many times, the high cost of using a form is the result of poor analysis or poor design. The purpose of this chapter is to provide the basic knowledge needed for effective forms analysis and design and to serve as a guide for forms analysts, procedure analysts, and systems analysts for achieving maximum economy through effective forms. Forms design is both an art and a science. Compliance with the rules of analysis and design should in no way compromise the aesthetics of the form itself.

16.4.1 Standard Techniques

Standard techniques for forms design should ensure that:

- The form is easy to fill in.
- The sequence of items is logical.
- The amount of effort or time needed to complete the form is minimal.
- The layout is functional.
- The form presents a good visual appearance.

Forms analysts usually devote the most time to the analysis phase. However, before a design can be put on paper, time must be spent studying design techniques and choosing the ones most appropriate for the specific form. More effective forms are created when these design techniques are applied consciously than when design options are exercised by chance or intuition.

16.4.2 Forms Design Tools and Aids

The tools and aids needed to design and lay out a form have traditionally been a design guide sheet, a triangle or ruler, pencils, and erasers. It is not necessary to be a skilled draftsperson or to use many items of drafting equipment to design an effective form. In fact, with the advent of microcomputer software, the task of forms layout has been moved from the drafting table to the computer.

A. Traditional tools

   The traditional tools of the forms designer still have a place in the forms design area. These provide a simple method for drafting a form design and are still employed when ordering forms to be printed by vendors. Following are the basic tools of the trade:

   1. Design guide sheet

      A design guide sheet helps to design a form quickly and accurately. A version of it is used by systems analysts and computer programmers to design computer printouts. It provides preprinted scales of measurement (in non-reproducible blue ink) that correspond to the space necessary for filling in the form easily by hand, typewriter, or computer printer.

      Laying out the form on a design guide sheet is usually done in pencil so that changes can be made easily as the design progresses. Two basic styles of general purpose guide sheets are available (from forms vendors or office supply stores):

      a. Open-faced style guide

         The open-faced style guide sheet has a blank design area, scaled along the borders in tenths, twelfths, sixths, and quarters of an inch. The scales provide commonly used measurements for the spaces needed for filling in information.

      b. Graph grid

         The graph (grid) style guide sheet is covered with one-inch squares that are divided into 1/10-inch squares. It is scaled along the borders.

   2. Pencils

      An ordinary black lead pencil is used for drawing lines and hand lettering. A number 2H lead pencil is recommended. Red and non-reproducible blue pencils are also useful.

3. Erasers

   Erasers on pencils can soon be worn out, so a pencil-styled eraser comes in handy for fine lines. Large hand-held erasers and soft gum erasers help clean large areas. If the forms design unit is particularly active, motor driven hand-held erasers might be considered.

4. Forms rulers

   A metal forms ruler is used as a straight-edge to draw lines. Metal rulers are available from form vendors or office supply stores. A typical forms ruler is metal, about sixteen inches long, with two useable sides. One edge will be subdivided into 1/10-inch spaces, while the other edges, back and front, will have other units of measurement.

   It also contains holes used to draw in tractor pin feed holes and binder holes. Some have templates of flow chart symbols.

5. Optional equipment

   The following items of equipment, although not essential, can be useful to a forms designer:

   • Clear plastic triangle.
   • Drafting table (preferably equipped with a parallel bar or drafting machine for ruling lines).
   • Light table or tracing table.
   • Ruling pens or non-smear, reproducible colored ballpoint pens with fine-to-medium points.
   • Lettering and symbol templates.
   • Artist's cutting tool with blades.
   • Clear cellophane tape.
   • Drafting masking tape.
   • Opaque white correction fluid.
   • Rubber cement.

B. Microcomputer Form Tools

For microcomputers there is a host of computer forms design software on the market. With the use of monochrome and color laser printers, camera ready art work can be made available for a printer.

Forms can be stored on a computer hard disk and called up as needed. This eliminates the need to stock supplies of different forms since the forms are printed as they are used. When using WordPerfect, Word or other software, letterhead, memos, and other forms can be stored on the microcomputer hard disk. WordPerfect has macro commands that can be used to pull up the needed form. A macro command contains a programmed set of instructions which only need to be entered once. Once programmed, the command can be executed to bring up the form on the screen as needed.

WordPerfect with soft fonts is an excellent forms design tool. By running WordPerfect with DrawPerfect this tool can be expanded to include graphics. A laser printer is a must to utilize this capability.

Comment:

A simpler computer forms design tool is Form Tool that retails for less than $100. It is not the only one of its kind on the market but, for the price, it is hard to beat. It lacks the power of the combination of WordPerfect, WordPerfect soft fonts, and DrawPerfect, but is easier to master and far less costly. The designed forms are stored on a hard disk and are easy to retrieve as needed. The manual is simple and easy to follow, and provides how-to information about forms design. Included with the design package is "Greatest Hits," which includes forms that can be used right away. These forms can be easily modified depending on need. Included with Greatest Hits is a tutorial to simplify the learning process. However, the use of this software should be mostly limited to the forms designer. If it is not controlled, there could be a serious problem with bootleg forms.

5. FORMS CONSTRUCTION

16.5 FORMS CONSTRUCTION

Every form has two major objectives: the first, its reason for existence, is to collect information; the second is to facilitate a standard form format. The facilitating task requires that a portion of every form be set aside for this standard format which includes: form title, the firm's name and sub-unit, instructions for completing the form, and routing instructions.

16.5.1 Form Facilitating Area

The area of the form devoted to the facilitating task is usually peripheral to its working area. This information is required to identify and handle the form, but it does not affect the data any more than pointers affect the data in the computer's database.

A. Identification

The first thing a person reads when using a form is the title. Some kind of identification is required to make the purpose of a form clear to the user. The title also facilitates requisitioning, stocking, and distributing. In addition to the title, identification includes the division or department's name, form number, date of edition, and any control symbols.

Different users, of course, are concerned with different parts of the identification. However, placement of identification data on the form is important to everyone.

1. Title and subtitle

The top left-hand corner is used for title and subtitle if the upper-right corner is reserved for filing information. Otherwise, the title may be centered at the top of the form. On a vertical file card, the top is reserved for filing data, and the title is placed at the bottom of the card.

On a visible index card, the title is placed at top of the card to prevent a break in the typing sequence. If the card is first filed in a visible file and later stored in a vertical file, the title is placed just above the "visible area." The visible area is that part of the card which shows when it is filed in visible equipment.

A subtitle may be desirable to explain or qualify the main title for the reader. If, for example, there is more than one "Invoice," each form should be distinguished by a subtitle, such as "Blanket Order," centered under the main title.

2. Form number

Some organizations require that the form number and edition or revision date be placed in the upper-left with the title. However, for most purposes the lower-right or lower-left margin is most advantageous, for the following reasons:

- This prevents obliterating the number when the form is stapled in the upper-left corner.

- This permits the form number to be seen readily when forms are bound at the top.
- This serves as an aid in stocking, particularly when forms are stocked in small quantities on supply shelves.

The form number should be printed in small type so as not to detract from the form's appearance. In addition, the number should be placed so it will not interfere with limited working area.

When a form consists of more than one page, the form number should appear on each page. Thus, if one page is separated from the others it can be quickly identified. When a form is printed on front and back, the form number should also appear on front and back. This aids the printer in backing up the face of the form correctly, and identifies forms when duplicated on a copy machine.

3. Edition date

   Each form should show the edition date or revision date. These are valuable for reference purposes in writing procedures, in ascertaining whether the current edition of a form is being used, in advising users if old editions of a form may be used, and in the disposition of obsolete stock. It is placed with the form number.

4. Page identification

   When a form has multiple pages and is folded or stapled, page numbers help:

   - Identify the form, particularly when pages are separated to fill in or process.
   - Key instructions to the form.
   - The printer assemble material for printing and collating after printing.

   Page numbers are usually placed in the upper-right corner. When continuation pages are used to complete a form and the number of the pages to be used is unknown at the outset, each page should be numbered as: "page 1 of _____ pages, page 2 of _____ pages." The total number of pages is entered in the blank spaces by the person completing the form.

5. Supersession notice

   It is helpful to have a method of notifying users and the supply room when an existing form is revised. This also applies when two or more forms are consolidated, or when an existing form is replaced by a new form. For this purpose, a supersession notice may be printed at the bottom margin of the form.

This notice should specify whether or not existing stocks of the replaced form may be used. If not, and if the new form has a different number, the number and date of the replaced form should be included in the supersession notice. If a sizable number of forms is superseded by one form, a separate notice may be more appropriate to inform affected personnel of the change. Examples of a supersession notice are shown in Exhibit 16-1.

6. Control symbols

When a form is subject to approval by an authorizing department of the firm, space should be provided for the approval number or legend. When a time limit is assigned to the use of the form, an expiration date is also included.

7. Logos and seals

Before placing a facsimile of an organization's seal or logo on any form, the use of the insignia must be authorized, or approval obtained, by the office initiating the form.

B. Readability

As a person struggles to grasp the content of a form, he/she responds favorably or unfavorably depending on its appearance and readability. Data entry error rates are affected by this factor.

Completed forms are often copied on a copy machine, or microfilmed, and the reproduced quality can be greatly affected by the color of paper and/or ink.

C. Instructions

Proper instructions aid completion of a form. They should be simple and easy to follow by a first-time user.

1. Brief instructions

Brief general instructions are placed at the top of the form, below or near the title, and tell the user immediately:

- How many copies are required.
- Who should submit the form.
- Where, when, and to whom copies should be sent.

When Revising an **Existing Form**, use one of the following:

- Previous editions are obsolete.

- Previous editions may be used until supply is exhausted.

- Existing stocks of (form number and edition date) will be used.

When Replacing an **Existing Form** with a **Different Number**, use one of the following:

- Replaces (form number and edition date) which is obsolete.

- Replaces (form number and edition date) which may be used until supply is exhausted.

For a **Combination** of the above supersession notices, use one of the following:

- Existing stocks of (form number and edition date) will be used.

- Replaces (form number and edition date) which is obsolete.

Exhibit 16-1. Supersession Notices

If detailed instructions appear elsewhere, reference should be included in the brief general instructions.

Instructions to amplify items of information or column heads are placed in parentheses after the item or head. Short instructions which relate to a specific section are placed with the section head. These points are illustrated in Exhibit 16-2.

2. Lengthy instructions

   Lengthy instructions are placed on:

   a. Front

      On the front of the form if there is sufficient space for both instructions and fill-in data.

   b. Back

      On the back of the form if there is not enough space on the front.

   c. Separate sheet

      On a separate sheet, or in a booklet.

   d. Procedure referral

      In a written procedure referring to the prescribed form.

   In no instance are instructions placed in entry spaces which are needed to expedite fill-in. If the form is printed front and back, all entry spaces are put, if possible, on the front of the form to eliminate having to turn the form over to complete and process it.

   Wide word spacing (the result of right justification produced by word processors and desktop publishing systems) must be guarded against in lengthy instructions. Because of the disproportionate spacing, words can appear to be more closely related to words in the lines above and below than the words that precede and/or follow. This can occur in text type forms, instructions on forms, or instructions in a separate issuance. Snug spacing between words makes each line an unbroken sequence that reads easily.

D. Layout instructions

   For the printer, hand lettering of lengthy instructions on the form layout is not necessary. An easy way to determine space and prepare copy is as follows:

Brief general instructions placed at top of form

Submit in duplicate, to
the Billing Department by
the 10th of each month

Reference to detailed instructions

PURCHASE ORDER
(See instructions on reverse)

Instructions to amplify other items of information

4. Name Formerly Used
   (If other than item 3)

Short instruction relating to specific section

PART D—PURCHASE REQUEST
(to be completed by purchasing dept.)

Exhibit 16-2. Where to Place Brief Instructions

1. Decide on the width of the printed column, the size of type to be used, and the number of characters in the printed column width. For example, a column 3 $1/_2$ inches wide to be set 14 characters to the inch will result in a column of 49 characters (14 characters to the inch multiplied by a column 3 $1/_2$ inches wide). On a separate sheet of paper, type the instructions, double spaced, in a printed column of 49 characters.

2. To determine the length of the printed column, divide the number of typed lines down the page by the number of lines to the inch of selected type. For example, if there are 56 lines and the type face measures 7 lines to the inch, including space between paragraphs, the length of the printing is 8 inches.

   For maximum readability, a 10- or 12-point Roman type is best for instructions. (When space is limited, it may be necessary to use an 8-point type.) When instructions are keyed to the form, it is easier to read if reference items or paragraph lead-ins are set in italic or boldface type.

3. With a blue pencil or a broken line, outline on the form layout the area in which the instructions are to be printed. Note on the form layout the source document for the copy to be printed.

4. The preceding process steps listed as 1, 2, and 3 can be omitted if camera-ready copy is prepared. This may be accomplished using a laser printer, hard or soft fonts, and a word processor or desktop publishing system.

E. Routing

The application of effective routing and mailing design techniques to multi-part forms reduces and simplifies handling of the papers. This also reduces the chance of error and helps speed up the distribution of the documents.

Whenever possible, a form should allow space in which to identify the addressor and the addressee. In this way, it becomes self-routing. Routing information in the spaces captioned "To" and "From" should be preprinted when the information remains constant. The spaces may be left blank for fill-in where the information varies.

When routing information is preprinted, use job titles rather than names that are likely to change. One change in personnel could make obsolete an entire stock of forms.

When addressing a form for multiple routing where the routing remains constant, the entries may be preprinted without X-boxes or they may be numbered. The order in which the addresses are printed should correspond to the workflow.

When routing a form to more than one address (multiple routing) when the addressees vary from time to time, preprint the addresses with X-boxes beside them. The person forwarding the form needs only to place an "X" in the box beside the appropriate address.

When multi-part distribution takes place using carbon forms, distribution appears at the bottom of each copy of the form. Printing the distribution in full on the original and all copies is more economical than printing the individual routing instructions on each copy. When the distribution is listed in full, all copies can be printed from one plate, there is no need to collate the form into sets, and those concerned will know what distribution is to be made of the form. A savings is also gained when all pages are the same color.

F. Mailing

Whether a form is designed for window mailing or as a self-mailer depends upon the method of addressing, the accompanying papers, and the volume. Current postal regulations must be checked when considering the mailing plan.

1. Window envelope mailing

    Postal regulations for mailing in a window envelope are shown in Exhibit 16-3. Although window envelopes cost slightly more than regular envelopes their use:

    a. Eliminates the addressing of envelopes.
    b. Avoids mailing a form in the wrong envelope.
    c. Precludes the possibility of errors in transcribing names and addresses from forms to envelopes.
    d. Simplifies envelope addressing when employing microcomputer printers.

2. Standard window placement

    A space four inches wide by one inch deep will accommodate most addresses and allow maximum utilization of space for the content of the form. The standard place for the window is on the left side of the envelope. However, envelopes are available with

- The address window must be parallel with the length of the envelope.

- The proper place for the address window is in the lower portion of the address side.

- Nothing but the name, address, zip code, and key number used by the mailer may appear through the address window.

- The return address should appear in the upper-left corner. If there is none, and delivery address does not show through the window, the piece will be handled as dead mail.

- The address showing through the window must be on white or a very light color paper.

- When used for registered mail, envelopes must have panels covering the opening. If transparent panels are glued to the envelopes, they may contain only matter without intrinsic value. If the panel is part of the envelope, the envelope may be used for all registered mail.

Exhibit 16-3. Window Envelope Postal Regulations

the window on either the right or the left side. Also, conditions may justify placing the window elsewhere. To keep supply costs to a minimum, utilize one size of envelopes for all form mailings.

The envelope size, window position, and addressing method must be known before beginning to design the form. This is important to insure that the address area on the form is aligned with the window when the form is folded and inserted in the envelope.

The address area is positioned first on the design guide sheet and the content of the form is designed around it. If the form is to be filled in by a typewriter, particular care must be taken to insure that proper spacing is maintained above, within, and below the window area. Marked corners for the allowable space will assist proper positioning.

3. Turn-around mailing

   A form can be designed to be returned to the originator. For example, one address area may be placed at the top for the recipient's name and address, and a second address area at the bottom for the originator's name and address. To return the form in a window envelope, the addressee simply refolds it. The form is then inserted in the envelope so that the originator's address, which may be preprinted to save typing time, is exposed in the window.

4. Self-mailers

   The use of envelopes and inserted forms may be eliminated by using "self-mailers." They can be used under the following conditions:

   a. The pieces should be folded flat, including those made up in zip code bundles, so the open edge is at the bottom when reading the address. Pieces folded to letter size aid distribution by postal employees. If possible, pieces should be folded to a size no larger than nine-by-twelve inches.

   b. Pieces should be fastened by a small sticker or a single wire staple on the longest open edge, except in quantity mailings where all pieces having the same zip code in the address are placed in a bundle.

   c. A clear rectangular space, not less than three-by-five inches, should be provided on the "self-mailer" for return address, penalty or postage indicia, name and address of addressee, postal endorsements, and other pertinent matter.

d. The paper should be of sufficient weight to facilitate handling by postal employees.

Self-mailers may be designed in the form of:

a. Postcards

Postcard sizes are governed by specifications contained in the Domestic Mail Manual (January 1, 1995). Sizes are to be no larger than $3\,^9/_{16}$-by-5 $^9/_{16}$ inches, or no smaller than $2\,^3/_4$-by-4 inches.

For turn-around mailing, two or more postcards may be attached by a horizontal perforation. One of the cards is detached by the respondent and returned as a reply. The return address and the postal bar code are preprinted, thus reducing the respondent's writing time. If the respondent is to pay the postage on a return reply, the turn-around postcard should show where to affix the stamp and the amount of postage.

b. Letter size return-mailers

Letter size return-mailers may be designed in one of two ways:

- Self-contained mailers in which a letter size sheet is folded over and stapled to be returned. (If the respondent is to pay the postage on returning the document, the amount of and place for the stamp should be noted.)

- A return window envelope is used which houses the enclosed document and displays the return address in the window.

16.5.2 Form Working Area

The form working area, often called the body of the form, is devoted to the work the form must do, or its reason for being. It is this area on a form that pulls information from an organization.

A. Arrangement

To make filling in the body of the form easier, its arrangement should make for continuous execution. Any other arrangement invites mistakes and lowers the quality and quantity of output. To introduce continuous execution into the design, three basic arrangement factors should be considered:

1. Grouping data

   If different persons are to enter data on the same form, the information to be completed by each person should be grouped according to the sequence of the processing steps involved. This eliminates searching or backtracking. Or, if a form is used as a source document to collect data on different types of material or on a different monitor, the items are grouped by related items or types of material.

   Sometimes it helps to identify the groupings in some way. The main grouping may be numbered and, if there are subgroupings, they may be lettered. Various ways of grouping items are illustrated in Exhibit 16-4.

2. Establishing sequence

   After related items are put together, they are placed in a sequence which both eliminates unnecessary writing motions and makes it easy to transcribe information from the form. This means comparable items which appear on related forms must be examined. For example, if the information on a form is entered onto a terminal screen, the sequence of the items on the form and the sequence on the monitor should be coordinated so that the information will be in proper order for data entry.

   Numbering the items on a form makes reference easier and faster. If an item has several component parts, these may be identified by following the traditional number-letter outline system.

3. Aligning data

   The data on a form are arranged so that the flow of writing is continuous from left to right and from top to bottom to correspond with people's visual habits. When this straight-line flow concept is observed, data can be entered on the form without any wasted motion. In addition, items on a form can be aligned vertically for a minimum of tabular and marginal stops.

B. Size

   The sizes of paper stock on which forms are printed should be standardized. A full sheet is cut into equal divisions which, when printed, provide finished forms in standard sizes. The sheet size most commonly used by vendors for printing is 22-by-34 inches. This will produce two 11-by-17 inch sheets or four 8 $1/_2$-by-11 inch sheets. The 8 $1/_2$-by-11 inch is now the industrial norm for a letterhead or form.

Step 1	TO BE COMPLETED BY DATA ENTRY CLERK

Step 2	TO BE COMPLETED BY DATA ENTRY OPERATOR

GROUP ITEMS

Group 1	HOURLY PERSONNEL

Group 2	SALARIED PERSONNEL

IDENTIFY GROUPS FOR REFERENCE

Group Numbered	SECTION III—REPLACEMENT PART

Sub-Group Lettered	PART A—WHY REPLACED

Exhibit 16-4. Correlated Items with Sequence of Processing Steps

The argument for standard size does not rest on reduced paper costs alone. The greatest economies are in the areas of machines, equipment, and supplies, all of which have been standardized in size, too. Anytime a non-standard size form forces use of other non-standard items, the cost rapidly mounts. Non-standard size filing cabinets, for example, cost about 25 to 40 percent more than standard size.

A form may be designed with either the small dimension or the large dimension as the reading width. The width is always referred to first, then the length. "Letter size," thus, is $8 \frac{1}{2}$-by-11 inches. Only if the sheet were to be turned sideways and used in that position would it be referred to as 11-by-$8 \frac{1}{2}$ inches. When using microcomputer printers, the normal $8 \frac{1}{2}$-by-11 is referred to as portrait, and 11-by-$8 \frac{1}{2}$ is called landscape.

C. Margins

Reproduction facilities require margins as working space for mechanically "gripping" the paper during the printing process and for trimming the paper when several copies of a form are printed on large sheets. Allow a minimum margin of 1/3 inch at the top, 1/2 inch at the bottom, and 3/10 inch at the sides. If card stock is used, allow at least 1/8 inch on all sides.

On some types of forms, the image must extend to the edge of the paper, for example, on a card form with limited space, or a group of forms which are overlapped to indicate comparative and cumulative figures. Extending the image to the edge of the paper requires printing on a sheet of paper larger than the trimmed and finished form size, and then trimming to the desired size. This is called "bleeding," which means to run off the edge of a trimmed printed sheet. If such a form is designed for offset printing, lines should be drawn beyond the image size. When trimmed, the lines will bleed off the edge of the paper, leaving a clean edge. Bleeding, when possible, should be avoided because of the increased cost.

D. Spacing

Horizontal and vertical space requirements are determined by the amount of fill-in to be entered and the printed matter, such as box captions, column and section heads, and text. The writing method, hand or typewriter, determines the amount of space to be allowed for the fill-in data.

Horizontal spacing is based on the number of characters written per inch and is controlled by the writing methods used to enter the data. Vertical spacing is based on the number of lines that can be written per inch. Exhibit 16-5 demonstrates these spacing requirements. Some forms are handwritten, some are typed, and a smaller percentage combine both methods.

E. Box Design

For posting typewritten entries the "box design" is the most favored method of forms design. It is sometimes called "upper left corner" (ULC) arrangement. Horizontal rules extend from the left to the right margin. Boxes are made by the insertion of vertical rules which are aligned whenever possible to keep the number of typewriter tabular stops to a minimum. The typing position of each line starts from a common left margin. Thus, the typewriter carriage is always returned to the same position.

Printed captions and items of information requested are placed in the upper-left corner of the boxes. Therefore, the captions are always visible when the form is in a typewriter, and the entire width of the boxes below the captions is available for the fill-in data. It is not uncommon for the box design to increase available space.

Each caption should be complete in itself but can be simplified, defined, or qualified by means of brief, amplifying statements in parentheses or in italics. A blank space reserved for future use by someone other than the person completing the form should be so labeled.

Because each space is clearly defined and each box is limited to one entry, there is never any doubt to which box a caption applies. Also, the typist does not have to space through printed captions to reach the fill-in area. He/she will not have to roll the typewriter platen up to see the caption and then back to type the entry.

Box design often produces a pleasing appearance because the aligning of vertical rules and a common left margin eliminate the cluttered appearance common to unplanned forms. The advantages of the box design are illustrated in Exhibit 16-6.

F. Columnar or Tabular

A columnar or tabular arrangement is used instead of the box design when several entries of the same type are to be listed under one heading. This eliminates the repetition of headings or captions, thus saving space.

WRITING METHOD	SPACE PER CHARACTER
Elite typewriter	$1/12$ inch
Pica typewriter	$1/10$ inch
Handwriting	$1/10$ to $1/6$ inch
Space per character determines	Horizontal space between ruled lines

WRITING METHOD	SPACE PER LINE
Typewriter	$1/6$ inch
Handwriting	$1/4$ inch
Handwriting and typing	$1/3$ inch
Space per line determines	Vertical spacing between horizontal ruled lines

Exhibit 16-5. Spacing Requirements

captions always visible,
entire writing line free

captions set in
small Gothic type

1. To	2. Department
3. From (person to contact)	4. Date
5. Project Title	6. Phone #

common
left margin

amplifying
statement

common
tabular stops

Exhibit 16-6. Box Design

In planning a columnar or tabular arrangement, the following should be considered:

1. Space heads

   The amount of fill-in data and the writing method determines the column width. The longest head determines the depth. One fill-in space should be allowed on each side of the entry to be made if space permits.

2. Determine depth of arrangement

   When the same information is wanted on known items, a preprinted stub is used with column heads. Its length determines the column length. If there is none, the estimated number of lines to be filled in determines the column length. Sometimes the number of lines needed to accommodate the fill-in data exceeds the number that can be provided on one sheet. If so, continuation sheets may be used which should carry complete identifying information.

3. Make reference and arithmetic as easy as possible.

   To aid the user, columns and lines should be identified. Columns are best identified by letters because there are seldom more than 26 columns, the number of letters in the alphabet. All horizontally preprinted items or lines can be numbered. For example, accompanying instructions which have been keyed to the lines and columns might read Section II, Line 3, Column (C). Column symbols may be repeated at the bottom of a large form.

4. Headings

   Primary or main heads are centered across the top of the sections which they describe. Information to be collected under primary heads can be subdivided into secondary heads, and further subdivided into tertiary heads. Column heads may be placed on two or more lines or abbreviated if the column width does not accommodate the printed caption on one line, provided they are fully intelligible. An abbreviation dictionary should be compiled to make certain that standard abbreviations are used throughout the organization. Explanation of column heads such as "specify kind" or "omit cents" can be placed under the column heads in italics or parentheses. If the form is to be handwritten, writing lines should be printed to assist the user. If the form is to be typewritten, the use of writing lines is optional.

G. Shading

Shading enhances the readability of a form when it is used to:

1. Block out entry spaces not to be used.

2. Emphasize entry spaces or sections to be filled in. Shading is a way of highlighting a specific item to call it to the attention of the person filling in the form.

3. Emphasize entries or sections to be processed. For example, a certain area of filled-in data could be surrounded by a screen to indicate that the numbers are to be totaled.

4. Reserve certain spaces for later entries. These spaces are not used by the person filling in the form but are reserved for later use, for example, in coding. In such cases, a suppressive screen is used. The fill-in data in the screened area are suppressed but legible. This technique is effective to easily distinguish one column of figures from another.

5. Emphasize column entries to be processed. For example, columns with preprinted figures are shaded so the entry columns stand out and are easily read by the form processor.

H. Answer boxes for X-entries

Answer boxes (X-entry boxes, ballot boxes, and check boxes are other names frequently used) can be used when:

1. A limited number of definite, preselected, optional answers such as "good," "better," or "best" can be preprinted on a form. The person filling in the form indicates the chosen answer with an "X" in the proper box.

2. A question can be answered "yes" or "no."

Answer boxes should always be marked "X" instead of check marked because:

a. There is no check mark on the typewriter.

b. If handwritten, the check mark may extend beyond the box and create a chance of error in reading.

c. Although handwritten X's may be large, the cross point of the X falls into the box and prevents doubt as to meaning. This can apply to scannable documents, too.

A $\frac{1}{6}$ inch box will accommodate most X-entries without hand positioning the form in the typewriter. The X-boxes should precede the captions. Sufficient space should be allowed between an answer box caption and the next box so there will be no doubt to which caption the box applies.

Align the boxes on the form to reduce tabular stops. Answer box captions may be numbered if the information is to be tabulated. A horizontal arrangement of answer boxes is preferred to a vertical arrangement.

6. FORMS PURCHASING

16.6 FORMS PURCHASING

There are national, regional and local independent forms sellers. Each has advantages and disadvantages. The national and regional forms sellers have their own mills. The local independent dealers work with forms sellers at the wholesale level and with more than one mill. They can place an order to fill a slack time at a mill and get a better price than a normally placed order.

The larger forms sellers can provide some services that might not be available from a local independent, such as: making camera-ready art work, providing microcomputer software for design layout efforts, and making engraved printing plates. The local independent, on the other hand, can often provide a better price, and help with technical assistance if so staffed. Local independent dealers have a vested interest in their firm, while a large firm's salespeople work on short-range commissions. They do not have to think about long-range customer relationships as much as the local independent dealers do. Large forms companies tend to deal with large firms that do not have to handhold their customers because the customers have their own forms staff.

Dealing with vendors requires a general universal procedure, as discussed in Chapter 15, Vendor Contracting. The procedures presented here will assist the buyer when dealing specifically with a forms vendor.

16.6.1 Vendor Selection

Selecting a vendor is based on what is wanted and needed. Make a list of these items and keep them clearly in mind throughout the selection process. Price is an issue, but not the only one; service can play a major role, too. What seems to be the best price is not if the payroll checks will not run through the printer.

Have the vendors bid on print jobs. Select one based both on price and on what you will get from the vendor. Do not place large orders with unproven vendors. Keep looking until a vendor is found that provides most of what is wanted at a reasonable price. This process is not the same thing as buying a computer. One major difference is the lead time required for placing a special order: it may take from two to three months.

16.6.2 Forms Trade Customs

There are traditional practices in the forms business that are defined as customs of the forms trade. These are not hard and fast rules, but they are standard practices that have evolved over time. The following cover flat forms and continuous forms produced for a customer order.

A. Forms layouts

All forms layouts supplied by the customer to the vendor remain the property of the customer. All forms layouts provided by the vendor remain the property of the vendor. They may not be used by the customer for dealing with other vendors. When form layouts are provided by the vendor, one copy must be signed, dated, and returned by the person placing the order for the form.

B. Proof alterations

Proof alterations must be well-defined on the proof. It should be signed and dated by the IS person or user manager involved in the form origination. It should also be signed by the form's representative. The party in error must be clearly identified. If the customer is in error there may be a charge for the change.

C. Art work and camera-ready material

All art work and camera-ready material is the property of the party providing or paying for it.

D. Storage of plates

The vendor is not required to store the plates used for printing after the job has been completed. If the forms are likely to become a reorder item, however, arrangements may be made with the vendor for storage.

E. Proof of stability and size

The vendor is required to state whether the proof is representative of the exact size, spacing, color, density, and shade of the order to be received. This is very important when the forms are to be used with high-speed machines.

F. Order placement

After orders are placed, they usually cannot be canceled. However, sometimes arrangements may be made with the vendor to compensate for canceling the order, cost depending on the state of the process at the time.

G. Consecutive numbering

Starting and ending numbers, lettering style, and number location must be specified when placing an order.

H. Form sizes

Standard sizes are stocked by the vendor. A non-standard size will cost more. This applies to both continuous and flat forms.

1. Continuous form sizes

Continuous blank forms paper is stocked by the vendor by the width size, weight, and number of carbons. Normal width sizes would be 8 $\frac{1}{2}$, 9 $\frac{1}{2}$, 11 and 12 inches. Other sizes may also be stocked, depending on the vendor. The 9 $\frac{1}{2}$- and 12-inch sizes are for forms for pin feeding printers. One-half inch on each side, to accommodate the pins, can be removed to produce an 8 $\frac{1}{2}$ and 11-inch form.

Any size that calls for a nonstandard width requires that a paper roll be cut down to size. For larger size paper the company will pay for cutting the roll to size, as well as for the paper itself. This results in a higher cost and a longer lead time for the purchase.

There is normally no problem with the form that is smaller in length than standard.

Printing equipment has the flexibility to perforate paper in any length desired.

2. Flat forms

The paper arrives at the vendor's printing operations in large paper flats. The paper may arrive in more than one size, but it eventually ends up as a standard size. Anything nonstandard will cost more for cutting and wasted paper.

Vendor printing costs are reduced when more than one form can be printed on a flat sheet of paper. It takes one press run and the paper is then cut down to the size of the forms.

The paper sizes (in inches) listed here are standard:

- A size 8 $\frac{1}{2}$ by 11.
- B size 11 by 17.
- C size 17 by 22.
- D size 22 by 34.
- E size 34 by 44.

16.6.3 Order Processing

When orders are placed through a purchase order, all supporting documents for what was ordered should be attached to the purchase order. The following should be considered when processing a forms order:

A. Quantity deviations

Orders are subject to a plus or minus quantity of ten percent of what was ordered.

B. Delivery

All shipments are FOB. Any part shipments will require negotiations.

C. Delivery delays

The vendor is not responsible for delivery delay due to: carrier delays, strikes, acts of war or riots, fires, government embargo, or acts of God.

D. Defective merchandise

If merchandise received is defective, notify accounts payable at once to hold up payment. Contact vendor's agent by phone, following up by letter with return receipt requested. The vendor is only liable for the cost of replacing the product and for shipping charges.

E. Form's performance

The form will be the same color as on the sample. Bar code and OCR text will be readable by properly operating machines. The machine that the form is to run on must be specified on the request for bid and the purchase order.

F. Verbal orders

Verbal orders will often be taken by vendors that the firm has done business with. In this case the vendor usually asks for a purchase order number. The actual purchase order (with the proper number) follows later.

G. Terms of payment

The purchase order will cover the invoice to be sent by the vendor. However, if there are discount terms, these should be given by the vendor before the purchase order is issued if possible. First-time customers have a delay to allow the vendor to confirm the credit status of the company.

H. Surcharge

Sometimes there are surcharges for small or rush orders. Make certain this information is known.

Chapter 17
E ND-USER IS DEVELOPMENT

1. END-USER IS DEVELOPMENT POLICY

17.1 END-USER IS DEVELOPMENT POLICY

End-user IS development policy focuses on autonomous individual and work group operations. However, this autonomy does not allow for the disregard of normal development practices found in industry. It is to follow the policies and procedures as recorded in this instrument.

End-user development will have a liaison relationship with corporate IS if no other relationship is defined, which will provide information and guidelines to be used to develop its microcomputer systems. These guidelines have been established to avoid corporate lawsuits and public embarrassment on the part of end-user system development.

The end-user management is fully responsible for any employees that do not abide by the information and guidelines provided by corporate information systems. Any repercussions resulting from noncompliance will be dealt with accordingly. The procedures offered here apply only to information and guidelines for end-user IS development.

2. END-USER IS PROJECT DEVELOPMENT

17.2 END-USER IS PROJECT DEVELOPMENT

End-user IS project development will focus on individual and work group operations. These activities can cover the following:

17-1

- Analyze end-user requirements.
- Analyze end-user workflows.
- Evaluate turnkey systems.
- Develop user applications from available software packages.
- Write user application programs using sanctioned software.
- Conduct feasibility studies.
- Conduct procedure analysis.
- Perform end-user systems design.
- Implement end-user systems.

Project development will include the following phases of project methodology:

- Identify a problem.
- Define the scope of the problem.
- Conduct a feasibility study.
- Assess the results of the feasibility study.
- Conduct a procedure analysis.
- Analyze the procedure.
- Select or develop the solution.
- Implement the solution.
- Evaluate the results.
- Document the operation for further implementation.

17.2.1 End-User IS Project Team

The concept of a project team has long been used by corporate IS which has involved users in a largely secondary role, if any. The end-user IS project team does not require corporate IS, but, depending on need, may request corporate IS systems' assistance. The relationship of corporate IS and the end-user project efforts will depend more on their individual cultures than their technology.

The end-user IS project team will be mostly representative of a single area of the company which, whether it be a division, department, or section, will have user management with a vested interest in the project. This interest is more than budgetary. The project team members will be mostly from this same area of the company.

The team will be formed to resolve a problem that has been identified within its own area. End-user management will appoint a project leader, who will be informed about the scope of the problem, and will request a feasibility study.

The project leader will conduct a feasibility study on his/her own. If any assistance is required, it may be drawn from the area being studied. After the feasibility study results are assessed and accepted by user management, the project undertaking will start. The selection of the end-user IS project team will be up to the project leader. All members of the project team, including the leader, will continue the duties of their primary jobs.

The job profile of the team members will vary with the needs of the project. The following are possible team member titles and the respective skills required:

A. Project leader

  1. Maturity

  The person must be recognized for his/her maturity.

  2. Administrator

  The person must be able to routinely perform day-to-day part-time administrative activities, such as reporting, requisitioning, memo writing, etc. This also includes the ability to set and follow schedules, meet deadlines, and handle resources and any budgets. A proactive administrator is much more desirable than a reactive administrator.

  3. IT skills

  The project leader must have the technical skill to gain the respect of the user staff and management.

  4. Company knowledge

  The person should know the formal organization chart, but also the informal organization to help the project progress smoothly.

  5. Delegator

  The person must be able to delegate and recognize that when a project team member is successful, that member gets all the credit. When the member fails, this failure is shared with the project leader.

6. Communicator

    The project leader must keep the project team, management, and others with vested interests in the project well informed. This includes informal day-to-day oral communication, written communication, formal presentations, teaching, and chairing meetings.

7. Innovator

    The project leader must not be limited to traditional solutions. He/she must be innovative and encourage others to be the same.

8. Leader

    The project team must be led through the most trying times. The leader must be able to work under pressure, remain calm, keep the project objective in focus, and still be sensitive to the team and others.

9. Maintain two jobs

    The leader will still have the responsibility of another job. The other position may be related to the users' IS operation or may not.

B. Project team members

    These people must possess skills needed for the project to be successful. They will be available part-time for the duration of the project, but will still retain their other primary responsibilities. The people could have the following project titles:

    • Programmer (Visual Basic, SASS, etc).

    • Project librarian

    • Project secretary.

    • Forms designer.

    • Data entry operator.

C. Corporate IS personnel on loan

    These personnel can be on loan for the user project for given time limits. They can act as consultants and/or project workers. They have talents that are normally not found in an end-user operation.

    • Systems analysts.

    • Systems and procedure analysts.

    • Analyst programmers.

    • Forms designers.

- Database designers.
- Senior programmers.
- Network specialists.

17.2.2 End-User IS Project Formulation

After the people have been selected by the project leader and approved by management, they meet to formalize and plan the project. The leader assigns tasks and with the team develops a schedule.

To complete an end-user project requires various skills and knowledge. At times the project may require the assistance of the corporate IS systems department which may be free or charged back to the user's budget. Tasks involved can be to:

- Utilize project management software packages.
- Perform feasibility studies.
- Document data flows and procedures.
- Design data collection tools.
- Conduct analysis interviews.
- Perform observations of current operations.
- Perform statistical analyses.
- Perform cost-benefit analyses.
- Design software application programs.
- Conduct software package evaluations.
- Write application programs.
- Design operator supporting materials.
- Sell users on the merits of alternative systems.
- Train users for the operation of systems.

The project planning and formalizing effort will:

- Determine the project scope and tasks.
- Confirm the team has the skills needed.
- Confirm that members have time for their duties.
- Determine what kind of assistance is needed from corporate IS and how much.
- Finalize planning tasks.

- Reassess member talent and required time available.
- Assign specific project tasks.
- Assign vendor contact person.

3. SYSTEM DOCUMENTATION

17.3 SYSTEM DOCUMENTATION

It is essential to understand the current system employed in the user's area before a new system can be devised to replace it. The current system must be completely documented.

This documentation requires the analyst to make personal contact with user operational personnel, giving him/her an opportunity to develop a rapport and establish a relationship based on trust with the current operators of the system. This is necessary to help insure positive attitudes toward the pending new system. In addition, the higher the level of cooperation the better the data collected will be.

Current system documentation activities should include the following:

- Define documentation scope.
- Study current published procedure.
- Study actual process.
- Document actual procedure.
- Confirm documentation
- Redefine scope
- Complete documentation of analysis.

17.3.1 Current System Documentation

Before any effort is expended on the development of an end-user system, a thorough understanding of the current system and a required needs analysis are prerequisites. This study may help avoid repeating the mistakes of the past.

A. Define documentation scope

The boundaries of any proposed system must be defined before any effort is spent because they delineate the scope of the operational activities to be utilized by the end-user information system.

The scope of an end-user information system seldom if ever extends beyond the boundaries of any one department or area of operation. The information collected for the defined area of scope may well reveal that what is expected is not possible. The scope of the study will all too often shift, expand, or even contract from its original definition.

It is important to identify key employees involved in the analysis. It is also important to reveal the critical operations and their priorities. The interpersonal, political, and micro-culture elements can attempt to alter the project scope. These must be carefully dealt with because the project requires the collaboration of all involved people to be successful.

B. Study current published procedures

The formal, published procedures should be studied before examining the actual procedures to provide information about those that were originally developed. Later, when studying the actual procedures, deviations will need to be investigated.

The reading of existing documentation starts with a general overview. This could include looking at organizational charts, annual reports, mission statements, former budgets, and the policies and procedures manual.

As the study becomes more involved, more specific aspects of the current operation will be examined, including such items as any former procedure analyses, cost studies, systems planning information, current forms and personnel staffing reports. The person doing this study will want to have his/her own file, so some documents will need to be copied.

C. Study actual process

To understand the actual current process the actual procedure should be followed through from beginning to end. This investigation can also cover the unstructured processes of the area under study. When a change from the prescribed procedure is discovered, the reason for it should be noted. If there is no formal documentation of these processes the analyst doing the study will have to record these findings in the project report, and complete the needed documentation.

D. Document actual procedure

The collected information will be documented in the form of flowcharts, forms, and written information. The actual procedure information will be collected in the form of worker interviews, observations, work sampling and questionnaires.

E. Confirm documentation

The analyst will verify the flowcharted procedures; while doing so he/she should note any problems that could accrue because of user management preferences, worker attitudes and the department's culture. The political and social environment, as well as worker personalities, are critical to the development of the end-user system.

F. Redefine scope

After collecting all the data, the scope of the project usually requires redefining. This information is then presented to the highest level of management within the department or division, most likely the person responsible for the project approval and budget. This person will always have the final responsibility for the scope, which can change from time to time.

G. Complete documentation of analysis

Completing the documentation and assembling it to prepare for the feasibility study shortens the project delivery date.

17.3.2 Information Collecting Techniques

Information must be collected when a system is being reengineered or created. The proposed operation may be a simple, short procedure or a complex end-user system application. But, whatever the end project, information is required for its design.

Members of the project team or IS personnel are responsible for this information gathering. There are a variety of techniques which make it possible to obtain the most current information needed to design an end-user system.

A. Document review

Printed materials utilized to operate a manual or computer system are collected. These items are then analyzed to provide as much information as possible about the operation: cost, job requirements, and detailed process information. The documents are grouped by type:

1. General documents
   - Organization charts.
   - Annual reports.
   - Department budgets.
   - Policy manual.
   - Job descriptions.

2. Procedure operations

- Procedural manuals.
- Process flowcharts.
- Former procedure studies.
- Work measurement studies
- Work sampling studies.
- Internal and external forms.

3. Current computer system

- System flowcharts.
- Dataflow diagrams.
- Document flowcharts.
- Data dictionary.
- Programming flowcharts.
- Monitor displays.
- Operation logs.
- Operation manuals.

B. Operational personnel interviews

Interviews are conducted in the same manner as presented in Chapter 3: Systems Analysis and Design, Section 3 Systems Analysis, Subsection 3 Information Gathering Interviews and Subsection 4 Document the Interviews (Section 3.3.4).

C. Work sampling studies

Work sampling is covered in Chapter 3 Systems Analysis and Design, Section 3 Systems Analysis, Subsection 5 (Section 3.3.5).

D. Current operating costs

Cost information for the operating department, including cost per measurable unit of output, is collected. Cost information should be broken down as follows:

1. Direct labor cost

This includes direct labor for the operating department, including per unit cost which is the cost of processing one unit through the operation. (Examples would be the cost per purchase order processed, or the cost to complete a customer order.) Costs will also note employee benefit expense.

2. Indirect labor cost

   This includes management, training, support, and corporate pro-rated indirect cost. The cost will be computed for the operating department. Per unit indirect labor cost will also be computed.

3. Direct material cost

   This is the direct material cost per unit processed.

4. Indirect material cost

   This the cost of supply items:

   - Paper clips.
   - Paper.
   - Printer toner and ribbons.
   - Expensed work aids.
   - Expensed computer software.
   - Computer disks.
   - Other general expensed office items.

   Indirect material cost will be reported as the total cost and also prorated to show the per unit cost of output.

5. Space cost

   This is the standard charge per square foot for the department's office space and utilities. This will be reported as the total cost and also as the prorated per unit cost of output.

6. Capital depreciation cost

   This is the annual capital depreciation cost to the department and the prorated per unit cost of output.

7. Other costs

   This includes all costs that have not been covered. (Examples would be employee bonding costs, software and hardware leased, etc.) This will be reported as the total unit cost and also as the prorated per unit cost of output.

E. Data dictionary

   If there is computer system in place, the data dictionary will need to be brought up-to-date.

4. END-USER FEASIBILITY STUDY

17.4 END-USER FEASIBILITY STUDY

The end-user IS feasibility study is conducted to determine the feasibility of proceeding with the innovation considered for the end-user work group or stand-alone computer system. The information collected by the end-user project team is a major input to this analysis.

For a new end-user system to be justified it must satisfy three feasibility requirements:

A. Economic feasibility

   Economic feasibility analysis determines if the solution meets measurements of cost effectiveness. This is justified on the basis of cost/benefit analyses.

B. Technical feasibility

   Technical feasibility analysis determines if the solution is technically practical: is the technology available and can the end-user and the facilities accommodate the solution?

C. Operational feasibility

   Operational feasibility analysis determines if the solution will meet end-user requirements: does the solution fit into the end-user operational environment and meet the requirements of an acceptable time schedule? It also ascertains if the human factors requirements will be met for the users, and if it fits into the social work scene.

17.4.1 End-User Feasibility Study File

When the feasibility study is started, a feasibility file folder will be labeled with the title of the study and will accumulate the following:

- an accumulated table of contents.
- all memos related to the study.
- e-mail documentation.
- vendor correspondence.
- vendor literature.
- accumulated costs data for the feasibility study.

- a log listing the calendar days and hours worked on the feasibility study.
- documentation of all meetings.
- a telephone log regarding all phone calls made and attempted.
- a copy of the final report.

17.4.2 Feasibility Study Report Requirements

The feasibility study report will be formatted in the following manner:

- Cover page, containing project title, author, and date.
- Overview of the request.
- Rationale for initiating the information systems project, or for changing an existing system.
- The body of the final report providing the details of the project.
- Exhibits.
- Summary, containing recommendations, estimated costs, estimated calendar time needed, and estimated man-hours of all persons involved in the project.

17.4.3 Economic Feasibility Analysis

The economic feasibility analysis determines if the solution can be justified on the basis of cost and benefits which are studied separately, if possible by two different people, then compared. The decision is affected by this cost/benefit analysis which looks at the payback calculations.

A. Cost identification

Costs are classified as:

1. Development costs

   There are one-time costs incurred while the system is being developed. Personnel time, including fringe benefits, is stated in dollars. Development costs can contain:

   - Personnel costs.
   - Hardware purchased.
   - Software development or purchase.
   - Document preparation.

- Site preparation.
- Furniture and fixtures.
- End-user training costs.

2. Operating costs

The operating costs are the ongoing costs incurred while the system is in operation.

- Operation personnel costs, plus benefits.
- Lease of hardware and software.
- Consumable supplies.
- Communication expense.
- Ongoing hardware and software upgrades and maintenance.
- Ongoing training.

3. Variable costs

These are costs based on production volume and include costs for such items as:

- Supplies that are based on the work load.
- Telephone and WAN line charges.
- Utilities used.
- Maintenance costs.
- Overtime costs.

4. Intangible costs

Intangible costs are those that cannot be easily converted into a dollar value. These can come in many forms; some examples are:

- Customer dissatisfaction.
- New system learning curve time lost.
- Learning errors incurred.
- Duties expanded due to creeping enlargement of scope.

B. Benefit identification

Benefits for end-user information systems can come in more than one form and must be totaled for a complete cost/benefit analysis. They can be classified as:

1. Tangible benefits.

- Personnel dollars saved.

> **Comment:**
> There is often a misconception about how to compute personnel dollars saved. One might think that if a new software package saves each company secretary one hour a week of work, then the 40 secretaries the company has will provide a savings equal to one secretary. Wrong!
>
> The company will most likely keep all 40 secretaries and the cost will still be the same: therefore, no direct savings. However, if the secretaries have been paid for overtime work, and overtime can be reduced, this can be credited as a savings.

- Intangible benefits.
- Morale improvement.

2. Cost-displacement benefits

   Cost-displacement benefits occur when the end-user information system provides for more efficient task performance. This, in effect, makes the end-user more productive by saving time or money.

   An example would be the use of a spreadsheet software package in the cost accounting department. If enough of these cost-displacement benefits assist the department, one or more cost accountants could be eliminated. Or, if a person left the department, he/she would not have to be replaced.

3. Value-added benefits

   These benefits occur when the end-user increases his/her effectiveness. Value-added benefits are long-term results based on short-term operation costs. One example is when the operation cost remains the same but the customer billing is increased. The cost of new technology subtracted from the benefits over time can produce a dollar savings. This technology also attracts new business because of the enhanced status of the organization. These value-added benefits are often realized with professional and managerial personnel. A good example would be the laptop computers (short-term cost) used by attorneys in court rooms (long-term results: elimination of time to transcribe notes, among others).

Value-added benefits can be obtained by:

- Providing more time for reviewing designs, proposals, or alternatives.
- Reducing the calendar time needed for designs, analysis, research, or planning.
- Reducing effort required for administrative duties.
- Permitting more opportunities for professional collaboration among colleagues in work-group efforts.

C. Cost/benefit analysis

After the total costs and benefits have been computed and verified, the cost/benefit analysis can begin. There is more than one technique available to do this, and one or more can be utilized.

Because of the short lifespans of hardware and software, lengthy payback periods should not be used. The time frame of three to five years is still reasonable. Whichever cost/benefit technique is employed, the analysis should be unbiased. The payback time should not be extended simply to justify the need, because maintenance costs can grow exponentially.

1. Payback analysis

    Payback analysis or cost/benefit comparison helps determine how long it will take for the proposed system to pay off the cost of developing and installing the new system. To compute the number of years necessary to recover costs:

    - Compute dollar total of expected benefits.
    - Compute dollar total of expected operation costs.
    - Subtract expected operating costs from expected dollar benefits.
    - Divide total development costs by average net annual expected benefit.

    This will give the number of years or payback period expected to recover this cost. The expected recovery cost is a one-time cost for the system development.

2. Operational benefits

    This is the estimated cost savings accrued during routine administrative operations of the proposed system.

3. Time-valued payback

Time-valued payback is the discount rate found in a present value table, which represents anticipated interest earning, inflation depreciation, etc., over a given time. An up-to-date present value table is essential to find the factor needed to determine the time-valued payback. The longer the payback the less the return on investment because the dollar's buying power becomes deflated because of interest revenue lost.

4. Net present value

Knowing the net present value allows the analyst to compute the time value of money and compare different investment opportunities which may have different costs, discount rates, and benefits.

To arrive at this figure, the costs and benefits for each given year of the system's life span are determined. The yearly adjusted costs and benefits are compared to the current dollar value of the investment. These figures are then compared with the adjusted costs and benefits to arrive at a final new present value, which can be positive or negative. A positive net present value indicates that the return exceeds the comparison rate, while a negative indicates that the proposed project return is less than the value of a comparative investment. A zero net present value indicates that either investment would be the same.

17.4.4 Technical Feasibility

The technical feasibility of the proposed solution is the practicality of its being able to adapt to the technology available. The technology can seldom, if ever, be altered for the sole convenience of the solution. This study must address all five of the following items:

A. Availability of technology

Information technology is expanding at a rapid rate. Many technical obstacles that existed a few years ago have now been overcome. If a technology problem does exist, the proposal may need to be shelved for a while until the technology is developed.

The technology needed to make a proposed innovation feasible may be waiting in the wings of the current stage production. By working with an informal information network and developing a good vendor relationship a member of the end-user project may be a party to this knowledge. This is one of the reasons some organizations use to justify becoming a Beta site.

Both hardware and software are upgraded frequently, bringing new technology to the market daily, and the project leader should follow these developments closely.

B. Practicality

The hardware and software technology needed to implement the proposed project may be available, but it must also be practical. Many questions must be asked:

- Is it affordable?
- Will the vendor be in business next year?
- Can the item be modified?
- Has the item been proven over time?
- What is its track record with users?
- Is the source code available?
- What about vendor support and documentation?

C. Availability of technical skills

The necessary end-user talent must also be available. If there is no in-house talent, the training cost and/or time required may or may not be justifiable. Outside assistance may or may not be practical.

D. Project delivery schedule

The project delivery schedule must be practical. When working back from a required finish date, the start date might have already passed. Or the vendor's promised delivery date might be too late to utilize the technology when needed.

E. Obsolescence problem

It is important to make certain, as much as possible, that the proposed process will perform as desired. The deliverable technology can become obsolete before the system is installed or too soon after installation. If this is so, the payback time might not be completed because of this obsolescence.

Hardware manufactures are no longer stocking replacement parts because of the shortening product lifecycles, and some supply items might also no longer be available.

17.4.5 Operation Feasibility

The operation feasibility analysis determines if the end-user IS requirements are feasible. These operation concerns cover the end-user's individual and group process and political needs. The proposed system or innovation will need to satisfy these requirements.

A. Is the problem worth correcting?

Will the new innovation be worth the effort for correcting the problem?

Comment:
A large Midwest teaching hospital installed an online laboratory information system. One of the supposed benefits was to have the billing information downloaded to the business computer, thereby reducing billing time and data entry cost. Except with the new system, laboratory technicians and medical doctors were entering the data. This resulted in a higher error rate than before, as well as lost time of key personnel.

B. What is user attitude?

The management is sold the new system and approves its creation. But the users are the ones that operate it. Because the new end-user system affects their daily work efforts and relationships, and their traditional ways of doing things, gaining users' acceptance can become a challenge.

Introducing new technology or a new system can create outright resistance, hostility, and even worker sabotage. This may be because it lowers a worker's importance within a group, diminishing the power and status that the former job provided. End-user work groups may lose their power, status, and credibility within the company.

This attitude can be strong enough to destroy a new system. The problem can be noticed during the interviewing phase of the systems analysis. Blind work group questionnaires will also be informative. Once attitudes have been recognized plans can be made to alter them. Some suggestions are:

- Have user management show strong visible support.
- Provide end-user education.
- Encourage end-user design involvement.
- Re-evaluate worker job description, presenting more opportunities.
- Provide new worker status symbols.
- Upgrade job titles.
- Present total picture to workers.
- Inform them of their new job responsibilities and the increased status, as well as value to the company, that the jobs will give them.
- Improve worker environment.
- Have an open house to show off the new system.
- Provide news coverage about the workers and their new system in the company newspaper.

To be effective, it is recommended that two or more of these suggestions be followed.

C. What is the political environment?

A political environment that is stable provides a better opportunity base for end-user IS development than one that is in transition or volatile. One major advantage of end-user IS development over corporate IS development is that end-user developers have a far better understanding of user political problems.

If there are political problems between departments, having two independent end-user IS operations may make more sense than a corporate-sponsored integrated system involving both. With warring departments it is best that corporate IS stay clear.

D. Are there end-user skill problems?

There can be end-user skill level problems. Senior management personnel cannot be expected to always have keyboard skills. Workers that have traditionally operated at lower level clerical positions can be very intimidated by a computer system. The terminology, the mystique, and the lack of skills can present a challenge to any group of workers.

This challenge can be met by providing hands-on opportunity for all personnel to play with the computer. If need be they can begin by playing simple games. There will be far less apprehension when a user can beat the computer in a game.

The next step is to present a slowly paced training program which should begin in formal classes and proceed to self-paced program learning, with tutorials last. A trainer should be available to work closely with these people. Some may not master the skills needed as fast as desired, but a skills handicap is like a physical handicap in that provisions must be made to circumvent them. Once these persons master the needed skills, they generally become dedicated employees.

5. END-USER PROCEDURE ANALYSIS

17.5 END-USER PROCEDURE ANALYSIS

After the feasibility study has been completed, a decision must be made by end-user management. The choices are:

- Abandon the project.
- Proceed with the installation (less complex undertakings or prototypes).
- Proceed with procedure analysis and systems design.

This section is concerned with the third possible decision: end-user procedure analysis. When designing a new system the proposed output should be the same as the old system or better, incorporating features that the current system does not provide. To deliver the desired new system the elements of the current system must be analyzed in detail.

Simple projects that do not have involved elements do not require a procedure analysis to begin. More complex projects, however, will utilize a prototype operation to expedite the process and correct any systems problems during the shake-down operation.

17.5.1 Detail Process Documentation

The process will be studied in detail from the input point to the finalization of the process within the scope of the project. For a current manual operation a detailed Procedure Flowchart will be drawn of the process elements. See Chapter 2.7.2 Procedure Flowchart for the process. For a current computer operation a Dataflow Diagram will be drawn down to the lowest detail level to show the process elements. See Chapter 2.7.3 Dataflow Diagrams for the process.

After the flowcharts are drawn they are examined by the employees performing each task to confirm their authenticity and should be examined by all the operational people involved in the process. Data information held in files should also be confirmed.

17.5.2 Procedure Data Analysis

The procedure data analysis covers current user opinions, operating costs, operations, and the actual procedures that drive the present system. While the end-user's opinions may be subjective, other collected data will be objective and correct but might not be totally representative.

Comment:
For one particular system, the data collected noted a weekly volume of 720 units processed. So the new system was designed to handle 750 units per week to be on the safe side. After the system was operational it was discovered that of the average 720 units processed in a week, 303 had to be processed on Mondays. The system could handle only 125 a day (750/5 days). The information collected was correct, but it was not all the information needed.

When analyzing the collected data, take care to insure that enough information is available.

A. Value of current operation

The effective points of the current operation will be addressed. How well does it actually perform?

- Does it satisfy current end-user management?
- Are the costs within reason?
- How well does it meet output needs?

B. Cause of problems

- What are the causes of the problems?
- Can the problems be corrected in a new system?

C. Achievability of project goals

- Will the proposed technology achieve the goals?
- Can goals be reached within the cost estimated?

D. Enhancement opportunities

How can the proposed system best add benefits to the present operation? These benefits will often be items that have not been considered by current end-users and their management. In fact, enhancements may be a by-product of the proposed technology.

17.5.3 Recording Analysis Information

The information collected will be recorded and placed in the project folder for future reference. A copy will be given to each project member and the project sponsoring management.

It will be documented in the following format:

A. Title page

This contains the project name, date, and project team members with their project and normal work titles.

B. Summary introduction

This is a one-page introduction and project summary report. It should note the end-user IS project objectives.

C. Body of report

This will contain the detail information collected and the analyzed results. Unfamiliar terms will be defined.

D. Appendices

- Sample of forms collected.
- Vendor literature.
- Flowcharts.
- Sample of any questionnaires used.
- Sample of any work sampling forms used.

If the report reveals any major items of concern, an information meeting will be held with end-user management and all members of the project team. The project leader will deliver an oral presentation covering the report and any of the concerns.

In preparing for the meeting, the project leader should

- Obtain a room.
- Send meeting notices, choosing time based on management availability.
- Prepare a presentation outline.
- Prepare visual aids (see 13.5.2 Presentation Devices).
- Rehearse the presentation in the room provided.
- Confirm that all invited management will attend.

After the meeting, resolve the issues discussed. Send out memos to this effect. If required, schedule a follow-up meeting.

6. END-USER IS DESIGN

17.6 END-USER IS DESIGN

After the detailed analysis is completed and no problems remain, the end-user IS project team may start the design phase. The designers do not have total freedom for synthesizing an optimal design. One or more factors beyond their control may influence the final design:

- Inflexibility of off-the-shelf software.
- No source code available for purchased software.
- Corporate policy constants.
- End-user political problems.
- Corporate IS's end-user policy.
- Budget reduction for proposed system.

The design process begins after the design scope and constants are identified. One of the major design constraints is the software which will drive the proposed system. The required software will come in one of the following forms:

- Off-the-shelf software.
- Purchased software, object code only.
- Purchased software, object and source code.
- Program(s) to be written.

This information should be known before the end-user IS design starts. The design tasks follow a given sequence as indicated.

17.6.1 Design Phase

The design process begins with a general design overview. Through successive iterations the general design evolves into a detail design level suitable for being turned into computer program instructions and/or manual procedure operations.

A. General logical system design

The general logical design concentrates on content components and the data handling operation of the system without regard to hardware or software needs. The logical concept is first drawn at the Context level of a Dataflow Diagram (see Chapter 2.7.3 Dataflow Diagrams).

B. General physical system design

This next step iteration includes the instruments needed to perform the tasks. Dataflow Diagram, Level Zero, will be utilized. At this level hardware, software, and people needs of the evolving system come into consideration.

C. Detail operation design

This next level uses Level One of the Dataflow Diagram. It defines which procedures will be followed by end-user operational personnel and which program modules will be required.

D. Program design level

At this level the monitor screen displays will be constructed. Output documents will be formatted. It uses the same illustrations as required for the Input-Output Prototype. See Chapter 3 Systems Analysis and Design, 3.5.2 Types of Prototyping Methods, D. Input-Output Prototype (Section 3.5.2.D).

This prototype does not have an operating program. The program design level also has no coded programs but has the detail information needed to write them. At this level the monitor screen displays and output forms can receive final approval or can be altered so that the next step, program implementation, can be started.

E. System programming

At this level the programming tasks are completed. This can consist of a written program, or can be a purchased program with the source coding provided. With off-the-shelf software, whatever customizing is possible will be done. All program documentation will be completed and placed in a program project folder.

17.6.2 Human Factor Considerations

There has been much in print about human factor problems in end-user operating systems. These problems are valid and occur when human needs are not taken into consideration by the system designers. One of the major concerns revolves around the fact that all people do not have the same size, weight, or environmental requirements.

A. Workstation Ergonomics

Adding a keyboard to the standard desk height, which is higher than a typing table, can cause problems. To be ergonomically correct, that is, most comfortable for a user, the keyboard should rest on an adjustable table top. The table top should be moveable so as to place the keyboard keys from about 25 to 32 inches from the floor.

The chair is the most important item of furniture at the work station. It is better without arms. The chair seat should be adjustable from about 15 to 21 inches from the floor. The back rest should also be adjustable, both up and down, and back and forward. The seat width and depth should be available in more than one size for workers. The chair should be supported by four or more casters.

The monitor should have an adjustable support so that the viewing screen can be set horizontal to the eye height. The light display should be adjustable for both output and contrast.

The desk or workstation should provide enough top space to spread out the items needed to work with and to store them. There should be a lockable area for personal items.

B. Office area

The general office area should be clean and neat. There should be sufficient electric outlets because computer outlets should not be shared with other electrical items. Power surge protectors and UPS may be considered, too.

Lighting is important when working all day at a work station. The ambient light should be fluorescent or indirect tungsten bulbs. Window light can be a problem if the light does not come from the north. To reduce glare, windows which do not face north should be to the left or right of the user at a monitor screen.

With laser and jet ink printers office noise is less of a problem today than it used to be. But drapes and other noise control devices should be used to reduce or mask noise if it is present.

C. Monitor screen display

It is still more difficult to read a monitor screen than a newspaper, and the laptop computers are even worse. Better and bigger monitors that reduce some of the problems are appearing on the market.

However, screen glare and reflection from current monitors have resulted in discomfort and eye strain. There is also a tendency for screens to be clearer in the middle than at its margins. Screen image sharpness has also left something to be desired. Contrast can be adjusted and a selection of three or four colored monitor screen covers may provide a solution for this.

The normal screen displays 80 columns wide by 25 rows high which is poor for desktop publishing. Now, however, there are vertical screens available which are more convenient.

D. Keyboard

There are increasing numbers of different keyboards appearing on the market. There are also a number using ergonomic-related design. More laptop keyboards provide for wrist rests and have built-in pointing devices.

E. Screen output display

Screens, as well as input documents and output hard copy, require ergonomic considerations. People in the U.S. still read from left to right and top to bottom whether it be hard copy or screen displays.

When designing the screen display, the following should be kept in mind:

- Avoid red and black combinations, because of the number of color-blind people who cannot see red as a distinct color.
- Know the users and their needs.
- Keep instructions for use simple.
- Optimize operations, using touch screen menus, pointers, etc.
- Keep screen commands simple.
- Be consistent with all systems.
- Place most often used items on the screen at the top left side.

17.6.3 Project Completion and Acceptance

After the design effort has been completed, the project should be wrapped up with the following:

A. Documentation

The design and operation documentation must be completed. The operator's instruction manuals will be completed and tested by a random selection of no less than 20 percent of the operating personnel. The documentation of the detail system design and programming must be accurate and complete so as to present no problems with maintenance later.

B. Training

Training should be provided to all operations personnel. Independent learning instructions should be provided to new employees. Provisions must be in place for independent learning of later modifications to the system.

C. End-user management presentation

The completed end-user IS design will be presented to end-user management for its final acceptance and support before implementation.

D. End-user operations presentation

This a presentation for all end users. End-user management is encouraged to be present to give its support to the new system.

 1. Introduction

 The senior end-user manager will make the introduction, explaining why the project was started. He/she will make it clear that end-user management wanted and supported the project and its objective from the beginning.

 2. General overview of the system

 The project leader will introduce all the project team members. He/she will give a general overview of the system and its benefits.

 The following will be stressed during the presentation:

 - It is the end-users' system.
 - There was a need for it.
 - It will be better for all concerned if everyone provides 100 percent support for the implementation and operation of the system.
 - There can be problems expected as with any new system. But the project team will be there to help. Users should not be afraid to ask questions or ask for help. There is a need also to learn the operation manual.

3. Close of the presentation

Just before the meeting ends, it should be opened to questions.

7. EXTERNAL END-USER ASSISTANCE

17.7 EXTERNAL END-USER ASSISTANCE

External assistance can be available either from within the company or outside the company. Depending on the corporate policy, the corporate IS organization can freely provide this service or it can be charged back to the requesting department. If it is not charged back and the corporate IS organization is capable of giving assistance in the time frame needed, its services should be utilized. If there is a charge, a cost estimate must be obtained.

If the corporate IS department is not available to supply the needed service, or cannot within an acceptable time frame, or does not have the expertise required, outside service bids will be issued. If the IS service is billable and available, outside bids should be issued to determine the least expensive source.

The service from an outside source can come in the form of consulting or contract services. See Chapter 15, Vendor Contracting for policies and procedures.

17.7.1 Software Vendors

With the growth of end-user IS software, vendors are being encouraged to market vertical software which is produced for a restricted market of common users. An example would be Solomon Software of Findlay, Ohio, which produces and markets accounting software limited to accounting end-users. Vertical market software can be found for the following areas (among others):

- Accounting.
- Human resource management.
- Car body repair shops.
- Manufacturing.
- Purchasing.
- Engineering.
- Construction.

- Billing.
- Scheduling.
- Publications.
- Drafting.
- Statistical analysis.
- Photography.

Another kind of software for general end-user applications is horizontal software. General applications are those used widely throughout companies. The three common types are word processing, spreadsheet, and database. This software may have a supplemental use by many company end-users but often has a primary use within some departments. Examples would be word processing for the typing pool, and spreadsheets for the cost estimating department.

As more microcomputers are used, off-the-shelf software demand increases. More and more vendors are developing end-user software and providing services, such as both free and billable Help Desk assistance, for the support of their customers.

One of the best sources of vertical software vendors has become professional publications where many ads are targeted for end-user applications. Horizontal software ads appear mostly in computer literature; however, they also appear in publications ranging from the daily *Wall Street Journal* to the weekly *US News and World Report*.

17.7.2 Seeking Vendor Assistance

Because end-user computing is found in a variety of user areas the assistance for such end-users is often beyond the resources of the corporate IS department. However, it can be found in the vendor market.

A. Full-service consulting vendors

These are most often nationwide firms that can provide a wide array of consulting services for the end-user IS project. Many are branches of well-known accounting firms. If quality were based on price, they would be the best because their cost is the highest in the business.

B. Specialty end-user vendors

These are consultants or service providers who have the skills for given areas of end-user applications.

C. Contract vendors

These vendors provide services across different end-user applications such as:

- Contract programming.
- Networking.
- Database.
- Client/server.

D. Turnkey vendors

These vendors provide the total system package, which may contain the following:

- Hardware.
- All the software.
- Network system.
- Database system.
- Training.
- Operational manuals.
- Help Desk.

E. Outsourcing vendors

These are vendors that install and/or operate end-user IS operations. These vendors are more involved in the operation than a turnkey package vendor would be because they also operate the system.

Finding vendors is becoming easier because of the growth of this industry. Local vendors advertise in the Yellow Pages, while national vendors advertise in national publications. Local vendors are a good source for a single site operation, but national firms would be better for multiple site operations.

National professional consulting societies and members of national professional societies are both sources for finding vendors. Another source would be published directories of consultants. The local library may also be a help.

17.7.3 Contacting Vendors

One way to contact a vendor is with a request for information letter (RFI). This gives the vendor an opportunity to analyze the client's needs and match it with what he/she has to offer. The RFI should provide the following information:

- The nature of the end-user IS application.
- The time window within which it is to be developed.
- The current resources available to the end-user.
- The expected goal of the project.
- The company contact person's name, phone number and Internet ID.

If the end-user has firmed up the plans and is seeking a vendor for a given service, a request for proposal (RFP) will be sent to vendors. This is a detailed document specifying the needed services, which may be in the form of a consulting service that is to provide contract services. See Chapter 15, Vendor Contracting for more information.

8. END-USER IS IMPLEMENTATION

17.8 END-USER IS IMPLEMENTATION

Implementation is the start-up of the end-user IS system. This should be scheduled for a lull (or slow) time in the end-user's cycle of operation. The new system should be presented to the end-users in a positive light.

The process is like launching a newly constructed ship. It will float or sink, or any possible variation in between. A lot will be riding on the attitude of the end-users, which can have a profound effect on the success of the system.

Comment:
The author worked on one project in which the end-users wanted the system to work at all costs. After a while, because of design problems, it had to be shut down. The users did not want to give up their system. They were upset and wanted to keep on trying.

17.8.1 Types of Implementations

The implementation can be carried out in any one of four ways, each having its pros and cons.

A. Parallel implementation

This is a popular and safe way of implementing a new system, definitely recommended for applications that are critical. The reason it is so safe is that the old system is not unplugged until the new system has proven itself. Both the new and the old are operated in parallel. The learning curve can also be allowed for and users brought up to the needed skill level before the conversion is made.

Parallel implementation also costs more than the other types. Extra people have to be recruited, trained, used, and then let go. In this situation, extra contract workers are the best solution.

However, implementing at the lull time will reduce the number of contract workers needed and, in some cases, the entire process could even be handled using only overtime.

B. Phased implementation

Phased implementation occurs when the new system is placed into operation in phases. This reduces the load that has to be carried by the end-users. There is less to learn at one time. And the new system can be pulled back if needed. This transition can proceed at the rate best suited for the situation.

However, not all end-user systems lend themselves to this type of conversion; it can also prolong the conversion over a longer time period.

C. Pilot/prototype implementation

This form involves choosing a developmental site that seems to offer the best chance of success with the new system. Then, if the system works, it can be implemented at other sites. Using a single site at first would be a safer procedure. The effort to train the end-user operations people can be extensive. In this situation, the workers can be pre-screened to obtain those attributes needed for a successful conversion. The pilot/prototype can be refined until it operates at the desired level of efficiency.

One problem with this method is that success at a pilot/prototype development site in Salt Lake City, Utah, would not guarantee the same success in New York City. People, local culture, and operations are not always the same. Another problem is that the process to convert all other sites at once would take more resources than are most often available.

D. Direct cut-over implementation

This type requires that operations be cut over to the new system at the same time the old system is terminated. Some applications can only be handled in this manner. It is a fast way of getting under way with a new end-user IS system, less costly than the other methods of conversion, especially the parallel implementation.

But any failure can be a disaster. While provisions to return to the old system must be in place, the credibility of the new system can be undermined if this is made public.

Comment:
There was a company in Michigan that went this route. The system was such a failure that a correct inventory list could not even be provided for the firm's bankruptcy auction.

17.8.2 Implementation Requirements

For the implementation to be successful a combination of factors and attitudes is required. Some of these factors are recognized as important long before the conversion is executed, but they are most effective if they all work in concert from the very beginning.

They are:

A. Systems design

The quality of the final product has all the earmarks of excellence. The project team, the end-users, and management are all elated about the delivery system; their attitudes alone will have impact on the success of the conversion.

The performance and reliability level of the system satisfies the users' requirements. The users are looking forward to using the new system, because it will do something for them.

B. User involvement

The end-users are very much a part of the new system because of their involvement in the analysis and the design. Their input has been recognized as important to the success of the implementation and operation of the new system. It is this esprit de corps that supplies the momentum essential to the undertaking; the end-users believe their system will not fail.

C. User-management commitment

Management commitment provides for the resources needed for the end-user project team. However, these resources alone will not guarantee success. Management must demonstrate its eagerness for the success of the project. It must set the tone for the workers.

D. Resources/value

The resources committed to the project are a testimonial of the value of the project to the company. The cost/benefit analysis can confirm this value and the resources committed to it. There should be a direct correlation between the two: the greater the value the more resources can be committed.

17.8.3 Implementation Success Factors

There are universal factors that affect the success of a project, including end-user IS projects:

A. Project size

The size of the project affects the risk factor. The larger the project the more calendar time is required. The longer the calendar time the more the opportunity for the requirements to change. The more the requirements change the less likely the implemented system will do the job needed, because the need is no longer the same.

The larger the project size the more members required for the project team. The more members on the project team the greater the communication problems. The greater the communication problems the more the opportunities for project errors and project delays.

It is better to have several smaller projects than one large one. The efficiency rates and success rates are much higher for smaller projects.

B. Complexity risk

The more complex the project the greater the risk for the implementation. There are just too many interdependent things that can go wrong.

Dividing a complex project into more than one can seldom be done. The success of this type of project would be enhanced using a pilot/prototype implementation.

C. Technology risk

The newer and the more complex the technology the greater the risks. The first release of a given software has more bugs than the third release.

A pilot/prototype is a good candidate for this form of implementation. Indeed, the direct cut over implementation of a project with this kind of risk has been called a Kamikaze implementation.

17.8.4 Implementation Follow-Up

All end-user IS implementations are required to have a follow-up evaluation needed to answer a number of questions:

- Is the system operating as planned?
- Are the end-users happy with the system?
- What parts of the system are not working?
- Was the system over-sold?
- Was the cost/benefit analysis correct?
- What else needs to be done?

The list can continue. No one point in time is the best time to begin implementation follow-up. Data should be collected as an ongoing process. Different types of problems happen at different time intervals and new corrective actions create new items to evaluate.

Reports of the follow-up findings should be given at monthly intervals until the operation is fine-tuned. Later, as the system becomes obsolete, the entire analysis and design process will begin again.

End-user IS evaluation should include the following:

A. Evaluation items

The items to be evaluated will come from end-user management, the project leader, project members, and corporate IS systems. The basic questions may address the evaluation of the total system and its parts.

B. Evaluation criteria

The criteria used will be provided by the same people who established the evaluation items. The criteria must be objective. Industrial norms may assist in the criteria selection.

C. Evaluation instruments

Evaluation instruments are items such as turnaround time, bench mark comparisons, errors per unit of process, ratio of customer complaints, worker overtime, etc.

D. Evaluation data

Data from the following sources should be collected: the Help Desk, system performance logs, operator questionnaires, error logs, customer complaints recorded, etc.

E. Analyze collected data

The data will be analyzed using past performance information and industrial standards.

F. Design corrective action

Corrective action will be designed and documented. The documentation will be sent, with a cover memo, to the end-user manager. On receipt of this document, end-user management, the project leader, other project members involved, and any outside persons who were involved will meet to design corrective action for resolution of any problems. The end-user manager will have to approve any designated corrective action.

G. Carry out the corrective action

The corrective action will be executed. At a given predetermined date, unless there is an emergency, the process will be evaluated again.

Chapter 18
E ND-USER IS OPERATIONS

---

1. END-USER IS POLICIES

18.1 END-USER IS POLICIES

End-user IS policies cover end-user IS work groups and end-user free-standing microcomputer operations which are autonomous. However, autonomy does not allow for end-user operations to disregard normal operation practices found in industry. They must follow the policies and procedures as recorded in this instrument. They will have a liaison relationship with corporate IS if no other relation is defined. Corporate IS will provide information and guidelines to be used to operate end-user information systems. These guidelines have been established to avoid corporate lawsuits and any public embarrassment.

The end-user management is fully responsible for any employees that do not abide by the information and guidelines provided by corporate information systems. Any repercussions resulting from noncompliance will be dealt with accordingly. The procedures offered here apply only to information and guidelines for end-user computer operations.

18.1.1 End-User Computer Work Groups

End-user computer work groups that are part of information systems can be to some extent autonomous. However, the more the group relies on information systems for assistance the less autonomy it will have. Even with "total" autonomy it will need to comply with universal standards for hardware and software utilization.

An end-user work group system can be a client/server operation employing an information systems server, or an autonomous work group with its own end-user server system. It can be a closed system or can be provided with a gateway for external network access. There is no restriction as to the hardware configuration of the end-user work group, as long as the equipment is justified by end-user management.

The company is responsible for complying with certain practices found in the industry. The responsibility for assuring that these practices are being followed by the end-user work group should be delegated by end-user management.

18.1.2 End-User Microcomputer Policies

Information systems controls site licensed software. The cost of software is paid by the user with charges based on quantity.

Departments may purchase their own software. However, if it is not on the list of software which the information systems department supports, they cannot expect any user support for that particular choice.

18.1.3 Personal Hardware and Software

No personal hardware or software is allowed. All hardware and software of any kind, including in-house developed programs, are the sole property of the firm. This policy is enforced to reduce problems with equipment, software failure, damage to data files, and the introduction of viruses. To restrict access to the firm's data and/or programs and prevent virus transmission, disks or tapes belonging to the firm are not to be used in personal home computers.

18.1.4 Backup Hardware and Software

End-user IS is responsible for maintaining backup hardware and software. Arrangements with the corporate computer store may be made by end-user management for the availability of hardware backup as needed, on a loan basis, to end-users.

18.1.5 End-User Training

The information systems department is responsible for coordinating and providing microcomputer training for end-users. This consists of both formal classes and individual, self-paced instruction.

2. END-USER WORK GROUP OPERATIONS

18.2 END-USER WORK GROUP OPERATIONS

End-user work group computer systems can vary, in configuration and process, from one area to another within the same corporation. However, the End-User Work Group Operations procedures applicable to "common procedures" are to be followed by all groups in the corporation. When operation needs are expanded beyond the common procedures, procedure documentation will conform to the requirements set by information systems.

18.2.1 General Operations

This subsection covers general operations to be followed by the end-user work group when operating the computer system. Each group will have a person appointed as the unit's computer coordinator (full- or part-time duty).

A. Computer coordinator's responsibilities

Following are the responsibilities of the coordinator:

- Anticipate possible hardware needs.
- Anticipate new software.
- Provide information and service for users.
- Provide for informal and formal training.
- Oversee operation policies.
- Be a source for operation documentation.
- Disseminate new operating information.
- Be the liaison between the end-user work group computer operation and corporate information systems.
- Be a knowledge source for user applications.
- Perform hardware maintenance.
- Perform software updates.
- Perform backup of files and database.
- Maintain a supply inventory.
- Be the facilitator for disaster recovery.
- Be on call for after-hours problems.

- Maintain computer security procedures.
- Police system for unauthorized software.
- Maintain an operation performance problem log.
- Write a monthly exception report to the end-user unit manager.

B. End-user terminal operations

Each terminal will be provided with a current operations manual. This may be supplemented by other manuals that are vendor-supplied or written in-house.

There are standard terminal operating procedures that apply to all terminals:

- Turning on the terminal.
- Daily housekeeping operations.
- Weekly housekeeping
- Turning off the terminal.

C. End-user operation rules and procedures

When providing the rules and procedures to be followed by all end-users, the computer coordinator will explain the rationale behind them.

- No food or beverages close to the terminal area.
- No smoking near software or hardware.
- No telephones near computer disks.
- No illegal copying of software.
- No personal software allowed.
- No personal use of computer system.
- No personal disks allowed.
- No hardware may be removed from the department.

End-user operators should inform the coordinator of any need for ergonomic devices. The devices available are:

- Keyboard wrist rest.
- Mouse wrist rest.
- Foot rest.
- Ergonomic keyboard.

- Arm support.
- Ergonomic adjustable chair.
- Adjustable workstations for special employees.
- Radiation and/or glare monitor screen cover.
- Special telephone needs.

3. IS CLIENT/SERVER PROCEDURES

18.3 IS CLIENT/SERVER PROCEDURES

In an end-user work group client/server operation, information systems computer operations provides the server. The following procedures for this type of end-user work group computer system operation are to help insure the safety of the IS computer operation. There could be more than one such end-user work group computer system within the corporation.

18.3.1 IS Client/Server Support

The IS computer operations Help Desk will provide support for general computer client/server operations. It will be available for end-user work group users with operation problems. If a problem cannot be handled by Help Desk employees, they will contact someone who can help.

The end-user work group's particular technical operation concerns will be addressed by a person from its end-user work area. This person will be appointed by the work group management and will be identified as the computer coordinator. This person will also be responsible for communicating the work group needs to IS computer operations and/or the systems unit.

The coordinator's responsibilities are to:

- Assist the IS trainer with end-user work group training needs.
- Provide informal training to computer terminal users.
- Be a knowledge source for user applications.
- Be the information systems' end-user work group contact.
- Maintain a reference library of publications for the end-user work group.

18.3.2 End-User Work Group Education

The end-user work group will receive information about and training for the use of its hardware and software. This will be the responsibility of the IS project management group installing the new system.

After it is operational, provisions must be made for instructions for subsequent system changes. The coordinator will assist with this task.

Provisions should be made for new employees utilizing the end-user work group system. There should be self-paced learning instruments, such as:

- Computer tutorials.
- Program learning manuals.
- Audio instruction tapes.
- VCR tapes.
- Operation manuals.

The coordinator will assist with the training of new end-user work group computer terminal users and will, in addition, be responsible for instructing the new end-user regarding the work group's utilization of the computer system. The coordinator will also inform end-users of pending operational changes and assist them once the changes are in place.

18.3.3 Terminal Operations

There are standard operating procedures for operators of terminals or work stations:

A. Turning on the system

    To turn on the system, the operator follows the operating manual's procedures and checks to see that the monitor display and all peripheral equipment are operating properly. If not, the operator consults the manual and proceeds when the system is ready. If the terminal is not working properly the Help Desk is contacted. Its telephone number should be on the first page of the manual.

    Before contacting anyone for assistance, the operator will:

    - Write down the details of what happened.
    - Make a list of what corrective measures were tried.
    - When assistance is available, bring the computer system up to the place where the problem occurred.

B. Turning off the system

Turn off the system in the following sequence:

1. Exit from the operating system.
2. Turn off peripheral equipment.
3. Turn off the terminal.
4. Remove all floppy disks.

C. Daily operations

Check hardware daily for:

1. Quality of the monitor display. Adjust as needed.
2. Cleanliness of the equipment. Cleaning the equipment as needed may be done at the start or end of each work day, and at other times during the day when there is high volume use.

If work station has a printer, do the following:

1. Check paper supply in printer. Add paper as needed.
2. Check quality of printing. Replace ribbons or printer cartridges as needed.

D. Weekly housekeeping

The end-user key operator/user will vacuum or dust off the keyboard and wipe clean the monitor glass once a week. High-use diskette heads will also be cleaned weekly. If the heads are not often used, a once-per-month cleaning will suffice.

E. Dust covers

In areas that have a higher than normal amount of airborne dust, dust covers should be used for microcomputers, keyboards, monitors, and other attached devices when not in use. For very dusty areas there are special keyboard covers that can be employed while using the keyboard which will require periodic replacement. Therefore, a supply should be maintained by the coordinator.

F. Floppy disk backup

When data is kept on floppy disks and not on a hard disk, the floppy disk is copied for backup. The two floppy disks, original and backup, must not be stored together. The backup copy must be write-protected.

18.3.4 Operation Rules

The following rules apply to all persons utilizing the end-user work group computer system:

- No food or beverage is to be placed on or near the hardware or software.
- No smoking is permitted near the hardware or software.
- The computer and disks must be at least two feet from telephones. Other magnetic devices should be kept away from the computer, disks, and tapes.
- No illegal copying of software is permitted.
- No hardware or software may be removed from the firm's premises without written permission.
- No personal hardware, software, or disk is permitted on the premises.
- No down- or up-loading of any non-company software or data will be permitted.

18.3.5 Accessories

Accessories are classified into two groups, ergonomic devices and productivity aids. The devices are to be purchased by the end-user work group department. The coordinator will be responsible for coordinating this effort. (The following items are not identified by brand name.)

A. Ergonomic devices

Terminal ergonomic devices are to help the human body interact with the computer system and function with the least amount of fatigue, error, and bodily harm. The following types are available:

- Keyboard wrist rest.
- Mouse wrist rest.
- Foot rest.
- Ergonomic keyboard.
- Arm support.
- Ergonomic adjustable chair.
- Adjustable workstations for special employees.
- Radiation and/or glare monitor screen cover.

B. Productivity aids

The following, if used properly, have been known to increase end-user productivity:

- Tilt'n turn monitor stand.
- Copy holders.
- Copy holder and light.
- Diskette storage devices.
- Desktop print stand and/or organizer
- PC roll-out keyboard system.
- Keyboard cover.
- Mouse pad.
- Mouse holder.
- Keyboard labels for F keys and/or other keys.
- Wastepaper container and paper shredder.
- Workstations (that include a drawer for personal items that can be locked).
- Speaker telephone.

4. END-USER MICROCOMPUTER COORDINATOR

18.4 END-USER MICROCOMPUTER COORDINATOR

The end-user microcomputer coordinator's duties and responsibilities will vary from one location to another, depending on needs. The actual title of coordinator may also vary depending on needs, but whatever the title, the objective of this person is to ensure that the microcomputer policies are enforced.

18.4.1 Responsibilities

Following are the responsibilities of the person assigned to the coordinator position:

A. Process requests for new hardware and software.

B. Keep abreast of end-user hardware and software needs.

C. Provide an on-going hardware and software troubleshooting service for end-users to handle day-to-day operating problems.

D. Provide informal and formal training assistance for microcomputer users.

E. Enforce policies regarding microcomputer hardware and software operations.

F. Disseminate new hardware/software information.

G. Provide backup service for microcomputer hardware and software.

H. Provide microcomputer LAN service and/or supervision.

I. Maintain a microcomputer electronic bulletin board for end-users' concerns.

18.4.2 In-House Consulting Service

The coordinator acts as an in-house consultant for end-users of sanctioned microcomputer equipment and software. The microcomputers can be in the form of desktop, transportable, laptop, or notebook machines. Assessing present and future needs of these machines is one of the services provided. The consulting service also covers the areas of microcomputer communications and networking. The coordinator is responsible for maintaining a compatible standard for microcomputer and LAN or WAN communications. He/she also works with personnel responsible for communications to ensure continuity and compatibility of the microcomputer systems.

Microcomputer access to mainframe databases requires approval by the coordinator before any contact is made with the database administrator and/or data manager.

The coordinator will maintain a daily log which is the data source for monthly reports of his/her activities. The daily log will record time spent on the following items (travel time will be also be included):

- Microcomputer hardware troubleshooting.
- Microcomputer software troubleshooting.
- Informal and formal training assistance.
- User consulting service.

The coordinator's indirect (administrative cost) time will be kept in the following categories:

- Reading and other education methods used to keep up with current technology.
- Communication network services.
- Electronic bulletin board usage and maintenance.
- User education and training preparation (when not charged to a given department).
- General administration duties, etc.

18.4.3 Microcomputer Training

The coordinator is the training provider for end-user microcomputer and computer terminal users and may enlist the services of the IS training unit or the firm's training department in carrying out this responsibility. Training may be provided on a group or individual basis. Charges for this service will follow established cost accounting practices. There is no service charge for the loan of text material, the use of self-paced instruction programs, or the loan of instructional hardware.

The coordinator will maintain an up-to-date library of reading material and self-instruction programs available for users. The latest versions of operating hardware and software manuals will be included.

Instructional programs will be developed in-house, contracted for with outside developers, and purchased "off-the-shelf." Unless developed or purchased for given departments, the cost will be applied to the indirect administrative training budget.

The coordinator will require a work area to house his/her office and training development effort. The whole area will be:

- Secured when not in use.
- Air conditioned and air purified.
- Equipped with furniture and storage facilities.
- Equipped with a classroom that can double as a meeting room.

A required minimum of capital equipment is needed for a microcomputer training operation. Most items will be stationary, but some may be portable and loaned to users. There should be on hand more than one of each item to be loaned. The following microcomputer training equipment is considered the minimum needed:

- White board.

> **Comment:**
> This is much more practical than a blackboard and can double as a projection screen.

- Table-top lectern.
- Portable overhead projector.
- Flip chart (floor model).
- 35mm slide projector.
- 35mm camera with flash attachment.
- Camera copy stand with lights. If daylight film is used, blue (daylight rendering) photo flood lights should be used to provide the correct color balance.
- VCR and color monitor.
- Supply items: non-permanent color markers, overhead transparencies (both write-on and laser printable), spare projection bulbs, flipchart paper, 35mm daylight slide film (film speed of 200 or more), slide trays, and erasers.

5. MICROCOMPUTER ACQUISITION

18.5 MICROCOMPUTER ACQUISITION

The coordinator will be responsible for the inventory control of all microcomputer hardware (desktop, transportable, laptop, and notebook) and software acquisitions, and should be attuned to microcomputer users' expected needs. He/she will also assist users with any future hardware and software requirements.

Purchase requisitions for microcomputer hardware, software, and service or consulting contracts are forwarded to the coordinator who approves the purchase requisitions and forwards them to the end-user manager, who in turn approves them and forwards them to the purchasing department. Purchase requisitions are used only for approved budgeted expenditures.

18.5.1 Hardware Acquisition

The procedures for hardware acquisition are as follows:

A. Approved hardware purchases

Departments with budget approval for hardware expenditures complete a purchase requisition and forward it to the coordinator who will check the capital expense budget listing and confirm that the purchase can be approved.

If the purchase is not on the approved list, the requisition is returned with a memo explaining the problem. If it is in order, the coordinator dates and signs the purchase requisition and forwards it to the end-user manager for his/her approval. It is then forwarded to the purchasing department.

B. Hardware loans

End-users requesting a loan of hardware from the coordinator will provide the following information:

- What is to be loaned.
- Expected length of time for the loan.
- Reason for the loan.
- The department and person requesting the loan.
- Where the equipment will be used.
- The person who will be using the equipment.

When the equipment is released, an "out card" with the date, time, equipment loaned, serial number, and to whom it is loaned will be completed and signed by the person receiving the equipment. The card will be filed, by date, until the item is returned when it will again be signed and dated by the person returning the item.

The "out card" file will be reviewed once per month. Delinquent borrowers will be contacted about returning the equipment. Cards for returned items will be held on file for one year.

If any damage is observed to the item it will be so noted on the card, and the card will become the source for a damage memo report to be completed by the coordinator. This memo will be sent to the end-user head of the borrower. Arrangements will be made to repair or replace the piece of equipment at a cost to be decided by the coordinator. That amount will be reported to the end-user head.

C. New hardware acquisition

The coordinator serves as an information source for future hardware acquisitions and maintains a published list of "approved" hardware, i.e., sanctioned for purchase. If the desired hardware is listed, the user need only provide budgeted funds to acquire the equipment.

The purchase of hardware that is not sanctioned will require a request either for a one-time purchase, or for the item to be placed on the approved list. The procedure for either action is to write a memo to the coordinator explaining the special request and containing the following information:

- Item's name, and vendor's name and address.
- Cost of the item.
- Quantity required.
- Reason special item is required.
- What happens if item is not approved.
- Personnel responsible for item's maintenance.
- Personnel responsible for training and operation support.

If required, a meeting will be held with the party interested in the new hardware and the coordinator. If an alternate piece of approved hardware is not acceptable to the user, and the request is not resolved, the coordinator will contact the head of information systems for disposition of the problem.

The information systems manager will inform the requesting party by memo of his/her decision. If the equipment acquisition is still not approved, the user may appeal in writing to the Microcomputer Advisory Panel whose decision is final.

18.5.2 Software Acquisition

Software may be developed in-house or be acquired from an outside source. In-house software development will only be pursued if no commercially available software can be found for less than the in-house cost. The availability of in-house programming end-user personnel is also a consideration. Arrangements for any in-house developed software will be made by the coordinator. The actual programming effort may be done in-house by end-user personnel or the corporate IS programming unit, or contracted out by the coordinator. The cost of this effort will require the end-user head's approval because it will be then charged to that department's budget.

Software can be purchased for multi-users or a single user. Most software is purchased from vendors, while some is only available for an annual fee. Also, up-grades are generally available for a single user or multi-users. Purchased "off-the-shelf" software is available in two forms: one is for the "horizontal" market, that is, for widespread use across many different kinds of firms (word processing or spreadsheet software); the other is for the "vertical" market, that is, for applications pertaining to given industries. This kind may be more flexible, because in some cases the source program is available. This can make it possible to alter the program to meet the user's own needs.

The coordinator will maintain a published list of approved microcomputer software which will be continually up-dated with newly approved equipment. It is the duty of the coordinator to continually seek and respond to needs for newer and better software. Only approved software may be used. In the event that the coordinator will not approve requested software, the requesting party may appeal in writing to the corporate Microcomputer Advisory Panel whose decision is final.

Software acquisition procedures are as follows:

A. Specially developed software

When a user requires software that is not available by purchase, the coordinator works with the user to define the needs and assigns the project to an end-user programmer. If one is not available the coordinator will submit a memo to the person responsible for corporate microcomputer programming systems and provide enough information so that a project proposal can be developed and the cost estimated.

Project proposal information is reviewed with the user requesting the program. If time and money are available, a formal request in writing is issued by the end-user management.

Program development is handled using the same standard procedures as for information systems program development. As long as no security problem exists, the new software will be made available to other microcomputer users.

B. Purchased software

The user sends a memo to the coordinator requesting the approved software. The coordinator reviews the request and, if it is in order, sends the software to the party requesting it. If need be, an internal charge will be made to the requesting department's account.

If the software is not in stock, the coordinator will issue a purchase requisition on behalf of the requesting department and send it to the end-user head for approval.

C.   Software registration

All software registration will be completed and mailed by the coordinator in the name of the company.

D.   Software library

Copies of all in-house developed microcomputer programs and the original licensed software, as well as backup copies of other purchased software, are maintained in the end-user software library which will be under the control of the coordinator. Users with one-of-a-kind software are encouraged to have backup copies housed here as well. All library software will be the most current version in use.

E.   Software demo disks

Software demo disks will be provided to users requesting them and will not be charged to the user's account. They can be provided by vendors or developed in-house.

Comment:

The software library may provide an opportunity for potential users to try software before obtaining their own copies. The library also contains proper documentation and user instructions so that software can be tested. The coordinator may be called on to demonstrate software or demo programs to potential users.

18.5.3 Communications Acquisition

Microcomputer communication systems require some planning on the part of the potential user and the coordinator. The coordinator acts as a resource person for microcomputer communications acquisitions; this requires the maintenance of an information file of LAN (and to a lesser degree, of WAN) hardware and software to be used when considering future acquisitions or upgrading. There are a variety of LAN systems today, including wired or wireless. There is even one that employs power supply lines as the transmitting media. Remote network users (mobile or home offices) utilize modems to link with LAN systems.

For modem acquisitions a user-request memo, signed by the user's superior and defining the modem needs, is sent to the coordinator. The user will be supplied with an "approved" modem with the required (or a higher) transmission rate. The appropriate hardware and software are supplied and installed by the coordinator.

Comment:
Fax-modems are now available which allow for double duty and convenience.

Microcomputer network communication acquisitions may require approval of the person responsible for corporate communications. This is especially true with WAN system interfacing or when linking two or more LAN systems. The gateway and modem selection will also require the approval of the organizational communication person. If not, the coordinator will be fully responsible for installing the micro-LAN communication hookup. Users are to be provided with the required instructions and operation manuals for the online communication systems by the coordinator.

LAN-based e-mail has started to replace information systems host-based systems. The pros, so far, outweigh the cons for this trend. Some of the major reasons for this move are: lower prices, availability of Windows support of LAN-based e-mail, and emerging mail-enabled applications.

Acquisitions of LAN-based e-mail systems, as well as their maintenance, upgrading, and support are the ongoing responsibility of the coordinator.

18.5.4 Database Access Acquisition

Microcomputer users requiring access to a mainframe database will consult with the coordinator who will then contact the IS microcomputer manager regarding their needs. The manager reviews these and contacts the database administrator for user access. If the organization has a data administrator, this person will also be informed of the user's needs. Both administrators' approvals are required for the user to access the information system's database. If it is that of another user (in the same end-user work group), or part of a network of microcomputers, the coordinator contacts the data administrator for written approval. If there is none, the coordinator resolves the problem with the user, and sends a requesting memo to the database administrator for access.

The coordinator also makes arrangements for new microcomputer users to access the database and provides training and an operation manual.

6. MICROCOMPUTER OPERATIONS

18.6 MICROCOMPUTER OPERATIONS

Microcomputer (desktop, transportable, laptop, and notebook) operations utilize recommended manufacturers' standards as outlined in the manufacturers' manuals supplemented by those provided by the information system's microcomputer manager. The supplemented manuals are both purchased and written in-house if not available from outside sources.

> **Comment:**
> Because manufacturers' manuals are often written to meet deadlines and need to be corrected after use, publishers have filled the need with some that are easier to understand.

Today's technology has encouraged the use of the microcomputer as a user information and learning instrument with the aid of self-paced tutorials or even the "help" key. This technology should not be overlooked by the person responsible for the organization's microcomputers.

Various microcomputer operations within the company may have differing degrees of autonomy, but the appropriate policies, enforced by the coordinator, apply to all microcomputer users.

18.6.1 Microcomputer Security

Desktop or any stationary microcomputers should be located in a safe environment. The person assigned a nonstationary microcomputer assumes full responsibility for the safekeeping of both the hardware and the software. Preventing unauthorized access of any microcomputer system should be of utmost concern to all employees. The following items address the microcomputer security issue:

A. Physical location

The room in which the computers are kept should be locked when not in use. If this is not possible, serious consideration should be given to employing a cable lock to deter any removal of the desktop computer hardware. Any transportable computers should be kept in a safe place at all times; this includes the time the hardware is in transit. All portable computers must be handled as "carry-on luggage" while in public transit. When microcomputers are being transported for a special event that does not permit them to be carried individually, permission must be requested in writing from the coordinator. Approval will be granted in writing, along with the special one-time procedures to be followed for the event.

If a desktop microcomputer is moved to a new permanent location within an area under the jurisdiction of the coordinator, he/she will be informed in writing within 24 hours of the move. In the event that the new location is not under the jurisdiction of the current coordinator, he/she must approve the move before it takes place and then inform both the asset manager and the new area's coordinator of the move.

B. Access security

Stationary microcomputers with a modem or network and/or hard drives with any restricted information will be required to have one of the following:

- A lock.
- An access security board.
- An access security board with a lock-slot, so the board can utilize a cable security system.
- Personal access code software (in the event the microcomputer does not have an available slot for an access security board).
- An access security board with a motion alarm. In the event that a building alarm is available, and the situation warrants, an external connection to the building alarm system should be made. The alarm may be set to notify IS operations, and the firm's own security force, or an outside security service.

C. Software and data security

Software disks will be stored in a locked place. Data disks and back-up tapes and disks will be stored in a PC media safe or other such comparable device if so warranted by the data administrator or coordinator.

18.6.2 Daily Operating Procedures

There are standard operating procedures that apply to all microcomputer operations:

A. Turning on the system

    To turn on the system, the operator follows the manufacturer's procedures.

Comment:
Approved power backup hardware is highly recommended in the event of a power failure. If there is no such device, care should be taken not to use the machines when a power failure is likely.

The operator checks to see that the monitor display and all peripheral equipment are operating properly and if it is not, consults the operating manual. He/she then proceeds when the system is ready.

Portable computers that have access to AC power supply will be checked for the status of their batteries. If they require recharging (or to prolong battery life), the available AC power supply will be used. If the power supplied is outside of the U.S., be sure that it is compatible with your hardware requirements.

B. Turning off the system

    When turning off the system:

    • Exit from the operating system.
    • Turn off peripheral equipment.
    • Turn off the computer.
    • Remove floppy disks.
    • Turn off the surge protect switch.
    • Check battery-powered microcomputers for recharging needs, and when necessary, recharge batteries as soon as possible.

C. Daily operations

    Systems are checked daily (by the key operator/user) for:

- Paper supply in printer. Add paper as needed.
- Quality of printing. Replace ribbons or printer cartridges as needed.
- Quality of monitor display. Adjust as needed.
- Cleanliness of the computer equipment. Cleaning the equipment as needed may be done at the start or end of each work day, and at other times during the day when there is high volume use.

D. Weekly housekeeping

The key operator/user will vacuum or dust off the keyboard and wipe clean the monitor glass once a week. High-use diskette heads will also be cleaned weekly. If the heads are not often used, a once per month cleaning will suffice.

E. Dust covers

In areas that have a higher than normal amount of airborne dust, dust covers should be used for microcomputers, keyboards, monitors, and other attached devices when not in use. For very dusty areas there are special keyboard covers that can be employed while using the keyboard which require periodic replacement. Therefore, a supply should be maintained by the coordinator/key operator.

18.6.3 Operation Rules and Procedures

The following rules and procedures apply to the operation of all microcomputers:

A. No food or beverage is to be placed on or near the hardware or software.

B. No smoking is permitted near the hardware or software.

C. A clean and cool and dry air working environment is recommended for the computer.

D. The computer disks and reading heads must be at least two feet from telephones. Other magnetic devices should be kept away from the computer, disks and tapes.

E. All computers and peripheral equipment must be plugged into a surge protection unit. Non-computer electric devices should not be plugged into the surge protection outlet or into the same wall plug with the surge protection device. Only grounded electrical outlets are to be used.

F. No illegal copying of software is permitted.

G. No hardware or software may be removed from the firm's premises without written permission, for each occasion, from the coordinator. Portable computer systems that are used away from the workplace will require a permission letter or ID card signed by the coordinator to be kept with the system at all times. The permission letter/ID card will identify who has permission to use and carry the authorized equipment and software. It will also contain the serial numbers of the units authorized and will identify the software contained in the system.

H. No personal hardware, software, or disk is allowed on the premises.

I. No hardware or software (including portable equipment) will be loaned to non-company persons.

J. Floppy disk labels will be written on with a permanent marker before they are applied to the disks.

K. Floppy disks will be kept in their disk containers or storage unit when not in use.

18.6.4 Backup Procedures

Depending on the area of use within the company, backup procedures may vary. Not all data and software have the same value (although it is better to be safe if not sure). The following backup procedures are recommended:

A. New software

New purchased software is backed up in accordance with the software manufacturer's specifications. If only one copy can be made, the backed up copy is sent to the coordinator for the software library. After being copied, the new software is tested. If a problem is found, the coordinator is contacted. All copied software disks and tapes will be write-protected.

B. Hard drive backup procedures

The following is recommended for hard drive backup procedures:

1. At the end of each work day, all new data should be backed up onto disks or tape. Some active transactions (such as word processing, billing, etc.) will need to be backed up more often.

2. A backup copy of the hard drive software is maintained on disk or tape.

C. Floppy disk data

When data is kept on floppy disks and not on a hard drive, the floppy disk is copied for backup. The two copies of the floppy disks are not stored together. It is recommended that the backup copy be write-protected.

18.6.5 Microcomputer System Crash

In the event of a microcomputer system crash, the operator turns off the power, writes down what occurred just prior to the crash, as well as the time of the crash, and contacts the coordinator or key operator for assistance. A sign should be posted on the computer stating that the system has crashed and the equipment is not to be used. Portable computers should be taken to the coordinator.

18.6.6 Hardware Problems

For hardware problems, the operator refers to the operating manual. If the problem cannot be corrected, the problem and its effect on the hardware are noted, and the coordinator or key operator is contacted. A sign is placed on the (desktop) microcomputer indicating that it is not working and is not to be used. If a peripheral device does not work, a sign is placed on the device noting that it is out of order and indicating whether or not the computer is useable without the device.

18.6.7 Software Problems

For software problems, the operator contacts the Help Desk. In the event that the Help Desk cannot resolve the problem, the operator contacts the coordinator.

Before contacting anyone for assistance, however, the operator will:

*   Write down the details of what happened.
*   Make a list of what corrective measures were tried.
*   When assistance becomes available, bring the software up on the computer at the place where the problem occurred.

18.6.8 Accessories and Supplies

Microcomputer accessories can improve productivity, reduce fatigue, and improve morale. These accessories and supply items will be on a "recommended or approved list" provided by the coordinator and carried by the corporate computer store. Other items not stocked will be listed, with their vendors, by the computer store. This information helps when ordering through the purchasing department. The approved list of items will be published, updated, and distributed by the coordinator.

The items can be purchased from the user's department petty cash fund or with a budget requisition. Accessories are classified as production aids or ergonomic devices. Supply items will be requisitioned from the unit responsible for office or computer supplies. The standard operating procedure for requisitioning office supplies or computer supplies will be followed.

Accessories come in two groups, ergonomic devices and productivity aids. (The following items are not identified by brand name.)

A. Ergonomic devices

Microcomputer ergonomic devices are to help the human body interact with the microcomputer system and function with the least amount of fatigue, error, and bodily harm. The following types are available on the "recommended list" provided by the microcomputer store:

- Keyboard wrist rest.
- Mouse wrist rest.
- Foot rest.
- Ergonomic keyboard.
- Arm support.
- Ergonomic adjustable chair.
- Adjustable workstations for special employees.
- Radiation and/or glare monitor screen.

Comment:
REMEMBER THE REQUIREMENTS FOR THE AMERICANS WITH DISABILITIES ACT!

B. Productivity aids

The following, if used properly, have been known to increase productivity:

- Tilt'n turn monitor stand.
- Copy holders (flex arm, attachable or standard).
- Copy holder light.
- Diskette storage devices.
- Cartridge storage devices.
- Desktop print stand and/or organizer.
- PC roll-out keyboard system.
- Keyboard cover.
- Mouse pad.
- Mouse holder.
- Keyboard labels for F keys and/or other keys.
- Wastepaper container and paper shredder.
- Workstations that include a drawer that can be locked for personal items.
- Speaker telephone.

7. END-USER ASSET MANAGEMENT

18.7 END-USER ASSET MANAGEMENT

Developing, installing, and operating an asset management system is a complex effort. The development and installation should be handled as an end-user asset management project, and the installation should provide a well-documented, operating end-user asset management system.

A project leader should be appointed who, in addition to having the qualities and skills of a good project leader, should also be familiar with end-user microcomputer hardware and software and understand software licenses and copyrights.

> **Comment:**
>
> The corporate computer asset manager should contact the Software Publishers Association at 1730 M St. NW Suite 700, Washington, DC 20036-4510, or call (800) 388-7478 for current microcomputer and client/server information. A copy of the Association's latest newsletter is available on the Internet at *www.sta.org*, and anti-piracy information is available through its home page. Software Publishers Association can provide information, courses, and membership opportunities. It would be advisable to have both the project manager and corporate computer asset manager attend a Software Publishers Association seminar.

18.7.1 Developing the Asset Management Plan

The project leader and the corporate computer asset manager develop the asset management plan, with the approval of the end-user head. The plan should contain the following:

A. Asset management project team

    An asset management project team will be formed, the size to be determined by the end-user head.

B. Preplanning survey

    The project team will develop a hardware and software asset management plan. Before the plan is completed, a survey will be conducted as to current

    - Internal hardware controls.
    - Internal software controls.
    - Acquisition procedures for hardware and software.
    - Microcomputer data and software protection.
    - Software license compliance.
    - Unauthorized microcomputer hardware.
    - Unauthorized microcomputer software.

This information will define the current status to be used as a control. It will also provide information as to how the asset management system can be installed with a minimum of conflict and effort.

C. Asset management plan

The plan will utilize the information from the preplanning survey to:

- Define components of the proposed asset management system.
- Draft a project timetable.
- Plan the selection of standard software.
- Plan for the communication and implementation.
- Plan for the needed controls.
- Select a user test area for the system.
- Determine project and operation costs.

18.7.2 Plan Implementation

The implementation of the plan will be a major part of the asset management project. Following are its major areas:

- Selecting and obtaining delivery of software.
- Installing the software.
- Testing the software.
- Training operational personnel.
- Setting up the Help Desk.
- Preparing for a system audit.
- Asset tagging the hardware and making an inventory of the software.
- Establishing proof of purchase.
- Taking corrective actions.
- Developing continual audit program.
- Putting in place an operating hardware/software acquisition system.
- Maintaining a microcomputer users' education program.
- Installing and maintaining a disaster recovery system.
- Providing a network security and virus system.

18.7.3 Implementation and Operation

The implementation may start in a prototype area, preferably one that will offer the best opportunity to debug the system. After a particular area is operational, the system can be implemented in additional areas. Following are steps to be followed to implement and operate the new asset management system:

A. Inventory of hardware

    The inventory should taken in the shortest calendar time possible. After each unit has been inventoried, an update procedure, augmented by random inventory spot checks, should be put in place to maintain a current inventory.

    Each hardware item will be tagged with a scannable inventory tag placed on the equipment in the same location for each type of hardware.

    Each new acquisition of hardware must be tagged before the system is operational. The cost, department, and employee-assigned ownership of the hardware will be input to the microcomputer inventory system.

B. Physical inventory of software

    The inventory of microcomputer software can be taken at the same time as the hardware inventory or later. This will depend on the system software selected. The software of each microcomputer and file server will be identified and logged in. Unauthorized software will be purged and recorded in order to identify to what degree, for each area and user, software violations have occurred.

    This software data, by each microcomputer (desktop, laptop and notebook system) and person responsible for that computer, will be input to the microcomputer inventory system. Cost, department, and employee-assigned ownership information relating to new microcomputer software added later will also be input to the system.

C. Microcomputer inventory system

    The microcomputer inventory system will be used by departments and employees within departments to maintain an ongoing microcomputer hardware and software inventory. The system will generate a physical inventory report by department after the first and each of the subsequent inventories. The report will also be run at the end of each fiscal year and upon demand by the software coordinator. A copy of the department report will be sent to the department head and to the software coordinator. It will list the following:

    *   The department name.
    *   The date the physical inventory was taken.

- The name, total quantity, and total cost of each software type.
- The total cost of the department's software inventory.
- The number of each kind of software removed.

A detailed listing of each employee and his/her assigned microcomputers will also be produced. A copy of this Department Users Report will be sent to the coordinator, the department head and will be available for the software coordinator, if requested. It will contain the department name and the date of the inventory. This report will also list the following by each employee:

- Hardware assigned.
- Software on each computer after inventory.
- Unauthorized software removed, by computer.
- Total cost of hardware.
- Total cost of software.
- Total cost of both hardware and software.

A Department Hardware Inventory Report will be run, after the Department Users Report, for each department. A copy will be sent to the department head, to the coordinator, and to the corporate computer asset manager. It will list:

- The department name.
- The date the report was run.
- The hardware type, quantity, and total cost of each type.
- The total cost of the department's hardware inventory.

A Total Hardware/Software Asset Report will be run, listing the hardware/software assets by department. There will be four columns across each page: department name, number of PCs, total original investment for hardware/software, and average age of department PCs. The bottom line will indicate totals of the same information for the whole company. This report is to be run at the end of the fiscal year and upon demand. It will be sent to the head of information systems, the controller, and the corporate computer asset manager.

Chapter 19
GLOSSARY OF IS TERMS

1. GLOSSARY

19.1 GLOSSARY

ABORT To cancel, or terminate, a program, command or operation while in process.

ACCESS To retrieve data or program instructions from "secondary storage" (hard disk, floppy disk, or tape) or another on-line computer device.

ACCESS CODE An identification code or password used to gain access to a computer system.

ACCESS SYSTEM MENU The menu which appears when a program identification is typed at a DOS or program menu prompt. This access system menu enables the program to begin.

ACCESS TIME The period that elapses between the time the system issues a command for data retrieval and the time the data is transferred from its source.

ACCORDION FOLD Two or more folds that open like the pleats in an accordion.

ACOUSTIC COUPLER A modem with cups that fit around the ear and mouthpiece of a standard telephone.

ACRONYM A word formed by joining the first letters of a series of words such as FORTRAN (FORmula TRANslator) or LAN (Local Area Network).

ADA A high-level programming language developed by the U.S. Department of Defense.

ADAPTER A circuit board that plugs into a computer's expansion bus and increases the computer's capability.

ADDRESS A unique identifier associated with a station, line, path, or unit. Addresses of main memory are for instructions or data locations. LAN addresses are assigned for each device on line. Random access storage requires an address locator to find the actual location address of the record sought. For example, finding John Smith's record in storage would require matching "John Smith" to the address location that holds the record. Tape devices have no address locations. A tape drive would have to read the name element of each record until it located the one for John Smith.

AFTERMARKET The market for peripherals or software which is created by the sale of large numbers of a specific brand of computer. For example, sales of the IBM 400 computer have created a market for software or hardware peripherals, which have been developed by companies other than IBM.

AGAINST THE GRAIN Folding or feeding paper at right angles to the grain of the paper.

ALGORITHM A specific set of mathematical and logical procedures which a computer can follow to solve a problem.

ALPHANUMERIC CHARACTERS Character letters (A to Z), numbers (0 to 9), punctuation, and special symbols.

AMERICAN NATIONAL STANDARDS INSTITUTE (ANSI) Organization devoted to the voluntary development of standards. It has worked with the computer industry to develop standards for languages such as FORTRAN and COBOL.

AMPLIFIER A device that reproduces and enlarges but does not regenerate an electrical signal.

ANALOG A continuously varying electrical signal with an infinite number of amplitudes.

ANSI SCREEN CONTROL A set of standards developed by ANSI to control the information display of computer CRT screens.

API (APPLICATION PROGRAM INTERFACE) A method of allowing an application to interact directly with certain functions of an operating system or another application.

APL (A Programming Language) A high-level language used for programming scientific or mathematical applications.

APPC (ADVANCED PROGRAM-TO-PROGRAM COMMUNICATIONS) A component of IBM's System Network Architecture, APPC is designed to allow communications, on a more or less peer-to-peer basis, between programs running on different systems.

APPLICATION A term used to refer to a software program that accomplishes a certain task.

APPLICATION LAYER The layer of the OSI model concerned with application programs such as electronic mail, database manager, and file server software.

APPROVED LIST This is a list of computer software for which the IS department will provide user support.

AR The acronym for automatic repeat request. A request for a repeat is initiated when incorrectly received data is rejected.

ARCHITECTURE A system's architecture is described by the type of components, interfaces, and protocols it uses and how these elements fit together.

ARCHIVAL BACKUP A procedure to backup or copy files in secondary storage onto another secondary storage device.

ARCNET A widely used LAN architecture developed by Datapoint Corporation that uses a logical token-passing access method at 2.5 Mbps.

ARPANET A wide area network developed by the Defense Advanced Research Projects Agency that primarily connects universities and government agencies that are on the Internet.

ASCII (AMERICAN STANDARD CODE FOR INFORMATION INTERCHANGE) A standard for encoding characters (including the upper and lowercase alphabet, numerals, punctuation, and control characters) using seven bits. The standard set is 128 characters; IBM expanded this to 256 by adding an eighth bit to each existing character. This expanded set provides graphic, mathematical, scientific, financial, and foreign language characters.

ASSEMBLER Software that transforms an assembly language source code program into machine language. One assembler instruction code produces one machine language instruction.

ASSEMBLY LANGUAGE A lower-level programming language in which one statement is written for each machine language step.

ASYNCHRONOUS COMMUNICATIONS SERVER A device on a LAN that provides the capability for network workstations to access ASCII applications via switched communications lines.

AUDIT TRAIL A means of locating the origin of specific data that appears on final reports.

AUIC (ATTACHED UNIT INTERFACE CABLE) A four-twisted-pair cable that connects an "Ethernet" device to an Ethernet external transceiver.

BACKBONE NETWORK A network that inter-connects other networks.

BACKGROUND PROCESS When a multi-tasking operating system allows an operation to run in the background while it runs a second operation in the foreground.

BACKUP A copy of a file, directory, or volume placed on a separate storage device for the purpose of retrieval in case the original is accidentally erased, damaged, or destroyed.

BAD BLOCK TABLE A list of blocks on a disk that are unuseable.

BALLOT BOX See "X-Box."

BAR CODE A printed pattern of vertical lines used to represent numerical codes in a scannable reading form.

BASIC A high-level programming language. The written source code utilizes a compiler to generate an operating object coded program. The compilers are developed to run on different computers, and each compiler generates object programs for a specific computer. The source coding is very much the same but the produced machine-coded object programs are not. Some of the early PC computers used an Interpreter Basic which performed in ROM. It had a Basic interpreter which read each Basic instruction, translated it into machine language instructions, and then returned to ROM for the next Basic step translation.

BATCH FILE An ASCII text file with a .BAT extension. When the file is run each command will execute in sequence as if it were typed from a DOS prompt.

BATCH PROCESSING When like transactions are grouped into a single batch for processing.

BAUD A unit of signaling speed, not necessarily the bit rate.

BAUD RATE The rate at which data are transferred over a serial interface.

BENCHMARK A standard measurement used to test the performance of hardware or software.

BINDING Joining a group of sheets of printed paper into a single unit or book. Binding may be accomplished by means of adhesives, sewing, stitching, etc.

BINDING EDGE The edge of a sheet, or web, where binding is to take place.

BINDING MARGIN The area along the edge of a form that is to be bound or fastened.

BIT A binary digit; must be either a zero (on) or a one (off). The smallest possible unit of information in a digital system.

BIT ORDER The order of transmission of a serial system. Typically, the least significant bit (LSB) is sent first.

BLEED The area of the printed image extending beyond the trim edge.

BLOCKOUT A printed pattern used to obscure information in selected areas of selected copies.

BLOWUP An enlargement of copy.

BODY TYPE Type used for the main body or text of a job.

BOLDFACE Heavy-face type in contrast to light-face type. Used for emphasis in headings, subheadings, titles, etc.

BOND PAPER A grade of writing or printing paper where strength, durability, and permanence are essential requirements. Used for letterheads, business forms, etc.

BOOK Group of forms, single or in sets, bound at one margin in some manner.

BOOTLEG FORM A unauthorized form outside the jurisdiction of the forms control program of an organization where such a program exists.

BORDER A design printed along the outer edges of a form, usually as a protective measure. Intricate borders on checks and stock certificates reduce the chance of illegal or unauthorized reproduction.

BORDER RULE Heavy rules at top or bottom of or completely around a printed form.

BOTTLENECK A factor that restricts the flow of data through a system. When a bottleneck exists, performance is limited.

BOTTOM STUB Unit set construction in which the stub is at the foot of the form.

BOX Any small square printed on a form to be marked by the user ("X" is preferred to a check mark) to denote the applicability of a related word or phrase. Also referred to as "x-box," check box, ballot box.

BOX DESIGN (In forms layout) A type of layout that uses boxes to define placement of entries on a form.

BREAK FOR COLOR To separate parts that are to be printed in different colors.

BROADBAND A transmission system in which signals are encoded and modulated into different frequencies which allow for transmission of more than one input signal over the same line simultaneously.

BROADCAST A LAN data transmission scheme in which data packets are heard by all stations on the network, but are only received by the intended station.

BROUTER A brouter is used as a bridge and a router at Layers 2 and 3, respectively.

BROWNOUT A period when there is low voltage electric power because of increased demands.

BUFFER A memory device which holds information temporarily to compensate for differences in speed between computer components.

BUG A programming error that causes a program or a computer system not to perform as expected.

BUNDLED SOFTWARE Software which is included with a hardware system as part of the total price.

BUS A common connection. Networks that broadcast to all stations, such as Ethernet broadcasting to ARCnet, are considered bus networks.

BUS (PC) The connectors on a PC motherboard into which expansion boards are plugged.

BYTE Eight continuous bits which represent one character in memory.

BURSTER Machine used to separate continuous forms into single-part forms or sets.

CACHE To read data into a memory buffer so the information is available whenever needed and does not have to be read from the disk again.

CACHE BUFFER An area in RAM used for caching.

CALENDAR TIME The actual duration of a project, from the date it starts to the date it is completed. This includes both work and nonwork days.

CAMERA-READY COPY Any material ready to be photographed for reproduction without further change. May be typewritten copy, reproduction proofs, art work, or previously printed material.

CAPS AND SMALL CAPS Two sizes of capital letters in one size of type, commonly used in most Roman typefaces.

CAPTION Printing associated with an individual item that indicates to the form user what is to be entered or that identifies information already entered.

CAPTURED DATA Data that is in machine-readable form.

CARBON Paper with a pigmented coating for the purpose of effective image transfer (write-through) under impact or pressure.

CARBON BLACK The actual coloring material, or pigment, used with most black, nonsolvent carbon formulas.

CARBON-INTERLEAVED FORM Any continuous or unit set employing carbon paper to effect write-through.

CARBON SPOTTING Layout of carbon coating only on selected areas of a sheet of carbon. Used with reference to striped or pattern carbon.

CARBONLESS PAPER Any stock coated, manufactured, or treated to provide multiple copies without use of carbon interleaves or a carbon-type coating. The "mated chemical carbonless" system requires two paper surfaces to come in contact with each other. Each has a different, relatively colorless coating that reacts under impact or pressure to form a visible image on one surface ("coated front or CF surface"). "Self-contained chemical carbonless" paper ("self-imaging" paper) has the two materials coated on or manufactured into the same sheet. These papers are used to print in-house multipage forms.

CARRIER A base analog signal that is modulated to carry information.

CASEBOUND A book bound with a hard cover. The cover and text are manufactured as separate items. The last binding operation is to fasten case and text together.

CATHODE RAY TUBE (CRT) A computer output monitor screen.

CD/ROM A read-only optical storage device employing compact optical disk.

CHARACTER Number, letter, or other symbol that is one unit of a font or type array.

CHARACTER READING Machine reading of printed characters by optical means.

CHARACTER SPACING Horizontal distance between corresponding reference points of a series of machine-printed characters (also called "pitch" or "escapement" with typewriters and similar devices).

CHIP A miniature electronic circuit which is mass produced on silicon wafers (also called chips).

CLC Caps and lowercase, normally used for headings or titles, consisting of type in which only the first letter of each word is capitalized.

CLIENT A computer that accesses the resources of a server. See "client/server."

CLIENT/SERVER A network system design in which a processor or computer designated as a server such as a file server or database server provides services to clients' workstations or microcomputers.

CLIP ART A collection of graphic images available for use with desktop publishing.

CLOCK A signal used to synchronize the transmitter and receiver in a synchronous system.

COATED FRONT OR CA SURFACE See "mated chemical carbonless."

COAXIAL CABLE A commonly used cable type that is relatively insensitive to noise interferences, consisting of one or two insulating layers and two conductors. A central conductor wire is surrounded by the first layer of insulation. An outer shielding conductor is laid over the first layer of insulation. Usually the cable is then covered with a second layer of insulation.

COBOL (Common Business Oriented Language) A high-level language for programming business applications. It employs a compiler that converts one line of source code to one or more object code instructions. In the first part of the source coding, the computer used for compiling and the computer on which the object code is to run are identified. The two computers need not be the same.

COLLATING Gathering sheets or computer records in proper pre-identified order.

COLOR CODING Use of different colored stock, tinting, or printed marks on individual parts of a set to aid in identification and distribution.

COLUMN HEAD A heading that identifies a series of entries to be made in columnar sequence below.

COLUMNAR DESIGN A type of layout that makes use of vertical rules for form columns in which items of similar data are entered in list form.

COMMUNICATIONS PROTOCOL A list of parameters and standards that govern communications between computers employing telecommunications.

COMPILER A program which reads high-level program coding statements (source code) and translates the statements into machine executable instructions (object code).

COMPOSITION Typographic material that has been set and/or assembled. Also, the process of preparing this material for printing.

COMPUTER SYSTEM A complete computer installation with all the required peripherals needed for elements to work with each other as one system.

CONCENTRATOR A 10 BASE-T hub. A multiport repeater for Ethernet/802.3 used over unshielded twisted-pair cable.

CONDENSED TYPE A narrow or slender typeface.

CONSOLE A computer display terminal consisting of a monitor and keyboard.

CONTACT PRINT A photographic print made from a negative or positive using sensitized paper, film, or a printing plate.

CONTINUOUS PAPER A long strip of paper with perforations separating the pages (with paper tractor feeding sides) so that it can be tractor-fed from a printer. Also, a long strip of paper with no cuts or perforations separating the pages.

CONTRAST The tonal gradation between highlights and dark areas on a monitor screen.

CONTROLLER BOARD A device that enables a computer to communicate with a particular device (such as a disk or tape drive). It manages input/output and regulates the operation of its associated device.

COPY Any material furnished (typewritten manuscript, pictures, art work, etc.) to be used in a product to be printed.

COPY PROTECTION The inclusion in a program of hidden instructions intended to prevent unauthorized copying of software.

CORRUPTED FILE A file that contains scrambled and unrecoverable data.

COST-BENEFIT ANALYSIS A projection of the costs incurred in and benefits derived from installing hardware, software, or a proposed system.

COVER PAPER Any of a great variety of papers used for the outside covers of catalogs, brochures, booklets, and similar pieces.

CPM (CRITICAL-PATH METHOD) A process used in project management for the planning and timing of tasks that relies on the identification of a critical path. The time needed for the series of tasks along the critical path determines the total project completion time.

CRC The acronym for cyclical redundancy check. This ensures the validity of received data.

CUSTOM FORM Form manufactured to unique order specifications by a vendor.

CUT FORMS Forms delivered as individual sheets, not bound or padded.

DAISYWHEEL PRINTER An impact printer that has the print characters on the pedal tips, used on office typewriters.

DAMS Database management system organized to control a collection of information.

DAT Digital audio tape. Popular tape back-up format.

DATA Units of information stored on some type of magnetic media that can be called into a computer program for use.

DATA COMMUNICATIONS The transfer of information from one computer to another.

DATA DICTIONARY A list of data elements used in database management programs. Each data element contains information about its use, its size, its characteristics, who can use it, who can alter it, who can remove it, and who can only view it.

DATA ELEMENT A field containing an element of information used in records found in database management systems. Examples would be: FICA number, name, part number, etc.

DATA INDEPENDENCE Data is stored in such a way that users can gain access to it in a database system without knowing where the data is actually located.

DATA MANAGER A person responsible for the management of all corporate data. The database manager may report directly or indirectly to this person.

DATA PROCESSING The preparing, storing, or manipulation of information within a computer system.

DATA RECORD A complete addressable unit of related data elements expressed in identified data fields used in files and database systems.

DATA REDUNDANCY The same data stored in more than one location.

DATABASE An organized collection of information, in random access secondary storage, made up of related data records. There can be more than one database in a computer system.

DATABASE MANAGEMENT PROGRAM A data application program that provides for the retrieval, modification, deletion, or insertion of data elements. Database systems tend to reduce "data redundancy."

DATABASE MANAGER The person responsible for managing the corporate IS database. This person reports to the head of corporate information systems, but can report to the corporate data manager, too.

DATABASE SERVER A database server is the back-end processor that manages the database and fulfills database requests in a client/server system.

dBase A popular microcomputer database management system.

DEBUGGING The procedure of locating and correcting program errors.

DECISION TREE A graphic representation of all possible conditions or processing alternatives and end results. It resembles the branches of a tree growing out from the main trunk.

DECOLLATOR Machine used to separate continuous forms into individual piles or to remove interleaved carbon(s).

DEDICATED FILE SERVER A file server that cannot be operated as a user's server workstation. See "file server."

DE FACTO STANDARD A standard based on broad usage and support.

DEFAULT A value or option that is chosen automatically when no other value is specified.

DEMODULATION The process of recovering information impressed on a carrier signal by modulation.

DESK CHECKING Checking for errors in a program listing or on a computer monitor screen.

DESKTOP PUBLISHING The use of a microcomputer to generate camera-ready copy for printing. Requires the use of one of the available desktop publishing software programs.

DIE CUTTING The use of sharp steel rules to cut special shapes, such as labels, boxes, and containers, from printed sheets. Die cutting can be done on either flat-bed or rotary presses.

DIMENSIONAL STABILITY Ability to maintain size and shape; resistance of paper or film to dimensional change with change in moisture content or relative humidity.

DINGBAT Stock symbol, such as a star, triangle, dot, or arrow, usually used for visual emphasis.

DIRECTORY An index to the files stored on a disk that can be displayed on the monitor.

DISK CHANNEL All components, including the disk(s), that connect a disk drive or drives to a file server. This includes the host adapter or disk controller and cables.

DISK CONTROLLER A hardware device associated with a disk drive that controls how data is written to and retrieved from the disk.

DISK DRIVE The unit in a computer which reads and writes information to and from disks.

DISK DUPLEXING A method of safeguarding data in which the data is copied simultaneously to two hard disks on separate channels. If one channel fails, the data on the other channel remains unharmed. When data is duplexed, read requests are sent to whichever disk in the pair can respond faster, decreasing the file server's response time.

DISK MIRRORING A method of safeguarding data in which the same data is copied to two hard disks on the same channel. If one of the disks fails, the data on the other disk is safe. Because the two disks are on the same channel, mirroring provides only limited data protection; a failure anywhere along the channel could shut down both disks and data would be lost. See also "disk duplexing."

DISPLAY TYPE Type set larger than the text type. Used to attract attention.

DISTRIBUTED PROCESSING SYSTEM A computer system designed for multiple users with fully functional computer access.

DO/WHILE LOOP A loop control structure that continues to carry out its functions as long as an external condition is satisfied in a program.

DOCUMENTATION The instructions and references that provide users with the necessary information to use computer programs and systems or alter them at a later date.

DOT-MATRIX PRINTER An impact printer that causes the ends of pins in the form of characters, numbers, etc., to strike against a ribbon for printing text.

DOUBLE SPREAD In printing, any two facing pages, e.g., two-page spread, center spread.

DOWNLOADABLE FONTS Printing fonts that are stored on a hard disk and transferred into printer memory prior to printing.

DOWNLOADING The reception and storage of data from one computer to another, often via data communications.

DROPOUT In printing, parts of originals that do not reproduce, especially colored lines or background areas.

DUMMY A preliminary layout showing the position of illustrations and text as they are to appear in the final reproduction. Also, a set of blank pages made up in advance to show the size, shape, form, and general style of a piece of printing.

DUMP The transfer of the contents of computer main memory to a printer or a secondary storage device.

ELECTRONIC MAIL (E-MAIL) A network service that enables users to send and receive messages via computer.

ELECTROSTATIC COPYING Image transfer system used in copiers and computer laser printers to produce images using electrostatic forces.

ELITE Twelve-characters-per-inch (horizontal) typewriter spacing.

EMULATOR A computer program that makes a programmable device imitate another computer, producing the same results.

END-USER A person who benefits directly or indirectly from a computer system.

ERGONOMICS The science of designing hardware, tools, and the working environment taking into account human factors so as to enable people to interact more comfortably and more productively.

ERROR MESSAGE A display on a computer screen or hard copy that states that a computer program is unable to perform as programmed.

ESCAPEMENT Horizontal distance between corresponding reference points of a series of machine-printed characters. Also "pitch." Terms used with typewriters and similar devices.

ETHERNET Trade name for a computer networking system.

EXPERT SYSTEM A computer program containing the knowledge used by an expert in a given area that assists non-experts when they attempt to perform duties in that same area.

FACING PAGES The two pages of a bound document that face each other.

FACSIMILE The exact reproduction of a letter, document, or signature. Sometimes abbreviated as "facsim" or "fax."

FAULT TOLERANCE Resistance to system failure or data loss.

FAX The transmission and reception of documents between two locations via telecommunications.

FAX SERVER A network device or service that provides a LAN workstation access to incoming or outgoing faxes across the LAN.

FEASIBILITY STUDY A study to determine the possibility of undertaking a systems project.

FILE A name given to a collection of information stored in a secondary storage medium such as a tape or disk.

FILE ALLOCATION TABLE A table on a disk that records the disk location of all the file parts.

FILE SERVER A computer that provides network stations with controlled access to shareable resources. The network operating system is loaded on the file server and most shareable devices, such as disk subsystems and printers, are attached to it. The file server controls system security. It also monitors station-to-station communications. A dedicated file server can be used online as a file server while it is on the network. A non-dedicated file server can be used simultaneously as a file server and a workstation.

FILE SHARING The ability for multiple users to share files. Concurrent file sharing is controlled by application software, the workstation operating system, and/or the file server/database server operating system.

FLOPPY DISK A removable secondary storage medium that uses a magnetically sensitive, flexible or firm disk enclosed in a plastic envelope or case. Disks come in 5 $1/_4$" and 3 $1/_2$" high and low density forms, and the Zip drive 100 MB 3 $1/_2$".

FLOW CHART Analysis tool consisting of a diagrammatic representation of a system process or abstract relationship, normally made up of labeled blocks or keyed symbols connected by lines.

FLUSH LEFT (OR RIGHT) Indicates type set to line up at the left (or right).

FLUSH PARAGRAPH A paragraph with no indention.

FOLD MARK Short line printed on a form to show where it should be folded for use either by the manufacturer or by the user (as in forms designed for window envelopes or heat sealing).

FONT Consists of characters and spacing material of different sizes and shapes. Computer generated fonts come in two forms, hard and soft fonts. Soft fonts are software stored in memory, and downloaded to the printer. Hard fonts come in the form of cartridge hardware, which plugs into the printer.

FOOT Bottom edge, or area at the bottom, of a form, held as it is normally read or used. The machine's finger grip area of unit sets is normally at the foot of the form.

FORM A preprinted document available as flat or continuous.

FORMAT The size, style, type page, margins, printing requirements, etc., of a printed piece.

FORMS DESIGN The art or science of devising a form to efficiently fill a given function or systems need; includes selection of materials, construction, and layout.

FORTRAN A high-level programming language (computer compiled) used for scientific or mathematical applications.

FRONT-END PROCESSOR A specialized computer that relieves the main CPU, taking over line control, message handling, code conversion, and error control.

FTAM File transfer, access, and management. A remote file service and protocol software.

GANTT CHART A project scheduling tool using graphic representations to show start, elapsed, and completion times of each task within a given project. It can also show the planned scheduled (S) time and the actual completed (C) time. (See example below.) The Gantt chart indicates the status of a given project at any point. A Gantt chart employing dollars can also illustrate money budgeting for given tasks vs. money spent. Gantt chart monitor screen displays are available with some project management software. This allows for on-line reference of the status of projects that can be networked. Gantt charts can also be drawn on various size sheets of paper. The 8 $1/_2$-by-11 size is inserted in binders for project progress recording. Larger size sheets of paper can be used for displaying Gantt charts in the project team work areas.

GANTT CHART

PROJECT: _____

PROJECT TASKS	S C	JAN	FEB	MAR	APR	MAY	JUNE
ANALYSIS							
DESIGN							
PROGRAMMING							
TESTING							
CONVERSION							

GATEWAY A device that provides routing and protocol conversion among physically dissimilar networks and/or computers.

GIGABYTE (GB, G-BYTE) A unit of measure of memory or disk storage capacity; two to the thirtieth power (1,073,741,824 bytes).

GRAIN The direction in which most fibers lie in a sheet of paper, corresponding with the direction of the paper being produced on a paper machine.

GRIPPER MARGIN Unprintable blank edge of paper on which grippers bear, usually $1/_2$ inch or less.

HACKER A technically knowledgeable computer enthusiast who enjoys programming but is not usually employed as a programmer.

HALFTONE An illustration in which the gradation of tone in a photograph is reproduced by a graduated system of dots of varying size, usually nearly invisible to the unaided eye. This effect is produced by interposing a cross-ruled screen directly in front of the sensitized plate or negative. Today, photographs, negatives, or slides can be read into a desktop publishing system to produce camera-ready copy with halftone illustrations included in the page layout.

HANDSHAKE A predetermined exchange between two computer systems in order to establish communication.

HARD COPY Printed output from a computer system or typewriter.

HARDWARE Electronic components, computers and peripherals that make up a computer system.

HEAD MARGIN The white space above the first line on a page.

HEAD-TO-HEAD See "two-sided form."

HEAD-TO-FOOT See "two-sided form."

HOST 1. A time-sharing computer accessed via terminals or terminal emulation. 2. A computer to which an expansion device attaches. For example, when a LAN card is installed in a microcomputer, that microcomputer becomes the host to that adapter.

HOST ADAPTER An adapter card which attaches a device to a computer's expansion bus.

IBM TOKEN RING IBM's version of the 802.5 token-passing ring network.

IMPACT PRINTER A printer that forms an image by pressing a physical representation of the character against the paper to make an impression. Most impact printers utilize an inked ribbon to transfer the image, and are required for multiple carbon copy output.

IN-HOUSE Denotes that the task is done within the company.

INPUT DEVICE Peripheral hardware that inputs data into a computer system.

INTELLIGENT WORKSTATION A terminal containing microcomputer processing capability that runs independently or in conjunction with a host computer.

INTERFACE A shared boundary between two systems, such as between data communications (terminating) equipment and data terminal equipment (DTE). Also a boundary between adjacent layers of the ISO model.

INTERNET The largest network in the world. Successor to ARPANET, Internet includes other large inter-networks. The Internet uses the TCP/IP protocol suite and connects universities, government agencies, businesses and individuals around the world.

INTER-NETWORK Two or more networks connected by bridges and/or routers, a network of networks.

ISO The International Standard Organization. ISO developed the milestone Open Systems Interconnection (OSI) model.

JUSTIFY In composition, to space out lines so that each one is a designated length.

KERNING Adjusting the spacing between two characters.

KEY CODE Copy coded by means of symbols, usually letters; insertions are sometimes "keyed" in.

KEYBOARDING The mechanism used to manually record data onto a microcomputer or terminal.

LAN The acronym for local area network. Typically, it denotes a short-distance, high-speed network.

LASER PRINTER A high resolution printer that uses electrostatic reproduction technology, like electrostatic copy machines, to fuse text or graphic images onto plain paper.

LAYOUT The drawing or sketch of a proposed printed piece.

LAYOUT SHEET Form with guidelines or scales along the margins to assist the forms designer in forms layout.

LEADERS In composition, dashes or dots used to guide the eye across a page to the intended word or figure. Used in tabular work, programs, etc.

LEASED LINE A full-time link between two or more locations leased from a local or inter-exchange carrier.

LEDGER PAPER A grade of business paper generally used for keeping records. It can be subjected to appreciable wear because it has a high degree of durability.

LETTERPRESS A method of printing from a raised surface, such as type, or metal, rubber, or plastic plates. This can be the final form of desktop publishing output.

LIBRARY A collection of programs and data files for a computer system's offline storage.

LINE COPY Any copy suitable for reproduction that does not require the use of a halftone screen. This includes output of desktop publishing that does not contain halftone illustrations.

LOCAL AREA NETWORK (LAN) The linkage of computers within a limited area so users can exchange information and share peripherals. This linkage can be wired or wireless.

LOGOTYPE (OR LOGO) The name of a company or product in a special design used as a trademark in public relations, advertising, and customer and vendor contacts.

LOWERCASE The small letters in type as distinguished from the capital letters.

LSB The acronym for least significant bit. It stands for the bit with the least binary weight in a character.

MAINFRAME A large computer, generally with high-level and multiprocessing power and the capacity to support many users at once.

MARGIN The blank area along any edge of a sheet that must be kept free of printing due to production considerations.

MARK A binary 1.

MATED CHEMICAL CARBONLESS A carbonless paper system which requires two paper surfaces to come in contact with each other. Each has a different, relatively colorless coating that reacts under impact or pressure to form a visible image on one surface ("coated front or CA surface"). See "carbonless paper."

MATTE FINISH Dull paper finish, without gloss or luster.

MEGABYTE (MG, M-BYTE) A unit of measure for memory or disk storage capacity. Two to the twentieth power (1,048,576 bytes).

MICROCOMPUTER Smaller computers that employ microprocessor chip technology. These can be identified as: palm type, mini-notebooks, notebooks, laptops, transportable, desktop, work stations and PCs (personal computers).

MICROCOMPUTER COORDINATOR An end-user person responsible for the coordination and operation of an end-user microcomputer operation. The person can have full or part-time responsibility for this duty, can be hourly or salaried, and union or nonunion.

MICROCOMPUTER MANAGER A person who has the responsibility for managing and providing support to and training for users of microcomputers. This person reports to IS management. Since this position is most often a full-time responsibility, it is advisable it be filled by a salaried worker.

MILESTONES Used with Gantt, CPM and PERT charting to show when measurable units of task(s) have been completed. With Gantt charts the actual milestones can be drawn on the charts.

MINICOMPUTER A multi-user computer, generally with more power than a personal computer yet not as large as a mainframe.

MODELING An analytical process based on mathematical network behavior formulas called models used to predict the performance of product designs.

MODEM A device that converts digital signals to analog and analog signals to digital between computers via telephone transmission.

MODULAR PROGRAMMING A style of programming which requires that program functions be broken into modules. It is a form of program segmentation and is now the correct way to code programs. This is also a good way to write reusable code. Quick BASIC and Visual BASIC programming require this type of program coding.

MONITOR Screen for viewing computer output. It is also called a CRT.

MULTIPLEXER An electronic device that combines several signals into one to save transmission cost. Time division multiplexing (TDM) and frequency division multiplexing (FDM) are used in various aspects of LAN data communications.

NEGATIVE Film containing an image in which the values of the original are reversed so that the dark areas appear light and vice versa.

NETWORK A series of points connected by communications channels. Public networks can be used by anyone; private networks are closed to outsiders.

NETWORK ADMINISTRATOR A local area network manager who is responsible for maintaining a network.

NETWORK INTERFACE CARD (NIC) A circuit board installed in each network station to allow communications with other stations.

NON-DEDICATED FILE SERVER A file server that also functions as a workstation.

OBJECT CODE The machine readable instructions created by a computer or assembler from source code.

OFFSET An adaptation of stone lithography in which the design is drawn or photographically reproduced on a thin, flexible metal plate or other medium from which the design is transferred.

ONE-TIME CARBON Carbon paper designed to be used within a form for just one writing or printing and then discarded.

ONLINE DEVICE A peripheral device externally attached to a computer.

PACKET A basic message unit grouped for transmission through a public network such as ITU-TSS X.25. A packet usually includes routing information, data, and sometimes error detection information.

PAPER MASTER A paper printing plate used on an offset duplicator. The image is made by hand drawing, typewriter, or laser printer.

PARALLEL PORT A printer interface that allows data to be transmitted a byte at a time, with eight bits moving in parallel.

PASSWORD A security identification used to authorize users of a computer system or given program.

PEER-TO-PEER A network design where each computer shares and uses devices on an equal basis.

PERIPHERAL A physical device (such as a printer or disk subsystem) that is externally attached to a workstation or directly attached to the network.

PERT Programmed Evaluation Review Technique is a planning and control tool for defining and controlling the tasks necessary to complete a given project. The PERT chart and CPM charts are one and the same. The only difference is the manner in which task time is computed. The CPM chart uses only one expected time. With the PERT system, the time required for each task is computed as follows: the longest expected time, the shortest expected time, and four times the expected time are totaled and divided by six. This gives the expected time needed.

PICA The standard of type measurement in the point system, equal to 12 points or about $1/6$ inch. (6 picas = 1 inch, 72 picas = 12 inches.) See also "point."

PITCH Horizontal distance between corresponding reference points of a series of machine-printed characters. Also "escapement." Terms used with typewriters and similar devices.

PLASTIC BINDING A solid-back comb rolled to make a cylinder of any thickness and inserted through slots punched along the binding side. Used for project proposals, procedures, instruction manuals, etc.

POINT The unit upon which the point system of measuring type is based. A point is nearly $1/_{72}$ inch (0.013837 inch).

PRESSURE-SENSITIVE PAPER Material with an adhesive coating, protected by a backing sheet until used, that will stick without moistening. Used for labels for disks, tapes, binders, etc.

PRINT SERVER A device and/or program that manages shared printers. Print service is often provided by the file server but can also be provided from a separate LAN microcomputer or other device.

PROOF Print made from a negative or from a plate or type form by some manual procedure, usually to provide an indication of the appearance of the final printed piece or to check composition accuracy.

PROGRAM RUN BOOK Operating instructions for the benefit of those who run a given program, including any restart procedures in case of program failure. Most often used by mainframe computer operators but can also be provided for minicomputer operators and microcomputer users.

PROJECT SLIPPAGE This occurs when a project's critical path milestone finish date is not met. The critical path of a PERT or CPM chart determines the project completion time. See "cpm." Projects that are not using a PERT or CPM technology can have project slippage, too. It is first recognized when it becomes obvious that the project finish date will be later than planned.

PROTOCOL A formal set of rules setting the format and control of data exchange between two devices or processes.

QUICK BASIC An improved form of BASIC that is available from Microsoft. It has been available as part of its Windows software. The programming must be written in a modular form.

REAM A package of five hundred sheets of paper.

RECOMMENDED LIST A list of software that the IS department recommends and for which it provides user support. The list can also contain recommended IT hardware for users.

RECORD LOCKING A data protection scheme that prevents different users from performing simultaneous writes to the same record in a shared file, thus preventing overlapping disk writes and ensuring record integrity.

REDIRECTOR In a workstation this device sends data to the network or keeps it in the workstation for local use, as appropriate.

REPEATER A device used to extend cabling distances by regenerating signals.

REUSABLE CODE Code that is written in a structured modular format that allows it to be used at a later time with no (or minor) changes for other programming efforts.

RING TOPOLOGY A close loop in which data passes in one direction from station to station on the LAN. Each workstation on the ring acts as a repeater, passing data on to the next workstation.

ROM Read-only memory that is found on CDs and permanent microcomputer main memory.

ROUTER Hardware and software that route data between similar or dissimilar networks at the network layer of the OSI model.

RUNNING HEAD A line at the top of a page showing either the title of the book, the project, the chapter, or the subject.

SCALING Determining the proper reduced or enlarged size of an image.

SCANNER A microcomputer input device that copies documents into computer memory.

SECONDARY STORAGE Any place where computer data or program instructions are stored, other than main memory (RAM or ROM).

SELF-CONTAINED OR SELF-IMAGING PAPER Carbonless paper with the ability to generate its own image by chemical or mechanical means. See "carbonless paper."

SERIAL PORT A port that allows data to be transmitted one bit at a time.

SERVER A network device that provides services to client stations. Servers include file servers, disk servers, and print servers. See "client/server."

SHIELDED TWISTED-PAIR CABLE Twisted-pair wire surrounded by a foil or mesh shield to reduce susceptibility to outside interference and noise during network transmission.

SIMULATION A technique for evaluating the performance of a network before downloading it. Simulation employs timers and sequences as opposed to mathematical models to reproduce network behavior.

SITE LICENSING Procedure in which software is licensed to be used only at a particular location.

SIZE SNOWBALL EFFECT The larger the project size and/or the longer the required project calendar time the more likely that additional time and effort will be needed to complete the project. As more time and effort are required, these snowball, which in turn extends the finish date and increases the final cost. The user's needs change over time. The longer a project takes, the more the user can justify changes to the final product. And the number of changes will snowball. In addition, these changes that are required for a useable product also take even more time to install— which can justifiably require more changes.

SOFT FONTS Software fonts that are available with word processing and desktop publishing software. There are also packages available that can be downloaded to word processing and desktop publishing software. They are available in many styles and are scalable to required sizes.

SOURCE CODE Written program code before the program has been compiled into machine instructions.

SPAGHETTI CODE The name given to the first method of computer program coding. Program steps were written without any formal structure and meandered through the program. Tracing these program steps was like following a string of spaghetti in a bowl. Contrasted to "structured programming."

SPECIALTY FORM Any form that requires special or unusual equipment for its manufacture by a vendor.

SPINE The bound edge of a book.

SPIRAL BINDING A type of binding using plastic or metal wires bent into a spiral shape that are inserted through holes punched along the binding side. Used for documents such as operator's procedure instructions, feasibility studies, proposals, etc.

SPOT CARBONIZING Applying carbon coating in a selective pattern directly to the back of a form to achieve selective write-through without carbon interleaves.

STAR TOPOLOGY A LAN topology in which each workstation connects to a central device.

STAR-WIRED TOPOLOGY A ring network (such as a token-passing ring) cabled through centralized hubs or connection devices to create a physical star topology. By using this, individual stations and whole sections of the network can be removed or added easily.

STATISTICAL MULTIPLEXER A multiplexer that allocates time on the channel to active inputs only. It greatly increases line capacity.

STRUCTURED PROGRAMMING A standard that requires programs to be written in modular forms without the use of GO TO statements. Structured and modular programming have replaced "spaghetti" coding.

SURGE PROTECTOR An electrical device that prevents high-voltage surges from reaching the computer system.

SYNCHRONOUS TRANSMISSION Transmission of data during which the components of the network are all controlled by a single timing source.

TERMINAL A keyboard and display screen through which users can access a host computer.

TERMINAL EMULATION Software that enables a personal computer to communicate with a host computer by transmitting in the form used by the host's terminals.

TEXT The body matter of a page, feasibility study, or book.

THIRD PARTY VENDOR A firm that markets hardware for manufacturers.

TINTING Applying a lightly printed shading to an area of a form.

TOKEN BUS A network that uses a logical token-passing network. A service can only transmit data on the network if it is on the token.

TOKEN-PASSING RING A LAN design in which each station is connected to an upstream station and a downstream station. An electronic signal, called the token, is passed from station to station around the ring. A station may not send a transmission to another station unless it has possession of a free token. Since only one token is allowed on the network, only one station may broadcast at a time.

TRIMMARKS Marks placed on the copy to indicate the edge of the paper. Also ticmarks or cutmarks.

TURNAROUND DOCUMENT A computer-generated document that is sent to the receiver who may add information to it before it is returned to its source. The document then becomes an input to the computer system. When the document is inputted it contains the information that was provided at its origin plus any information that may have been added by its receiver. This form of document handling reduces data entry efforts and error rates. Examples of such documents are utility bills, credit card billing, and monthly mail order clubs.

TURNKEY SYSTEM A system in which the vendor takes full responsibility for complete system design and provides the required hardware, software, operations manual and user training.

TWISTED-PAIR CABLE Wiring used by local telephone systems.

TWO-SIDED FORM The top of a form is called the head and the bottom is called the foot. When a two-sided form is to be placed in a two- or three-ring binder, both the back and front of the form are printed with the heads back to back or "head-to-head." This allows the form page to be turned and read as with a book. When a two-sided form is to be placed in a binder that attaches the first page at its head, the second side of the form, if printed head-to-head, will require the binder to be rotated to be read. To provide for continuous reading of the forms in this kind of binder, the forms are printed head-to-foot. The first page will have the head of the form attached at the top, while the second page will be attached at the foot or bottom of the form.

TYPEFACE Style of type with respect to the design of the characters. Typefaces are divided broadly into Roman (serif) and Gothic (sans serif). Within a given typeface, there is a range of sizes (series) and variations (bold, condensed, italic).

UPPERCASE Capital letter in type as distinguished from the small letters.

UPS (UNINTERRUPTED POWER SOURCE) A device that provides electric back-up power to a computer system or other devices when the normal electric power fails. This occurs so quickly that the operation of devices that depend on electricity is not interrupted.

USER FRIENDLY A computer system which is easy for persons with no computer experience to use, causing little or no frustration or upset.

VISUAL BASIC A more advanced form of programming than Quick BASIC, available from Microsoft. Program operation is screen driven, which makes the program user friendly. As with Quick BASIC, it too uses modular programming. Programmed subroutines are available, either for purchase or with the payment of royalty.

WALKTHROUGH A technical review of a newly designed program or system. The review is conducted by interested parties such as programmers, systems analysts, users, and/or auditors. Program walkthroughs are conducted by peer programmers to detect program errors. In a walkthrough, people play the role of "devil's advocate" in reviewing another person/team's effort.

WAN The acronym for a Wide Area Network which is any network extending more than a few miles. It can use more than one form of message carrying.

WITH THE GRAIN Parallel to the grain of the paper.

WORK SAMPLING Consists of a large number of random observations of predetermined tasks an employee or group of employees may perform. Data collected by the work sampling observations will identify the amount of time spent on each task.

WORKSTATION A highly intelligent terminal often found on a LAN or client/server system. Some workstations do not require floppy disk drives because data and/or programs are downloaded from a computer server.

WRITE-THROUGH The process of transferring an image (using carbon paper) under impact or pressure.

X-BOX Any small square printed on a form to be marked by the user ("X" is preferred to a check mark) to denote the applicability of a related word or phrase. Also referred to as box, check box, ballot box.

INDEX